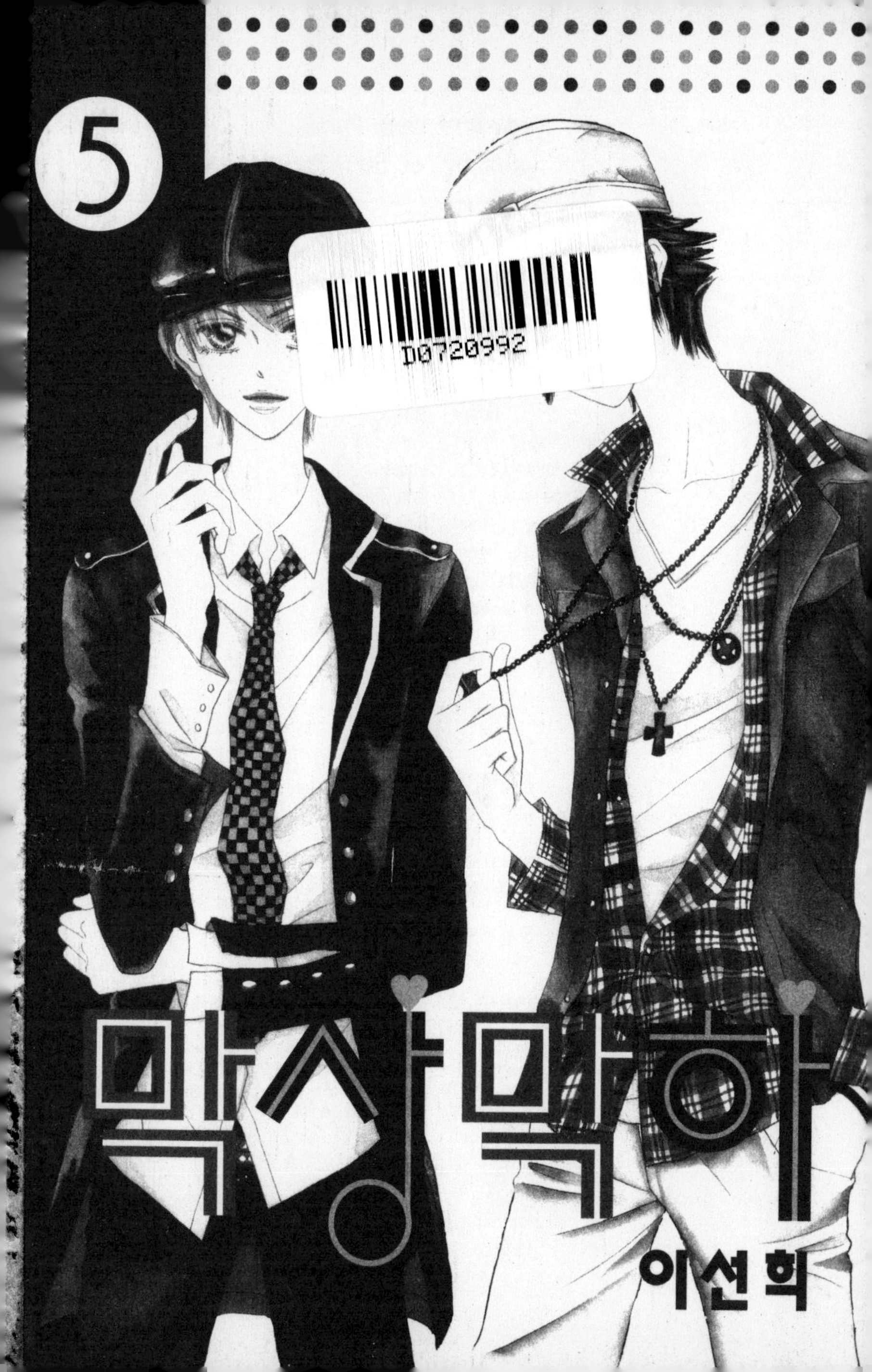
5
막상막하
이선희

Neck and Neck Vol. 5
Created by Lee Sun-Hee

Translation - Sunah Kim Schultz
English Adaptation - Magda Sniegocki
Retouch and Lettering - Fawn Lau
Cover Design - Chris Tjalsma

Editor - Tim Beedle
Digital Imaging Manager - Chris Buford
Managing Editor - Lindsey Johnston
VP of Production - Ron Klamert
Editor-in-Chief - Rob Tokar
Publisher - Mike Kiley
President and C.O.O. - John Parker
C.E.O. and Chief Creative Director - Stuart Levy

A  Manga

TOKYOPOP Inc.
5900 Wilshire Blvd. Suite 2000
Los Angeles, CA 90036

E-mail: info@TOKYOPOP.com
Come visit us online at www.TOKYOPOP.com

ISBN: 1-59816-099-0

First TOKYOPOP printing: May 2006
10 9 8 7 6 5 4 3 2 1
Printed in Canada

Vol. 5

by
Lee Sun-Hee

HAMBURG // LONDON // LOS ANGELES // TOKYO

My name is Dabin Choi, and I'm 15 years old. All my life, I've lived with my father, and I can't imagine things any other way. Now, if you didn't know, my dad is kind of... special. He's the boss of one of the largest and most powerful organized crime families in Korea. Obviously, considering his position, my father has a lot of people working for him. So many, in fact, that I can hardly even remember all their names...with one big, glaring, oh-so-beautiful exception. Eugene Sung's father and my father were good friends when they were younger. Eugene and I pretty much grew up together. When he became a teenager, Daddy gave Eugene a job helping him handle some of his more legitimate business deals. This meant that I got to see Eugene a lot more, but it still wasn't enough for me. You see, if it's not obvious by now, I have the world's biggest crush on Eugene, and I won't be satisfied until he's fallen completely head over heels for me.

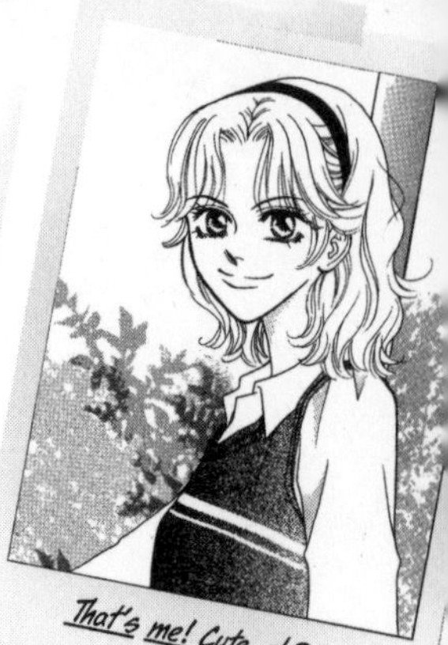

That's me! Cute, eh?

The problem is that Eugene views me as a little sister rather than a potential prom date. To change this, I convinced my father to allow me to transfer to Eugene's high school (when you're Daddy's ONLY little girl, these sort of requests come easily). However, this hasn't proven to be the thrill that I thought it would be. Yes, Eugene and I have gotten a lot closer, and yes, I've made some great new friends. However, they're not the problem. The problem is Shihu Myoung.

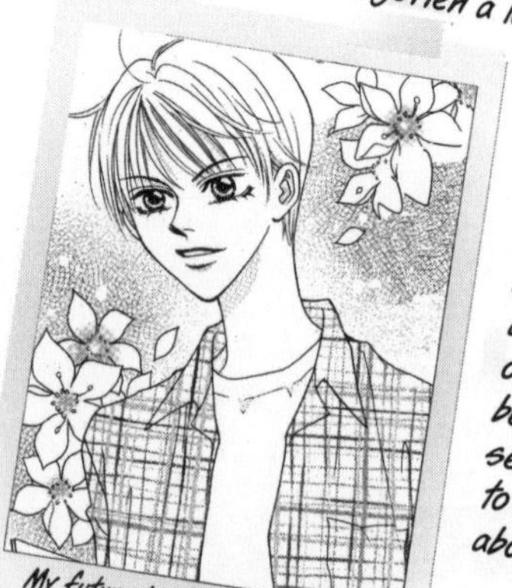

My future boyfriend. Eugene is such a dreamboat!

Shihu seems intent on making my life a living hell. That is, when he's not being really nice to me. Shihu's behavior just confuses me. I can't tell if he likes me or hates me at times, and it's probably better if I never try to figure him out. You see, Shihu's father and my father used to be partners. Daddy doesn't like to talk about it, but several years ago, they had

Neck and Neck

Story So Far

about it, but several years ago, they had some sort of falling out and now they're enemies. This war between them is becoming quite a problem. Even our assistant Ilsoo is concerned. That's probably why he asked Shihu to be my bodyguard. He sees it as a way of reuniting the families. I know he's just trying to help, but jeez! He's just making things even crazier!

Shihu's not my only problem. Not even close. Black Rose was my worst enemy at my old high school, and now she's been running rampant at my new school. That can only mean trouble. Particularly since she's been spotted with Minhyuk Kwon. Minhyuk is the Captain of the Senior Class, but he's a real jerk. (He scared people into voting for him.) I really don't want to think of what Minhyuk and Rose are capable of when they put their filthy minds together, but lately, it seems I have no choice.

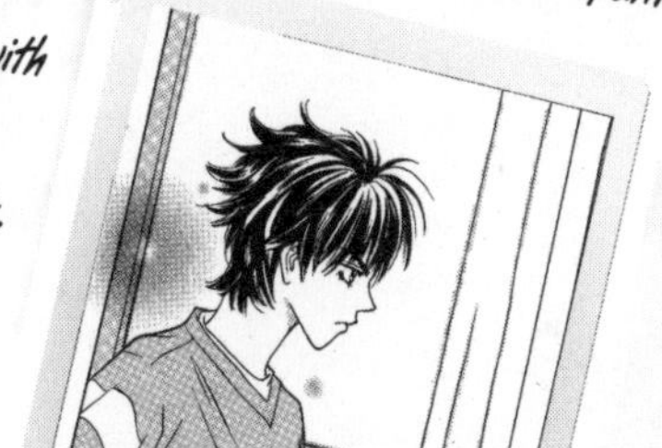

Shihu has the whole angst thing going for him. But that's about it.

However, my big problem right now, the one that's currently got my stress level well into the red, is the upcoming PTA meeting at school. Yeah, I know what you're thinking, but it's not my grades. I'm not worried about Daddy meeting my teachers. It's the possibility of my father running into Shihu's father that has me scared. This calls for immediate action!

| Cute | Sweet | Bright | Fresh |

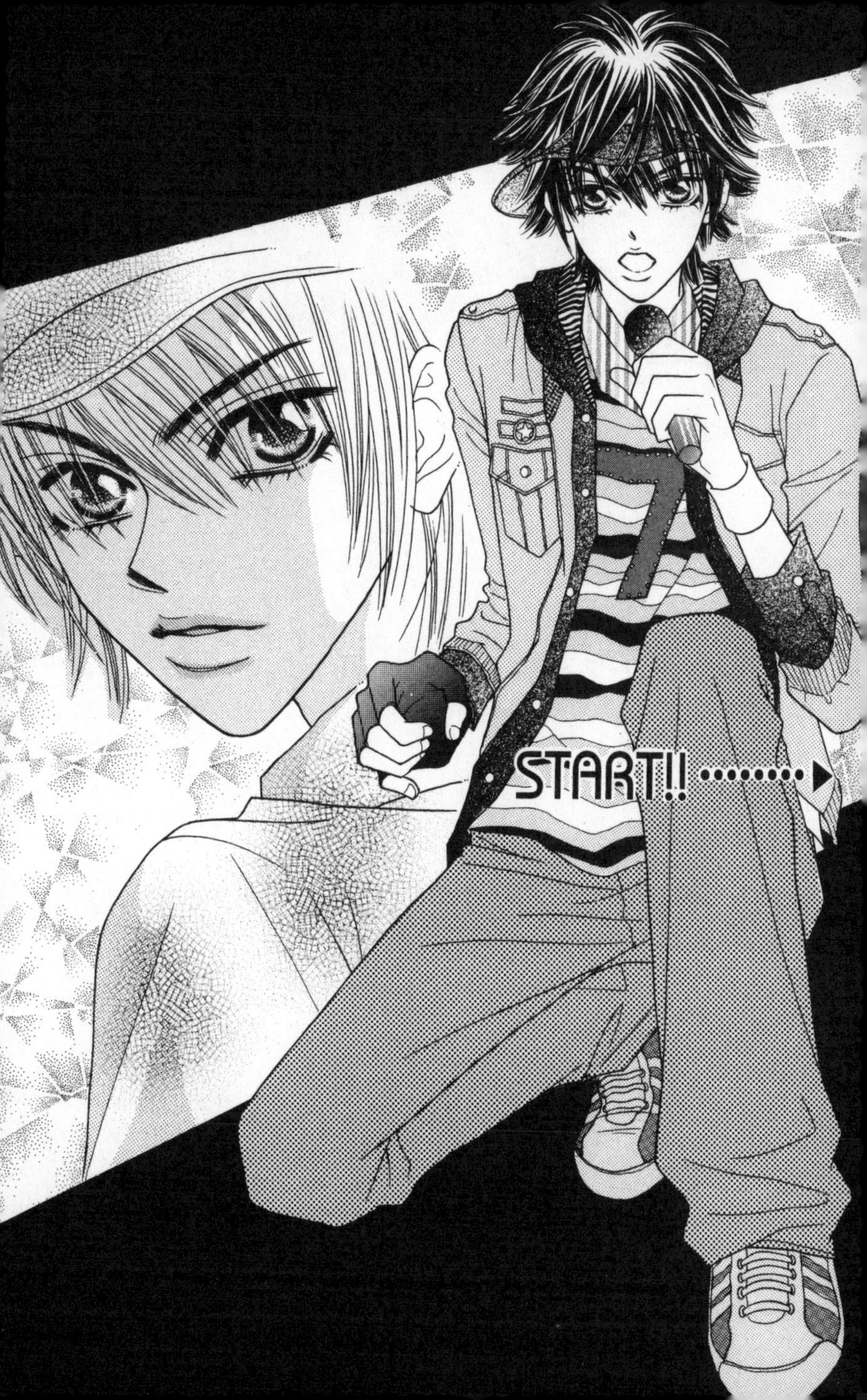
START!! ....▶

CONSIDERING THE WAY THOSE TWO FEEL ABOUT EACH OTHER...
Sure didn't expect to see your ugly mug again.
You're one to talk, baldy!
파지직
...IF THEY RUN INTO EACH OTHER AT YOUR SCHOOL, IT'S NOT GOING TO BE PRETTY.

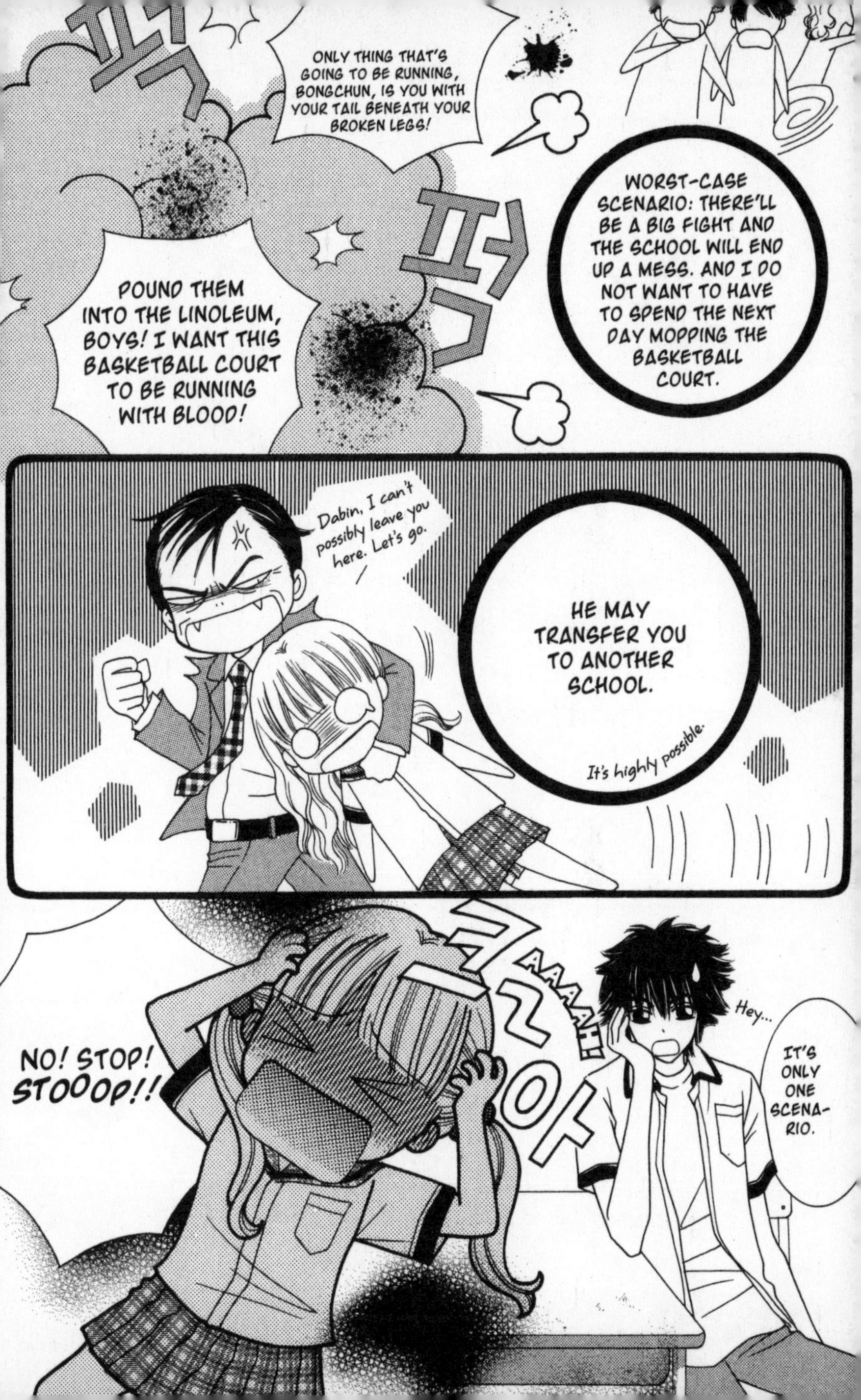
ONLY THING THAT'S GOING TO BE RUNNING, BONGCHUN, IS YOU WITH YOUR TAIL BENEATH YOUR BROKEN LEGS!
POUND THEM INTO THE LINOLEUM, BOYS! I WANT THIS BASKETBALL COURT TO BE RUNNING WITH BLOOD!
WORST-CASE SCENARIO: THERE'LL BE A BIG FIGHT AND THE SCHOOL WILL END UP A MESS. AND I DO NOT WANT TO HAVE TO SPEND THE NEXT DAY MOPPING THE BASKETBALL COURT.
Dabin, I can't possibly leave you here. Let's go.
HE MAY TRANSFER YOU TO ANOTHER SCHOOL.
It's highly possible.
NO! STOP! STOOOP!!
AAAAH!!
Hey...
IT'S ONLY ONE SCENA-RIO.

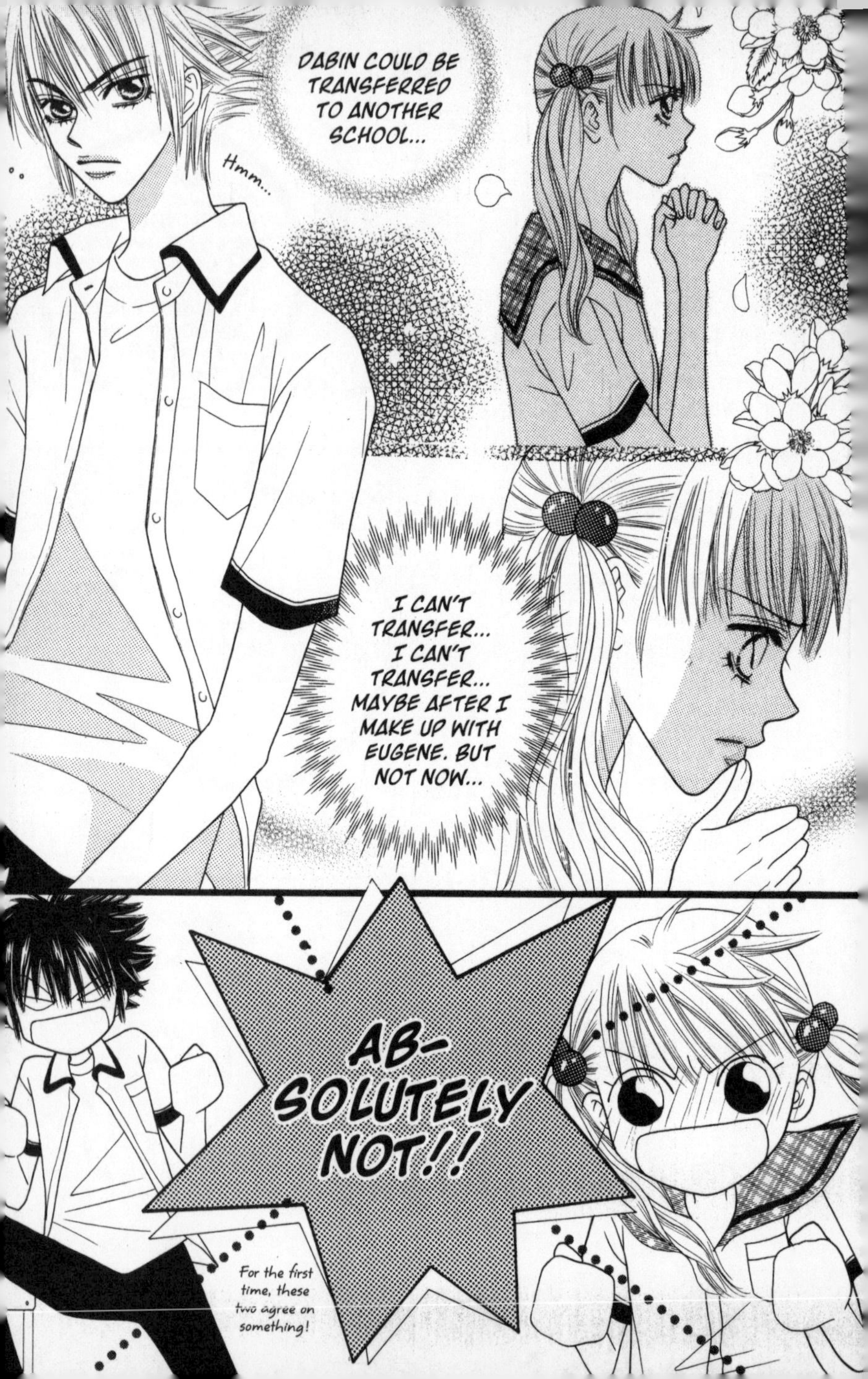
DABIN COULD BE TRANSFERRED TO ANOTHER SCHOOL...
Hmm...
I CAN'T TRANSFER... I CAN'T TRANSFER... MAYBE AFTER I MAKE UP WITH EUGENE. BUT NOT NOW...
AB-SOLUTELY NOT!!
For the first time, these two agree on something!

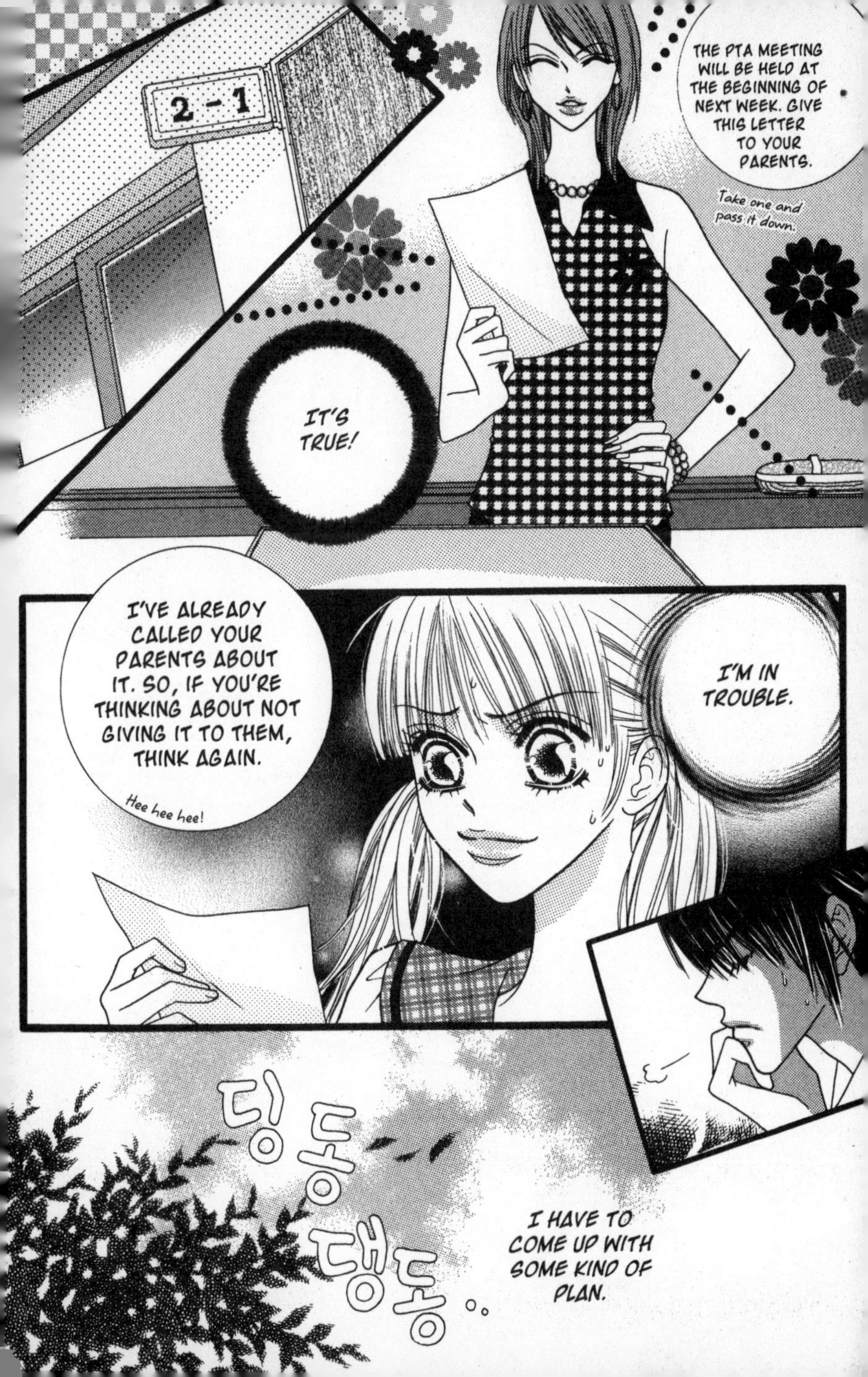

2-1
THE PTA MEETING WILL BE HELD AT THE BEGINNING OF NEXT WEEK. GIVE THIS LETTER TO YOUR PARENTS.
Take one and pass it down.
IT'S TRUE!
I'VE ALREADY CALLED YOUR PARENTS ABOUT IT. SO, IF YOU'RE THINKING ABOUT NOT GIVING IT TO THEM, THINK AGAIN.
Hee hee hee!
I'M IN TROUBLE.
딩동댕동 ..
I HAVE TO COME UP WITH SOME KIND OF PLAN.

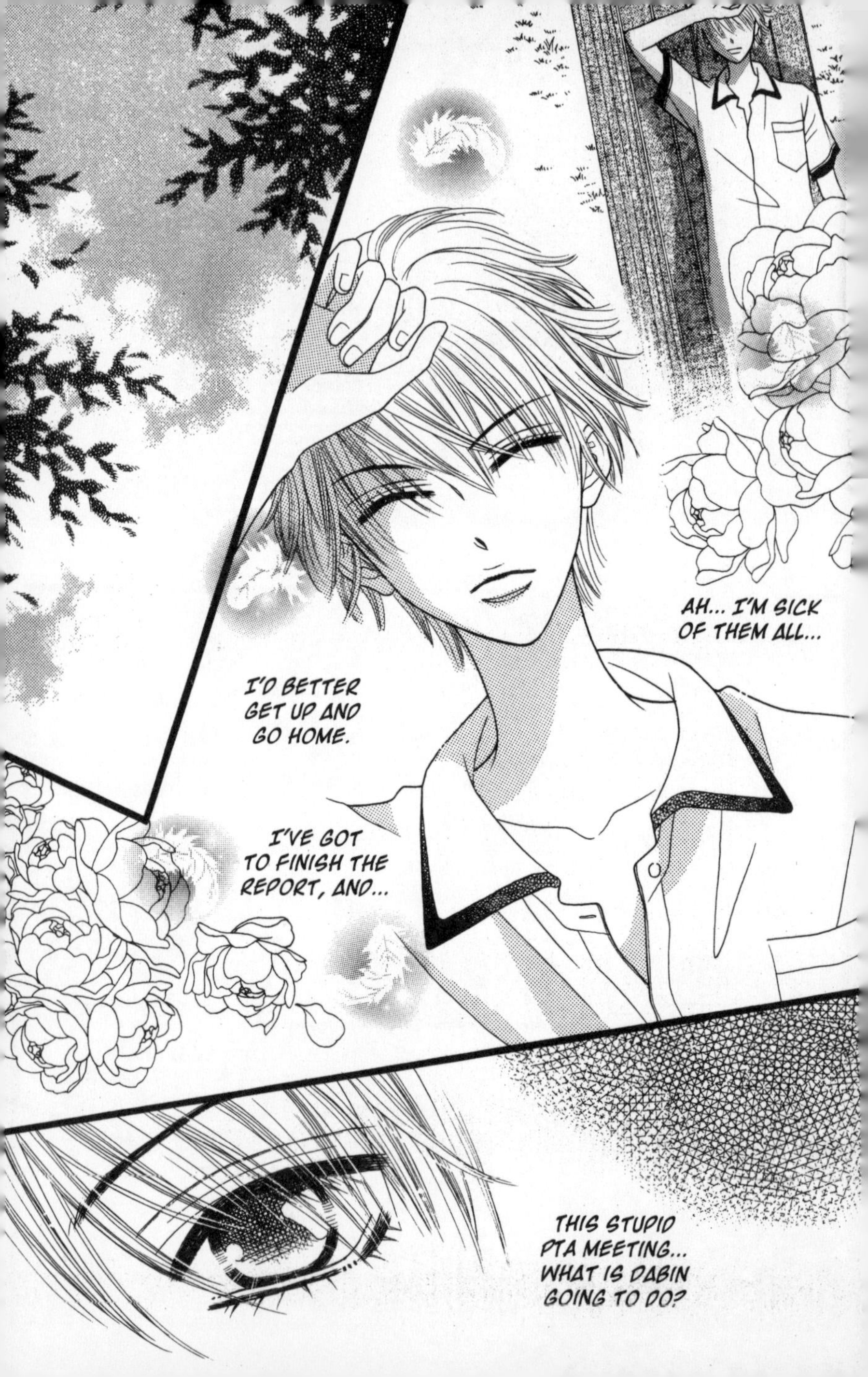
AH... I'M SICK OF THEM ALL...
I'D BETTER GET UP AND GO HOME.
I'VE GOT TO FINISH THE REPORT, AND...
THIS STUPID PTA MEETING... WHAT IS DABIN GOING TO DO?

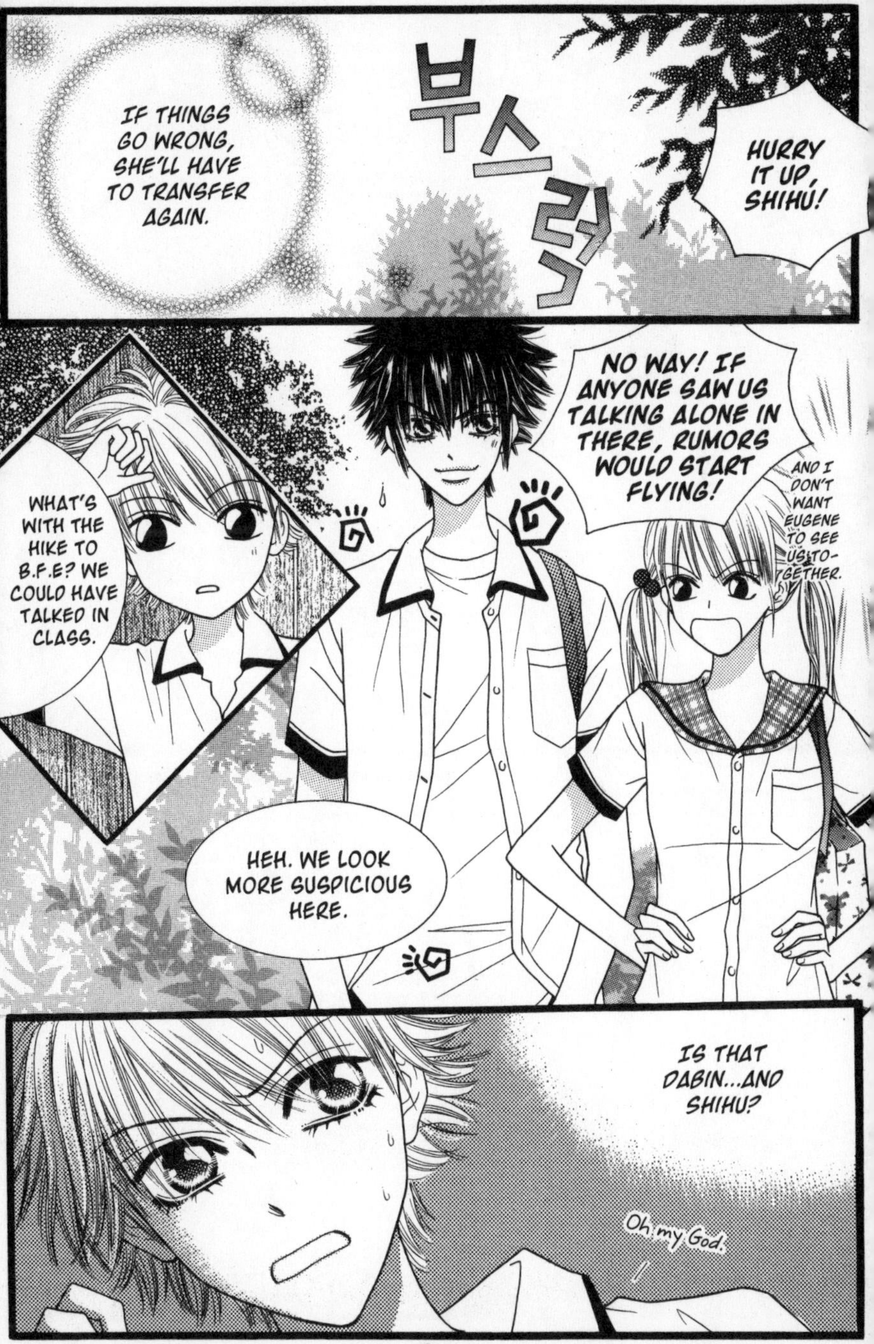
IF THINGS GO WRONG, SHE'LL HAVE TO TRANSFER AGAIN.
부스럭
HURRY IT UP, SHIHU!
WHAT'S WITH THE HIKE TO B.F.E? WE COULD HAVE TALKED IN CLASS.
HEH. WE LOOK MORE SUSPICIOUS HERE.
NO WAY! IF ANYONE SAW US TALKING ALONE IN THERE, RUMORS WOULD START FLYING!
AND I DON'T WANT EUGENE TO SEE US TO-GETHER.
IS THAT DABIN...AND SHIHU?
Oh my God.

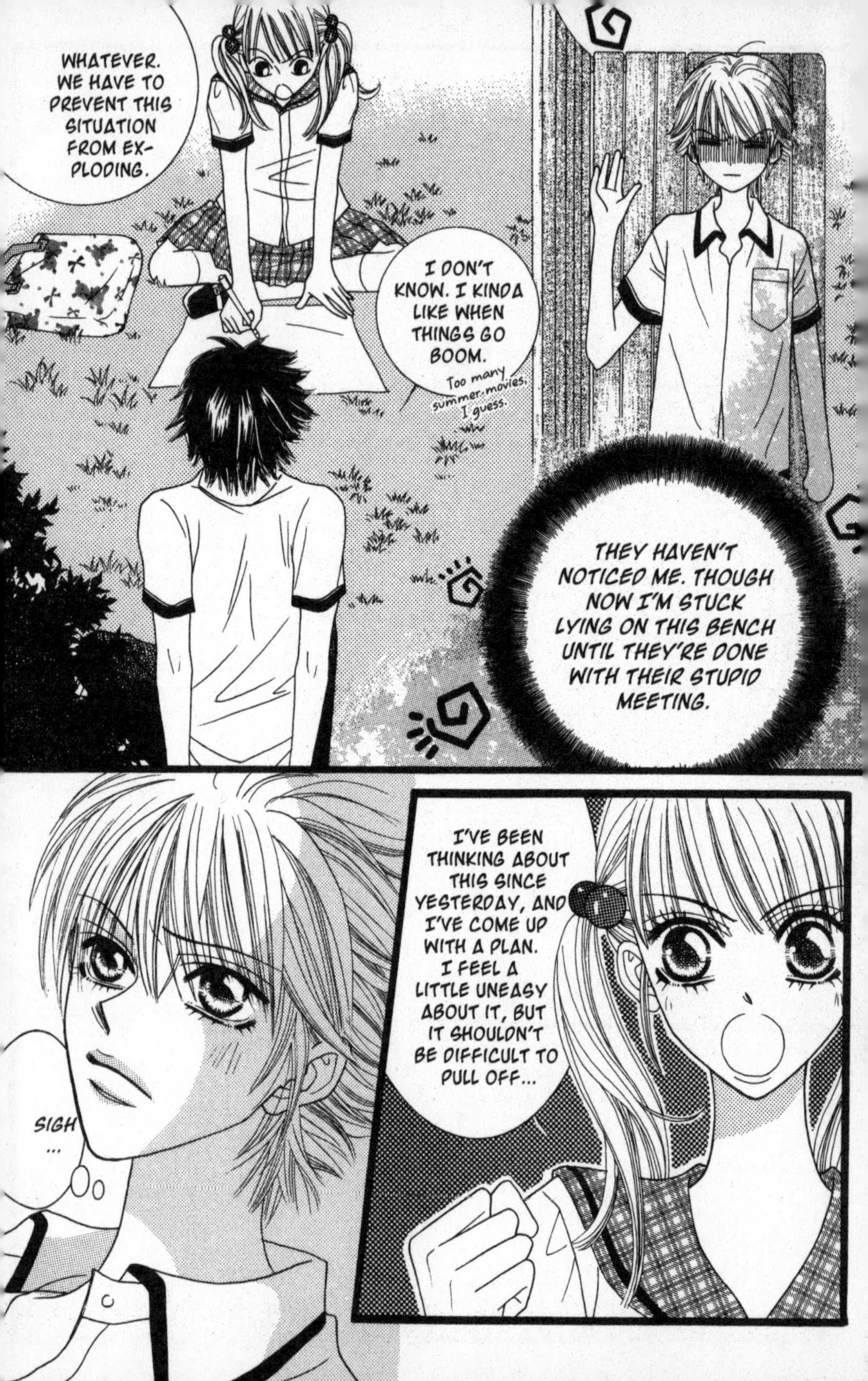
WHATEVER. WE HAVE TO PREVENT THIS SITUATION FROM EX-PLODING.
I DON'T KNOW. I KINDA LIKE WHEN THINGS GO BOOM.
Too many summer movies, I guess.
THEY HAVEN'T NOTICED ME. THOUGH NOW I'M STUCK LYING ON THIS BENCH UNTIL THEY'RE DONE WITH THEIR STUPID MEETING.
SIGH ...
I'VE BEEN THINKING ABOUT THIS SINCE YESTERDAY, AND I'VE COME UP WITH A PLAN. I FEEL A LITTLE UNEASY ABOUT IT, BUT IT SHOULDN'T BE DIFFICULT TO PULL OFF...

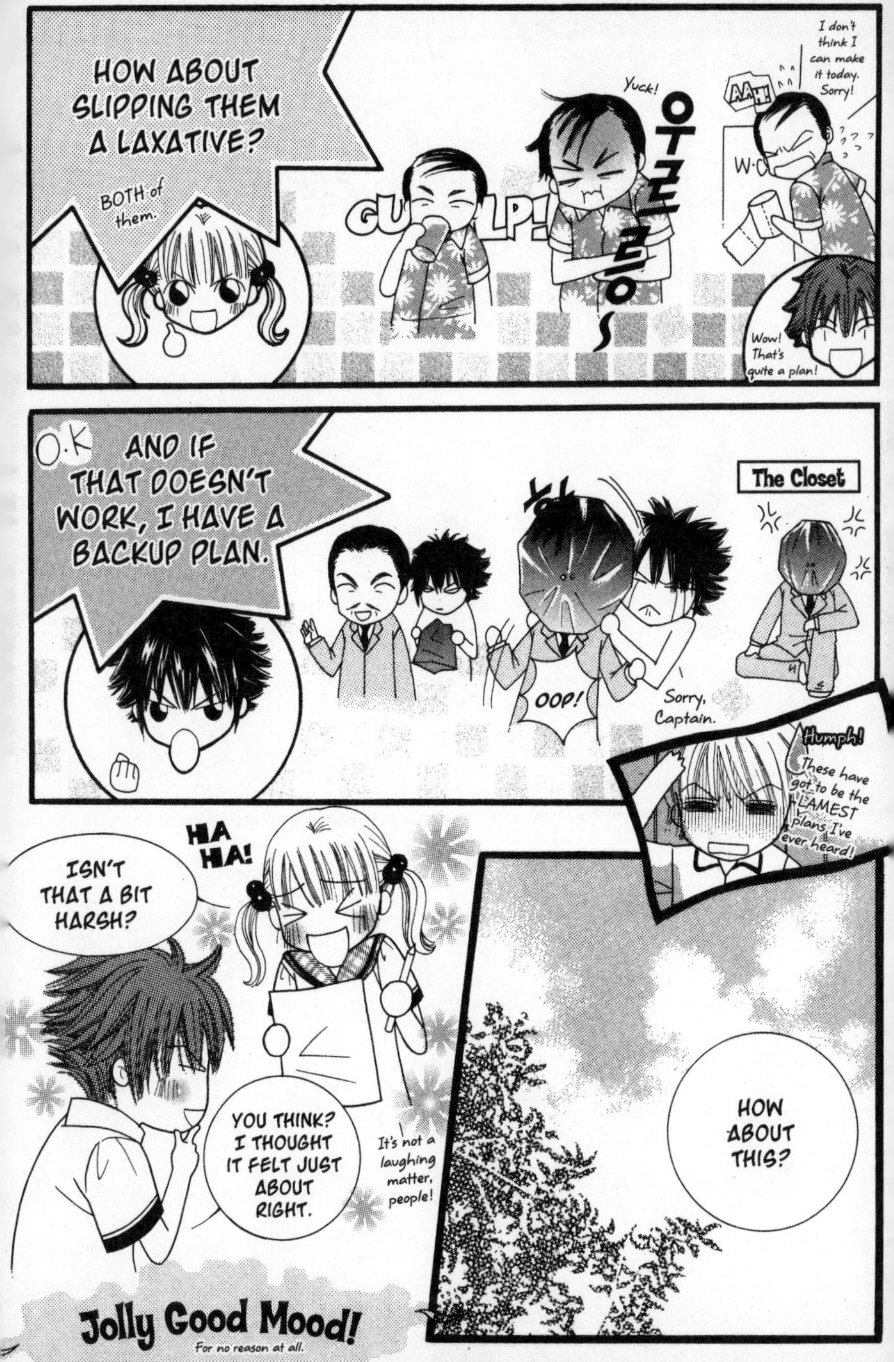
HOW ABOUT SLIPPING THEM A LAXATIVE?
BOTH of them.
GULP!
Yuck!
AAH!
I don't think I can make it today. Sorry!
W.C
Wow! That's quite a plan!
O.K
AND IF THAT DOESN'T WORK, I HAVE A BACKUP PLAN.
The Closet
OOP!
Sorry, Captain.
Humph!
These have got to be the LAMEST plans I've ever heard!
ISN'T THAT A BIT HARSH?
HA HA!
YOU THINK? I THOUGHT IT FELT JUST ABOUT RIGHT.
It's not a laughing matter, people!
HOW ABOUT THIS?
Jolly Good Mood!
For no reason at all.

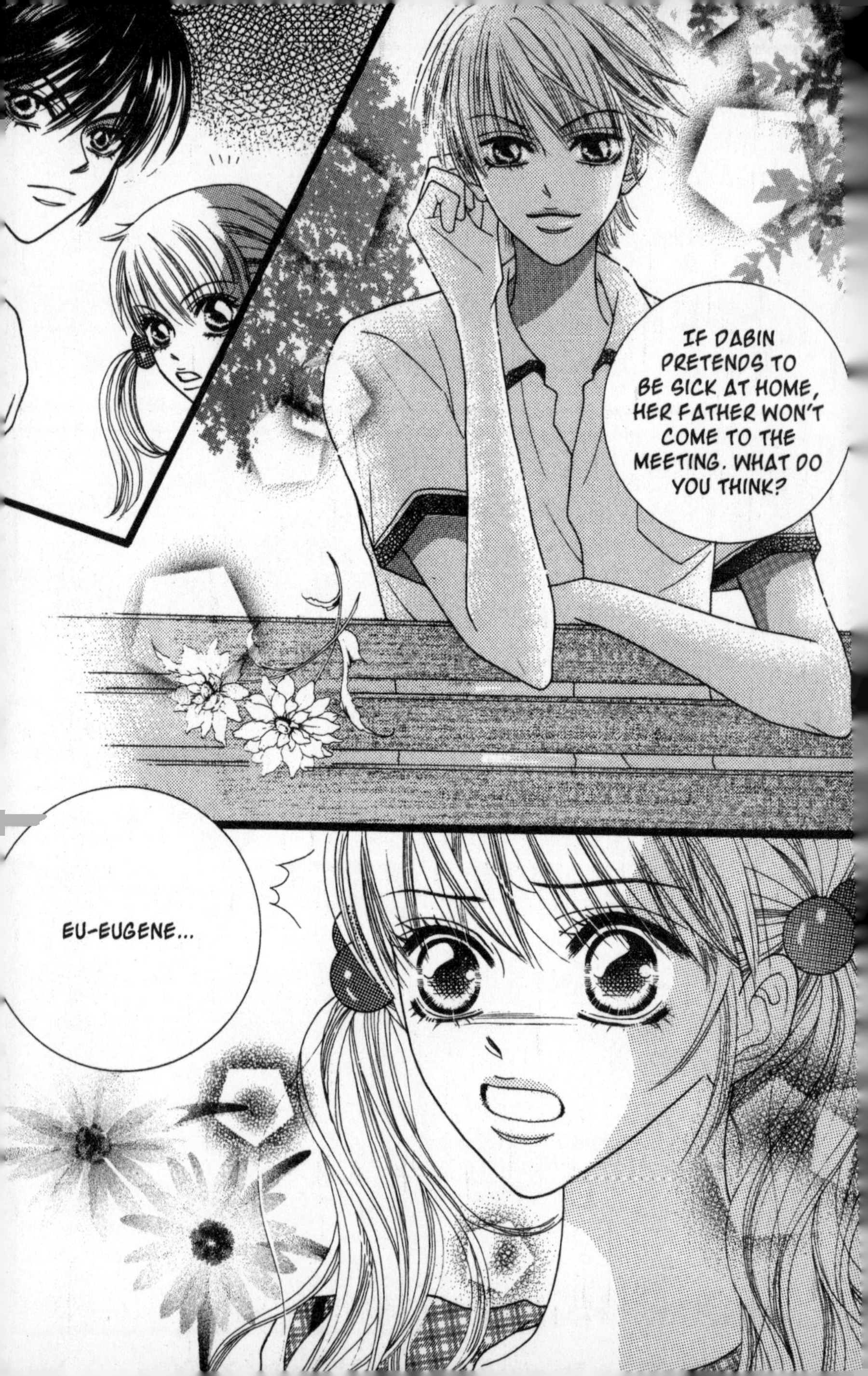
IF DABIN PRETENDS TO BE SICK AT HOME, HER FATHER WON'T COME TO THE MEETING. WHAT DO YOU THINK?
EU-EUGENE...

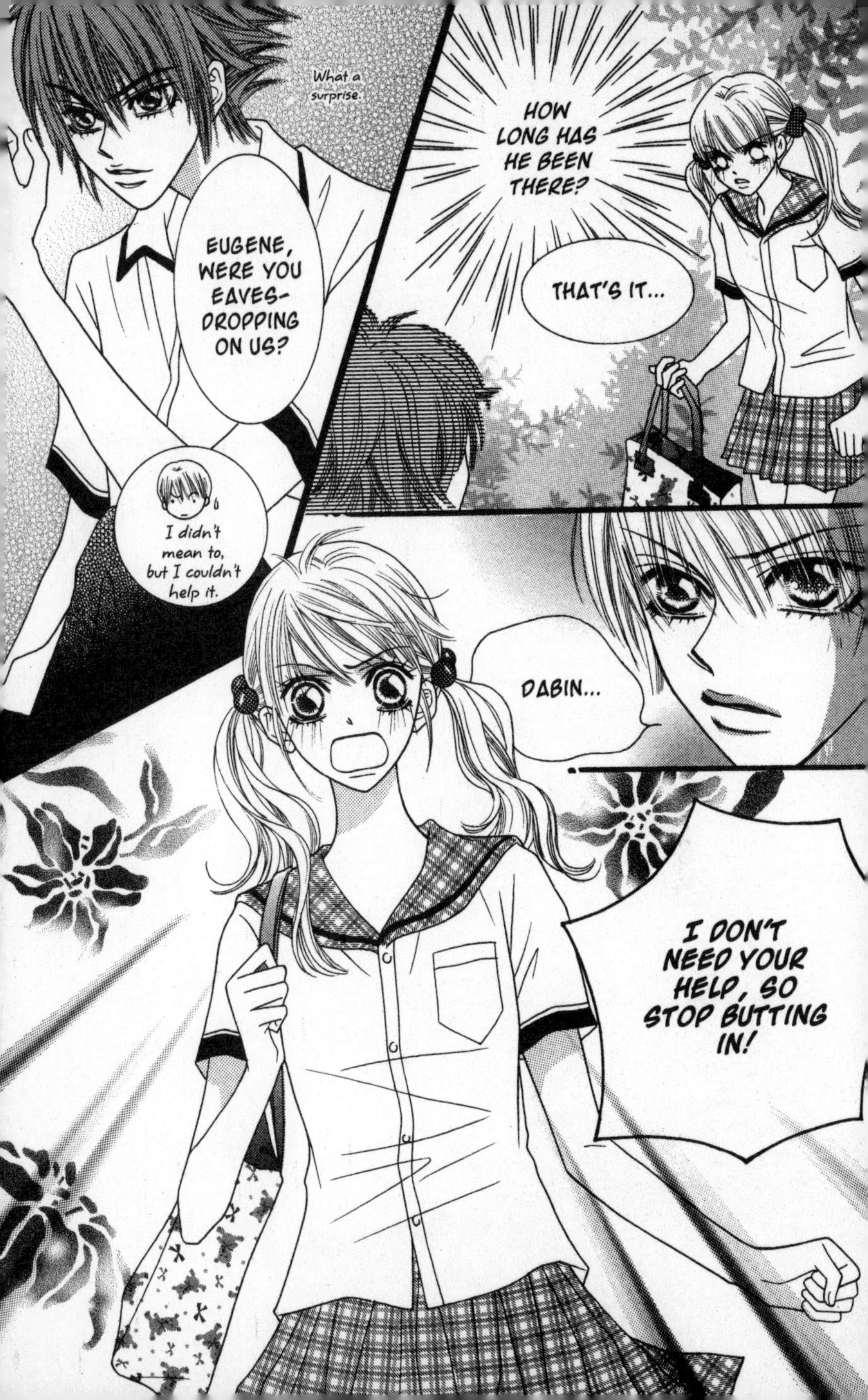
What a surprise.
EUGENE, WERE YOU EAVES-DROPPING ON US?
I didn't mean to, but I couldn't help it.
HOW LONG HAS HE BEEN THERE?
THAT'S IT...
DABIN...
I DON'T NEED YOUR HELP, SO STOP BUTTING IN!

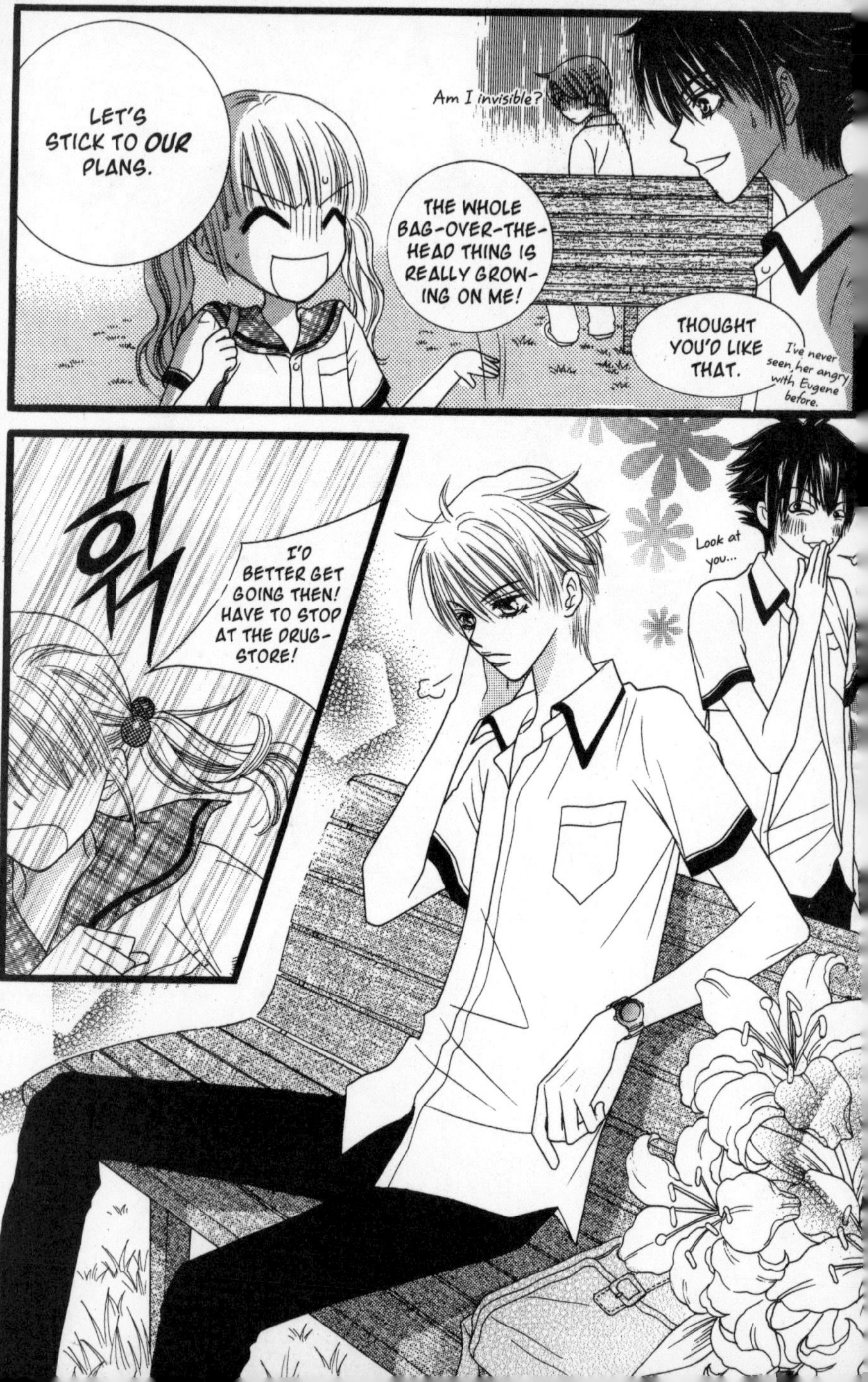
LET'S STICK TO *OUR* PLANS.
Am I invisible?
THE WHOLE BAG-OVER-THE-HEAD THING IS REALLY GROWING ON ME!
THOUGHT YOU'D LIKE THAT.
I've never seen her angry with Eugene before.
휙
I'D BETTER GET GOING THEN! HAVE TO STOP AT THE DRUG-STORE!
Look at you...

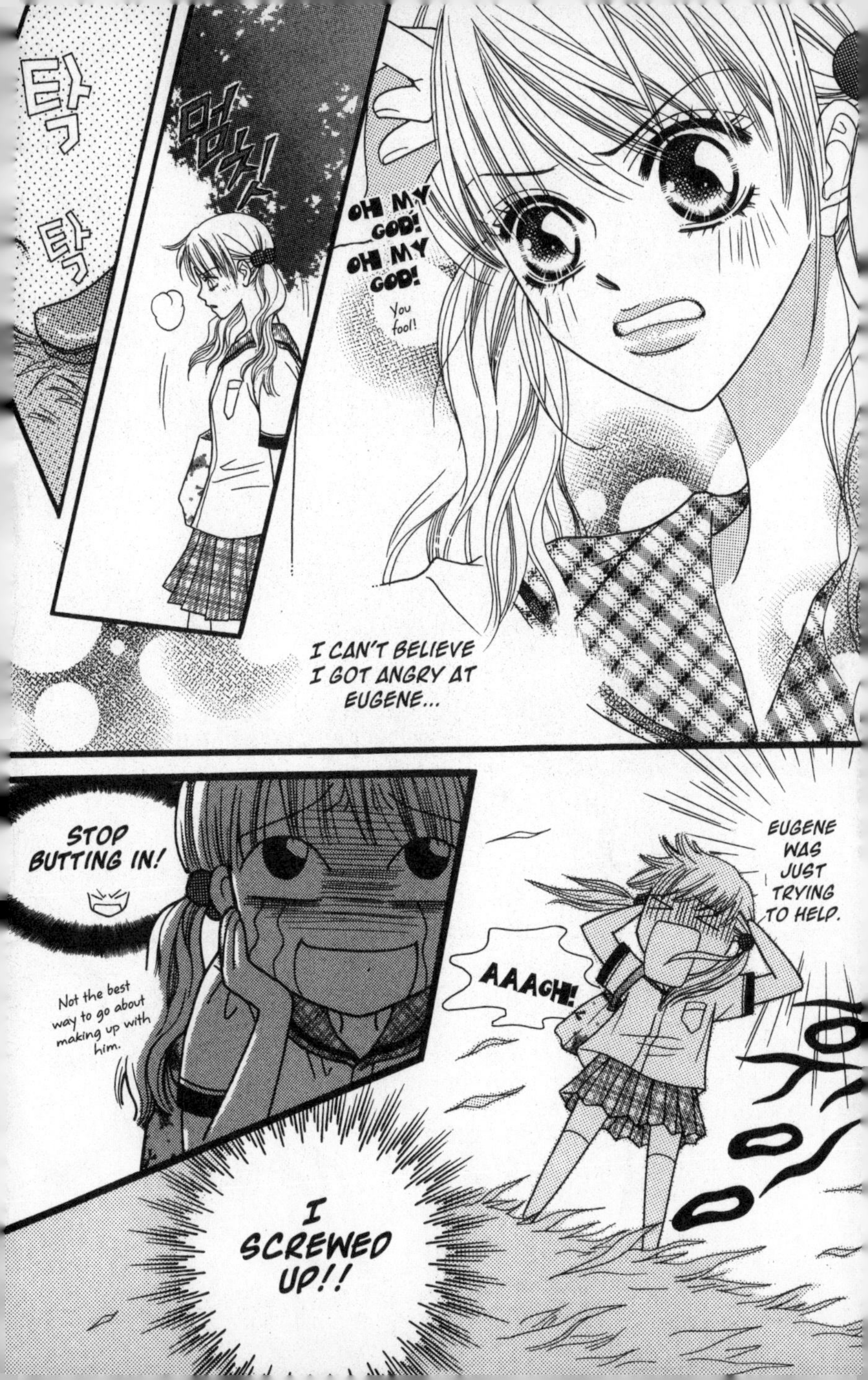
탁
탁
멈칫!
OH MY GOD! OH MY GOD!
You fool!
I CAN'T BELIEVE I GOT ANGRY AT EUGENE...
STOP BUTTING IN!
Not the best way to go about making up with him.
EUGENE WAS JUST TRYING TO HELP.
AAACH!
I SCREWED UP!!

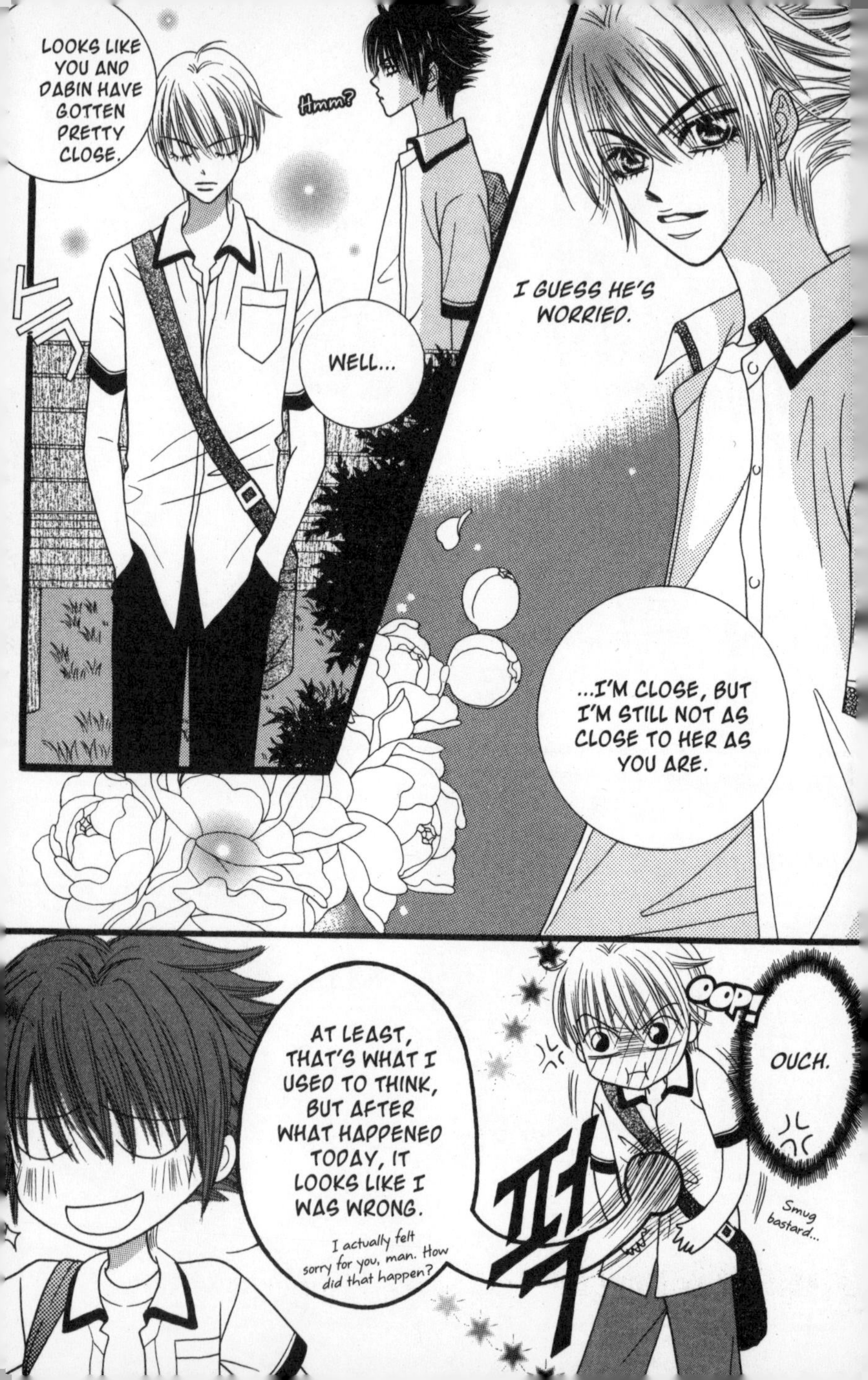
LOOKS LIKE YOU AND DABIN HAVE GOTTEN PRETTY CLOSE.
Hmm?
WELL...
I GUESS HE'S WORRIED.
...I'M CLOSE, BUT I'M STILL NOT AS CLOSE TO HER AS YOU ARE.
AT LEAST, THAT'S WHAT I USED TO THINK, BUT AFTER WHAT HAPPENED TODAY, IT LOOKS LIKE I WAS WRONG.
I actually felt sorry for you, man. How did that happen?
OOP!
OUCH.
Smug bastard...

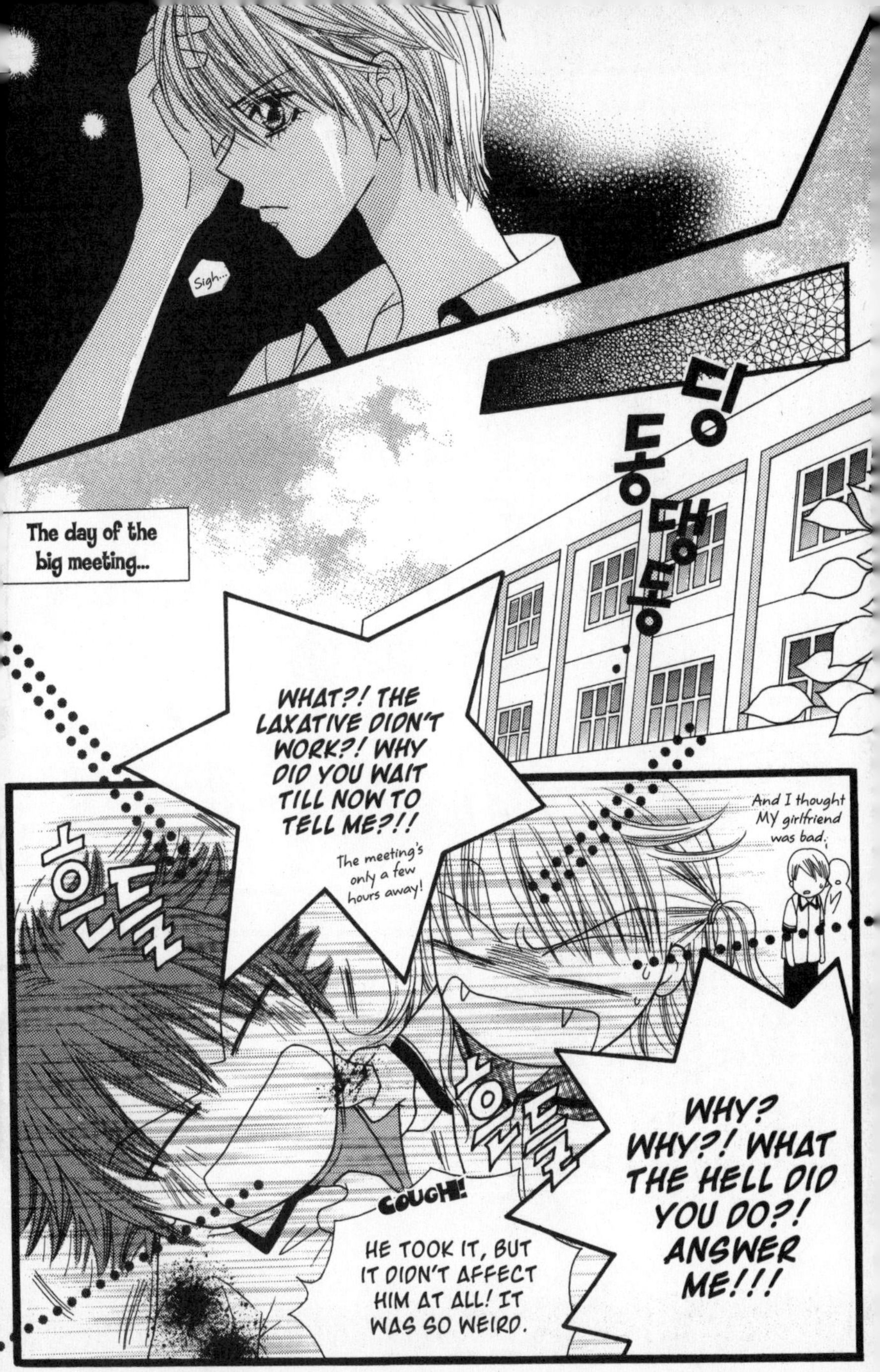
Sigh...
The day of the big meeting...
딩동댕동
WHAT?! THE LAXATIVE DIDN'T WORK?! WHY DID YOU WAIT TILL NOW TO TELL ME?!!
The meeting's only a few hours away!
And I thought MY girlfriend was bad.
COUGH!
HE TOOK IT, BUT IT DIDN'T AFFECT HIM AT ALL! IT WAS SO WEIRD.
WHY? WHY?! WHAT THE HELL DID YOU DO?! ANSWER ME!!!

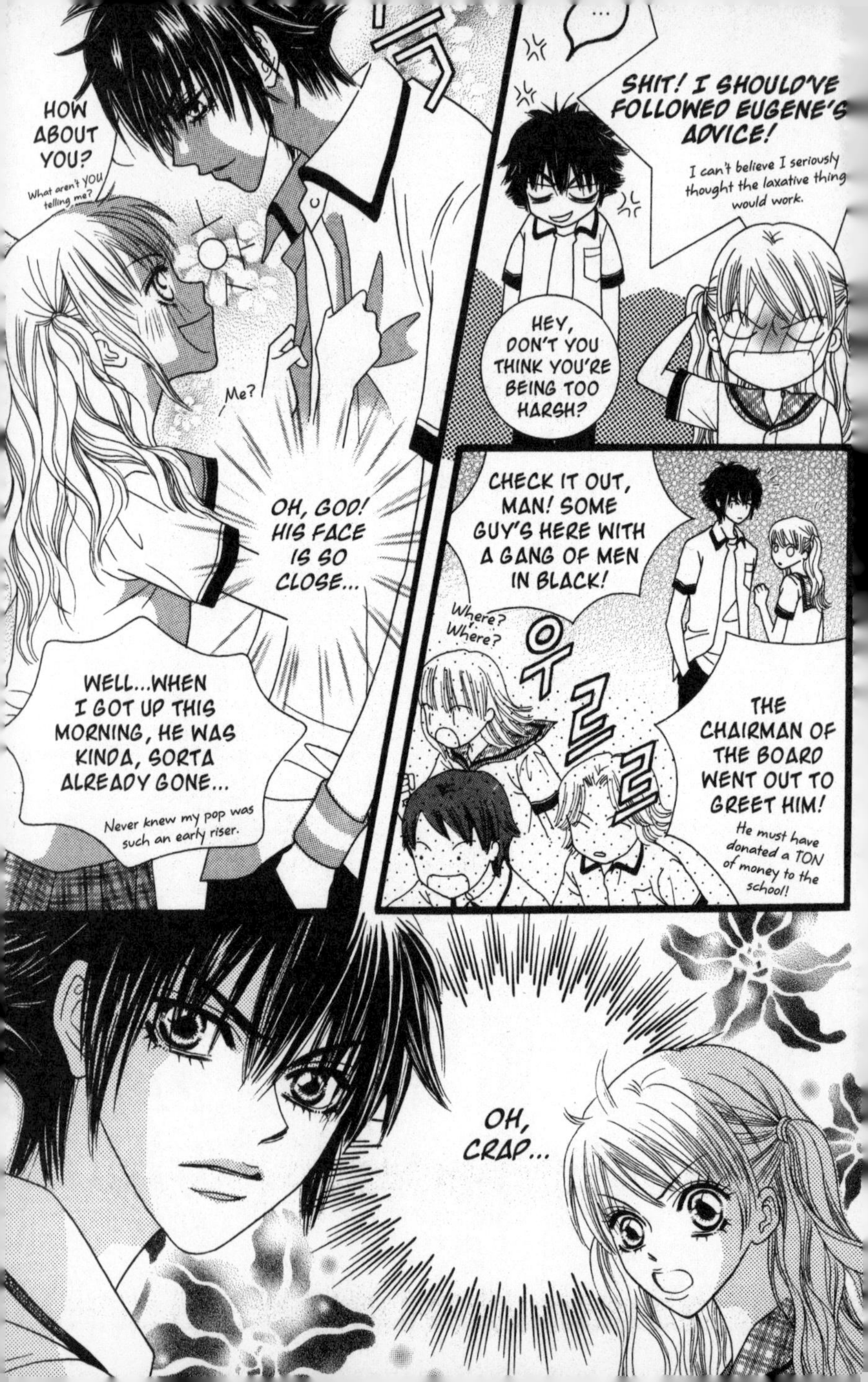
HOW ABOUT YOU?
What aren't YOU telling me?
Me?
OH, GOD! HIS FACE IS SO CLOSE...
WELL...WHEN I GOT UP THIS MORNING, HE WAS KINDA, SORTA ALREADY GONE...
Never knew my pop was such an early riser.
...
SHIT! I SHOULD'VE FOLLOWED EUGENE'S ADVICE!
I can't believe I seriously thought the laxative thing would work.
HEY, DON'T YOU THINK YOU'RE BEING TOO HARSH?
CHECK IT OUT, MAN! SOME GUY'S HERE WITH A GANG OF MEN IN BLACK!
Where? Where?
THE CHAIRMAN OF THE BOARD WENT OUT TO GREET HIM!
He must have donated a TON of money to the school!
OH, CRAP...

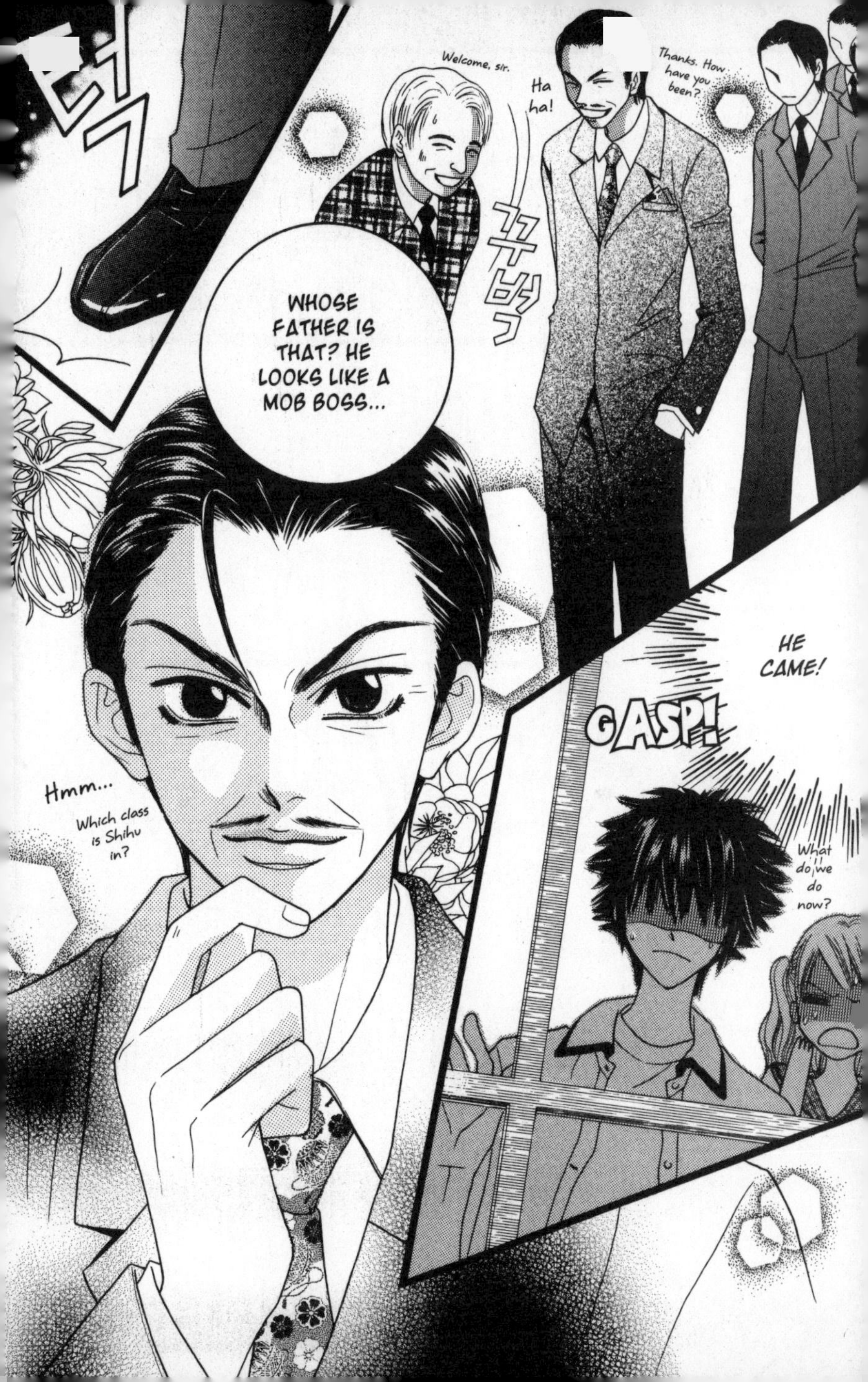
Welcome, sir.
Ha ha!
Thanks. How have you been?
꾸벅
WHOSE FATHER IS THAT? HE LOOKS LIKE A MOB BOSS...
Hmm...
Which class is Shihu in?
HE CAME!
GASP!
What do we do now?

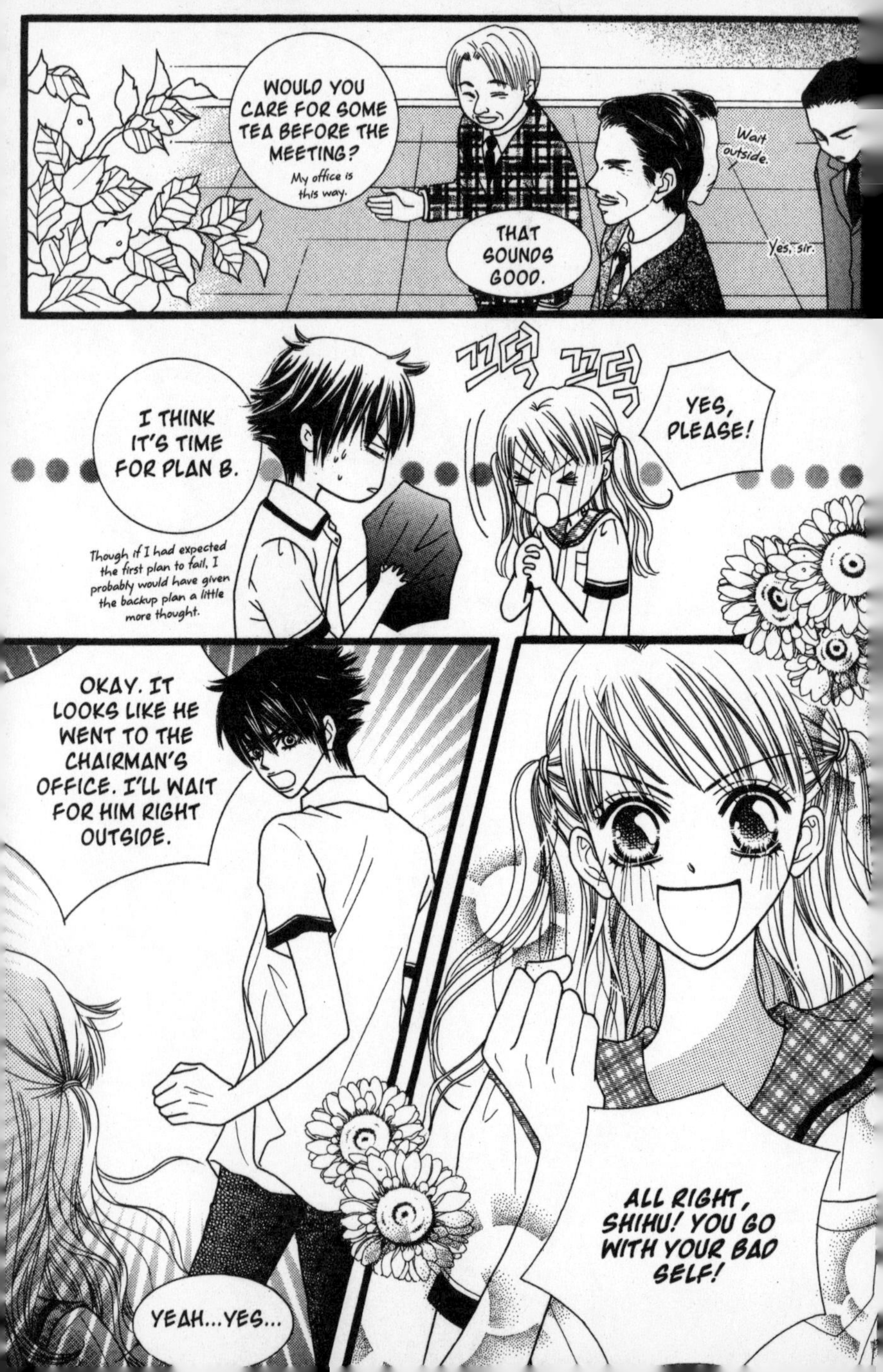
WOULD YOU CARE FOR SOME TEA BEFORE THE MEETING?
My office is this way.
THAT SOUNDS GOOD.
Wait outside.
Yes, sir.
I THINK IT'S TIME FOR PLAN B.
Though if I had expected the first plan to fail, I probably would have given the backup plan a little more thought.
끄덕 끄덕
YES, PLEASE!
OKAY. IT LOOKS LIKE HE WENT TO THE CHAIRMAN'S OFFICE. I'LL WAIT FOR HIM RIGHT OUTSIDE.
YEAH...YES...
ALL RIGHT, SHIHU! YOU GO WITH YOUR BAD SELF!

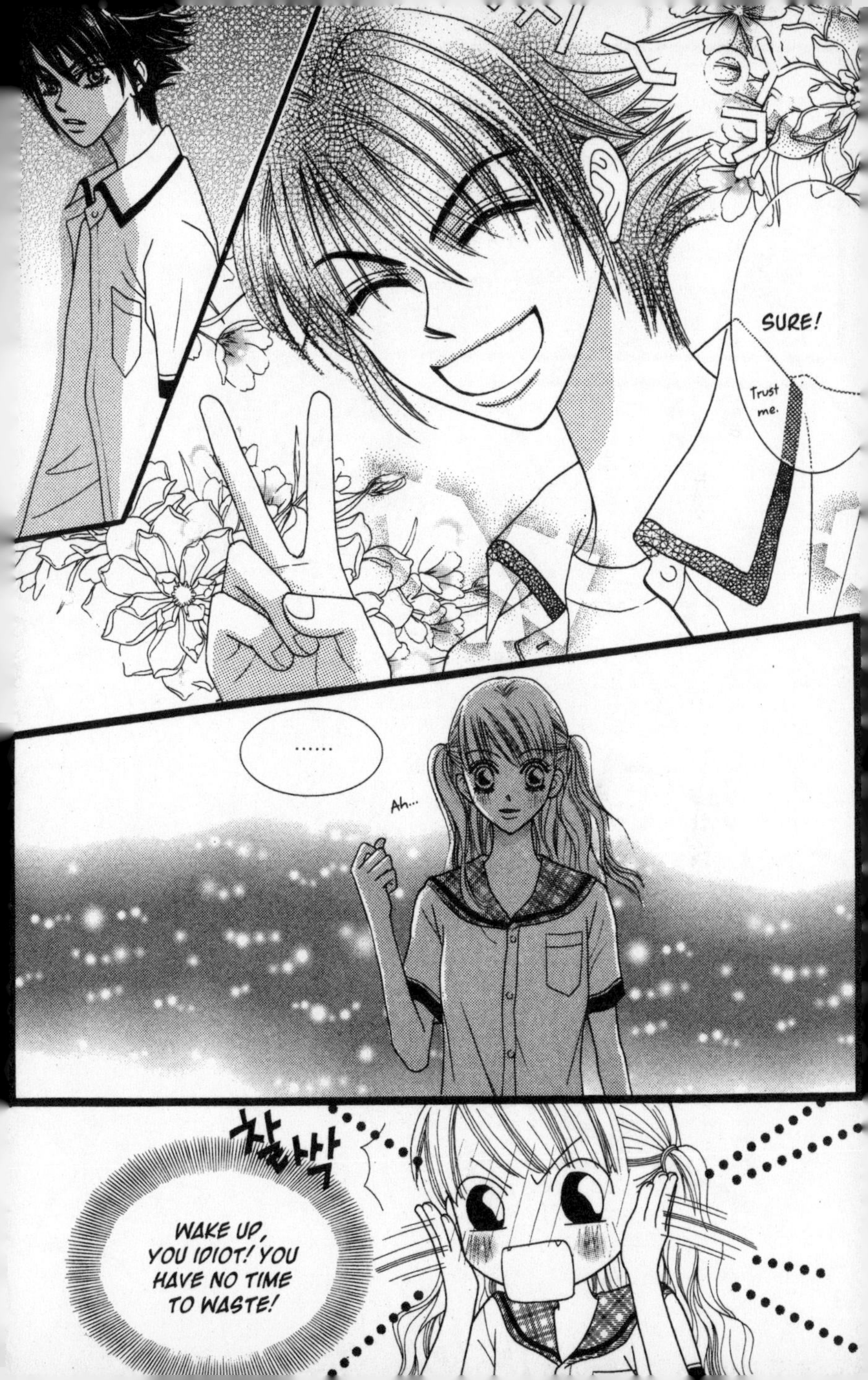
SURE!
Trust me.
......
Ah...
찰싹
WAKE UP, YOU IDIOT! YOU HAVE NO TIME TO WASTE!

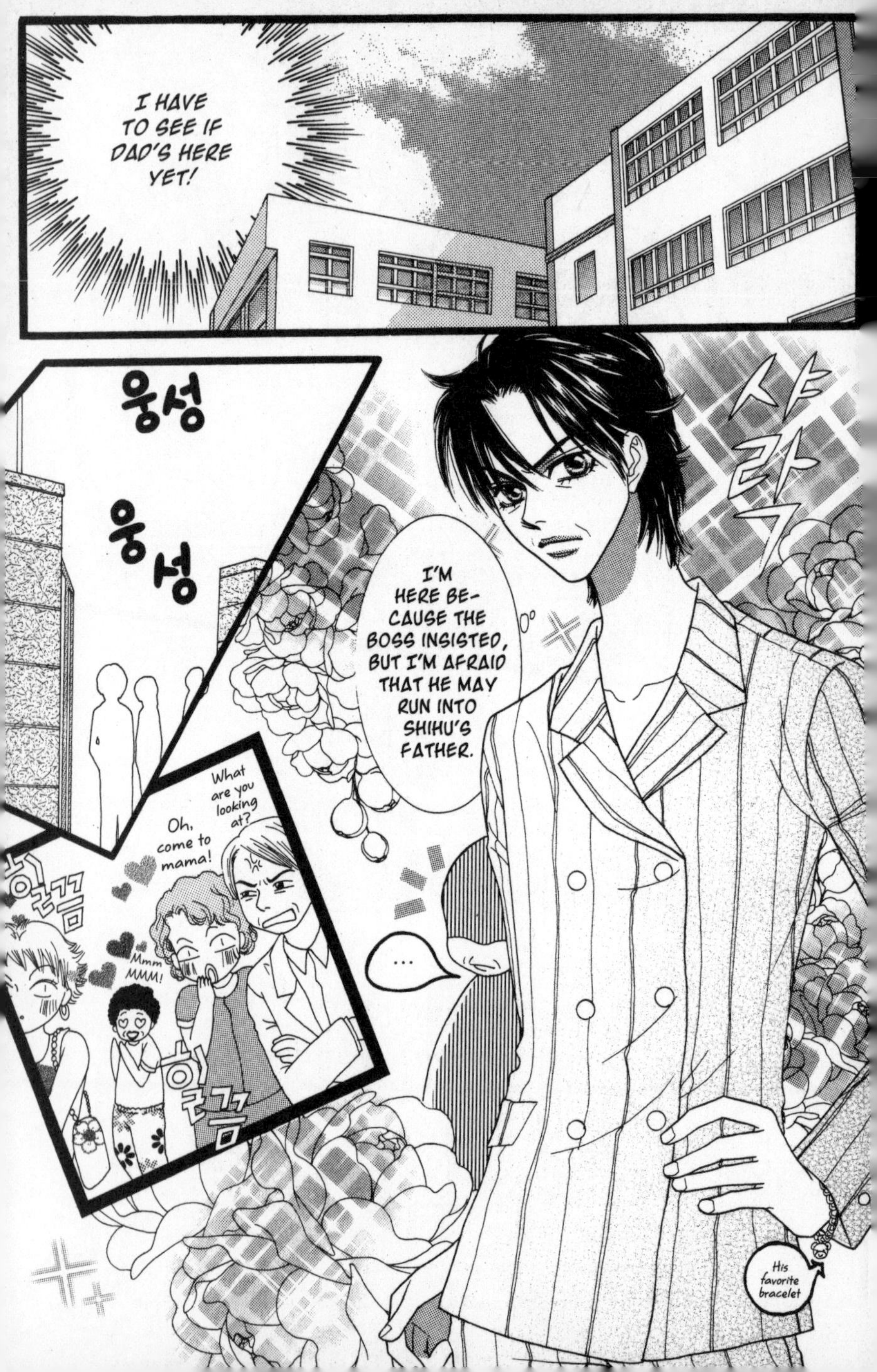
I HAVE TO SEE IF DAD'S HERE YET!
웅성 웅성
What are you looking at?
Oh, come to mama!
Mmm MMM!
힐끔
힐끔
샤락
I'M HERE BECAUSE THE BOSS INSISTED, BUT I'M AFRAID THAT HE MAY RUN INTO SHIHU'S FATHER.
...
His favorite bracelet

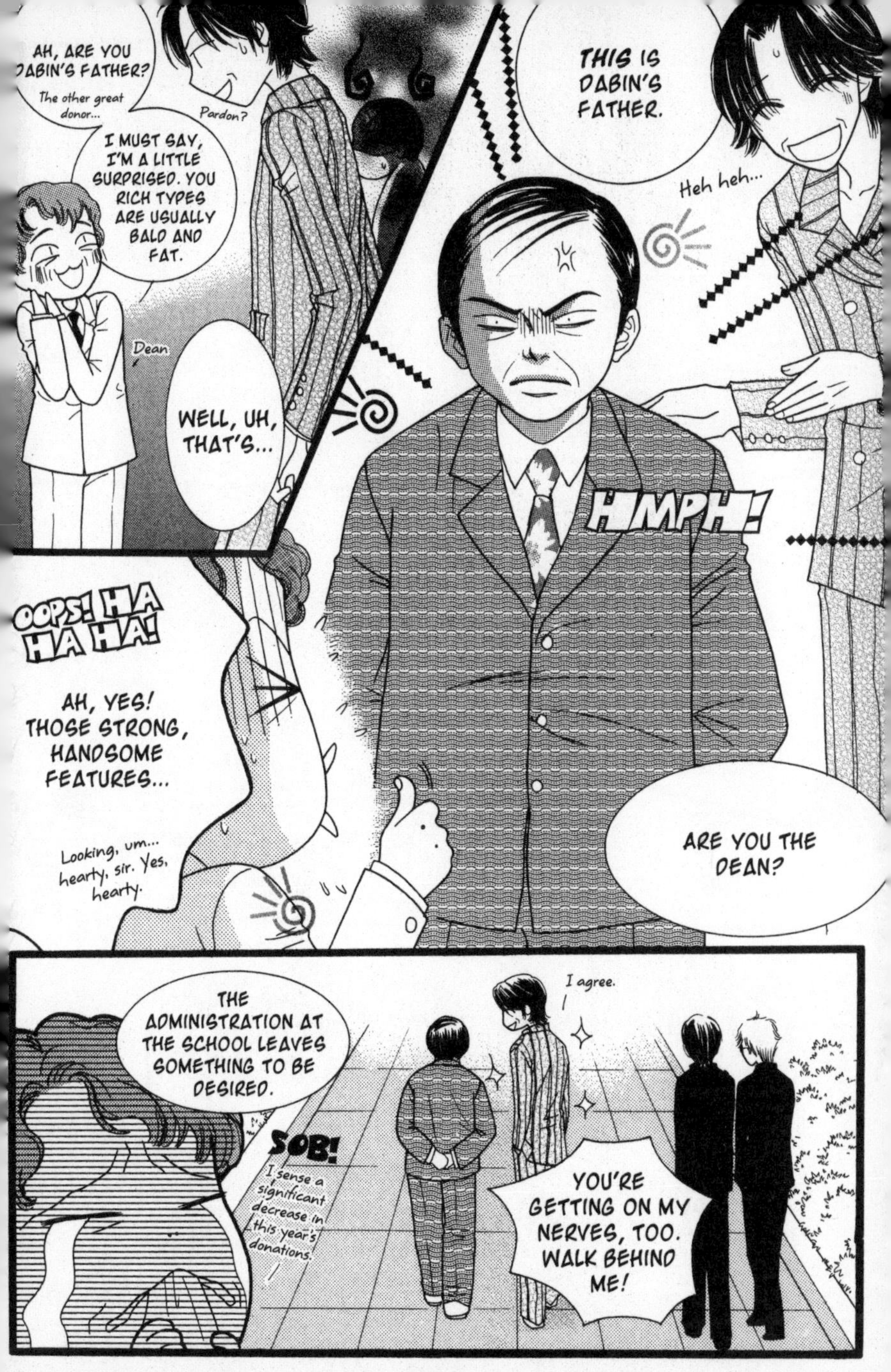
AH, ARE YOU DABIN'S FATHER?
The other great donor...
Pardon?
I MUST SAY, I'M A LITTLE SURPRISED. YOU RICH TYPES ARE USUALLY BALD AND FAT.
Dean
WELL, UH, THAT'S...
THIS IS DABIN'S FATHER.
Heh heh...
HMPH!
OOPS! HA HA HA!
AH, YES! THOSE STRONG, HANDSOME FEATURES...
Looking, um... hearty, sir. Yes, hearty.
ARE YOU THE DEAN?
THE ADMINISTRATION AT THE SCHOOL LEAVES SOMETHING TO BE DESIRED.
SOB!
I sense a significant decrease in this year's donations.
I agree.
YOU'RE GETTING ON MY NERVES, TOO. WALK BEHIND ME!

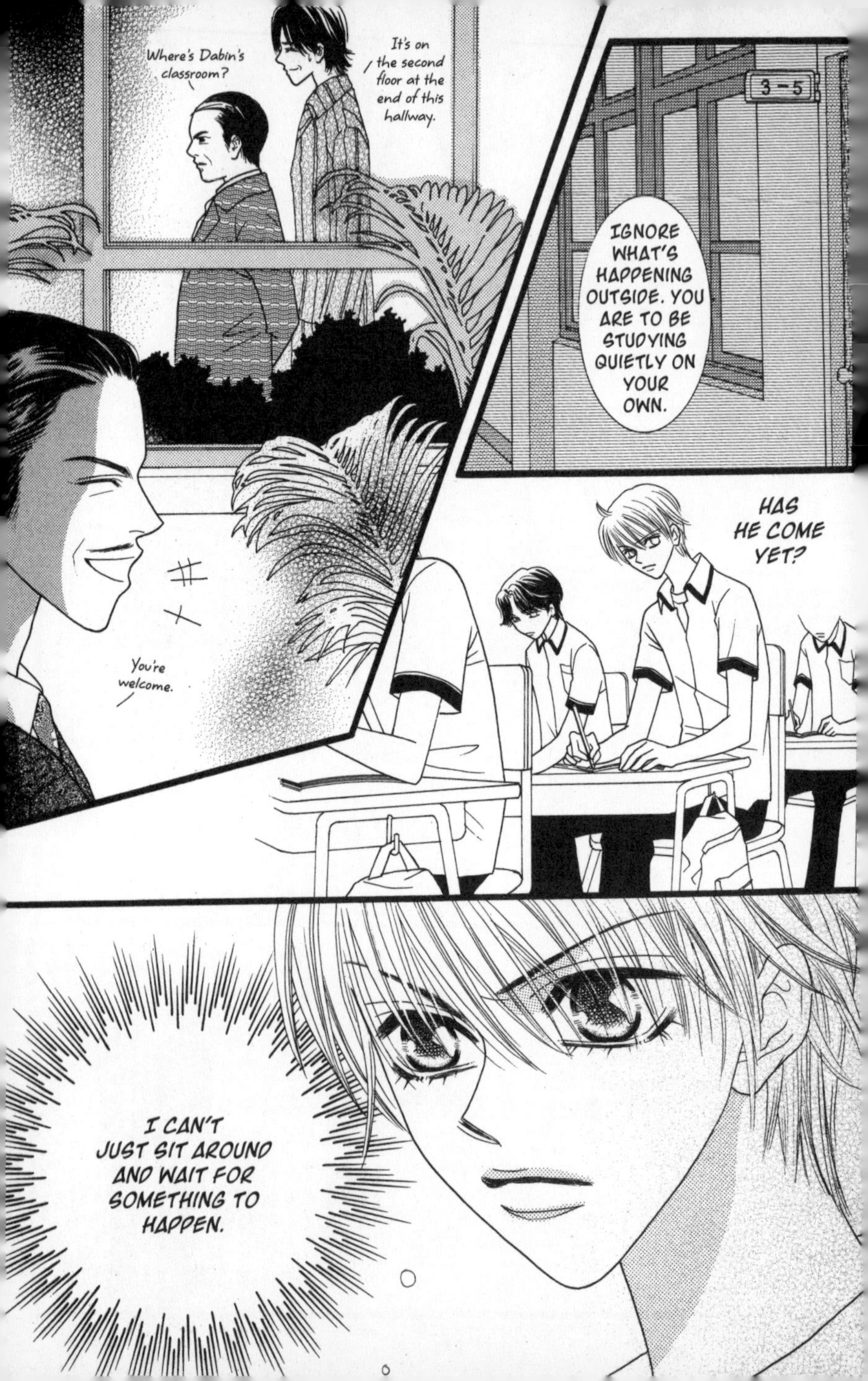
Where's Dabin's classroom?
It's on the second floor at the end of this hallway.
You're welcome.
3-5
IGNORE WHAT'S HAPPENING OUTSIDE. YOU ARE TO BE STUDYING QUIETLY ON YOUR OWN.
HAS HE COME YET?
I CAN'T JUST SIT AROUND AND WAIT FOR SOMETHING TO HAPPEN.

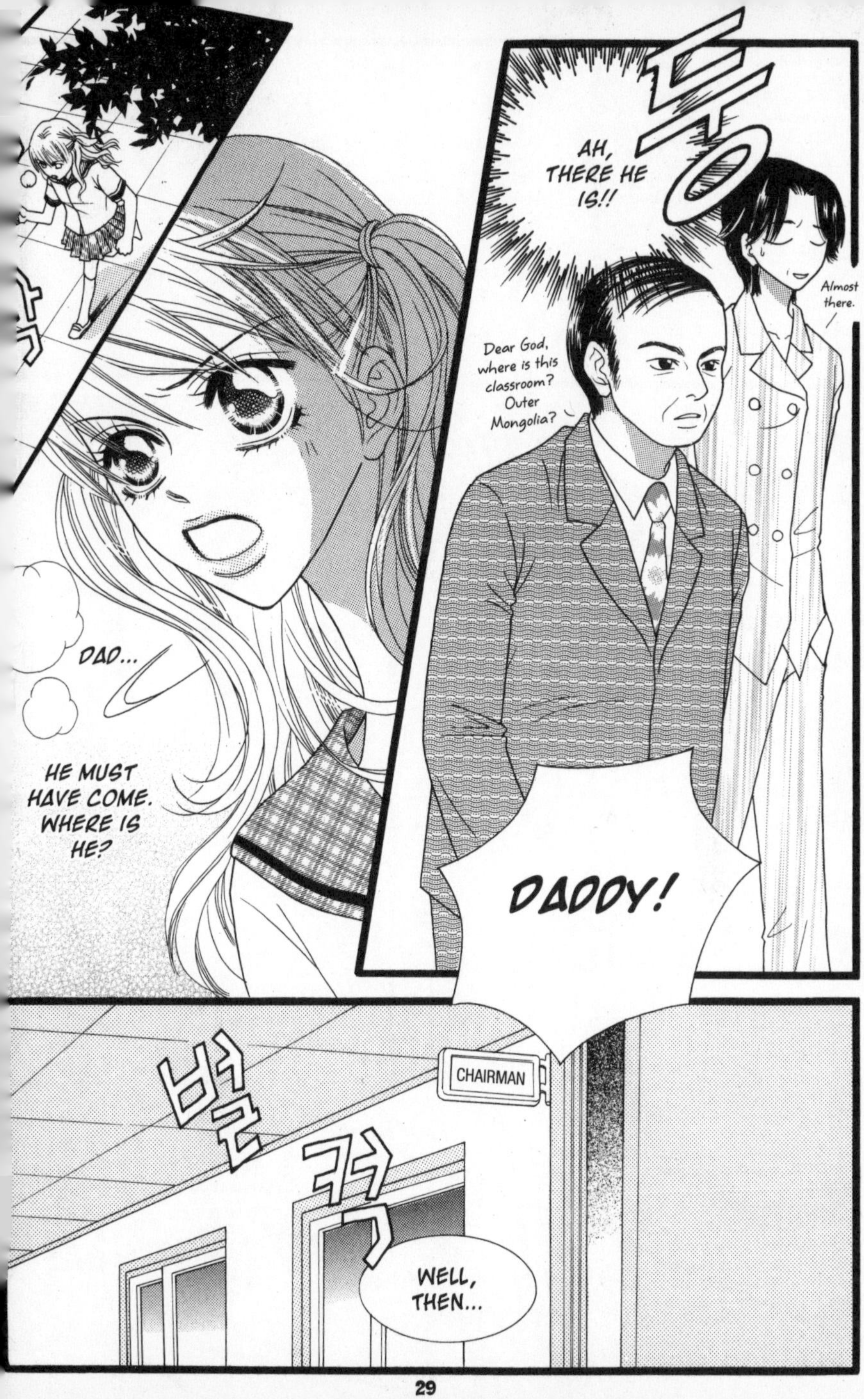
DAD...
HE MUST HAVE COME. WHERE IS HE?
AH, THERE HE IS!!
Dear God, where is this classroom? Outer Mongolia?
Almost there.
DADDY!
CHAIRMAN
WELL, THEN...

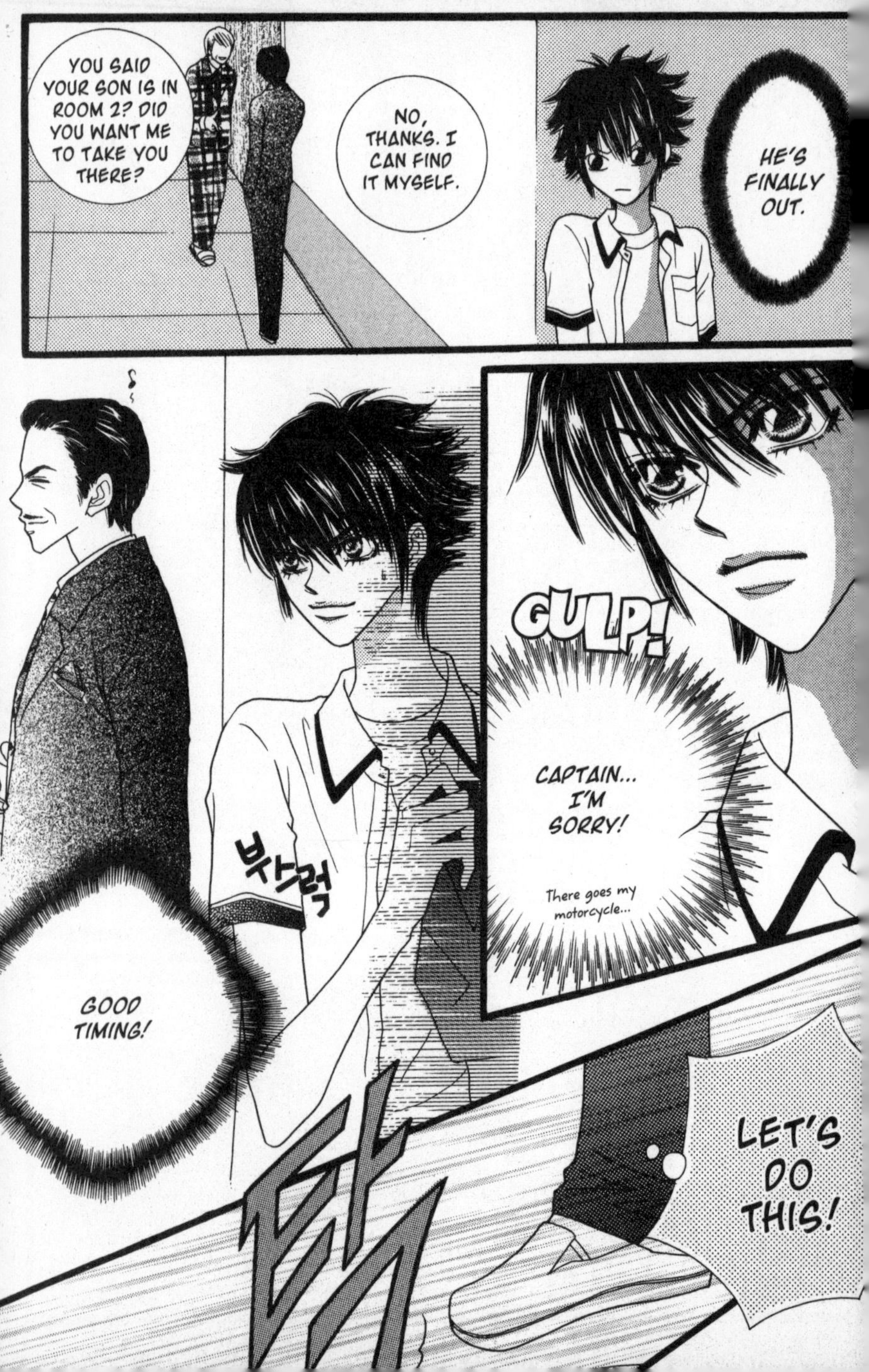
YOU SAID YOUR SON IS IN ROOM 2? DID YOU WANT ME TO TAKE YOU THERE?
NO, THANKS. I CAN FIND IT MYSELF.
HE'S FINALLY OUT.
GOOD TIMING!
GULP!
CAPTAIN... I'M SORRY!
There goes my motorcycle...
LET'S DO THIS!

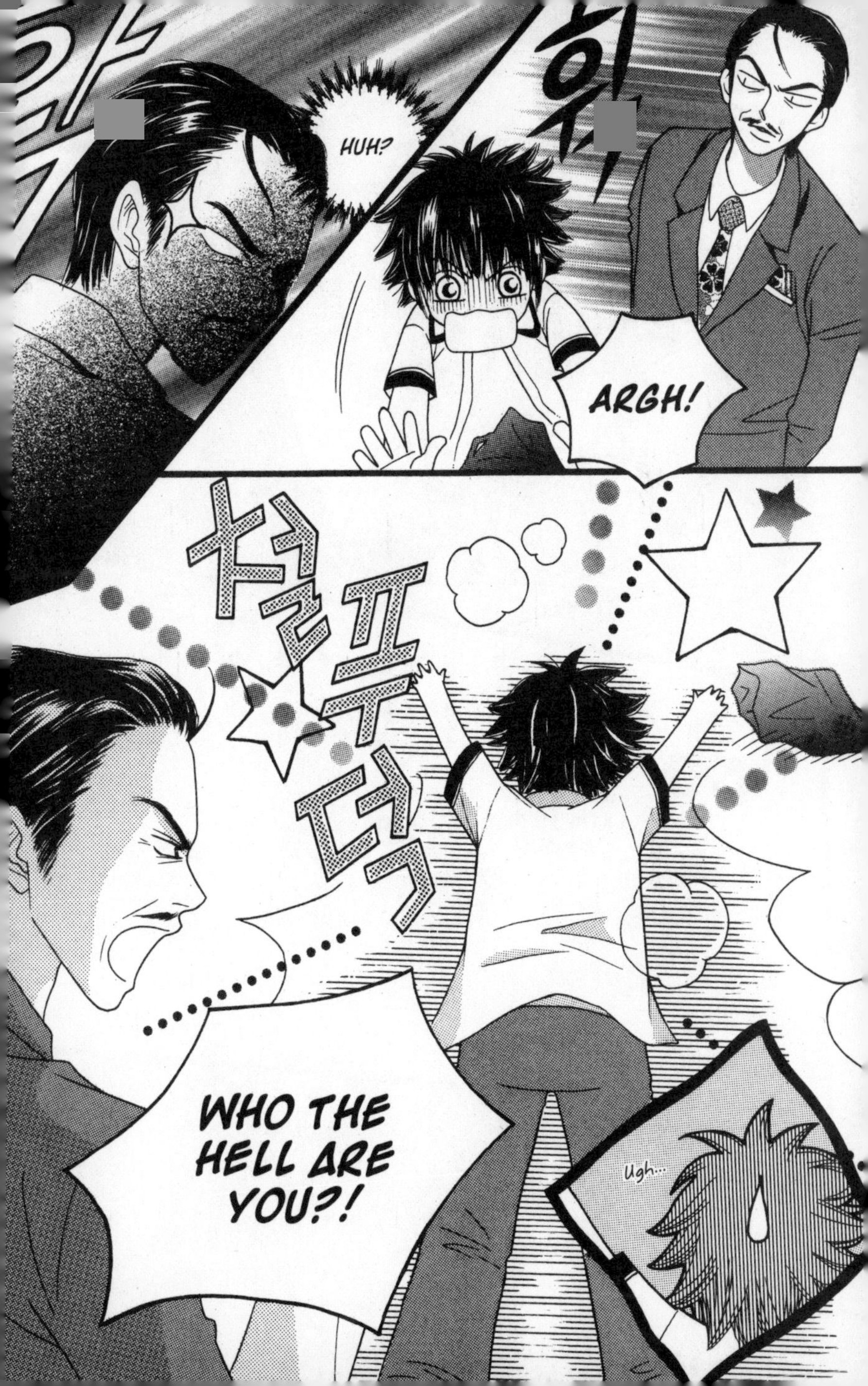
HUH?
ARGH!
철푸덕
WHO THE HELL ARE YOU?!
Ugh...

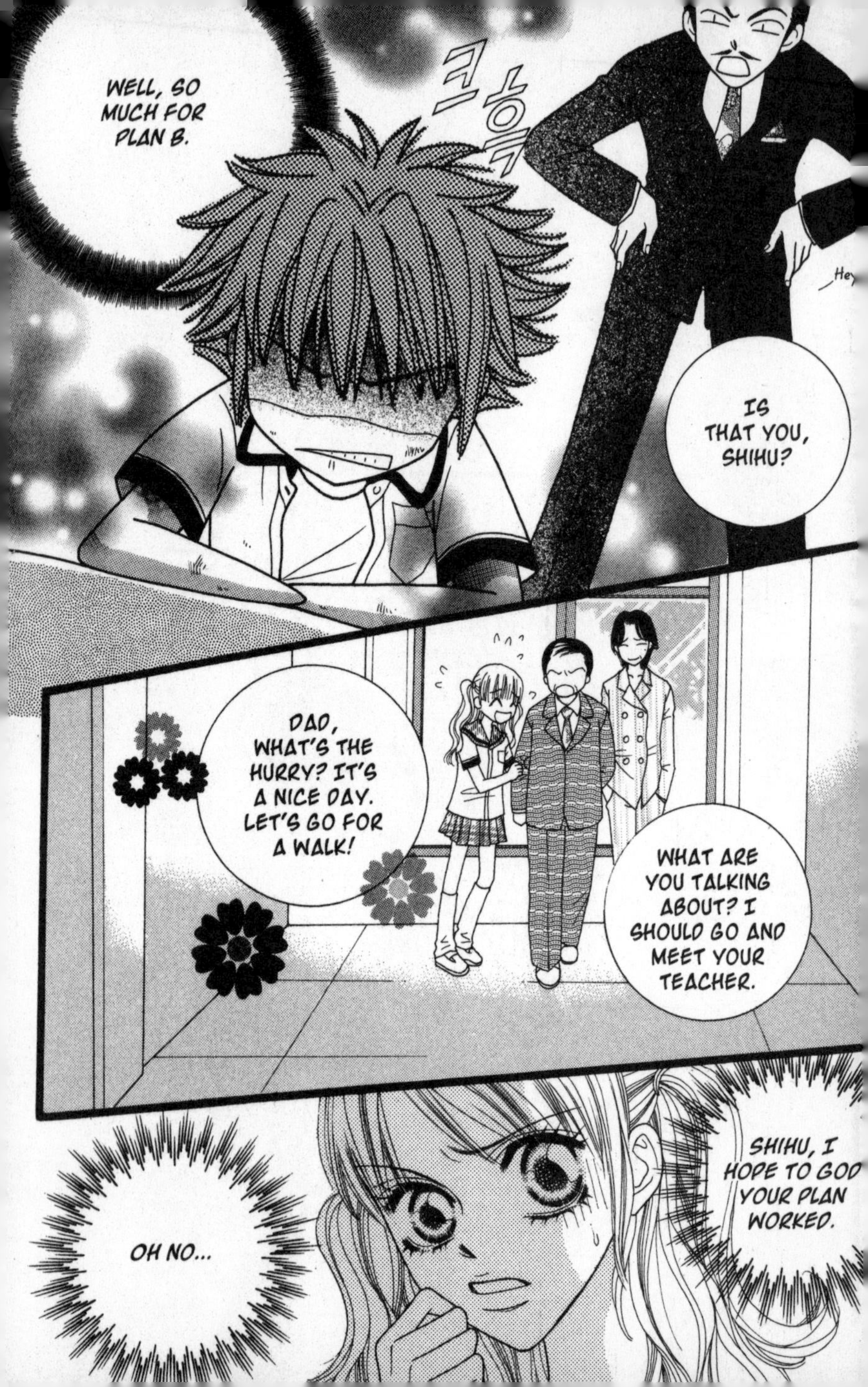
WELL, SO MUCH FOR PLAN B.
Hey
IS THAT YOU, SHIHU?
DAD, WHAT'S THE HURRY? IT'S A NICE DAY. LET'S GO FOR A WALK!
WHAT ARE YOU TALKING ABOUT? I SHOULD GO AND MEET YOUR TEACHER.
OH NO...
SHIHU, I HOPE TO GOD YOUR PLAN WORKED.

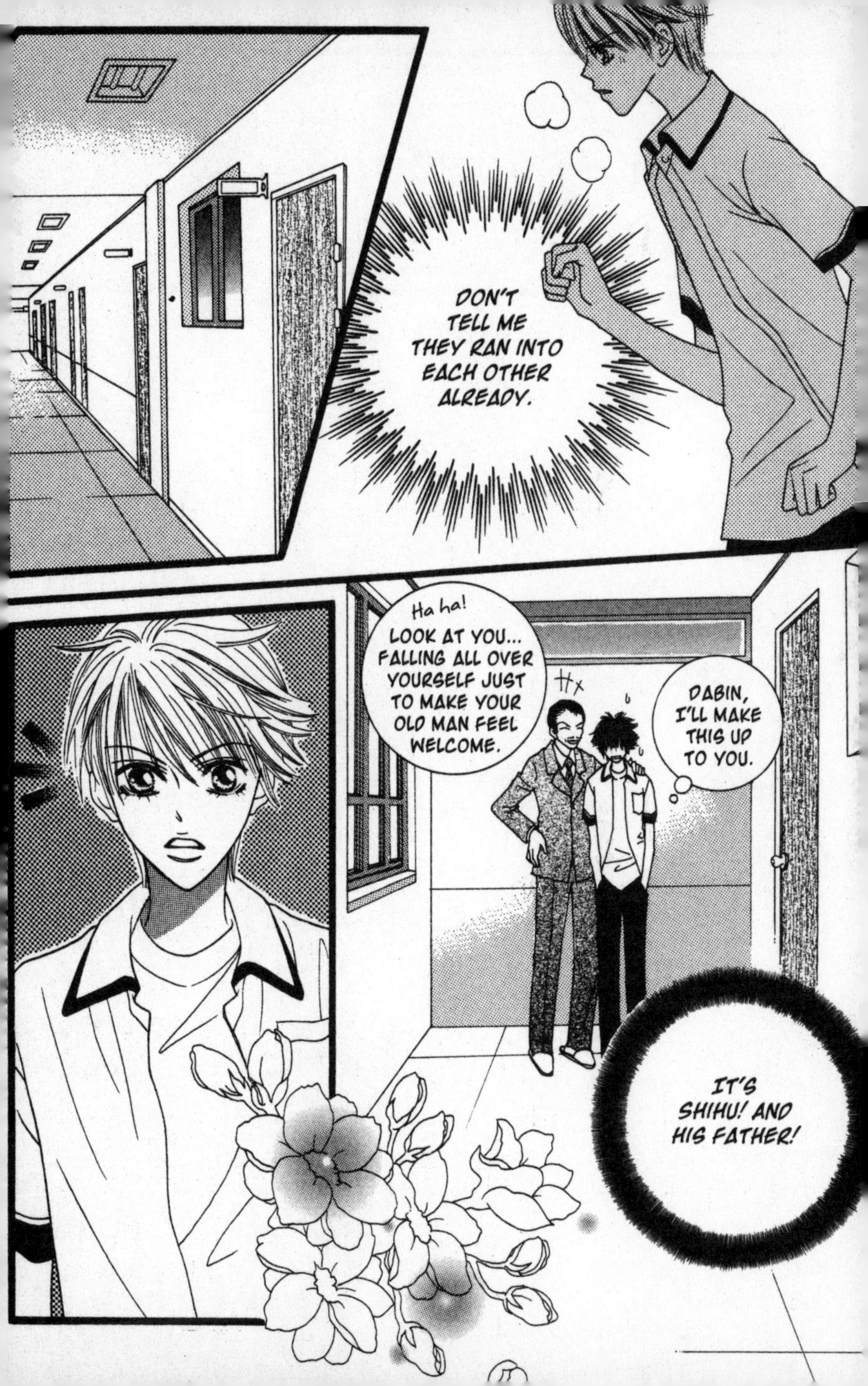
DON'T TELL ME THEY RAN INTO EACH OTHER ALREADY.
Ha ha! LOOK AT YOU... FALLING ALL OVER YOURSELF JUST TO MAKE YOUR OLD MAN FEEL WELCOME.
DABIN, I'LL MAKE THIS UP TO YOU.
IT'S SHIHU! AND HIS FATHER!

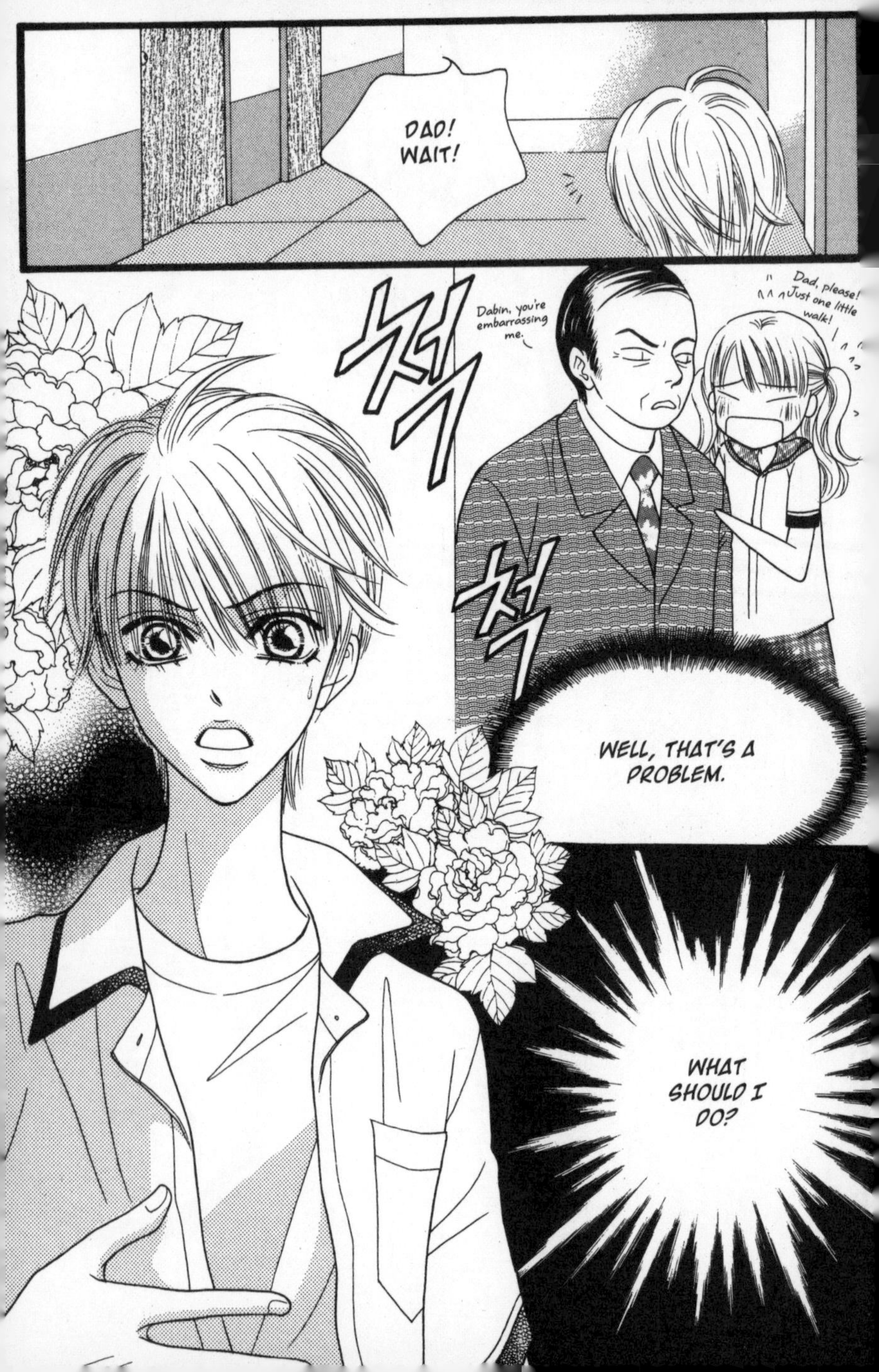
DAD! WAIT!
Dabin, you're embarrassing me.
Dad, please! Just one little walk!
WELL, THAT'S A PROBLEM.
WHAT SHOULD I DO?

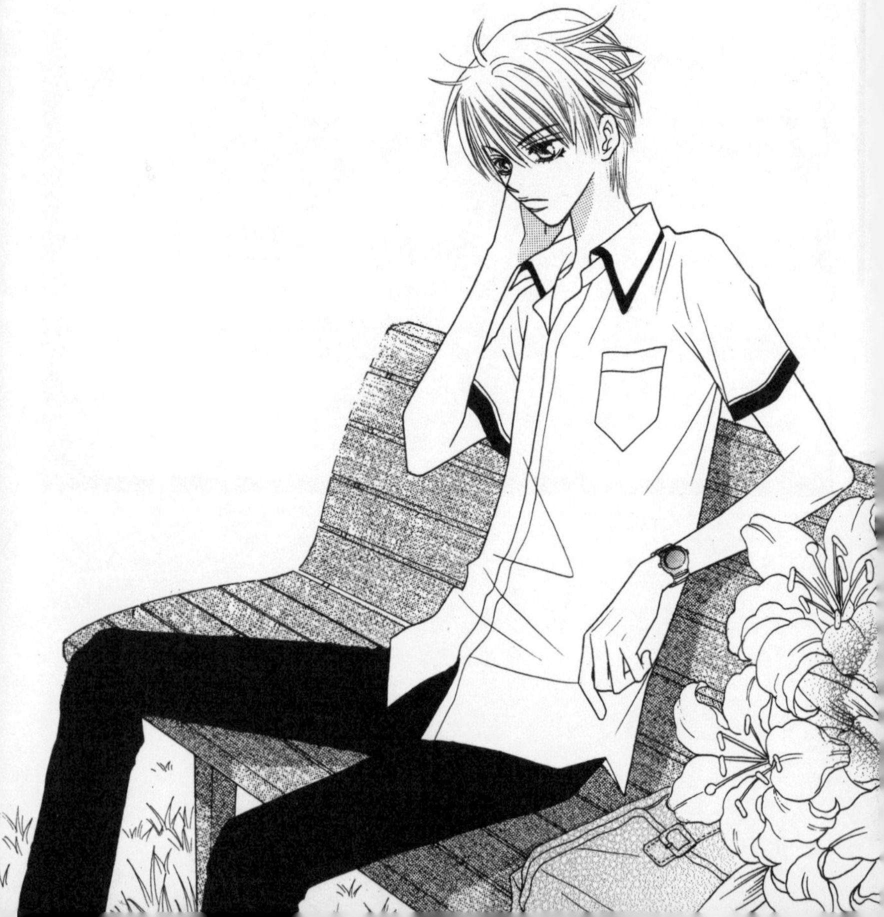

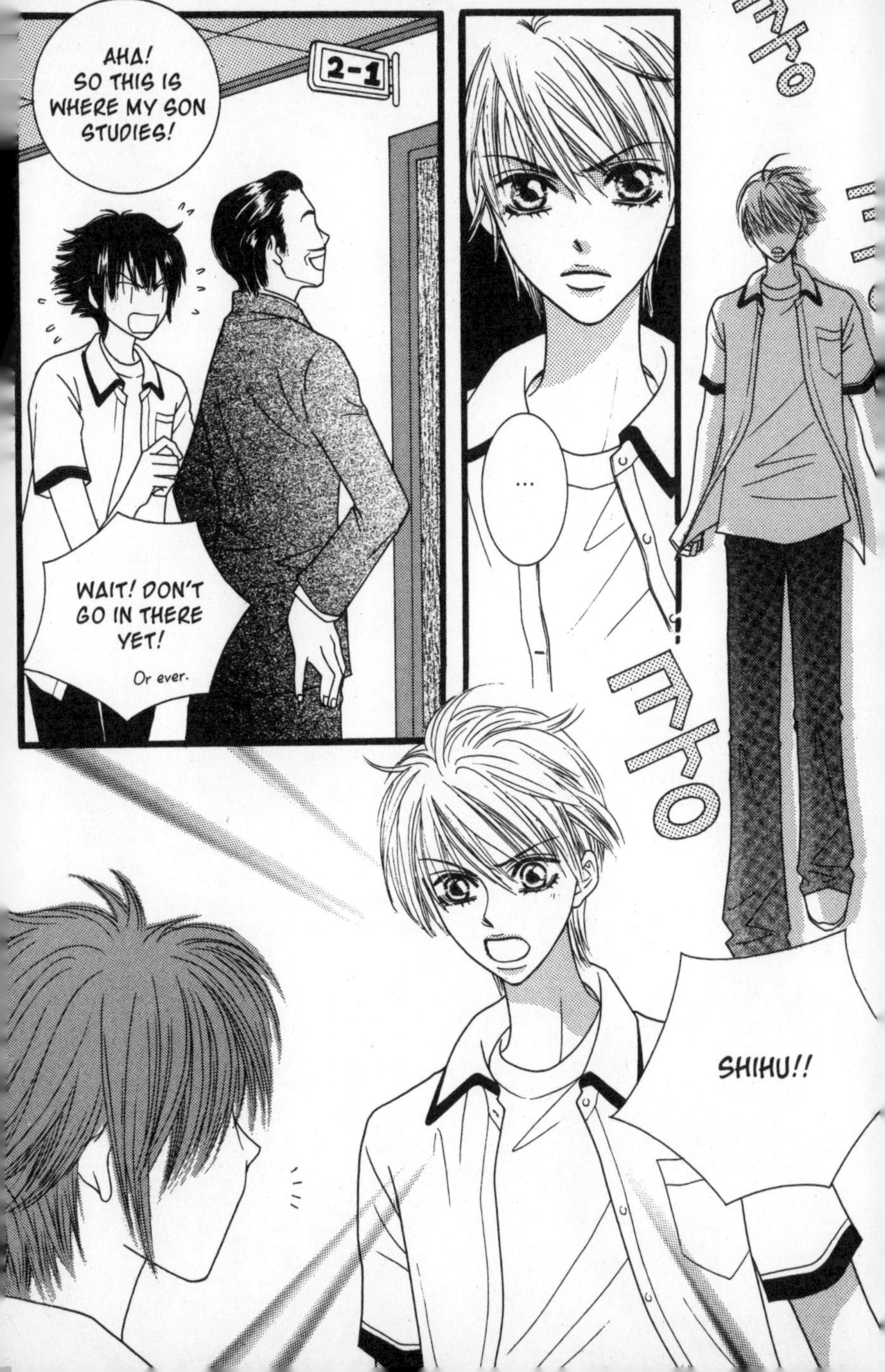
AHA! SO THIS IS WHERE MY SON STUDIES!
2-1
WAIT! DON'T GO IN THERE YET!
Or ever.
...
SHIHU!!

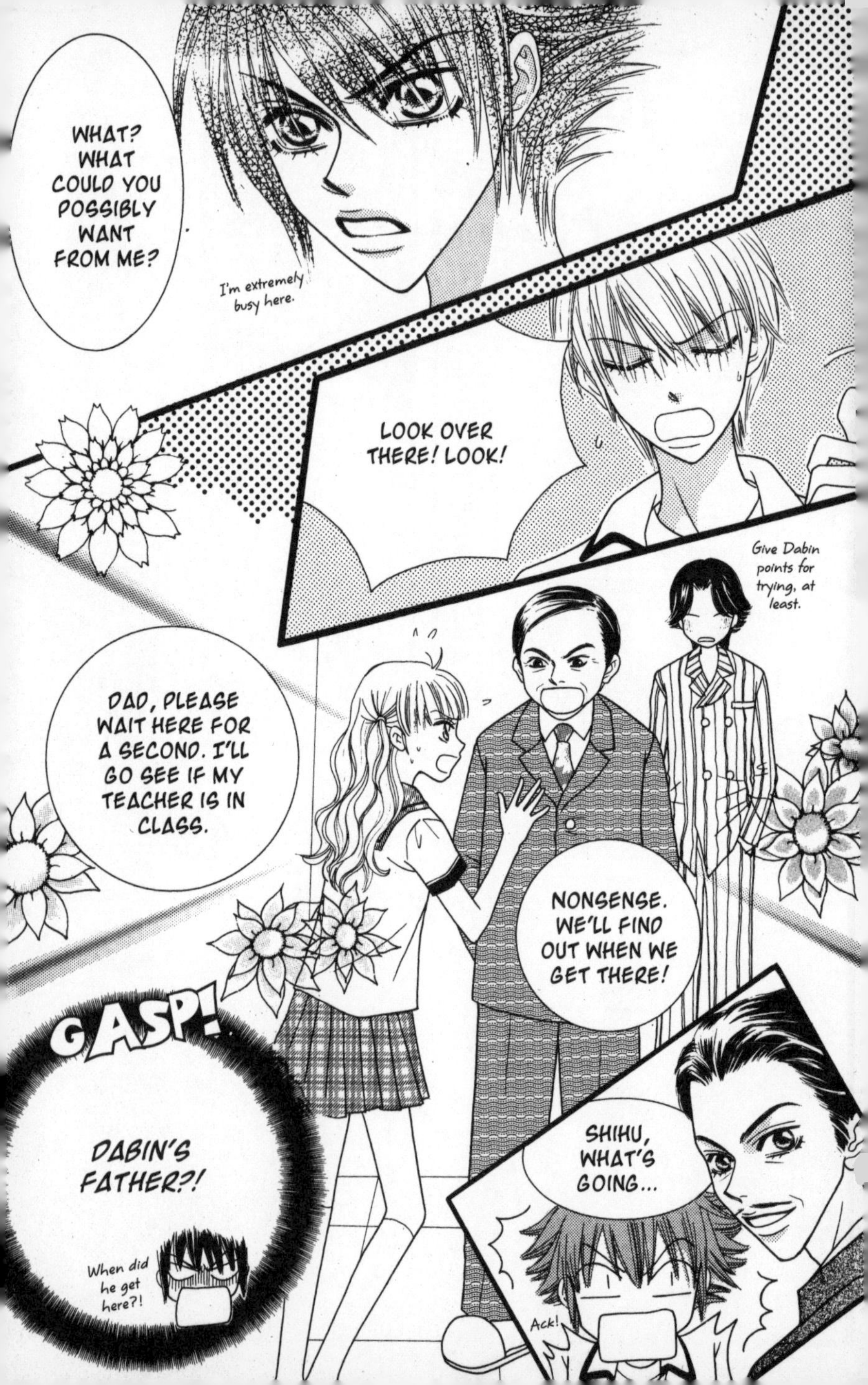
WHAT? WHAT COULD YOU POSSIBLY WANT FROM ME?
I'm extremely busy here.
LOOK OVER THERE! LOOK!
Give Dabin points for trying, at least.
DAD, PLEASE WAIT HERE FOR A SECOND. I'LL GO SEE IF MY TEACHER IS IN CLASS.
NONSENSE. WE'LL FIND OUT WHEN WE GET THERE!
GASP!
DABIN'S FATHER?!
When did he get here?!
SHIHU, WHAT'S GOING...
Ack!

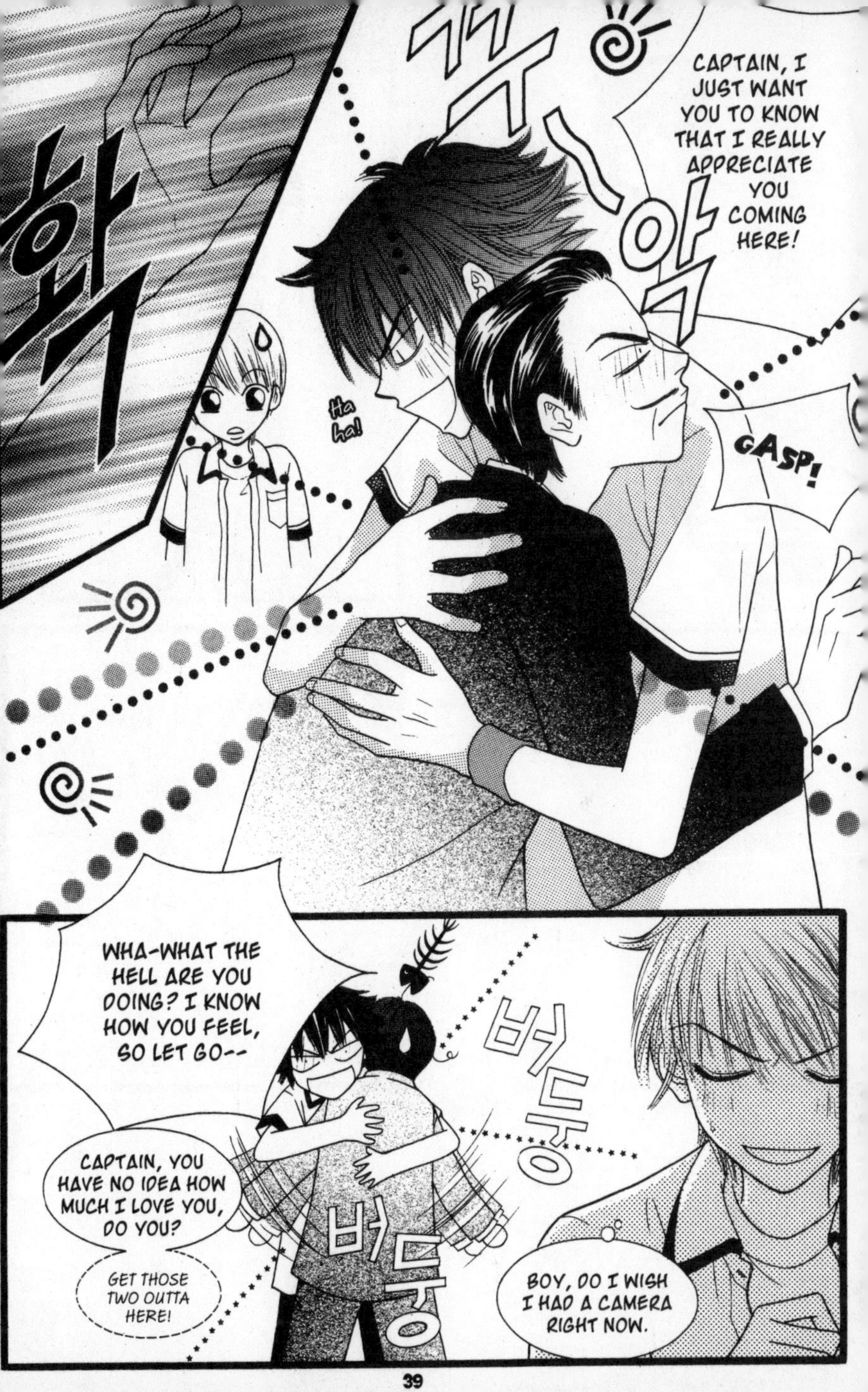
확
Ha ha!
CAPTAIN, I JUST WANT YOU TO KNOW THAT I REALLY APPRECIATE YOU COMING HERE!
GASP!
WHA-WHAT THE HELL ARE YOU DOING? I KNOW HOW YOU FEEL, SO LET GO--
CAPTAIN, YOU HAVE NO IDEA HOW MUCH I LOVE YOU, DO YOU?
GET THOSE TWO OUTTA HERE!
버둥
버둥
BOY, DO I WISH I HAD A CAMERA RIGHT NOW.

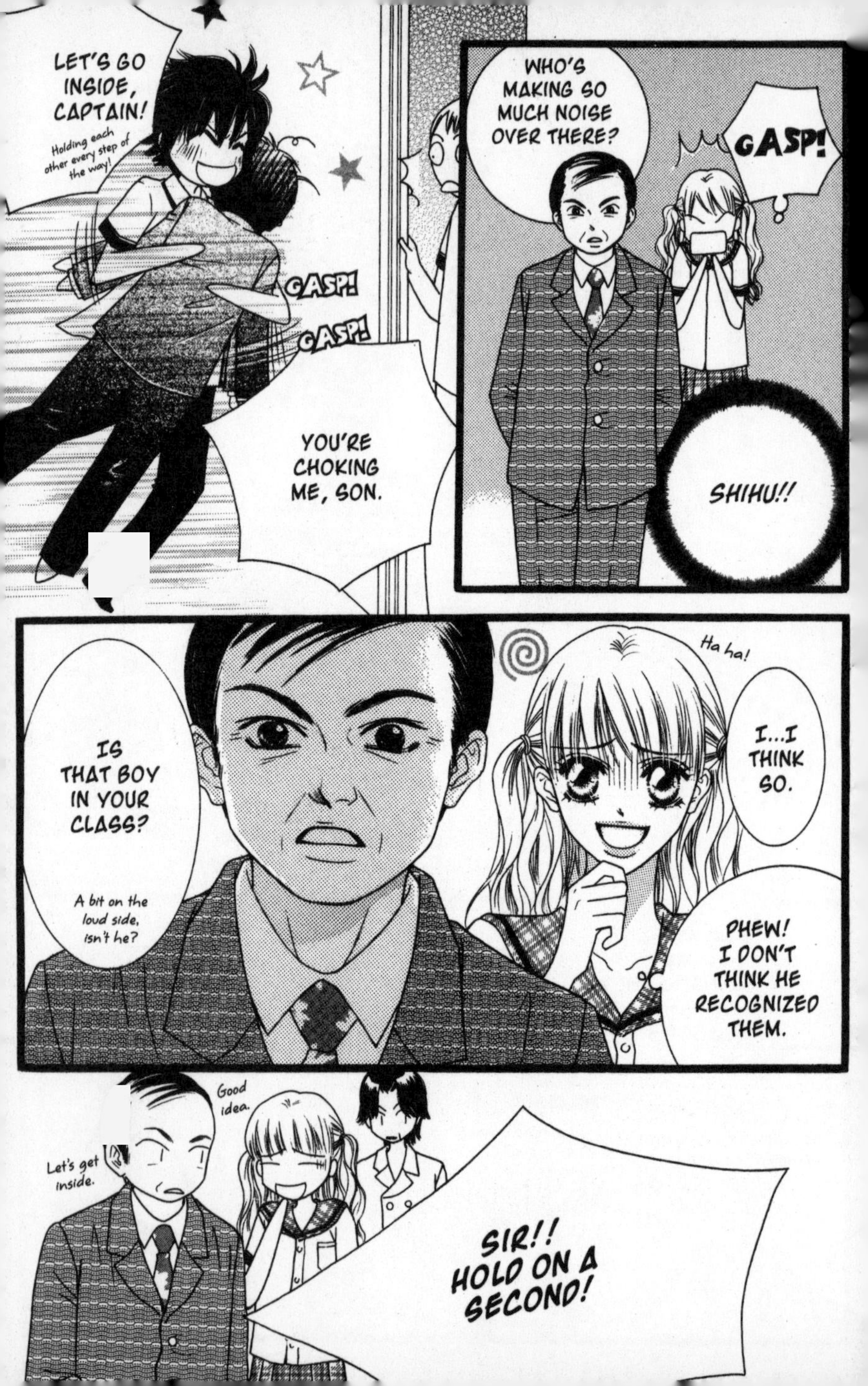
LET'S GO INSIDE, CAPTAIN!
Holding each other every step of the way!
GASP!
GASP!
YOU'RE CHOKING ME, SON.
WHO'S MAKING SO MUCH NOISE OVER THERE?
GASP!
SHIHU!!
IS THAT BOY IN YOUR CLASS?
A bit on the loud side, isn't he?
Ha ha!
I...I THINK SO.
PHEW! I DON'T THINK HE RECOGNIZED THEM.
Let's get inside.
Good idea.
SIR!! HOLD ON A SECOND!

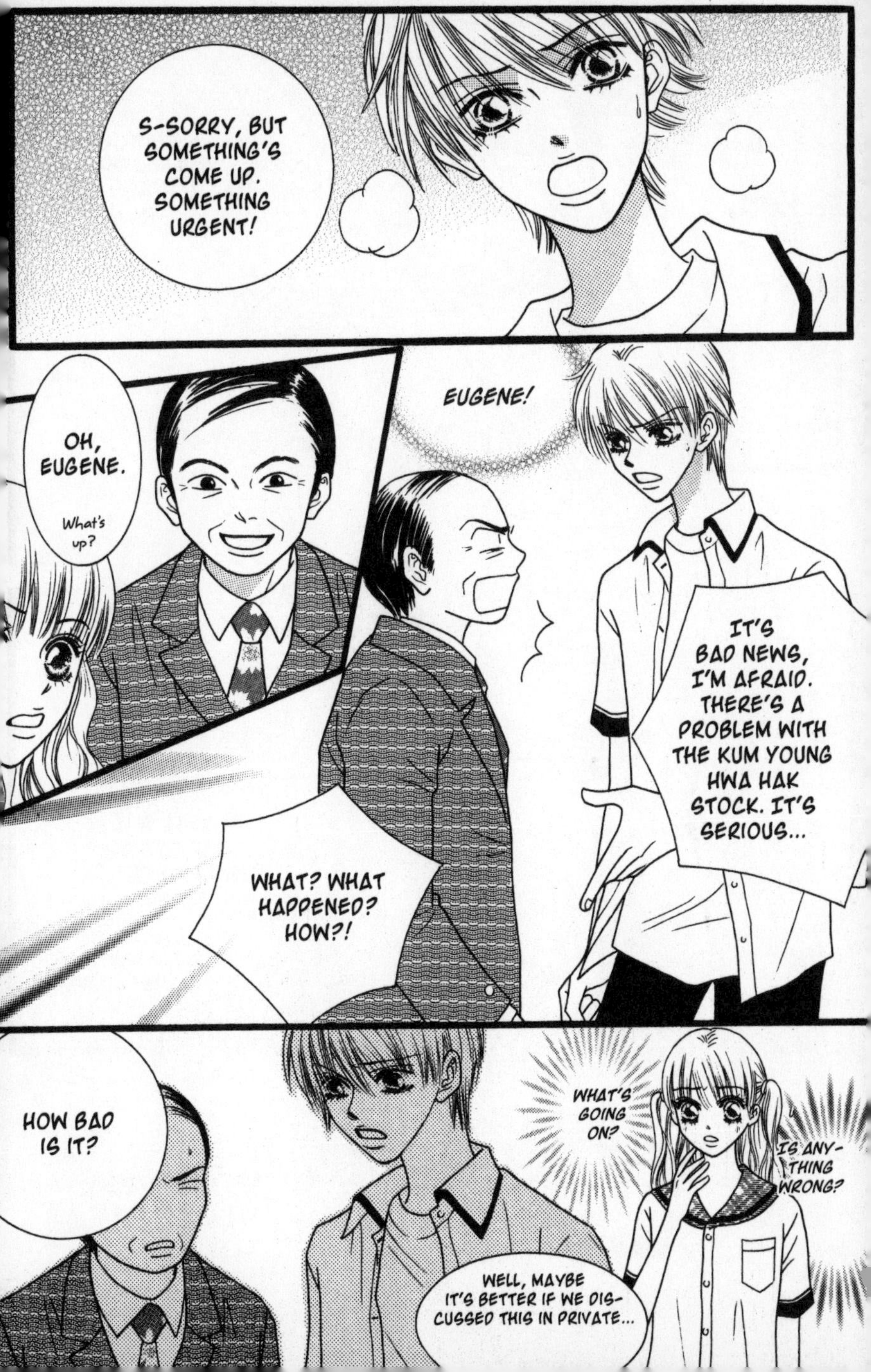
S-SORRY, BUT SOMETHING'S COME UP. SOMETHING URGENT!
OH, EUGENE.
What's up?
EUGENE!
IT'S BAD NEWS, I'M AFRAID. THERE'S A PROBLEM WITH THE KUM YOUNG HWA HAK STOCK. IT'S SERIOUS...
WHAT? WHAT HAPPENED? HOW?!
HOW BAD IS IT?
WHAT'S GOING ON?
IS ANYTHING WRONG?
WELL, MAYBE IT'S BETTER IF WE DISCUSSED THIS IN PRIVATE...

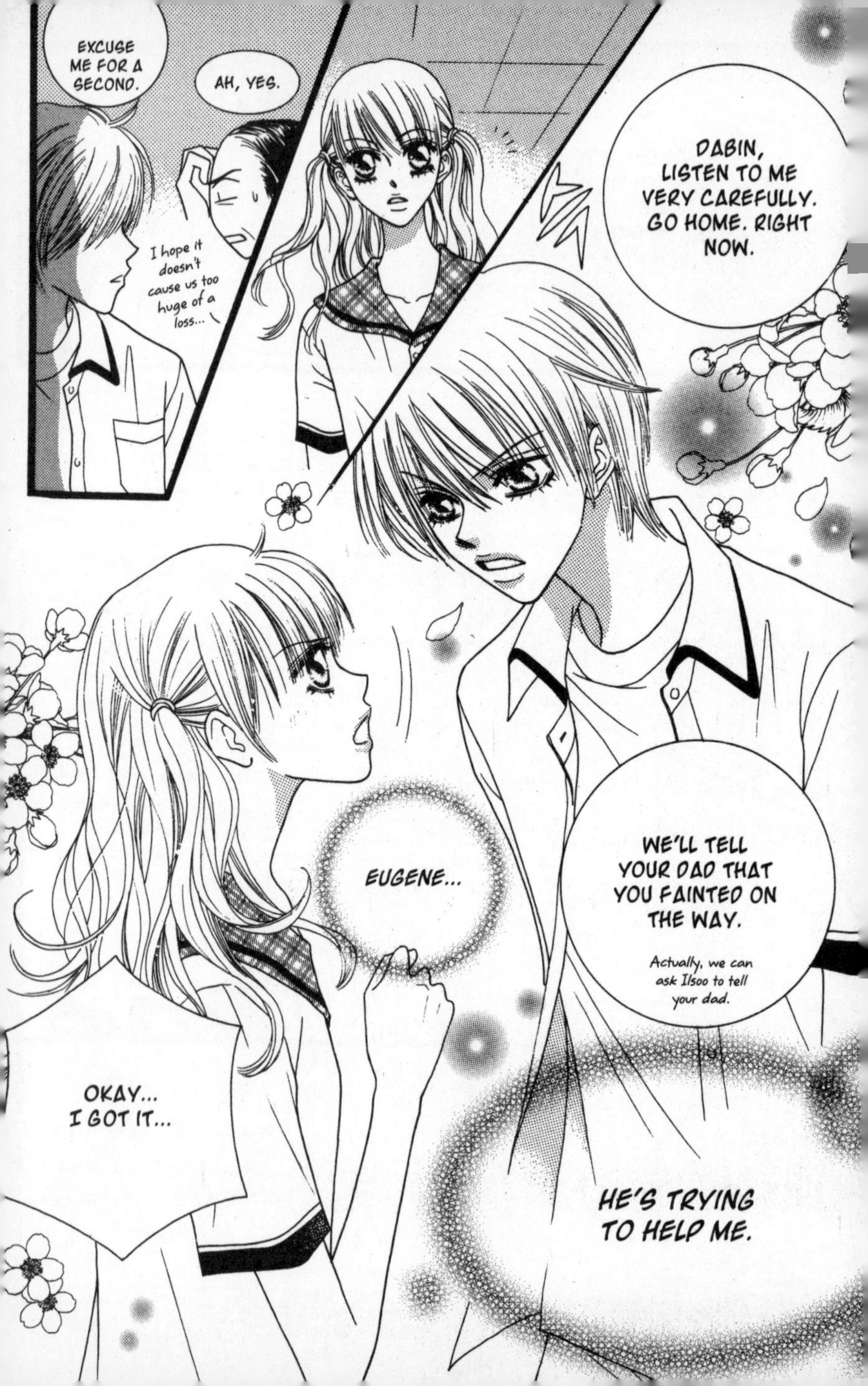
EXCUSE ME FOR A SECOND.
AH, YES.
I hope it doesn't cause us too huge of a loss...
DABIN, LISTEN TO ME VERY CAREFULLY. GO HOME. RIGHT NOW.
EUGENE...
WE'LL TELL YOUR DAD THAT YOU FAINTED ON THE WAY.
Actually, we can ask Ilsoo to tell your dad.
OKAY... I GOT IT...
HE'S TRYING TO HELP ME.

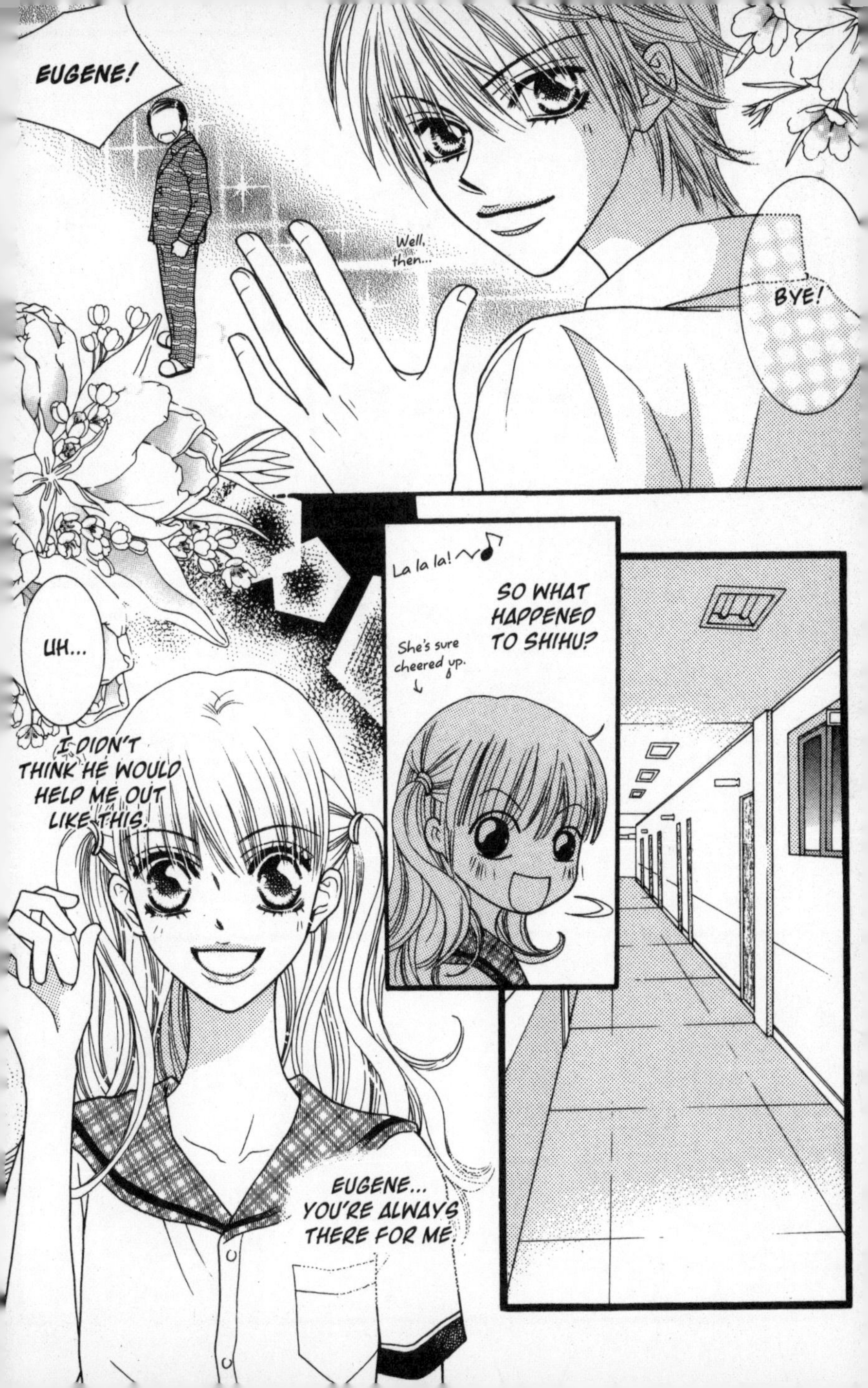
EUGENE!
Well, then...
BYE!
UH...
I DIDN'T THINK HE WOULD HELP ME OUT LIKE THIS.
EUGENE... YOU'RE ALWAYS THERE FOR ME.
La la la!
She's sure cheered up.
SO WHAT HAPPENED TO SHIHU?

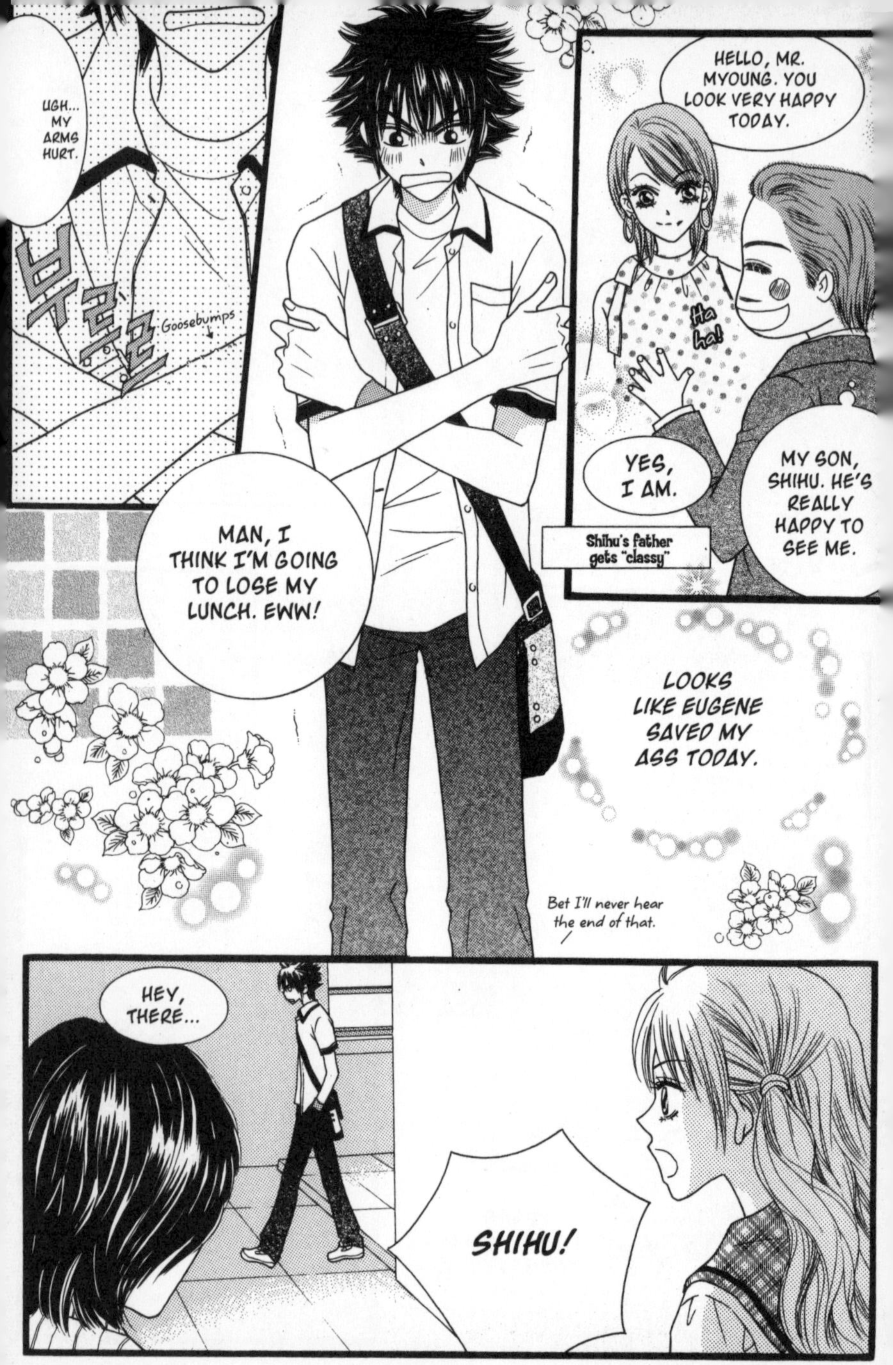

UGH... MY ARMS HURT.
Goosebumps
MAN, I THINK I'M GOING TO LOSE MY LUNCH. EWW!
HELLO, MR. MYOUNG. YOU LOOK VERY HAPPY TODAY.
Ha ha!
YES, I AM.
MY SON, SHIHU. HE'S REALLY HAPPY TO SEE ME.
Shihu's father gets "classy"
LOOKS LIKE EUGENE SAVED MY ASS TODAY.
Bet I'll never hear the end of that.
HEY, THERE...
SHIHU!

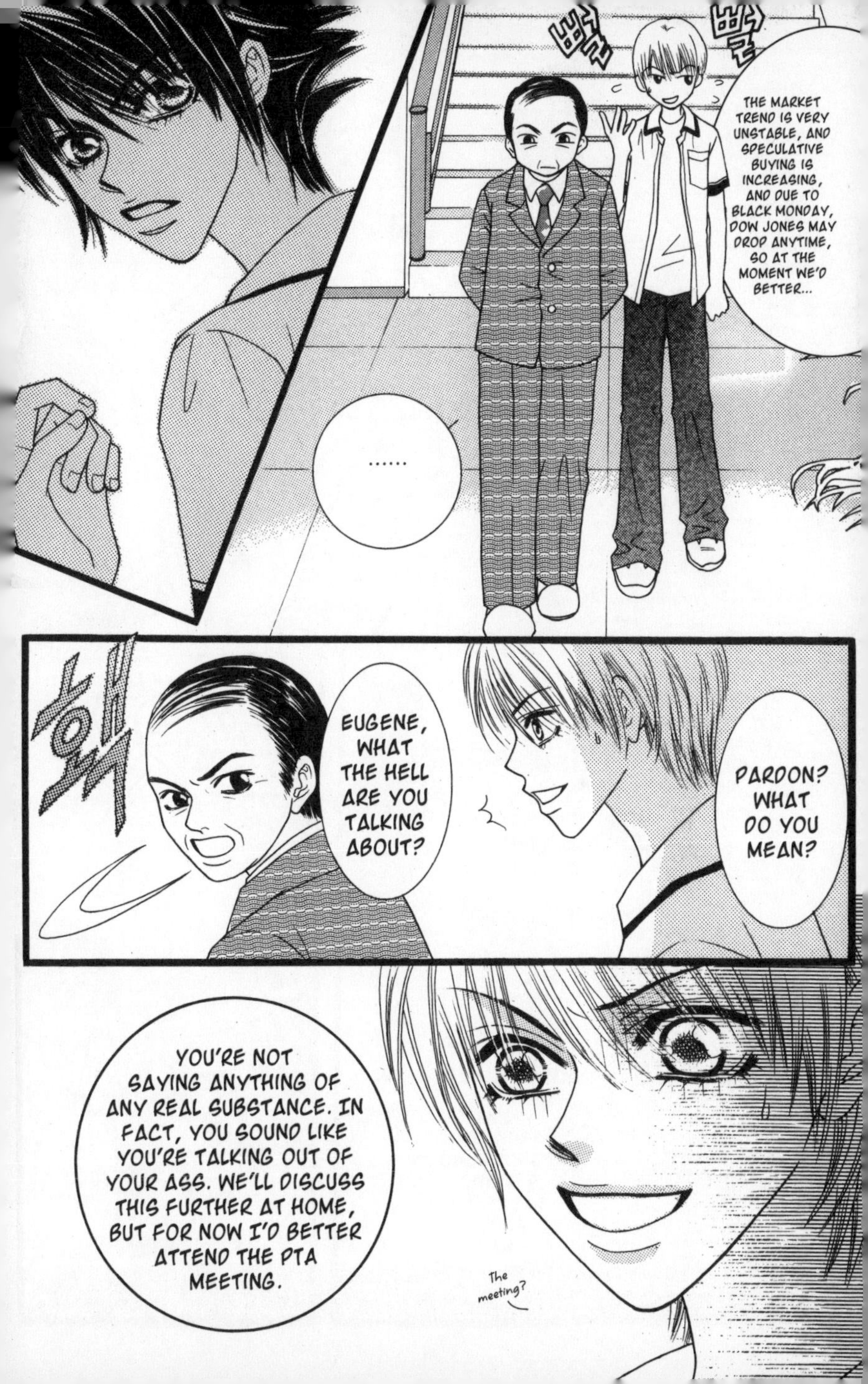
THE MARKET TREND IS VERY UNSTABLE, AND SPECULATIVE BUYING IS INCREASING, AND DUE TO BLACK MONDAY, DOW JONES MAY DROP ANYTIME, SO AT THE MOMENT WE'D BETTER...
......
EUGENE, WHAT THE HELL ARE YOU TALKING ABOUT?
PARDON? WHAT DO YOU MEAN?
YOU'RE NOT SAYING ANYTHING OF ANY REAL SUBSTANCE. IN FACT, YOU SOUND LIKE YOU'RE TALKING OUT OF YOUR ASS. WE'LL DISCUSS THIS FURTHER AT HOME, BUT FOR NOW I'D BETTER ATTEND THE PTA MEETING.
The meeting?

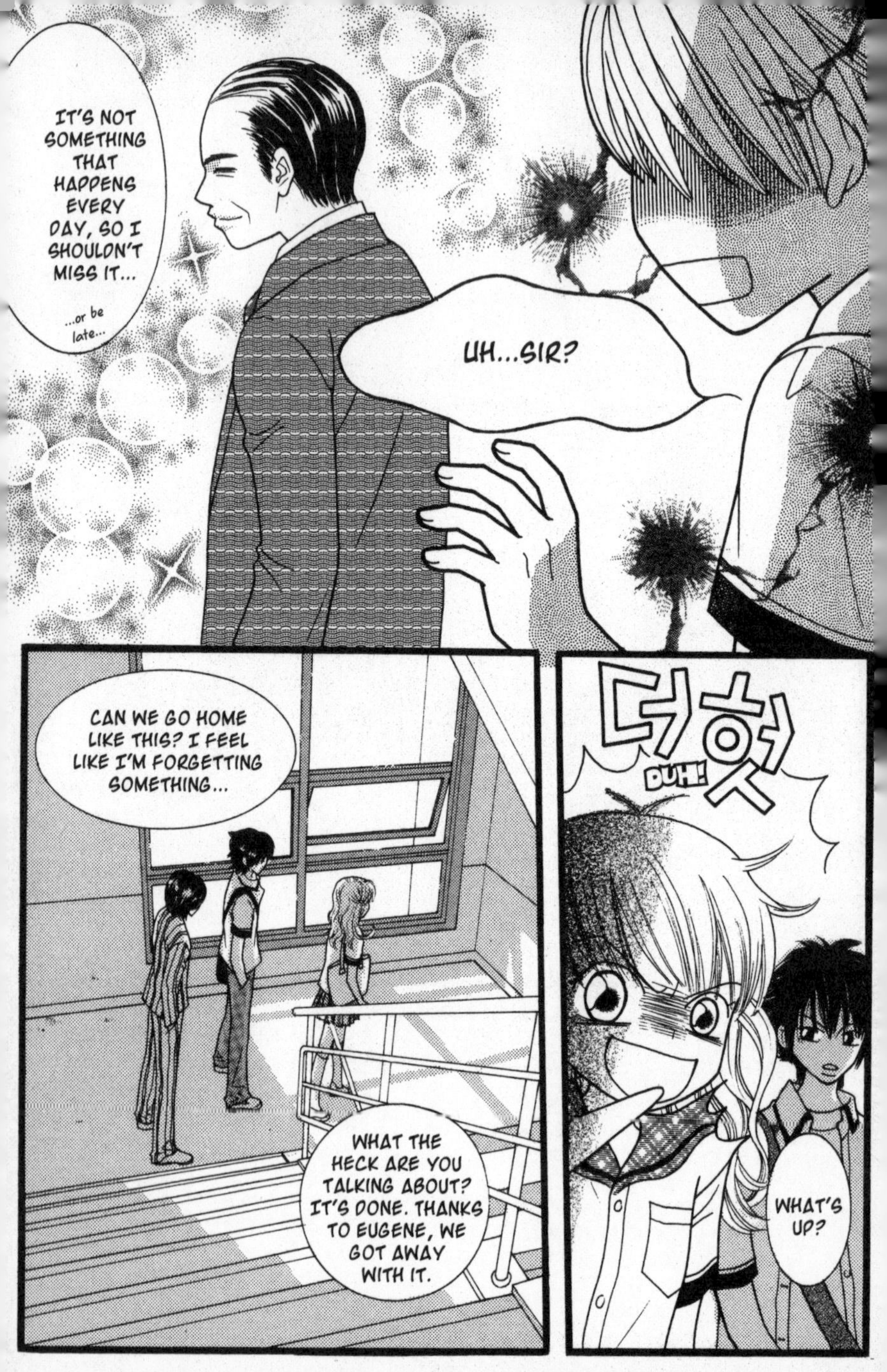
IT'S NOT SOMETHING THAT HAPPENS EVERY DAY, SO I SHOULDN'T MISS IT...
...or be late...
UH...SIR?
CAN WE GO HOME LIKE THIS? I FEEL LIKE I'M FORGETTING SOMETHING...
WHAT THE HECK ARE YOU TALKING ABOUT? IT'S DONE. THANKS TO EUGENE, WE GOT AWAY WITH IT.
더헛
DUH!
WHAT'S UP?

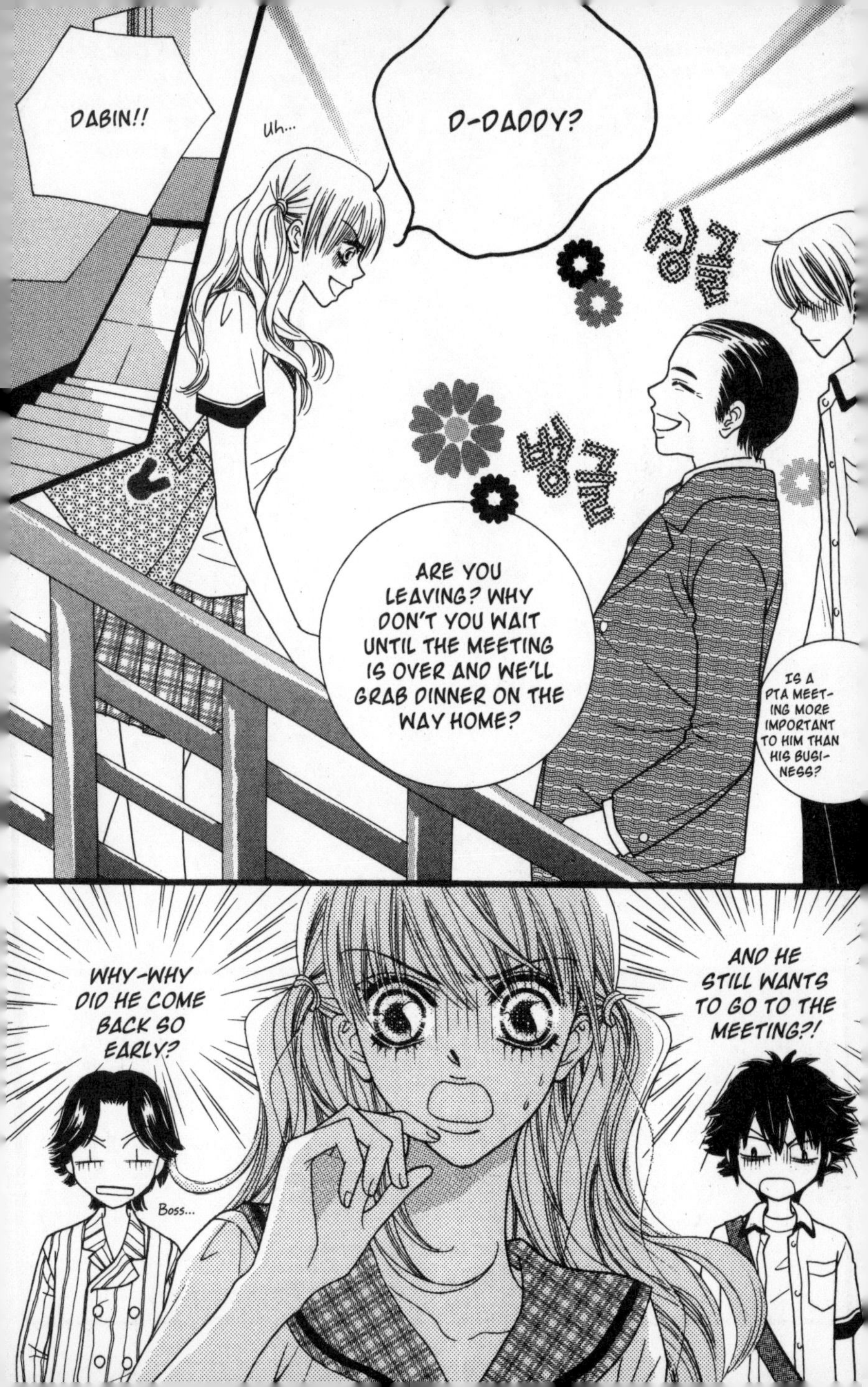
DABIN!!
Uh...
D-DADDY?
싱글
벙글
ARE YOU LEAVING? WHY DON'T YOU WAIT UNTIL THE MEETING IS OVER AND WE'LL GRAB DINNER ON THE WAY HOME?
IS A PTA MEETING MORE IMPORTANT TO HIM THAN HIS BUSINESS?
WHY-WHY DID HE COME BACK SO EARLY?
Boss...
AND HE STILL WANTS TO GO TO THE MEETING?!

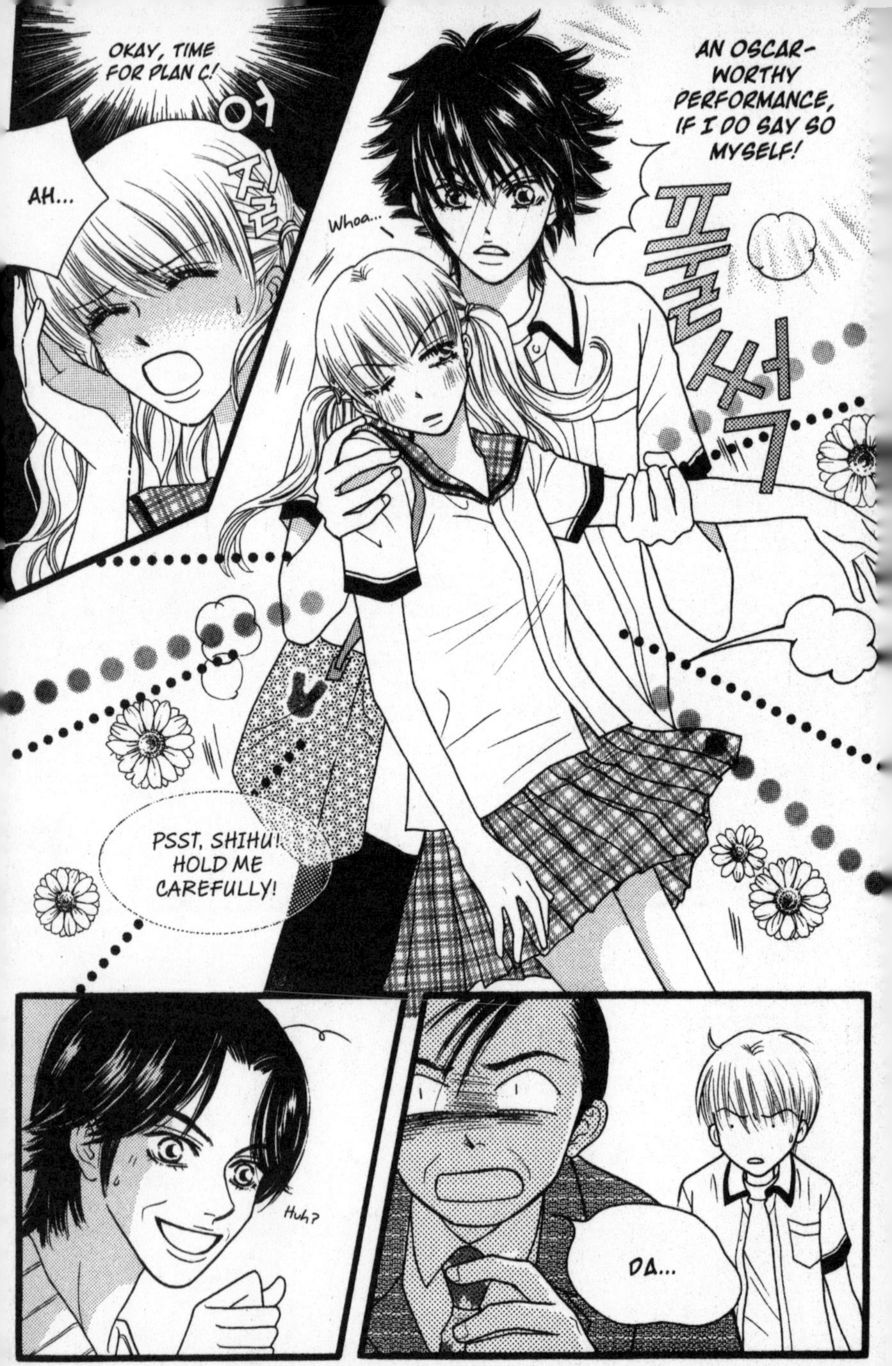
OKAY, TIME FOR PLAN C!
AH...
Whoa...
AN OSCAR-WORTHY PERFORMANCE, IF I DO SAY SO MYSELF!
PSST, SHIHU! HOLD ME CAREFULLY!
Huh?
DA...

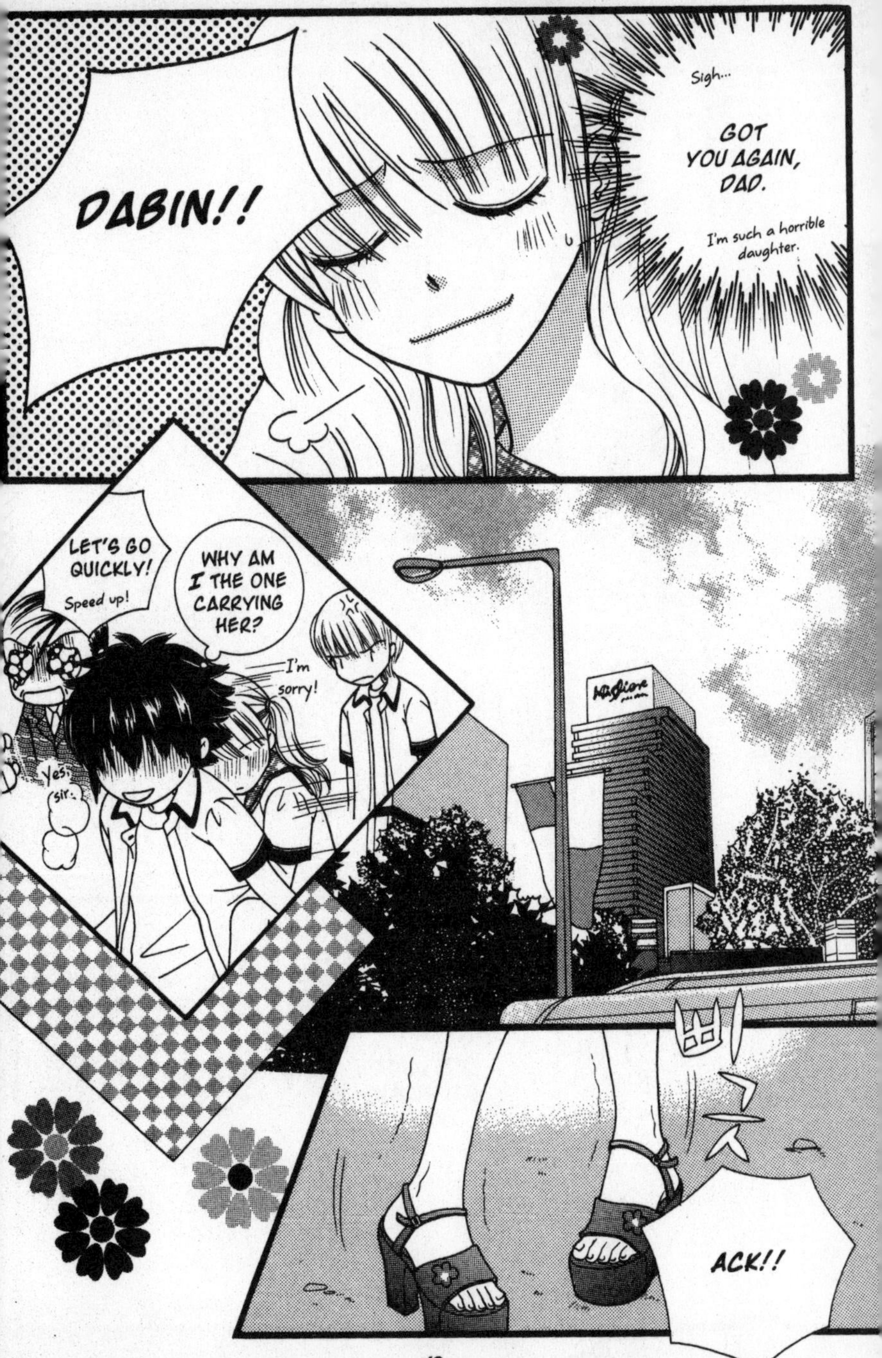
DABIN!!
Sigh...
GOT YOU AGAIN, DAD.
I'm such a horrible daughter.
LET'S GO QUICKLY!
Speed up!
WHY AM I THE ONE CARRYING HER?
I'm sorry!
Yes, sir.
ACK!!

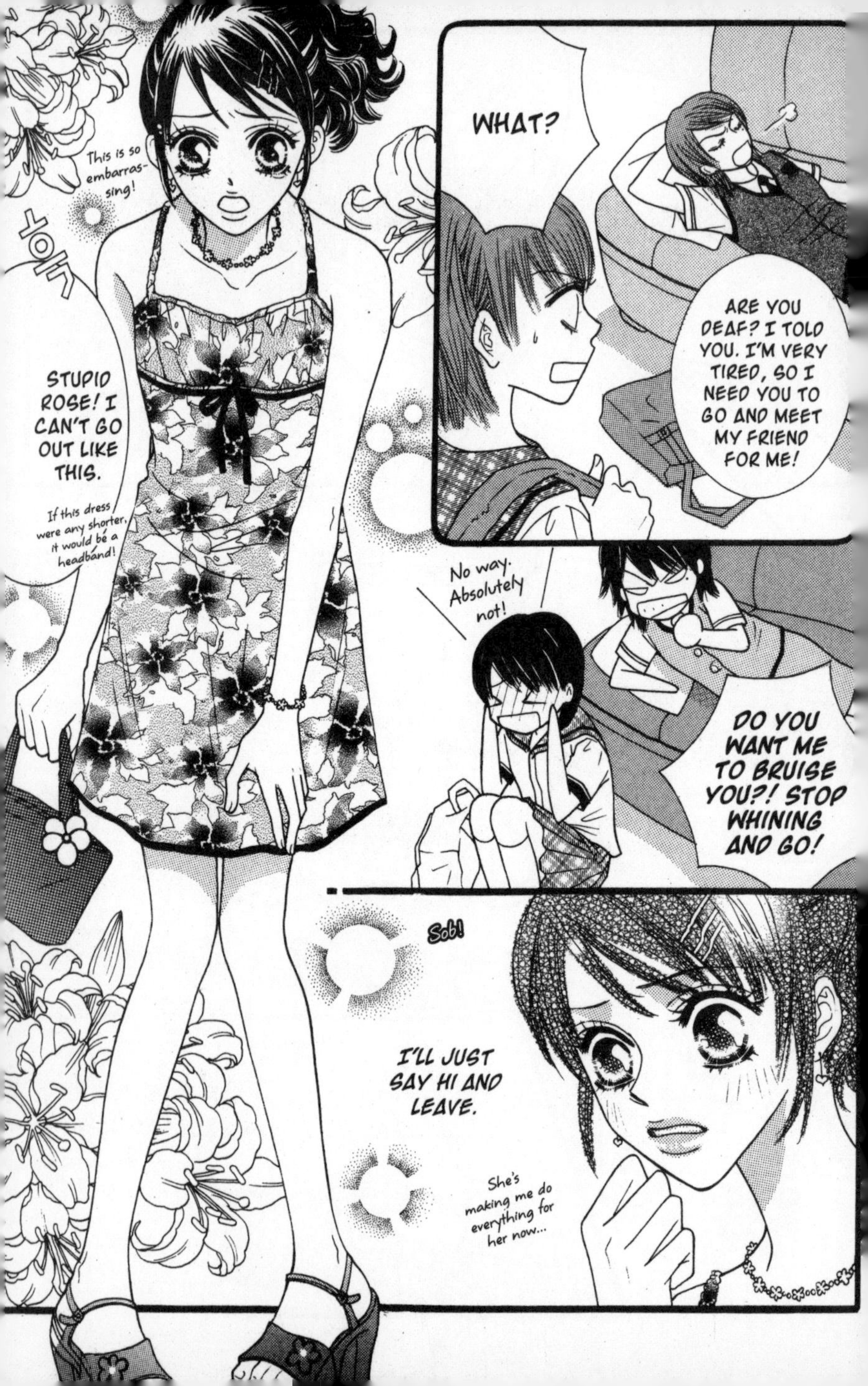
This is so embarrassing!
STUPID ROSE! I CAN'T GO OUT LIKE THIS.
If this dress were any shorter, it would be a headband!
WHAT?
ARE YOU DEAF? I TOLD YOU. I'M VERY TIRED, SO I NEED YOU TO GO AND MEET MY FRIEND FOR ME!
No way. Absolutely not!
DO YOU WANT ME TO BRUISE YOU?! STOP WHINING AND GO!
Sob!
I'LL JUST SAY HI AND LEAVE.
She's making me do everything for her now...

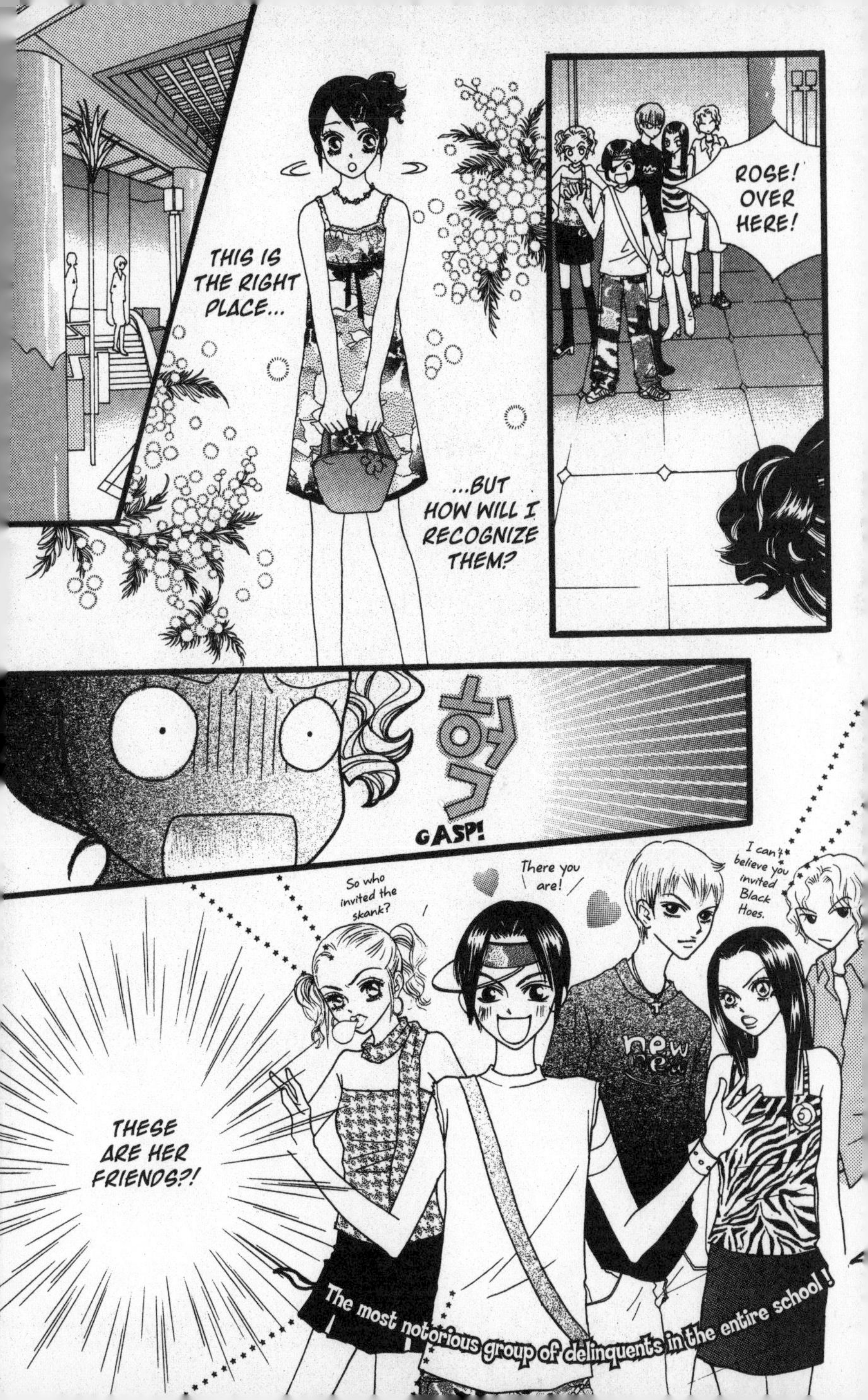
THIS IS THE RIGHT PLACE...
...BUT HOW WILL I RECOGNIZE THEM?
ROSE! OVER HERE!
헉
GASP!
So who invited the skank?
There you are!
I can't believe you invited Black Hoes.
THESE ARE HER FRIENDS?!
The most notorious group of delinquents in the entire school!

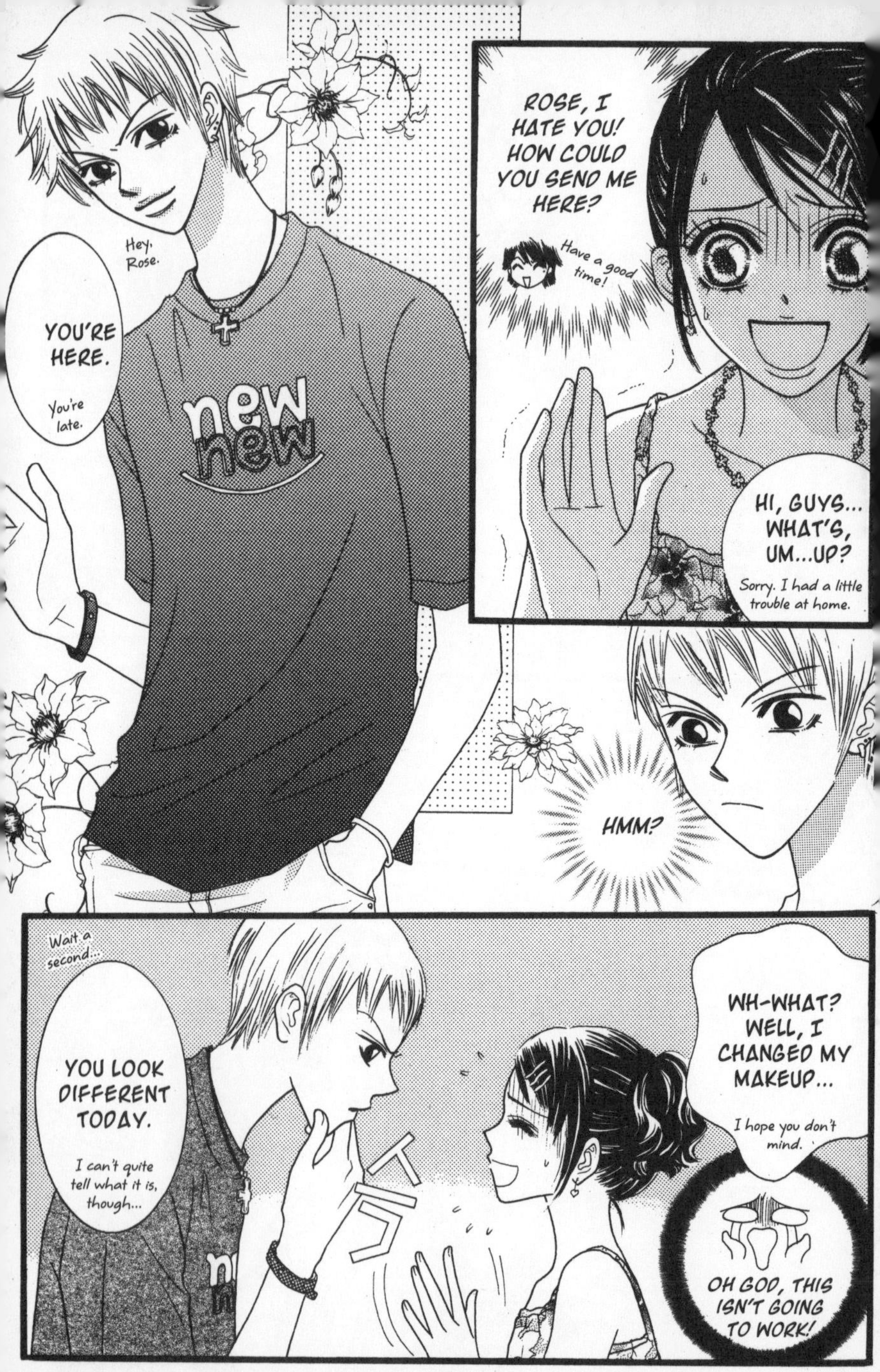
Hey, Rose.
YOU'RE HERE.
You're late.
ROSE, I HATE YOU! HOW COULD YOU SEND ME HERE?
Have a good time!
HI, GUYS... WHAT'S, UM...UP?
Sorry. I had a little trouble at home.
HMM?
Wait a second...
YOU LOOK DIFFERENT TODAY.
I can't quite tell what it is, though...
イラ
WH-WHAT? WELL, I CHANGED MY MAKEUP...
I hope you don't mind.
OH GOD, THIS ISN'T GOING TO WORK!

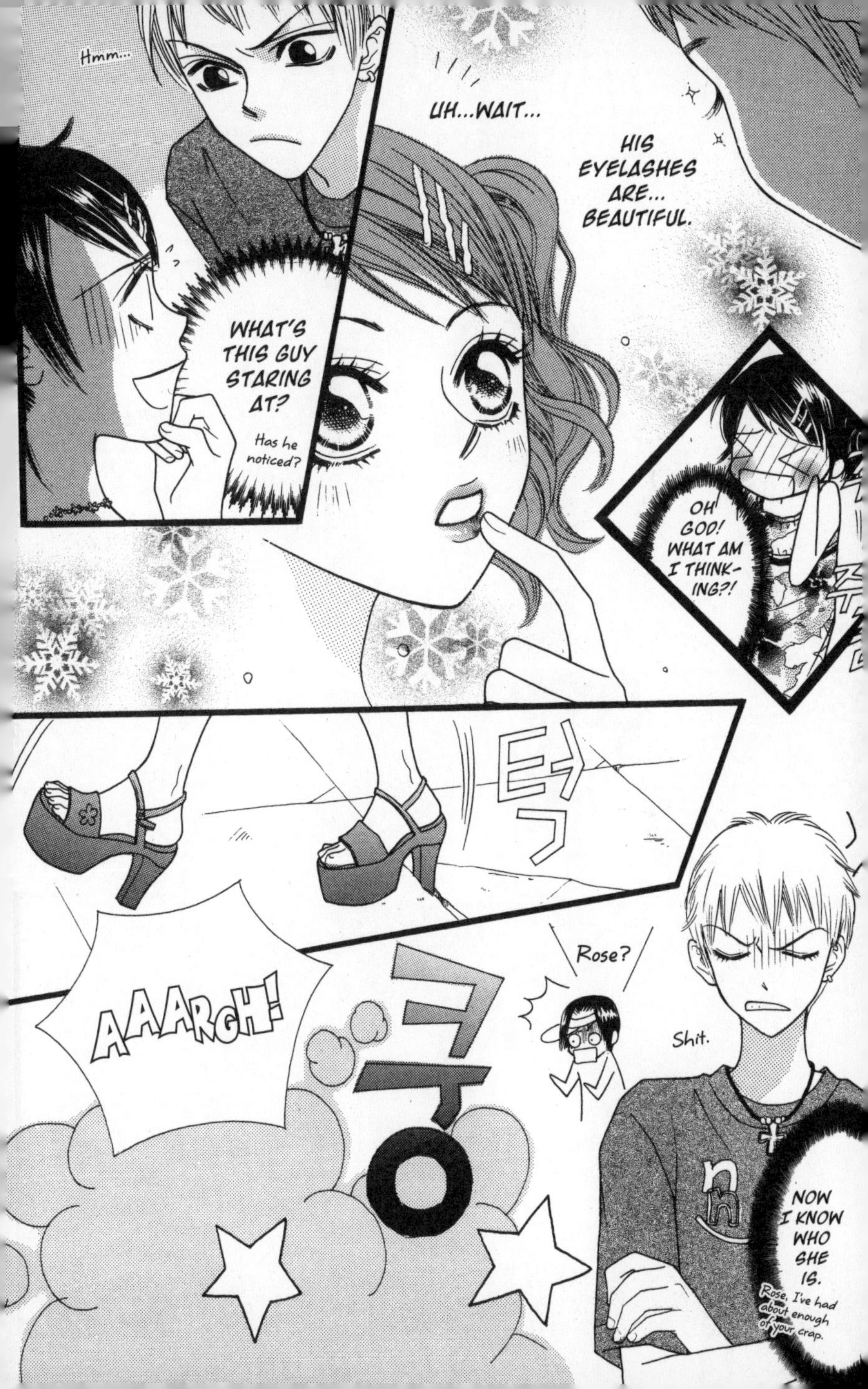
Hmm...
WHAT'S THIS GUY STARING AT?
Has he noticed?
UH...WAIT...
HIS EYELASHES ARE... BEAUTIFUL.
OH GOD! WHAT AM I THINKING?!
AAARGH!
Rose?
Shit.
NOW I KNOW WHO SHE IS.
Rose, I've had about enough of your crap.

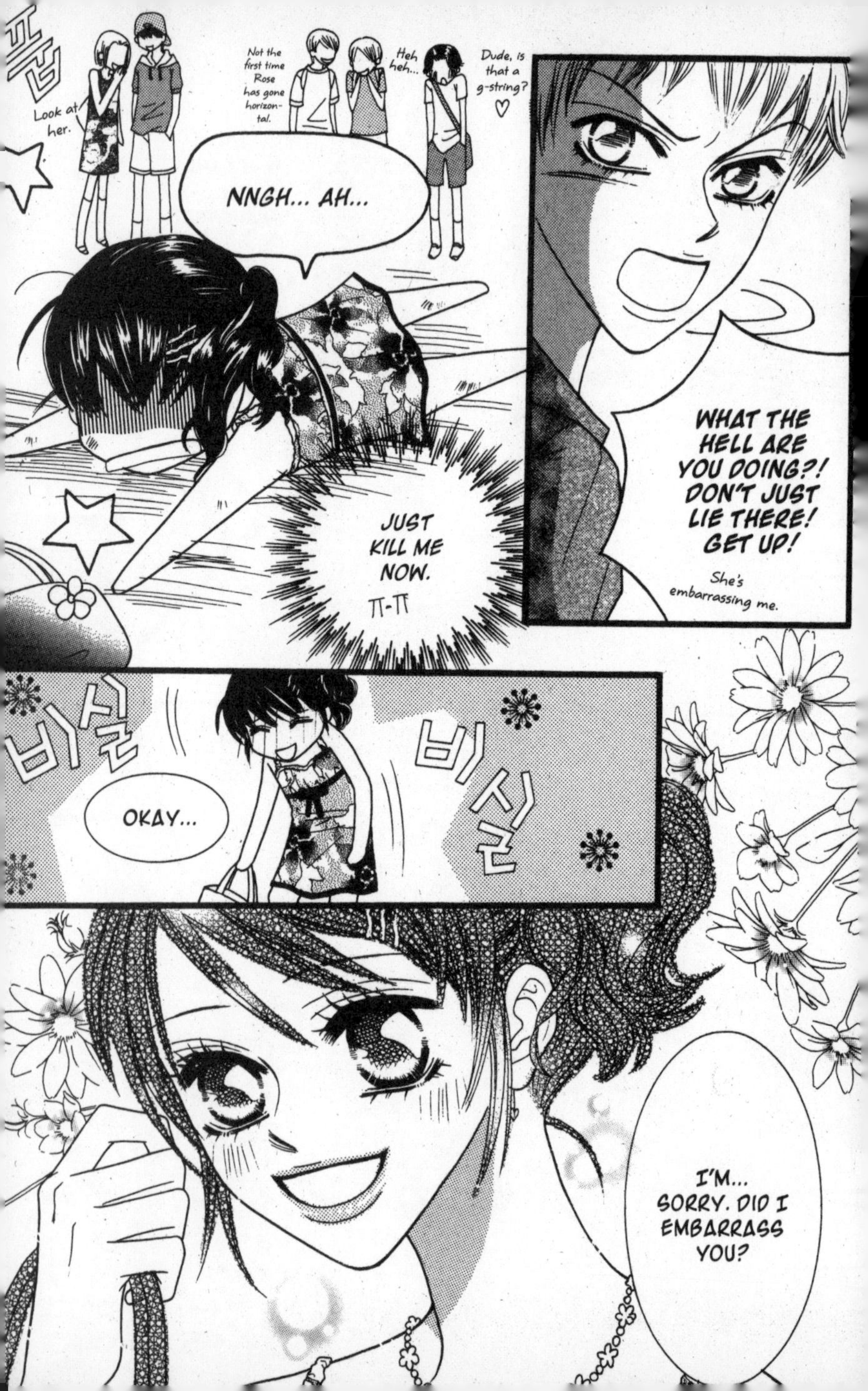
Look at her.
Not the first time Rose has gone horizontal.
Heh heh...
Dude, is that a g-string? ♡
NNGH... AH...
JUST KILL ME NOW. π-π
WHAT THE HELL ARE YOU DOING?! DON'T JUST LIE THERE! GET UP!
She's embarrassing me.
비실
OKAY...
비실
I'M... SORRY. DID I EMBARRASS YOU?

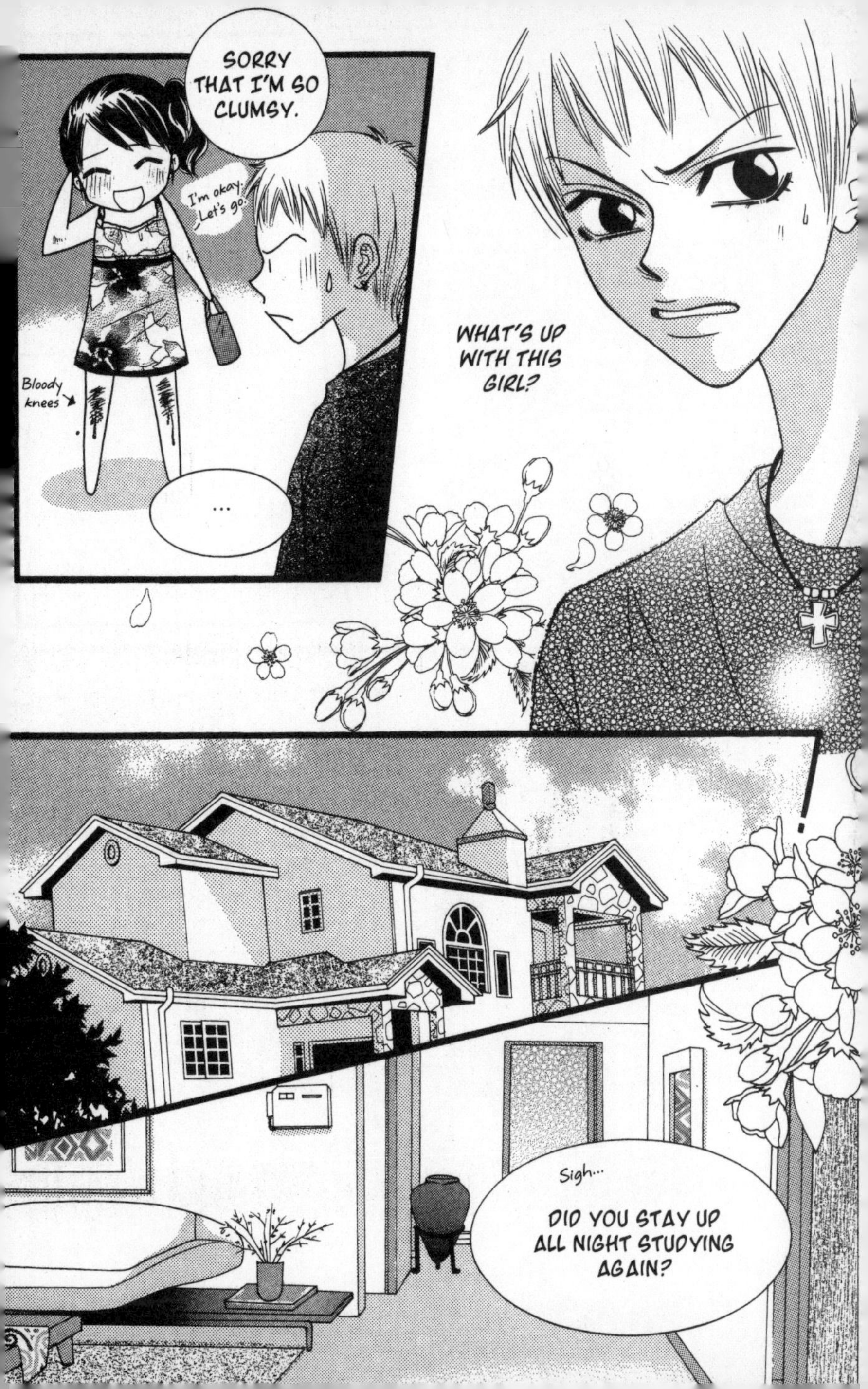
SORRY THAT I'M SO CLUMSY.
I'm okay. Let's go.
Bloody knees
...
WHAT'S UP WITH THIS GIRL?
Sigh...
DID YOU STAY UP ALL NIGHT STUDYING AGAIN?

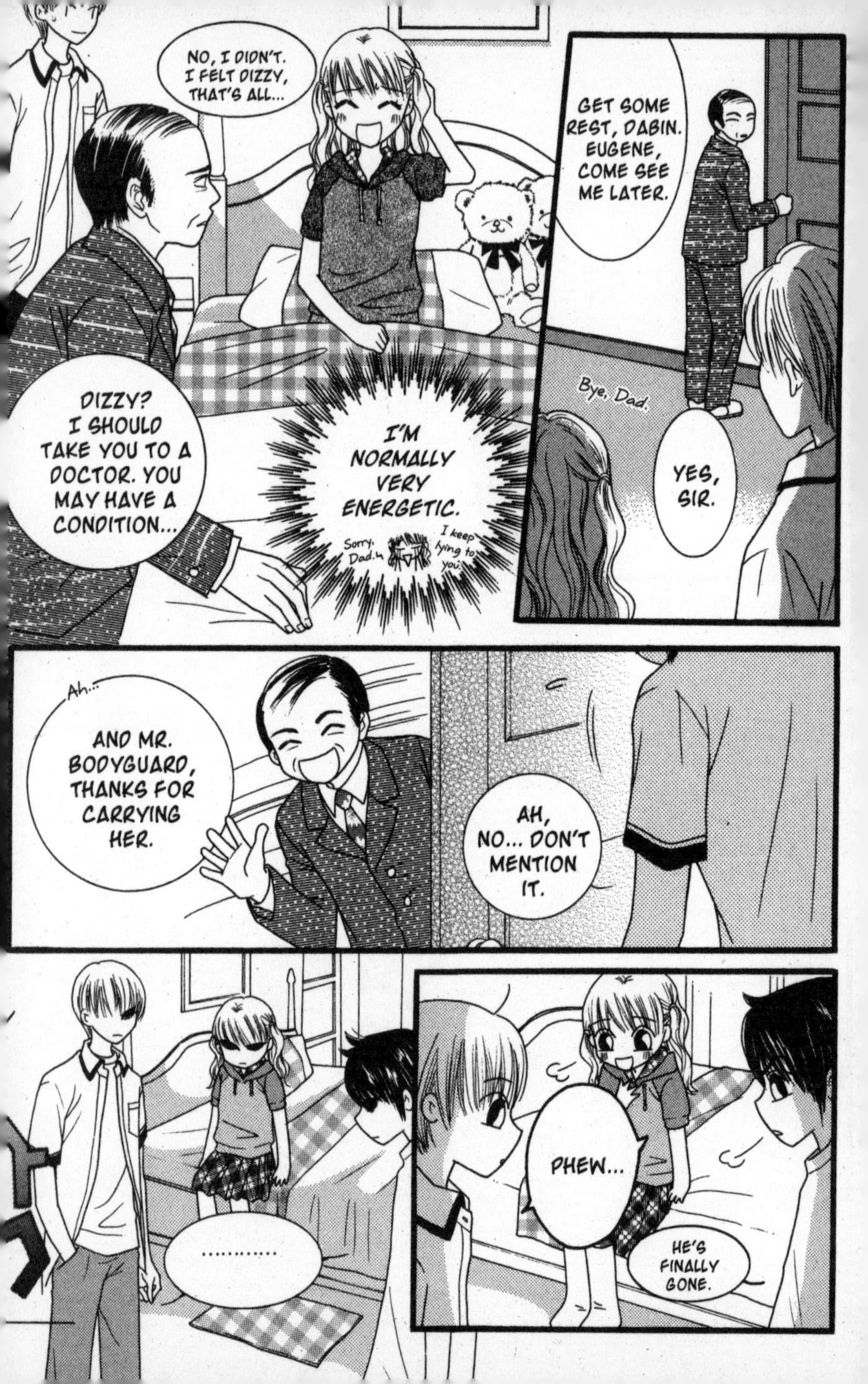
NO, I DIDN'T. I FELT DIZZY, THAT'S ALL...
DIZZY? I SHOULD TAKE YOU TO A DOCTOR. YOU MAY HAVE A CONDITION...
I'M NORMALLY VERY ENERGETIC.
Sorry, Dad.
I keep lying to you.
GET SOME REST, DABIN. EUGENE, COME SEE ME LATER.
Bye, Dad.
YES, SIR.
Ah...
AND MR. BODYGUARD, THANKS FOR CARRYING HER.
AH, NO... DON'T MENTION IT.
....
PHEW...
HE'S FINALLY GONE.

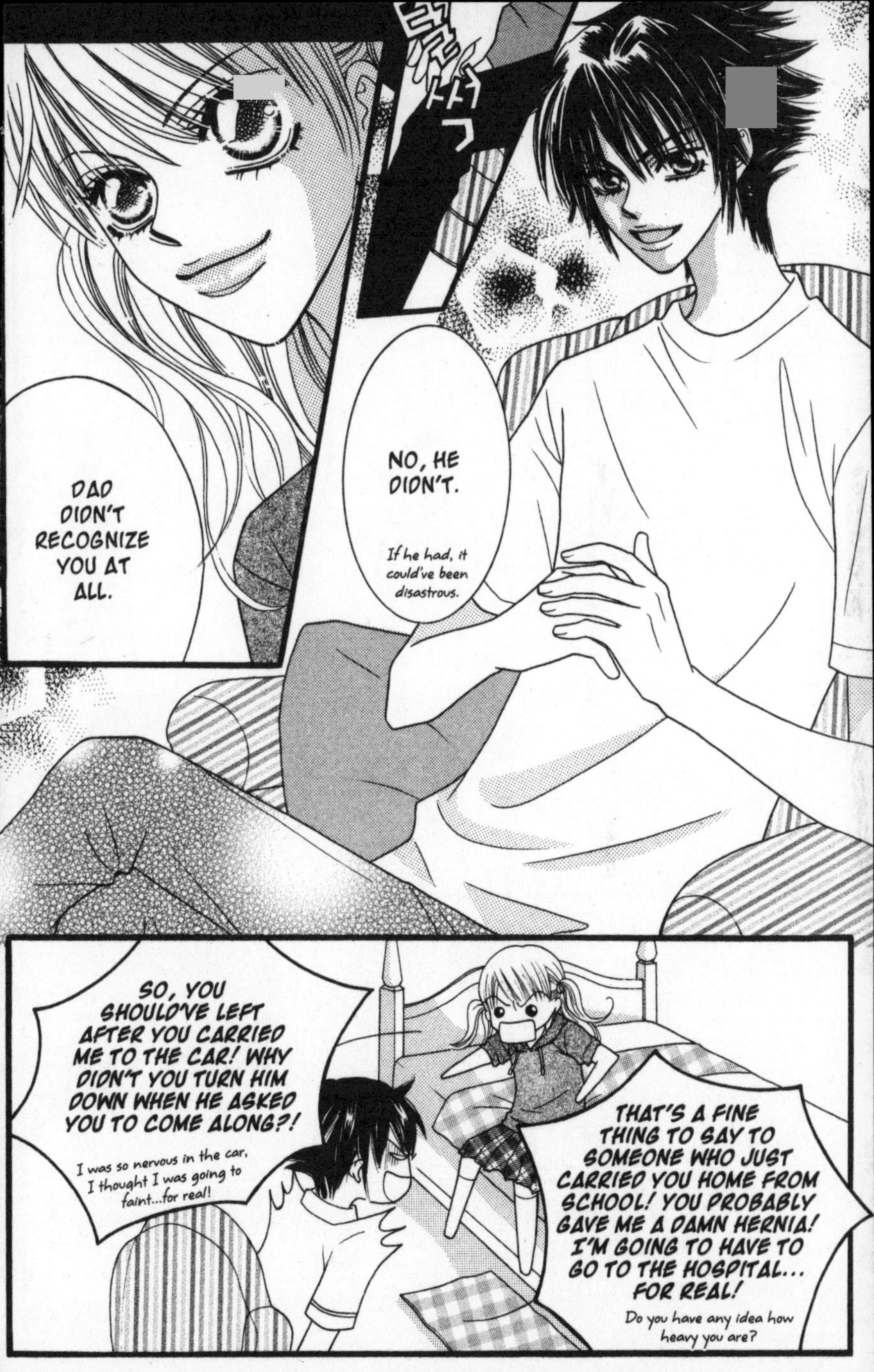
DAD DIDN'T RECOGNIZE YOU AT ALL.
NO, HE DIDN'T.
If he had, it could've been disastrous.
SO, YOU SHOULD'VE LEFT AFTER YOU CARRIED ME TO THE CAR! WHY DIDN'T YOU TURN HIM DOWN WHEN HE ASKED YOU TO COME ALONG?!
I was so nervous in the car, I thought I was going to faint...for real!
THAT'S A FINE THING TO SAY TO SOMEONE WHO JUST CARRIED YOU HOME FROM SCHOOL! YOU PROBABLY GAVE ME A DAMN HERNIA! I'M GOING TO HAVE TO GO TO THE HOSPITAL... FOR REAL!
Do you have any idea how heavy you are?

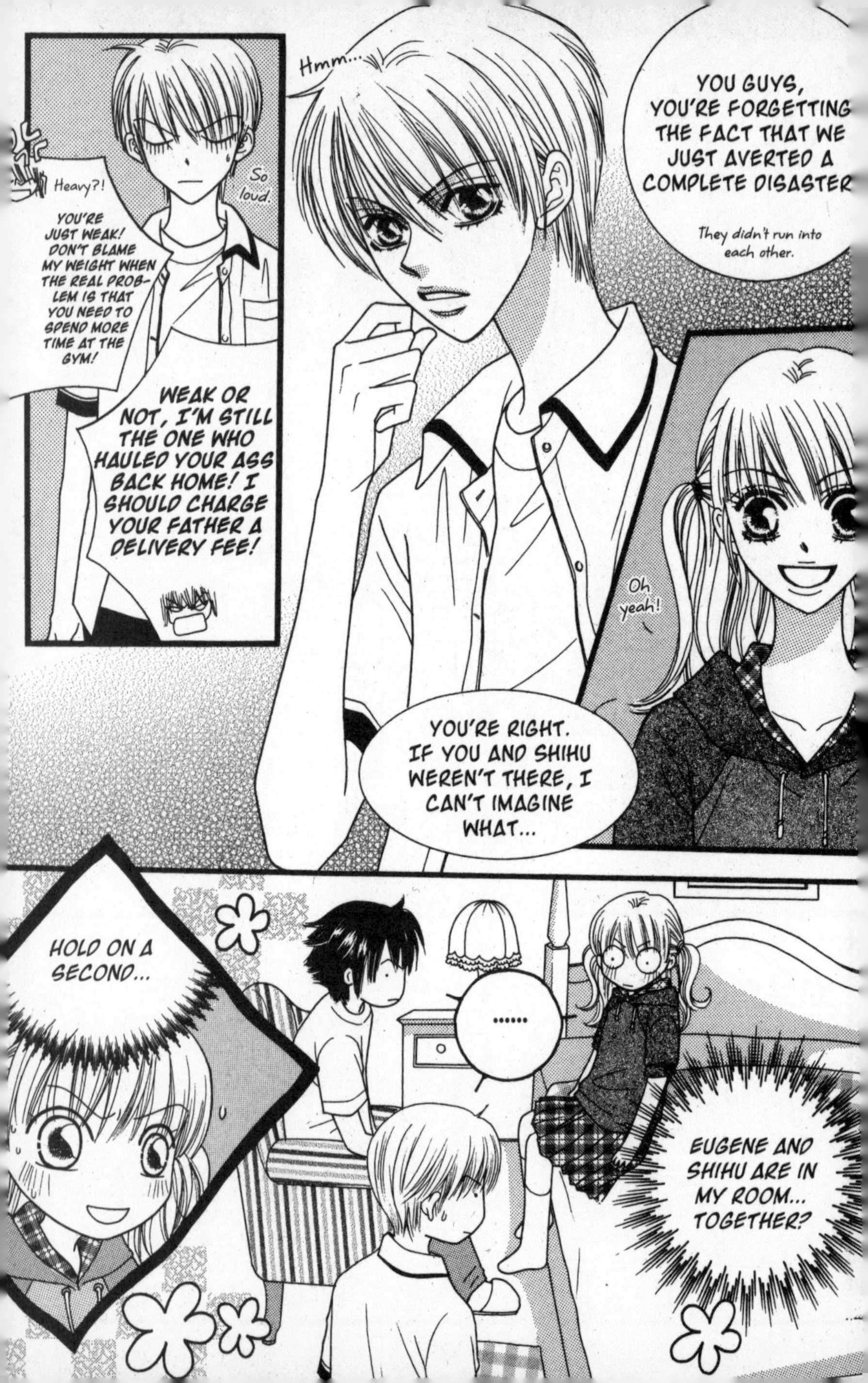
Heavy?!
YOU'RE JUST WEAK! DON'T BLAME MY WEIGHT WHEN THE REAL PROBLEM IS THAT YOU NEED TO SPEND MORE TIME AT THE GYM!
So loud.
WEAK OR NOT, I'M STILL THE ONE WHO HAULED YOUR ASS BACK HOME! I SHOULD CHARGE YOUR FATHER A DELIVERY FEE!
Hmm...
YOU GUYS, YOU'RE FORGETTING THE FACT THAT WE JUST AVERTED A COMPLETE DISASTER
They didn't run into each other.
Oh yeah!
YOU'RE RIGHT. IF YOU AND SHIHU WEREN'T THERE, I CAN'T IMAGINE WHAT...
HOLD ON A SECOND...
......
EUGENE AND SHIHU ARE IN MY ROOM... TOGETHER?

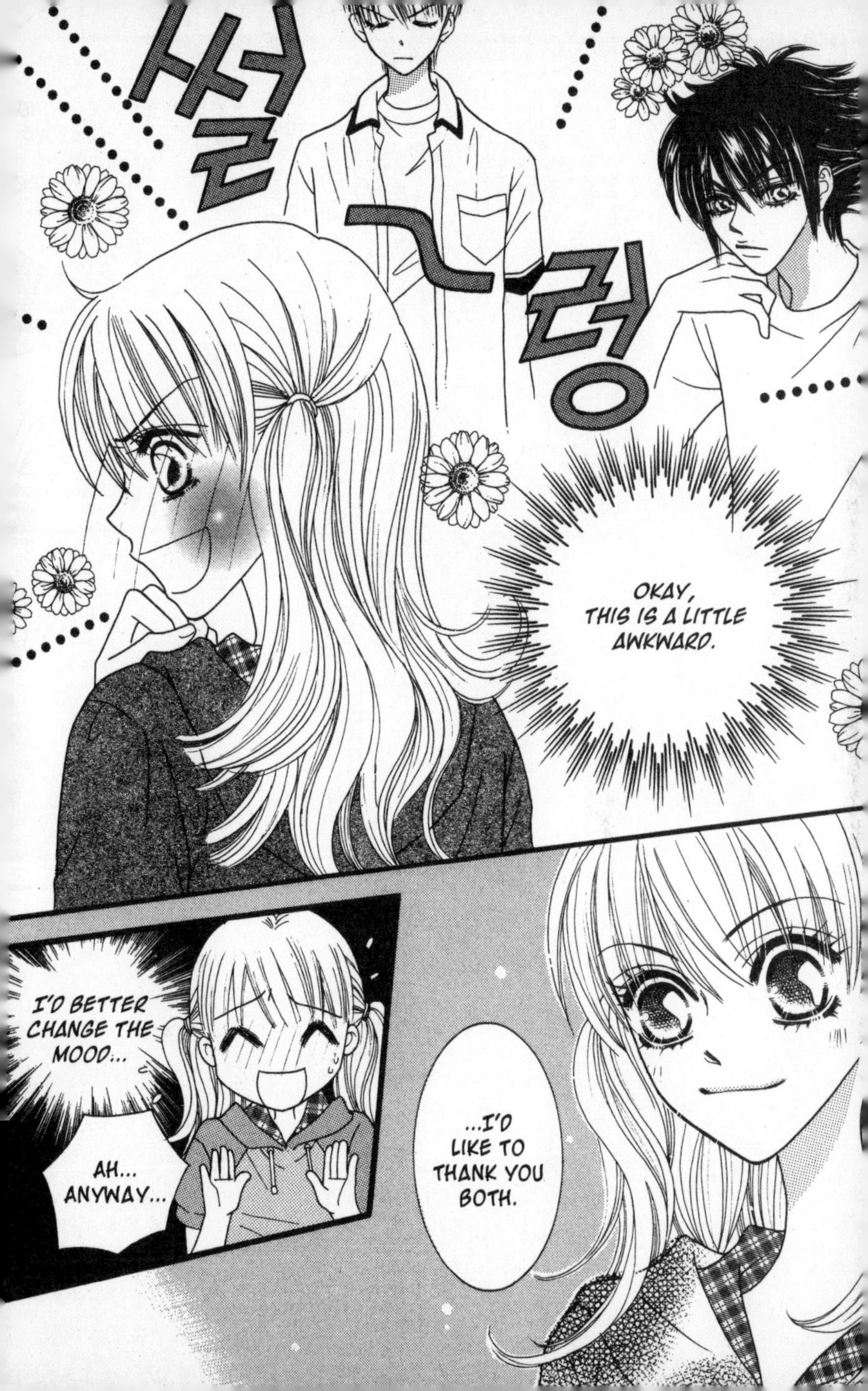
썰~렁
OKAY, THIS IS A LITTLE AWKWARD.
I'D BETTER CHANGE THE MOOD...
AH... ANYWAY...
...I'D LIKE TO THANK YOU BOTH.

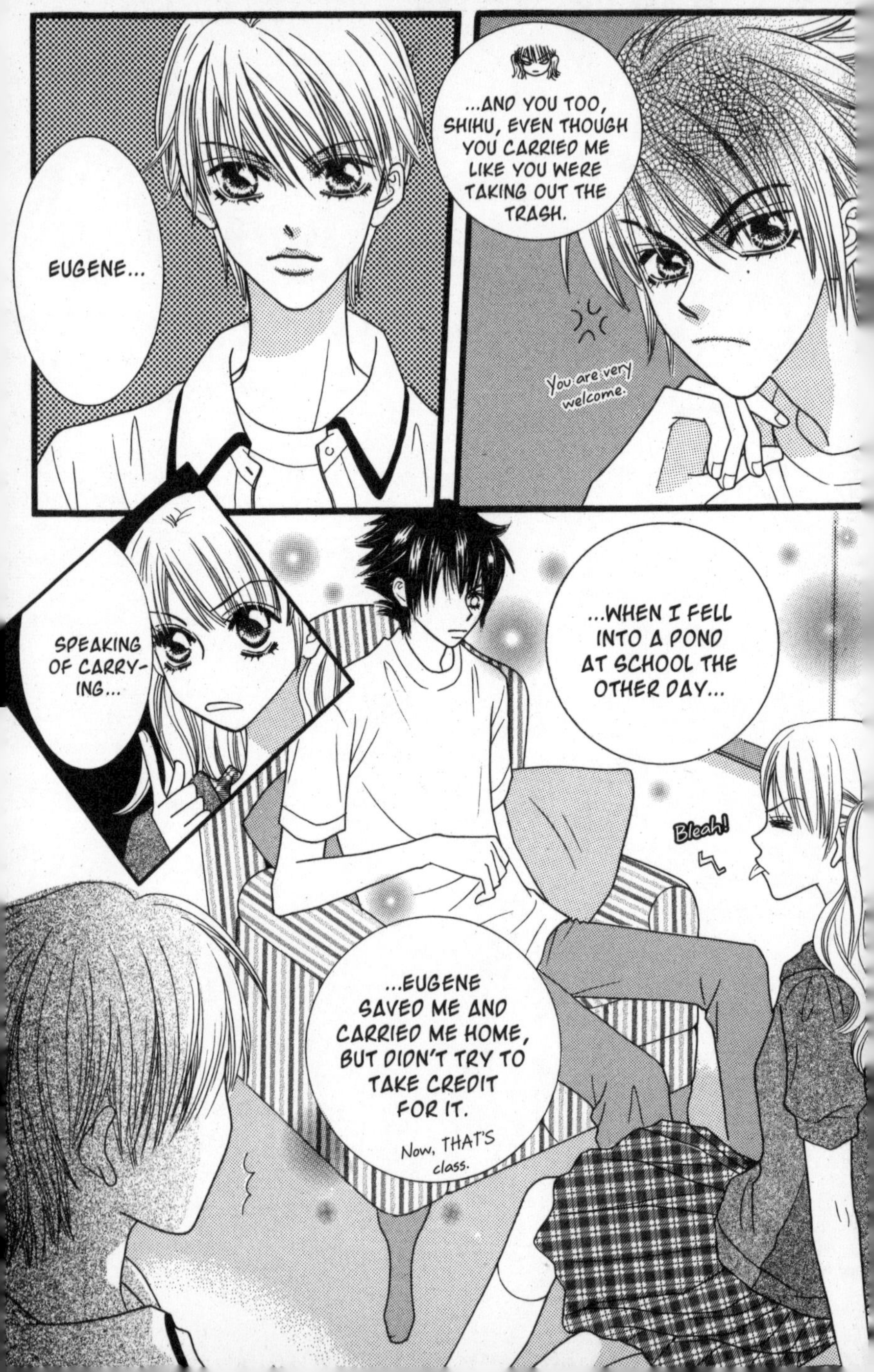
EUGENE...
...AND YOU TOO, SHIHU, EVEN THOUGH YOU CARRIED ME LIKE YOU WERE TAKING OUT THE TRASH.
You are very welcome.
SPEAKING OF CARRY-ING...
...WHEN I FELL INTO A POND AT SCHOOL THE OTHER DAY...
Bleah!
...EUGENE SAVED ME AND CARRIED ME HOME, BUT DIDN'T TRY TO TAKE CREDIT FOR IT.
Now, THAT'S class.

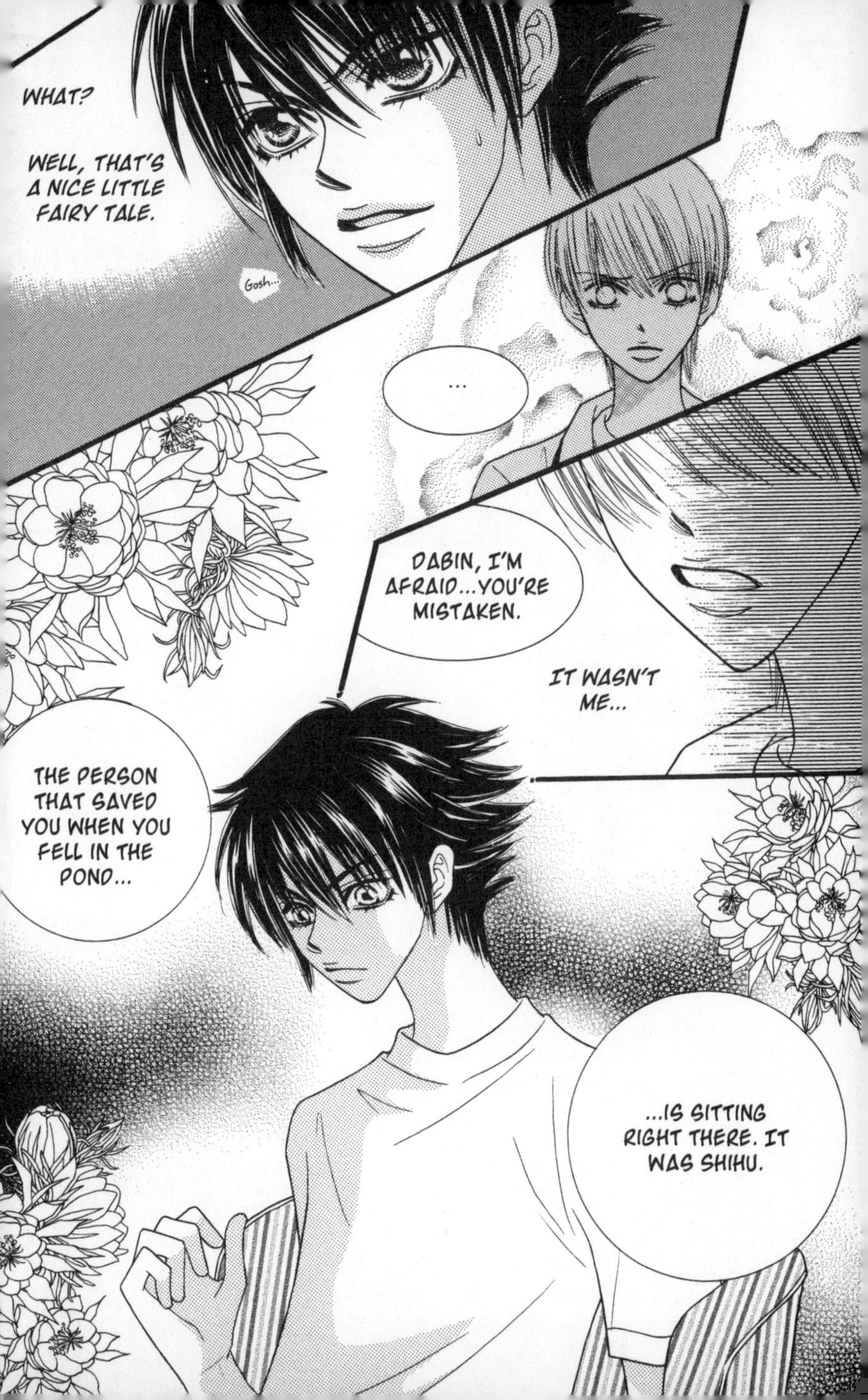
WHAT?
WELL, THAT'S A NICE LITTLE FAIRY TALE.
Gosh...
...
DABIN, I'M AFRAID...YOU'RE MISTAKEN.
IT WASN'T ME...
THE PERSON THAT SAVED YOU WHEN YOU FELL IN THE POND...
...IS SITTING RIGHT THERE. IT WAS SHIHU.

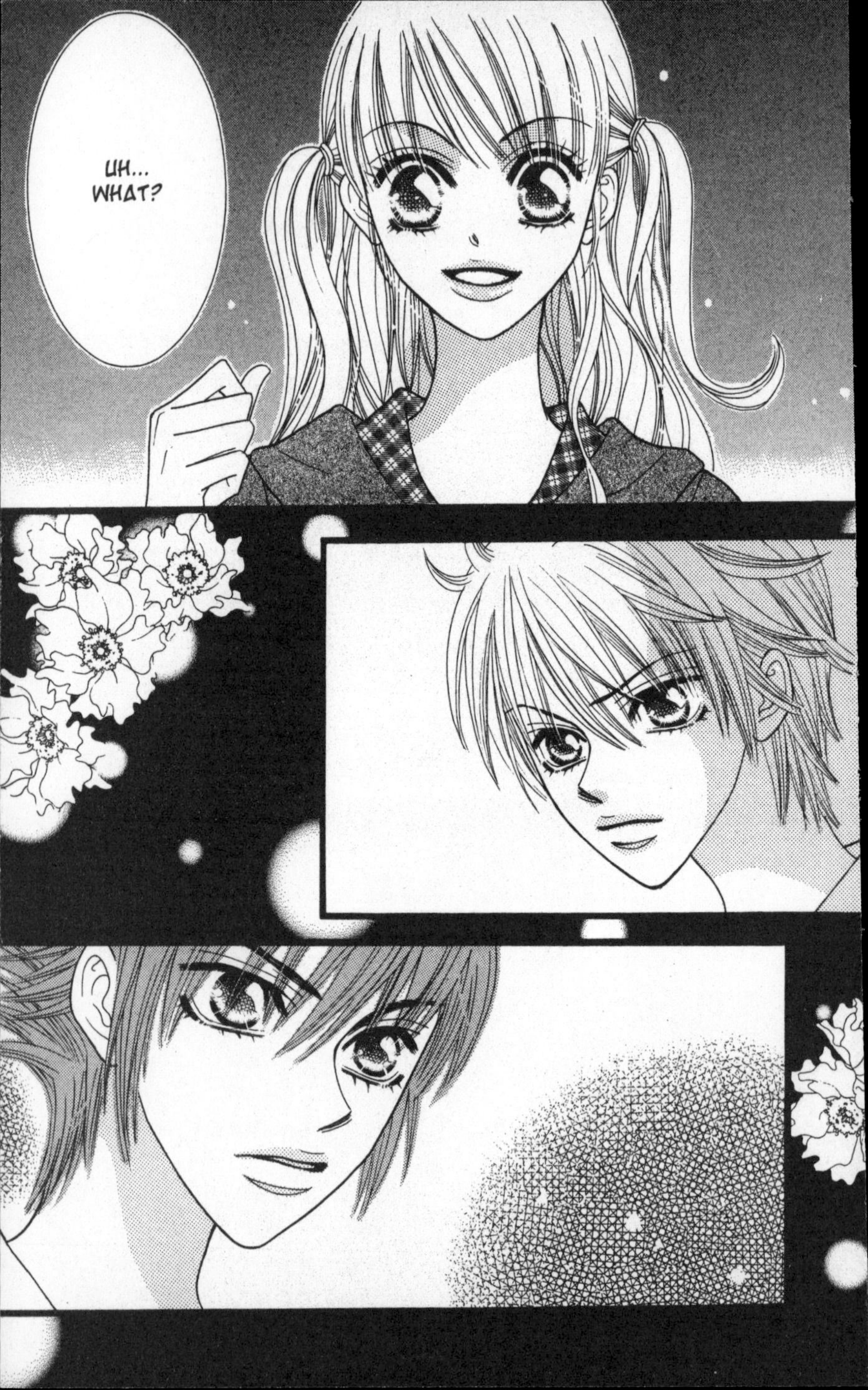
UH... WHAT?

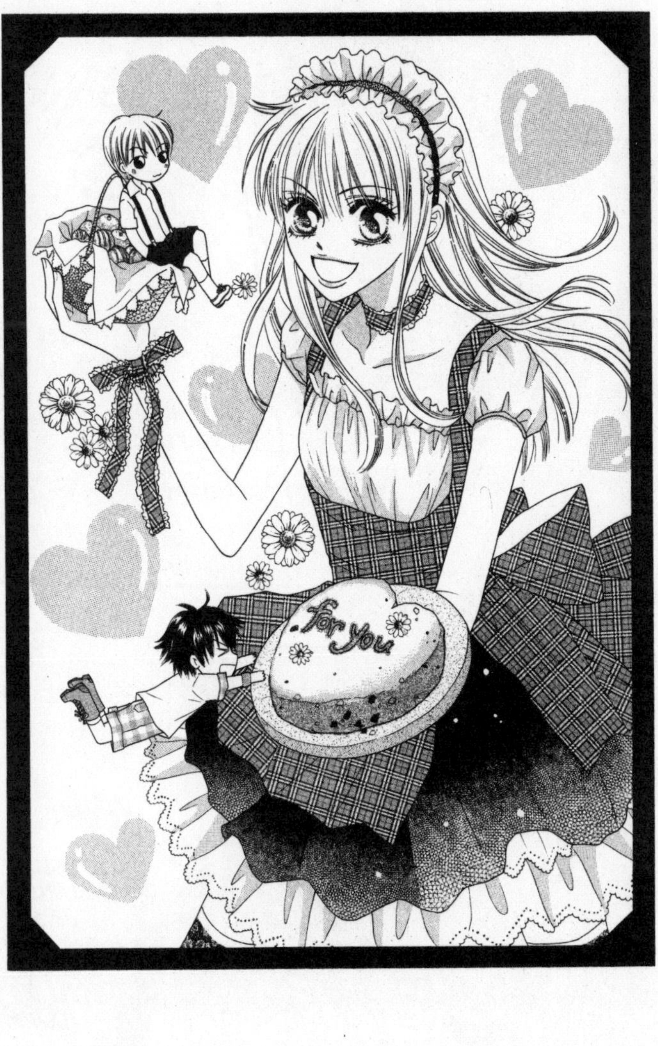
for you

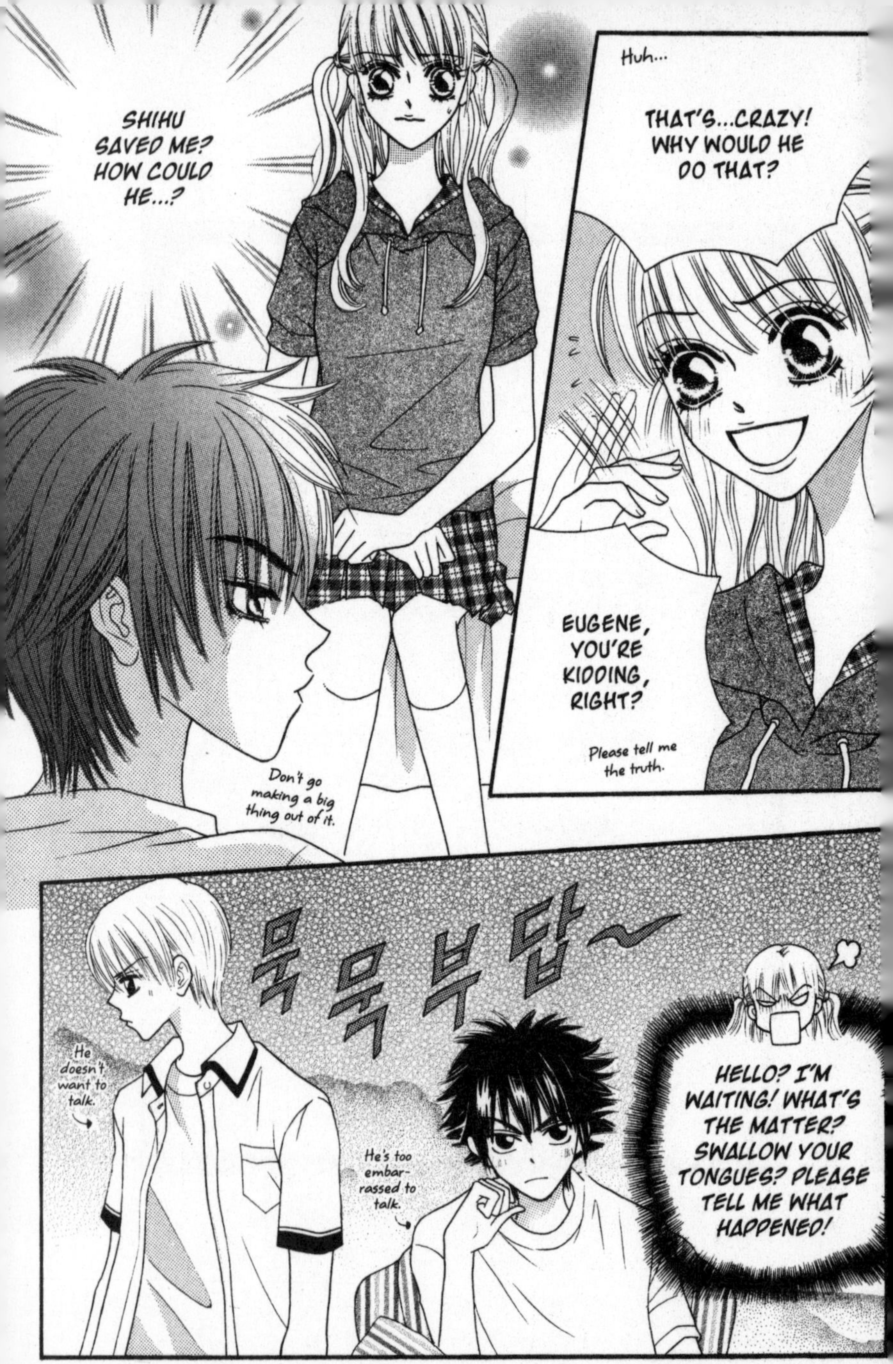
SHIHU SAVED ME? HOW COULD HE...?
Don't go making a big thing out of it.
Huh...
THAT'S...CRAZY! WHY WOULD HE DO THAT?
EUGENE, YOU'RE KIDDING, RIGHT?
Please tell me the truth.
묵묵부답~
He doesn't want to talk.
He's too embar-rassed to talk.
HELLO? I'M WAITING! WHAT'S THE MATTER? SWALLOW YOUR TONGUES? PLEASE TELL ME WHAT HAPPENED!

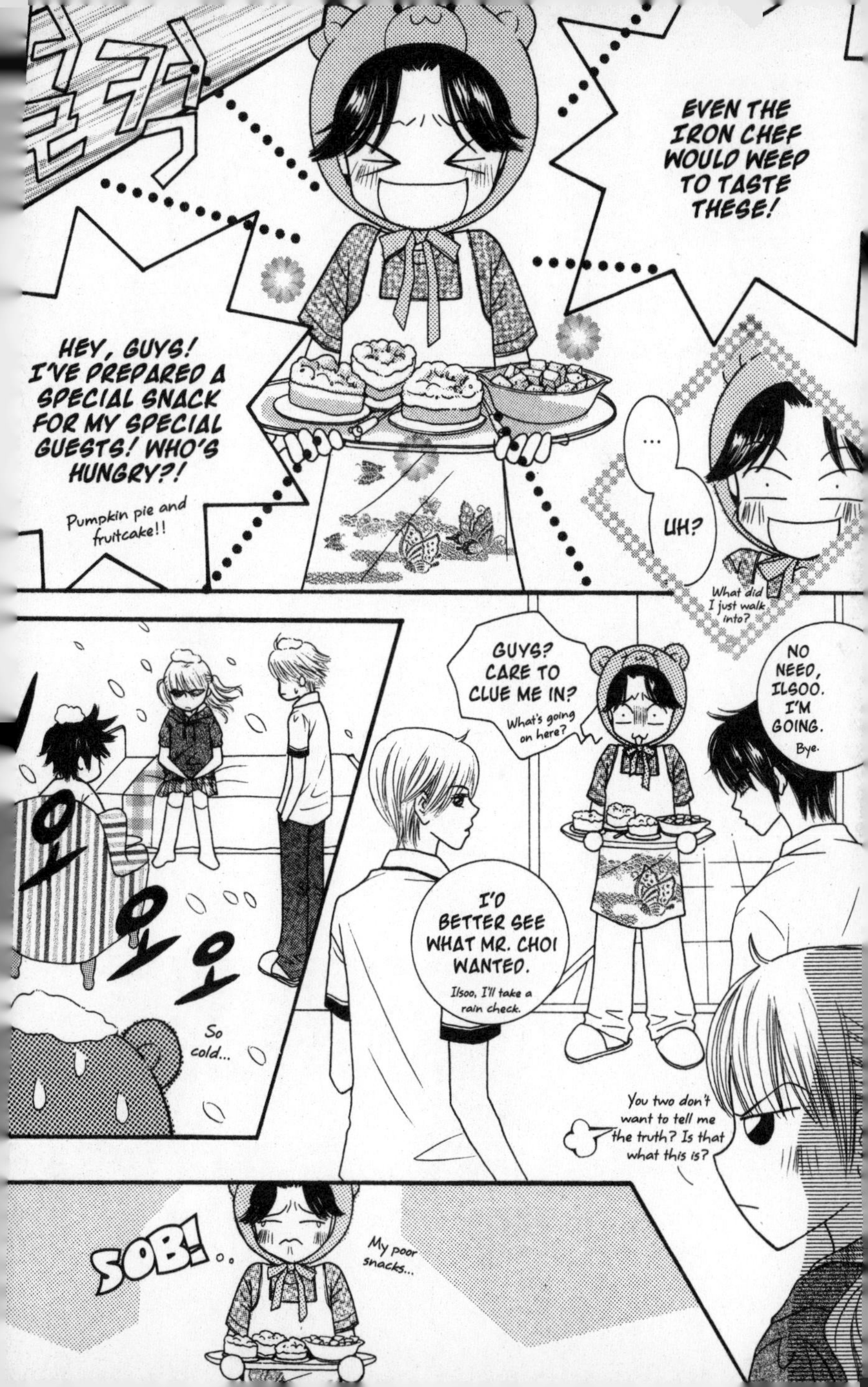
HEY, GUYS! I'VE PREPARED A SPECIAL SNACK FOR MY SPECIAL GUESTS! WHO'S HUNGRY?!
Pumpkin pie and fruitcake!!
EVEN THE IRON CHEF WOULD WEEP TO TASTE THESE!
...
UH?
What did I just walk into?
So cold...
GUYS? CARE TO CLUE ME IN?
What's going on here?
NO NEED, ILSOO. I'M GOING.
Bye.
I'D BETTER SEE WHAT MR. CHOI WANTED.
Ilsoo, I'll take a rain check.
You two don't want to tell me the truth? Is that what this is?
SOB!
My poor snacks...

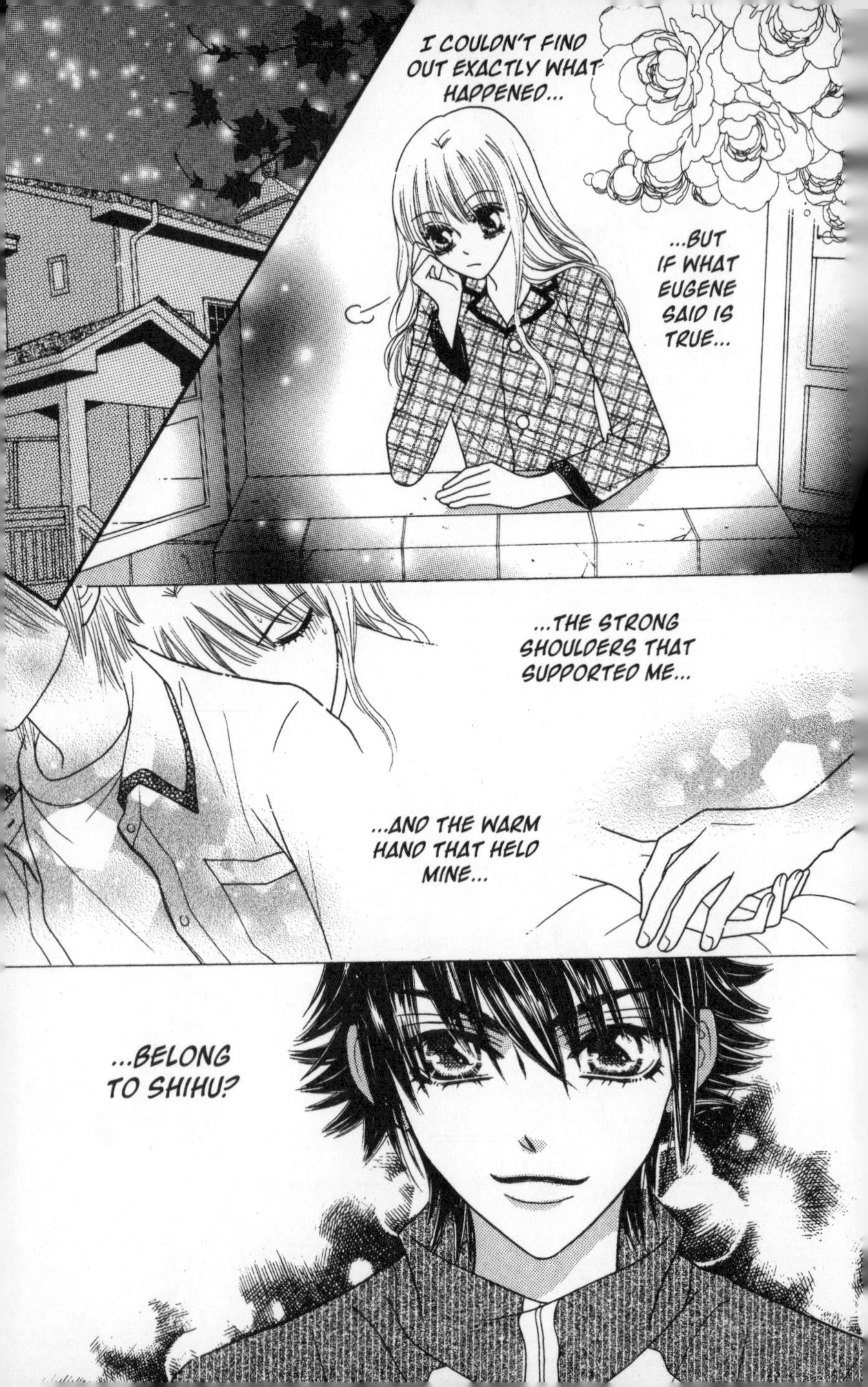
I COULDN'T FIND OUT EXACTLY WHAT HAPPENED...
...BUT IF WHAT EUGENE SAID IS TRUE...
...THE STRONG SHOULDERS THAT SUPPORTED ME...
...AND THE WARM HAND THAT HELD MINE...
...BELONG TO SHIHU?

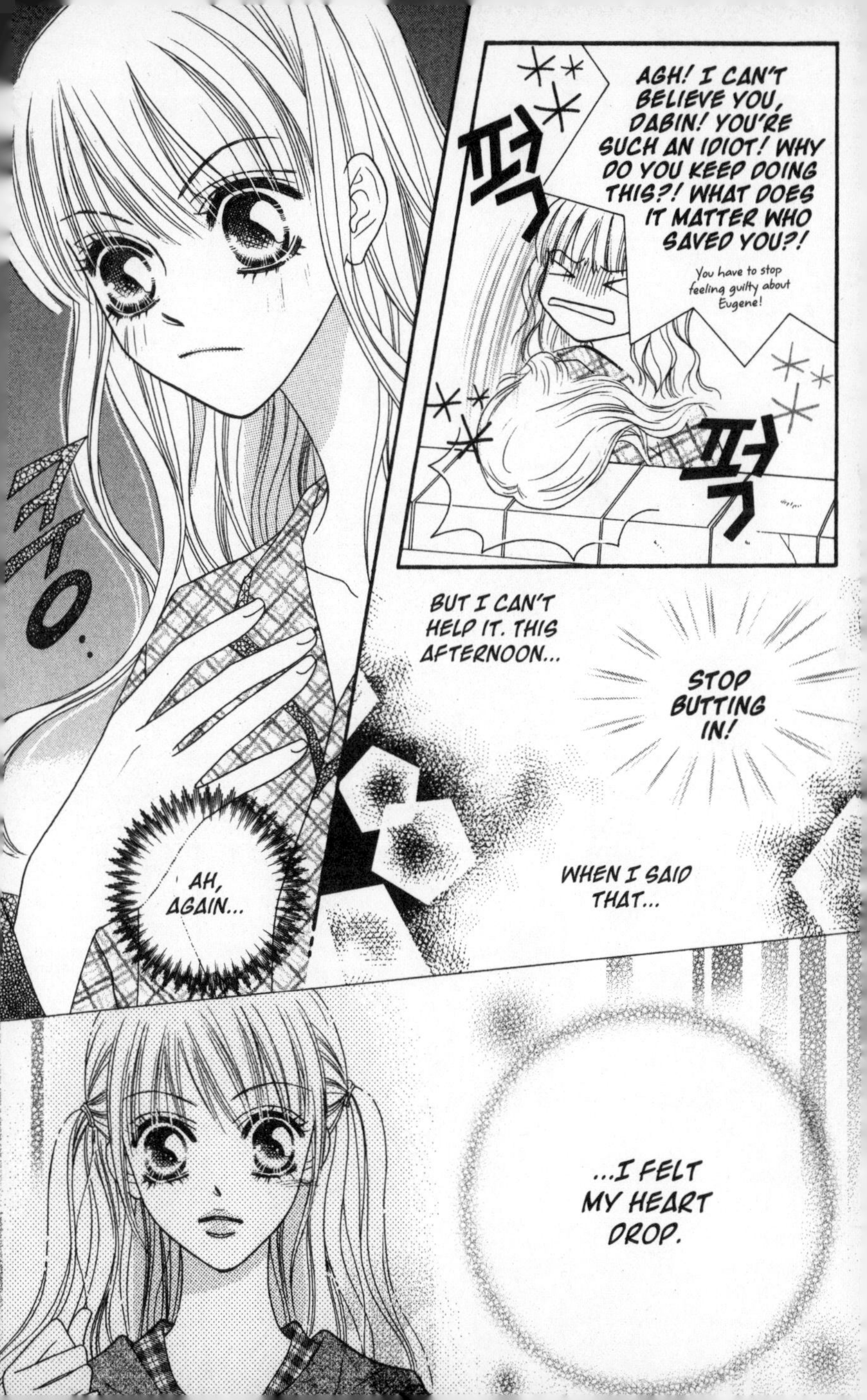
AH, AGAIN...
AGH! I CAN'T BELIEVE YOU, DABIN! YOU'RE SUCH AN IDIOT! WHY DO YOU KEEP DOING THIS?! WHAT DOES IT MATTER WHO SAVED YOU?!
You have to stop feeling guilty about Eugene!
BUT I CAN'T HELP IT. THIS AFTERNOON...
STOP BUTTING IN!
WHEN I SAID THAT...
...I FELT MY HEART DROP.

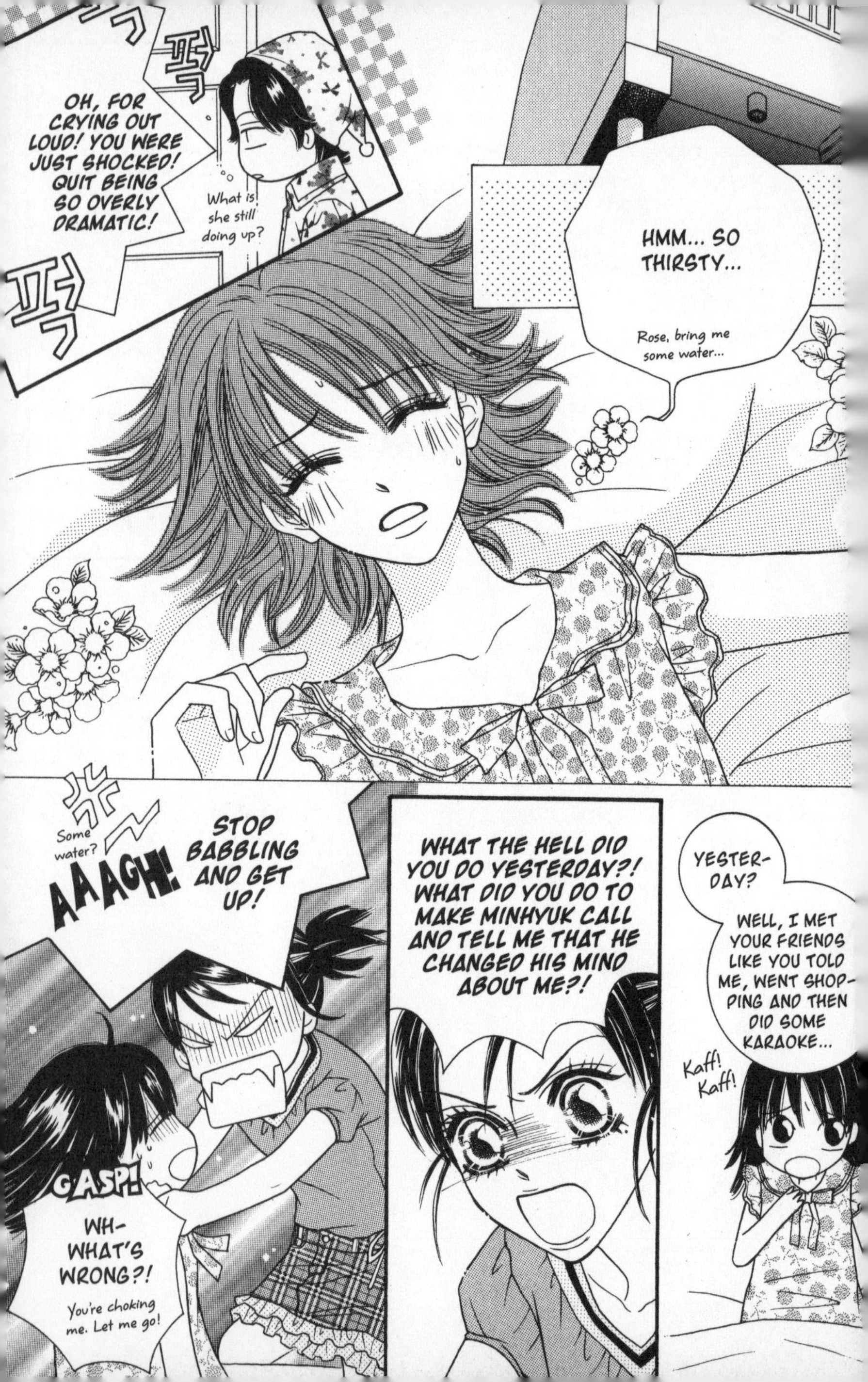
OH, FOR CRYING OUT LOUD! YOU WERE JUST SHOCKED! QUIT BEING SO OVERLY DRAMATIC!
What is she still doing up?
HMM... SO THIRSTY...
Rose, bring me some water...
Some water?
AAAGH!
STOP BABBLING AND GET UP!
GASP!
WH- WHAT'S WRONG?!
You're choking me. Let me go!
WHAT THE HELL DID YOU DO YESTERDAY?! WHAT DID YOU DO TO MAKE MINHYUK CALL AND TELL ME THAT HE CHANGED HIS MIND ABOUT ME?!
YESTER-DAY?
WELL, I MET YOUR FRIENDS LIKE YOU TOLD ME, WENT SHOP-PING AND THEN DID SOME KARAOKE...
Kaff! Kaff!

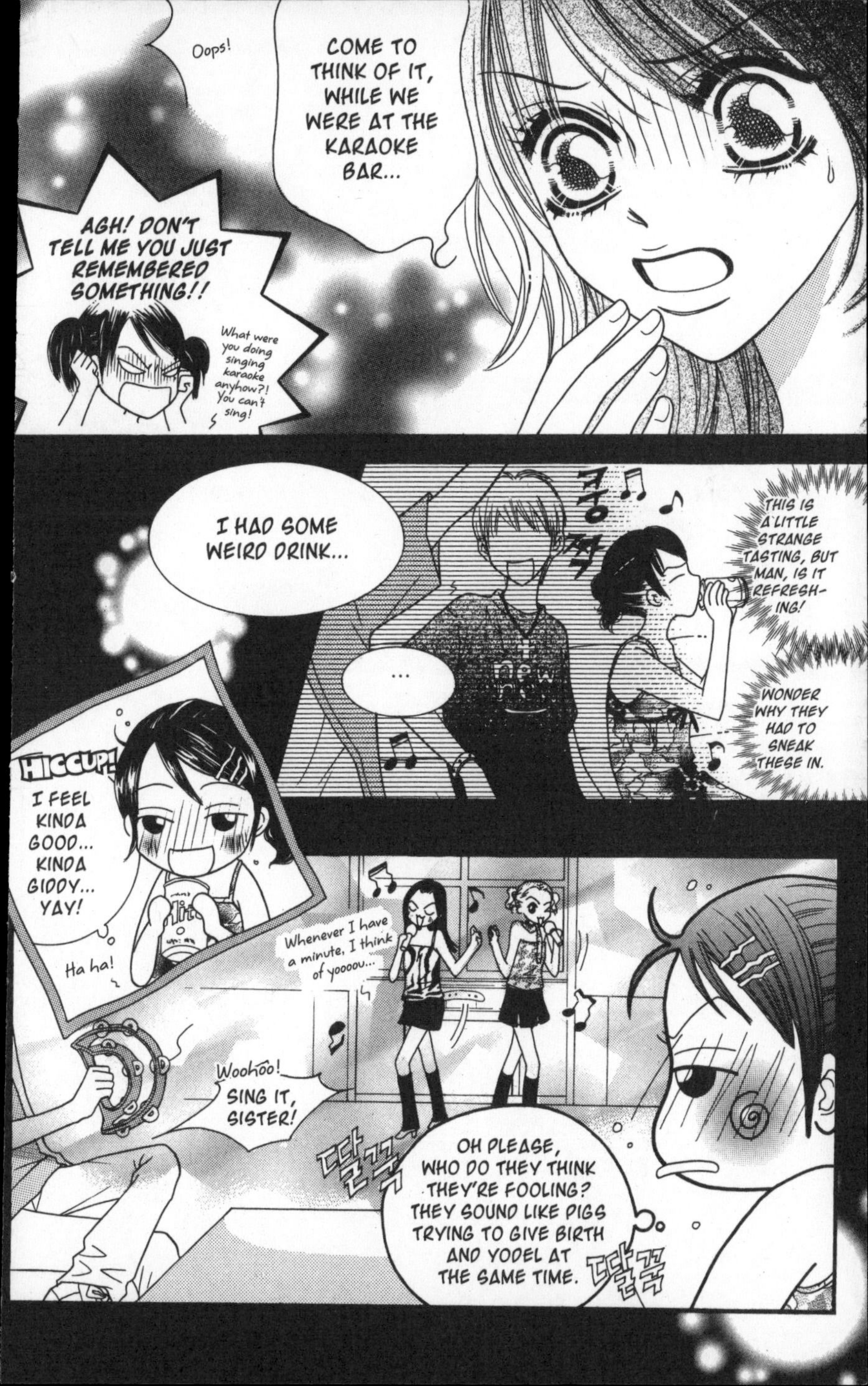
COME TO THINK OF IT, WHILE WE WERE AT THE KARAOKE BAR...
Oops!
AGH! DON'T TELL ME YOU JUST REMEMBERED SOMETHING!!
What were you doing singing karaoke anyhow?! You can't sing!
THIS IS A LITTLE STRANGE TASTING, BUT MAN, IS IT REFRESHING!
I HAD SOME WEIRD DRINK...
WONDER WHY THEY HAD TO SNEAK THESE IN.
...
HICCUP!
I FEEL KINDA GOOD... KINDA GIDDY... YAY!
Ha ha!
OH PLEASE, WHO DO THEY THINK THEY'RE FOOLING? THEY SOUND LIKE PIGS TRYING TO GIVE BIRTH AND YODEL AT THE SAME TIME.
Whenever I have a minute, I think of yoooou...
Woohoo! SING IT, SISTER!

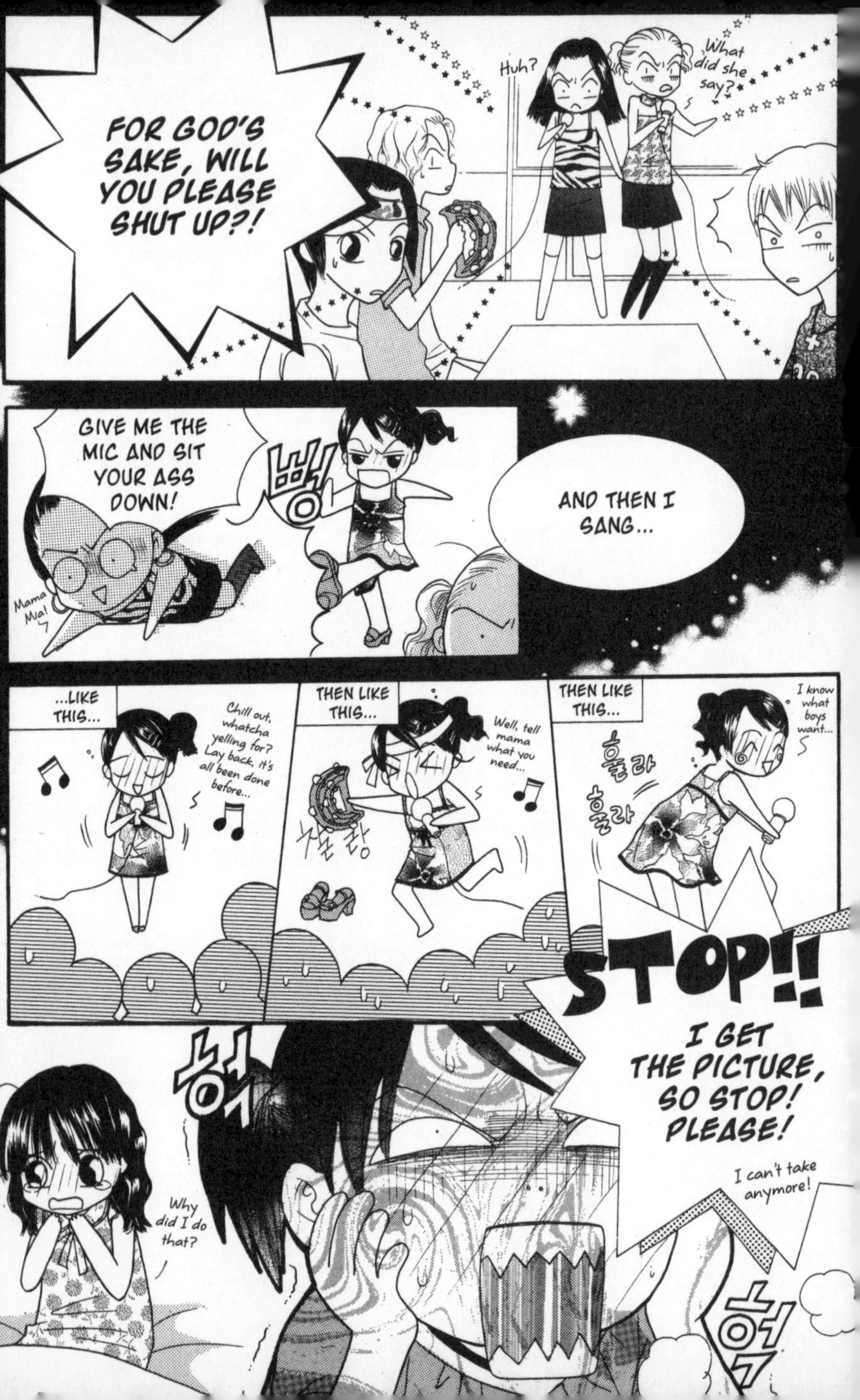

FOR GOD'S SAKE, WILL YOU PLEASE SHUT UP?!
Huh?
What did she say?
GIVE ME THE MIC AND SIT YOUR ASS DOWN!
Mama Mia!
AND THEN I SANG...
...LIKE THIS...
Chill out, whatcha yelling for? Lay back, it's all been done before...
THEN LIKE THIS...
Well, tell mama what you need...
THEN LIKE THIS...
I know what boys want...
STOP!!
I GET THE PICTURE, SO STOP! PLEASE!
Why did I do that?
I can't take anymore!

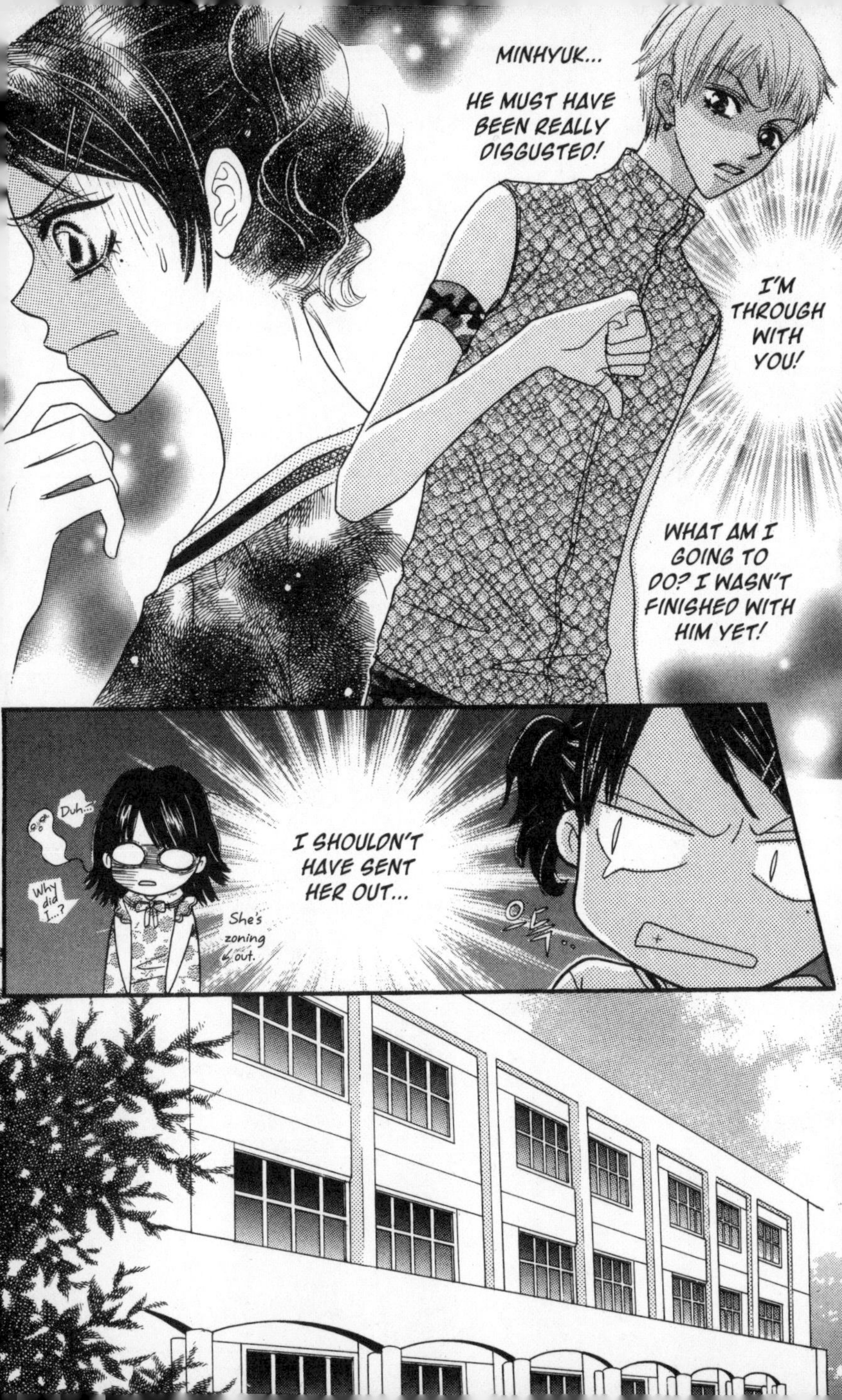
MINHYUK...
HE MUST HAVE BEEN REALLY DISGUSTED!
I'M THROUGH WITH YOU!
WHAT AM I GOING TO DO? I WASN'T FINISHED WITH HIM YET!
Duh...
Why did I...?
She's zoning out.
I SHOULDN'T HAVE SENT HER OUT...

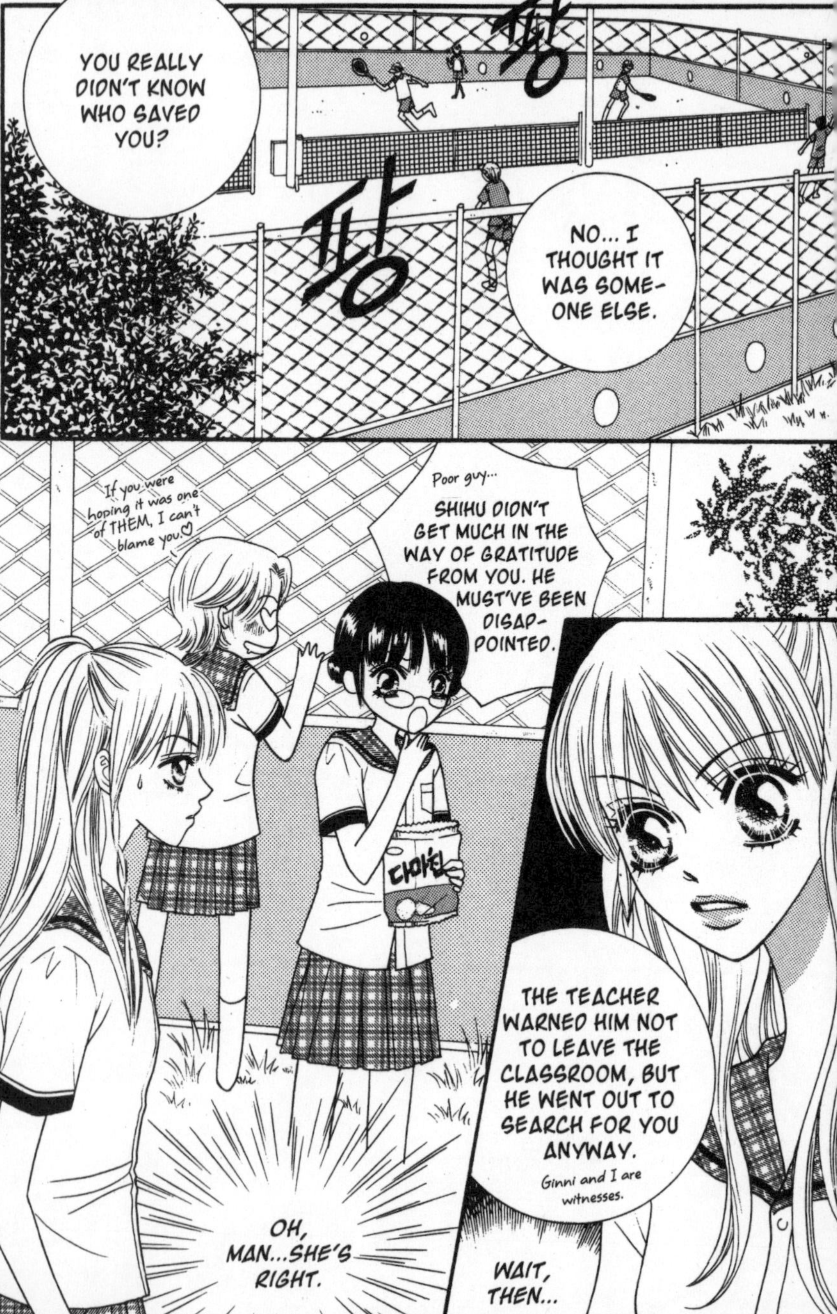
YOU REALLY DIDN'T KNOW WHO SAVED YOU?
팡
팡
NO... I THOUGHT IT WAS SOME-ONE ELSE.
If you were hoping it was one of THEM, I can't blame you.♡
Poor guy...
SHIHU DIDN'T GET MUCH IN THE WAY OF GRATITUDE FROM YOU. HE MUST'VE BEEN DISAP-POINTED.
OH, MAN...SHE'S RIGHT.
THE TEACHER WARNED HIM NOT TO LEAVE THE CLASSROOM, BUT HE WENT OUT TO SEARCH FOR YOU ANYWAY.
Ginni and I are witnesses.
WAIT, THEN...

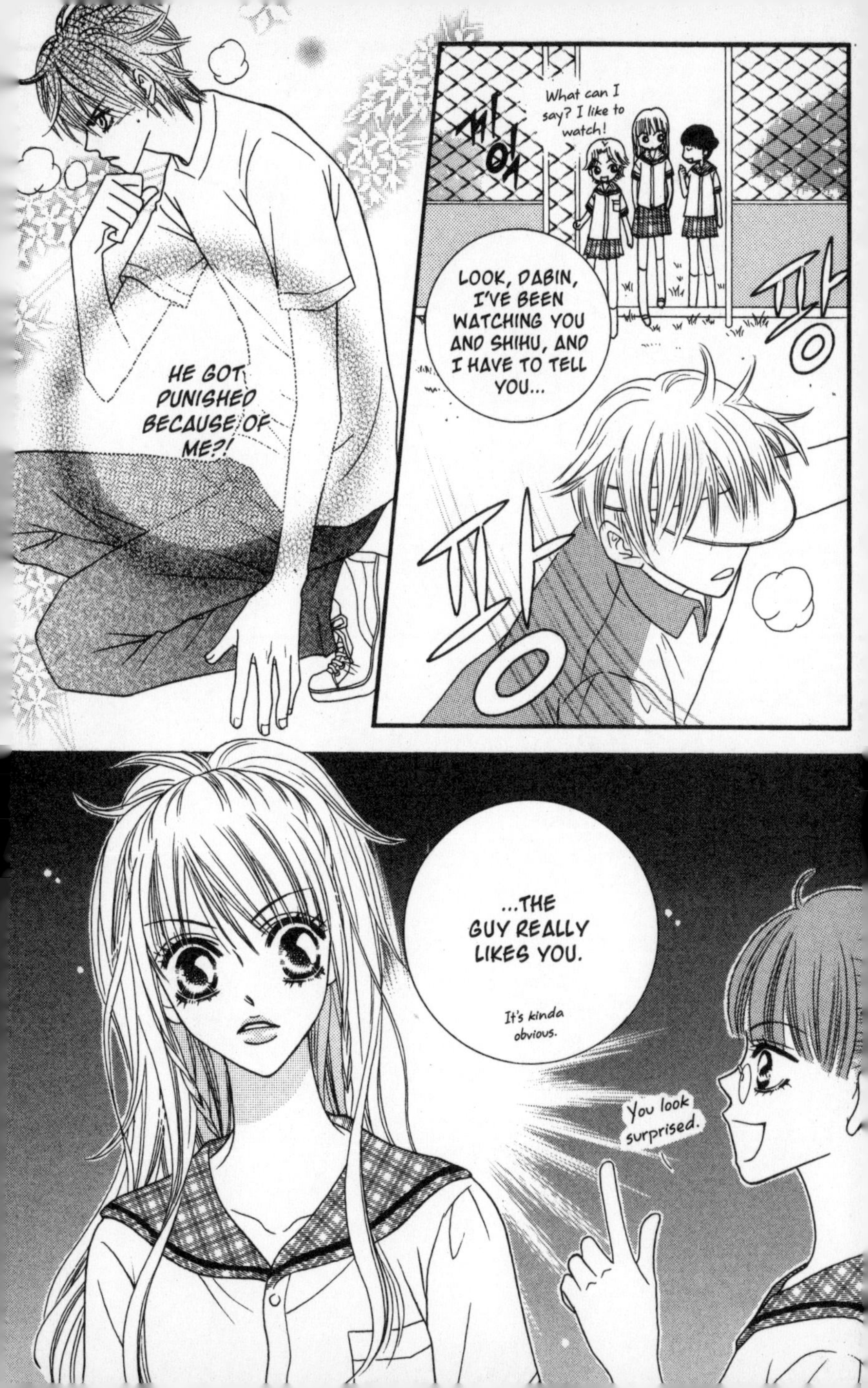
HE GOT PUNISHED BECAUSE OF ME?!
What can I say? I like to watch!
LOOK, DABIN, I'VE BEEN WATCHING YOU AND SHIHU, AND I HAVE TO TELL YOU...
...THE GUY REALLY LIKES YOU.
It's kinda obvious.
You look surprised.

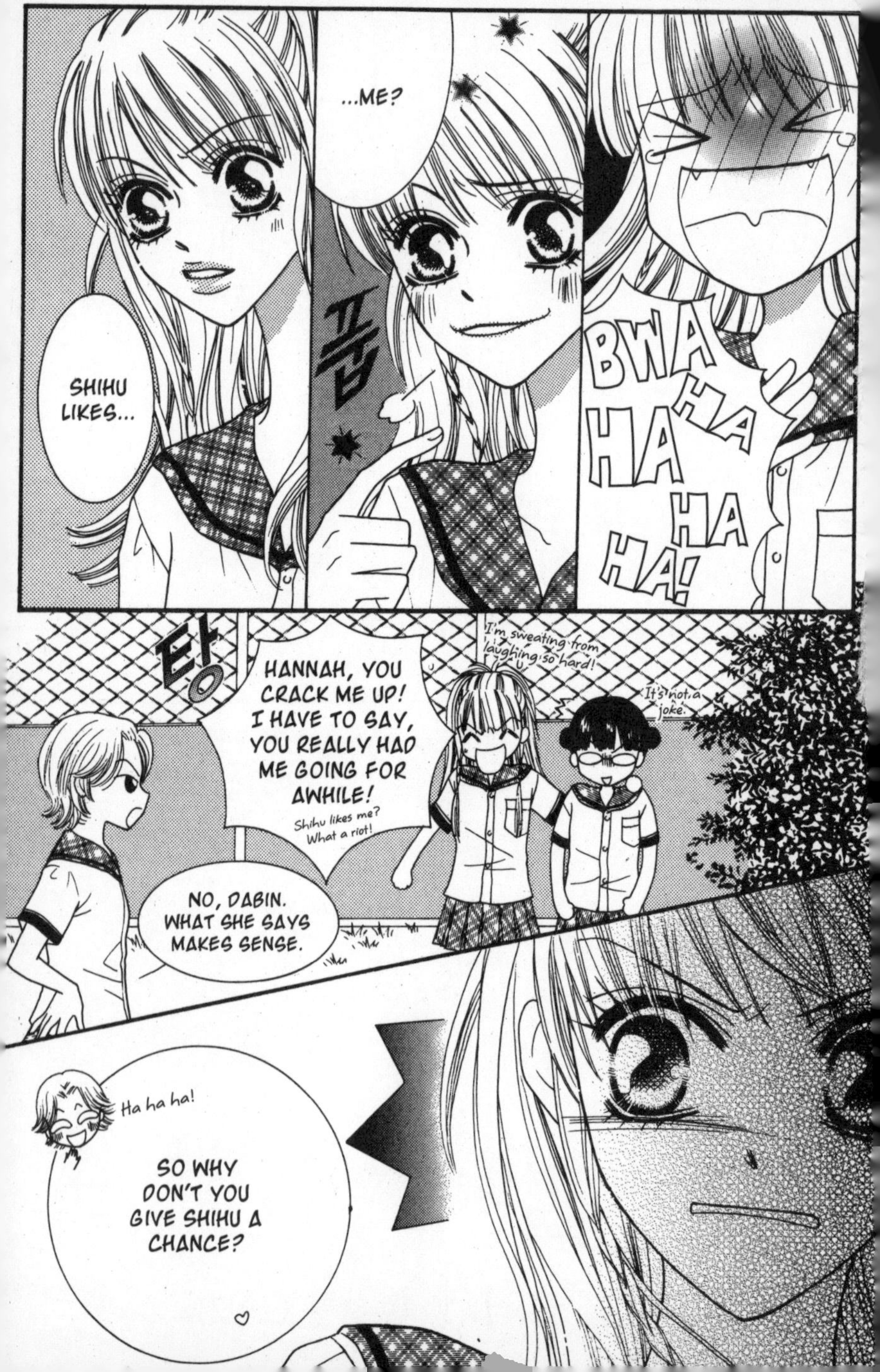
SHIHU LIKES...
...ME?
끄덕
BWAHAHAHAHAHA!
탁
HANNAH, YOU CRACK ME UP! I HAVE TO SAY, YOU REALLY HAD ME GOING FOR AWHILE!
Shihu likes me? What a riot!
I'm sweating from laughing so hard!
It's not a joke.
NO, DABIN. WHAT SHE SAYS MAKES SENSE.
Ha ha ha!
SO WHY DON'T YOU GIVE SHIHU A CHANCE?

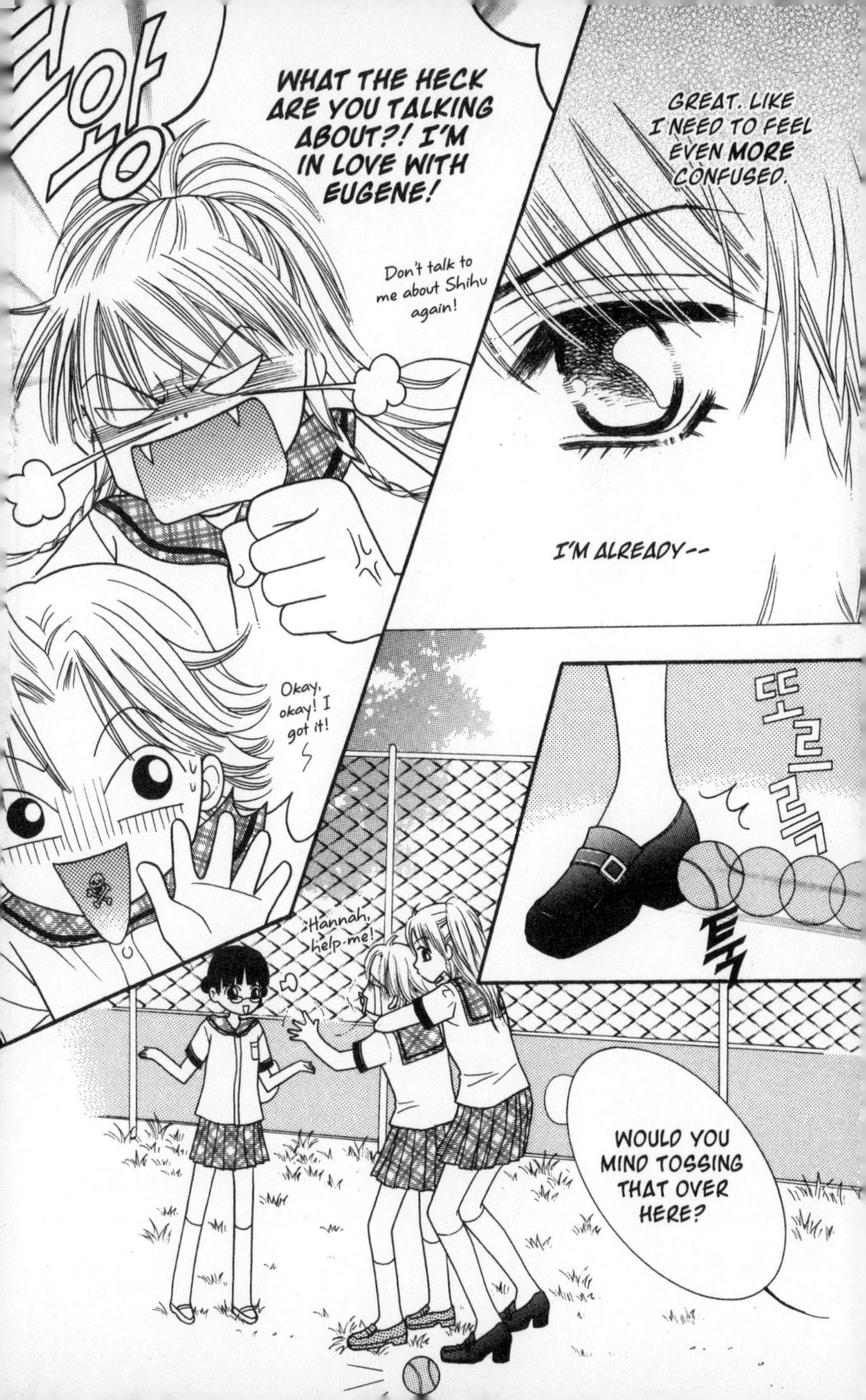
WHAT THE HECK ARE YOU TALKING ABOUT?! I'M IN LOVE WITH EUGENE!
Don't talk to me about Shihu again!
Okay, okay! I got it!
GREAT. LIKE I NEED TO FEEL EVEN MORE CONFUSED.
I'M ALREADY--
Hannah, help me!
WOULD YOU MIND TOSSING THAT OVER HERE?

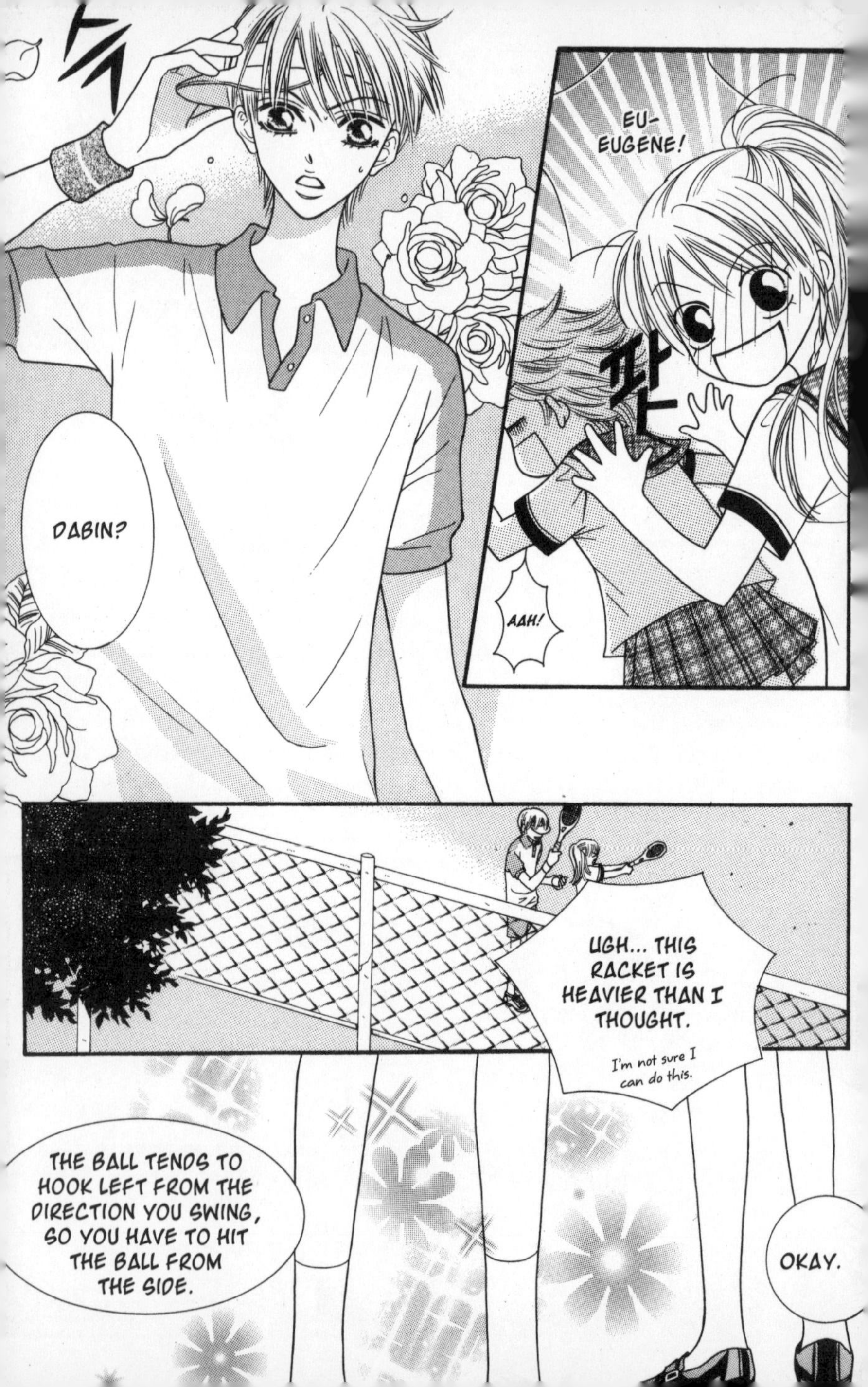
DABIN?
EU- EUGENE!
AAH!
UGH... THIS RACKET IS HEAVIER THAN I THOUGHT.
I'm not sure I can do this.
THE BALL TENDS TO HOOK LEFT FROM THE DIRECTION YOU SWING, SO YOU HAVE TO HIT THE BALL FROM THE SIDE.
OKAY.

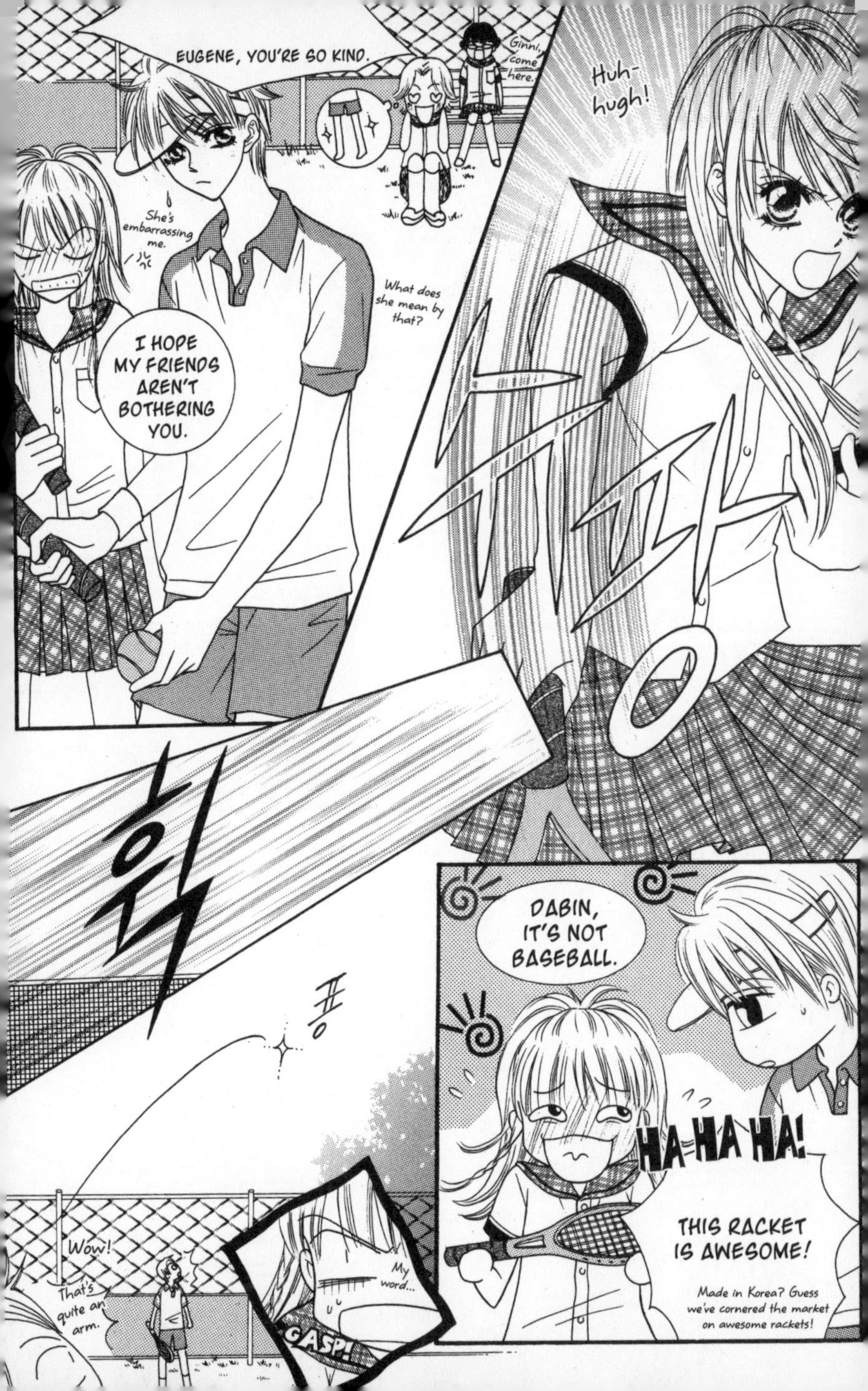
EUGENE, YOU'RE SO KIND.
Ginni, come here.
She's embarrassing me.
I HOPE MY FRIENDS AREN'T BOTHERING YOU.
What does she mean by that?
Huh-hugh!
Wow!
That's quite an arm.
My word...
GASP!
DABIN, IT'S NOT BASEBALL.
HA-HA HA!
THIS RACKET IS AWESOME!
Made in Korea? Guess we've cornered the market on awesome rackets!

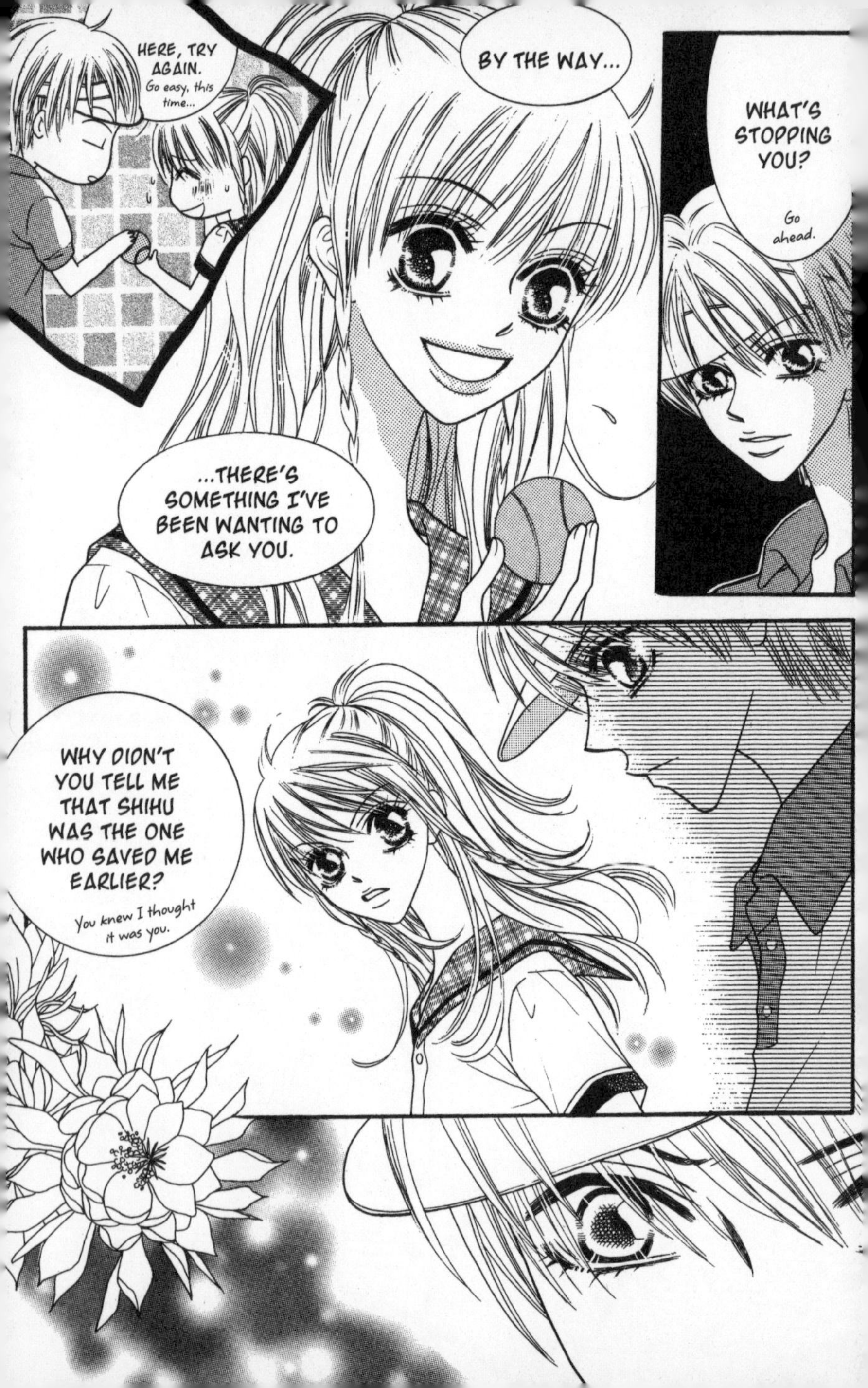
HERE, TRY AGAIN.
Go easy, this time...
BY THE WAY...
...THERE'S SOMETHING I'VE BEEN WANTING TO ASK YOU.
WHAT'S STOPPING YOU?
Go ahead.
WHY DIDN'T YOU TELL ME THAT SHIHU WAS THE ONE WHO SAVED ME EARLIER?
You knew I thought it was you.

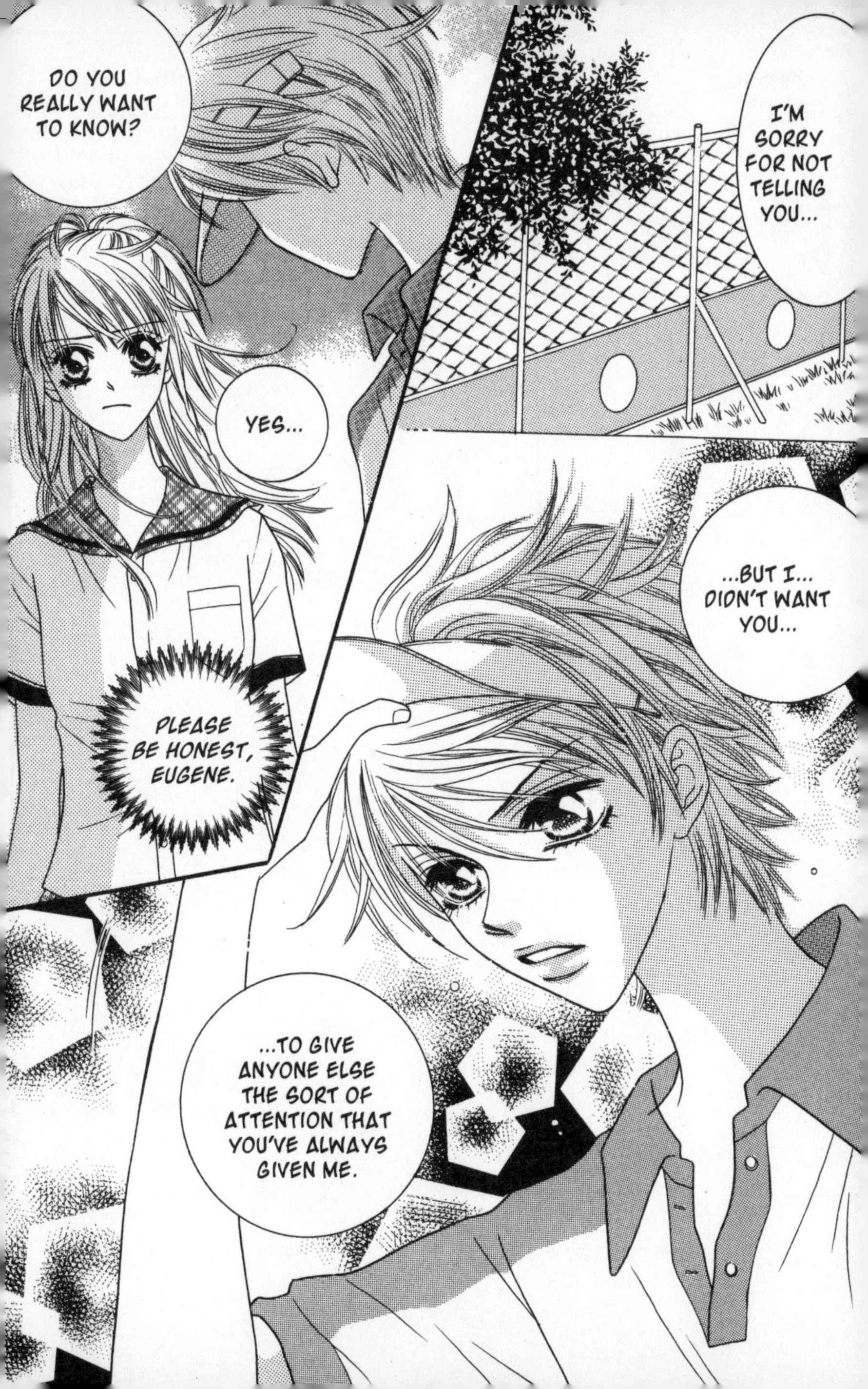
DO YOU REALLY WANT TO KNOW?
YES...
PLEASE BE HONEST, EUGENE.
I'M SORRY FOR NOT TELLING YOU...
...BUT I... DIDN'T WANT YOU...
...TO GIVE ANYONE ELSE THE SORT OF ATTENTION THAT YOU'VE ALWAYS GIVEN ME.

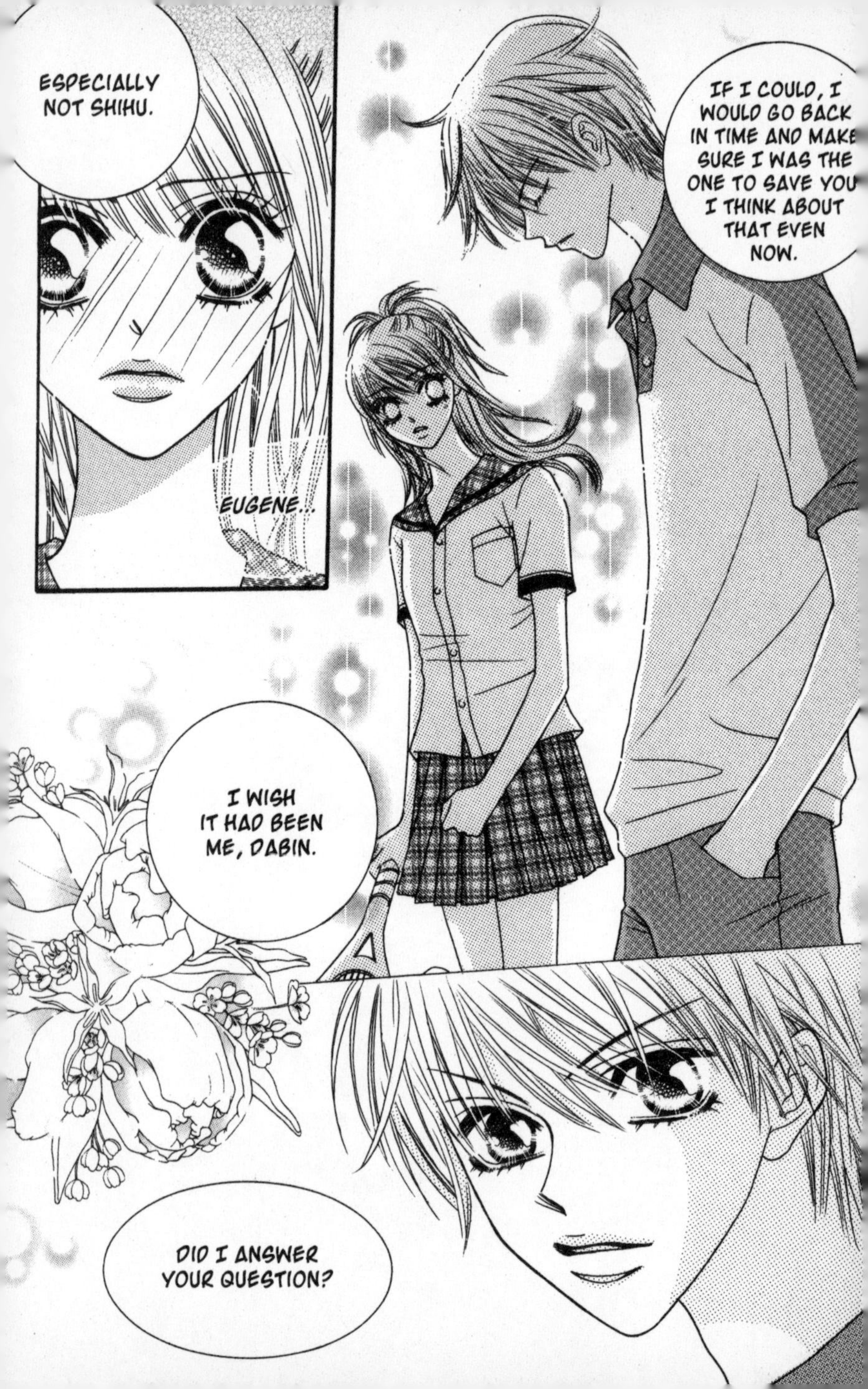
ESPECIALLY NOT SHIHU.
EUGENE...
IF I COULD, I WOULD GO BACK IN TIME AND MAKE SURE I WAS THE ONE TO SAVE YOU I THINK ABOUT THAT EVEN NOW.
I WISH IT HAD BEEN ME, DABIN.
DID I ANSWER YOUR QUESTION?

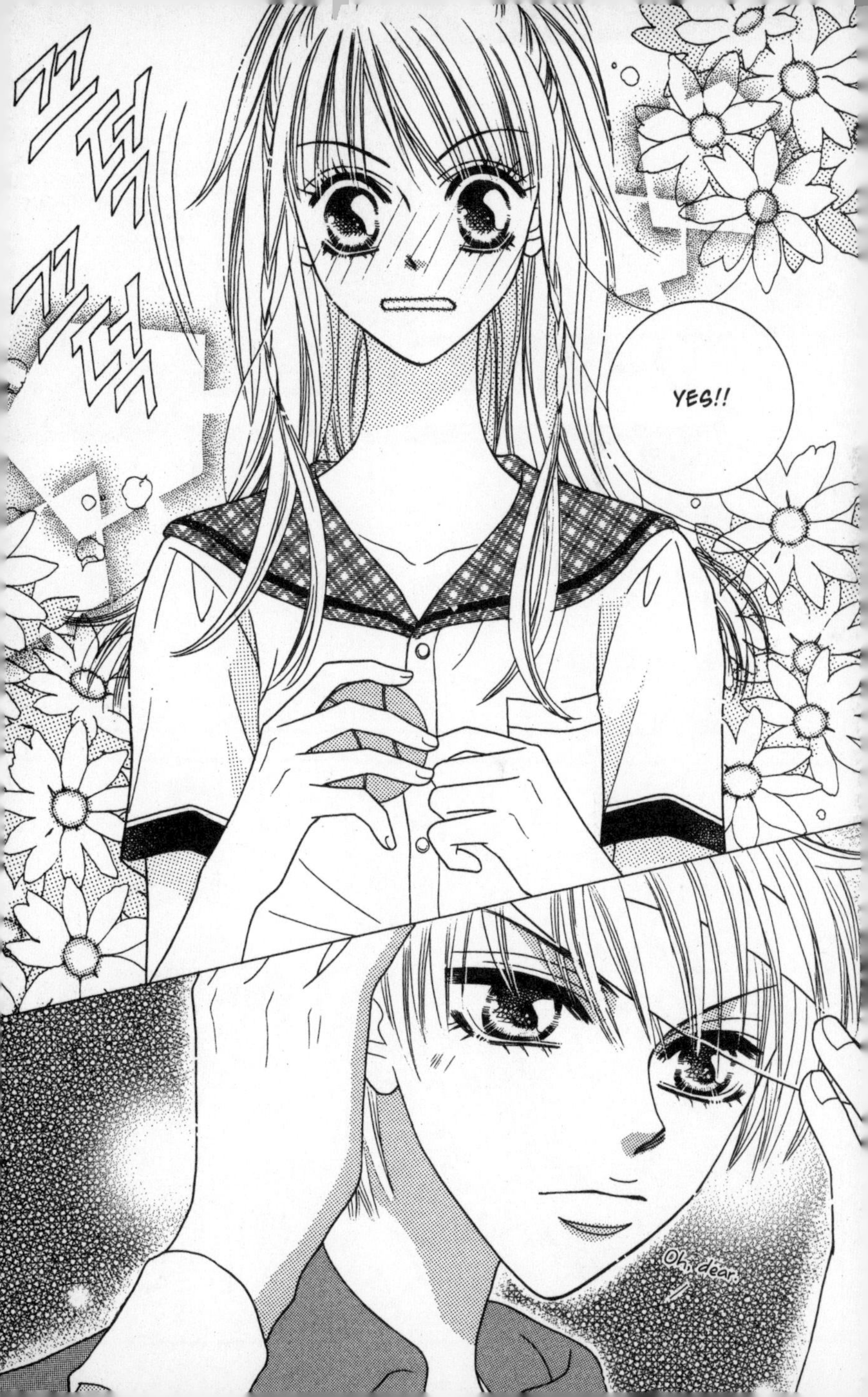
끄덕 끄덕
YES!!
Oh, dear.

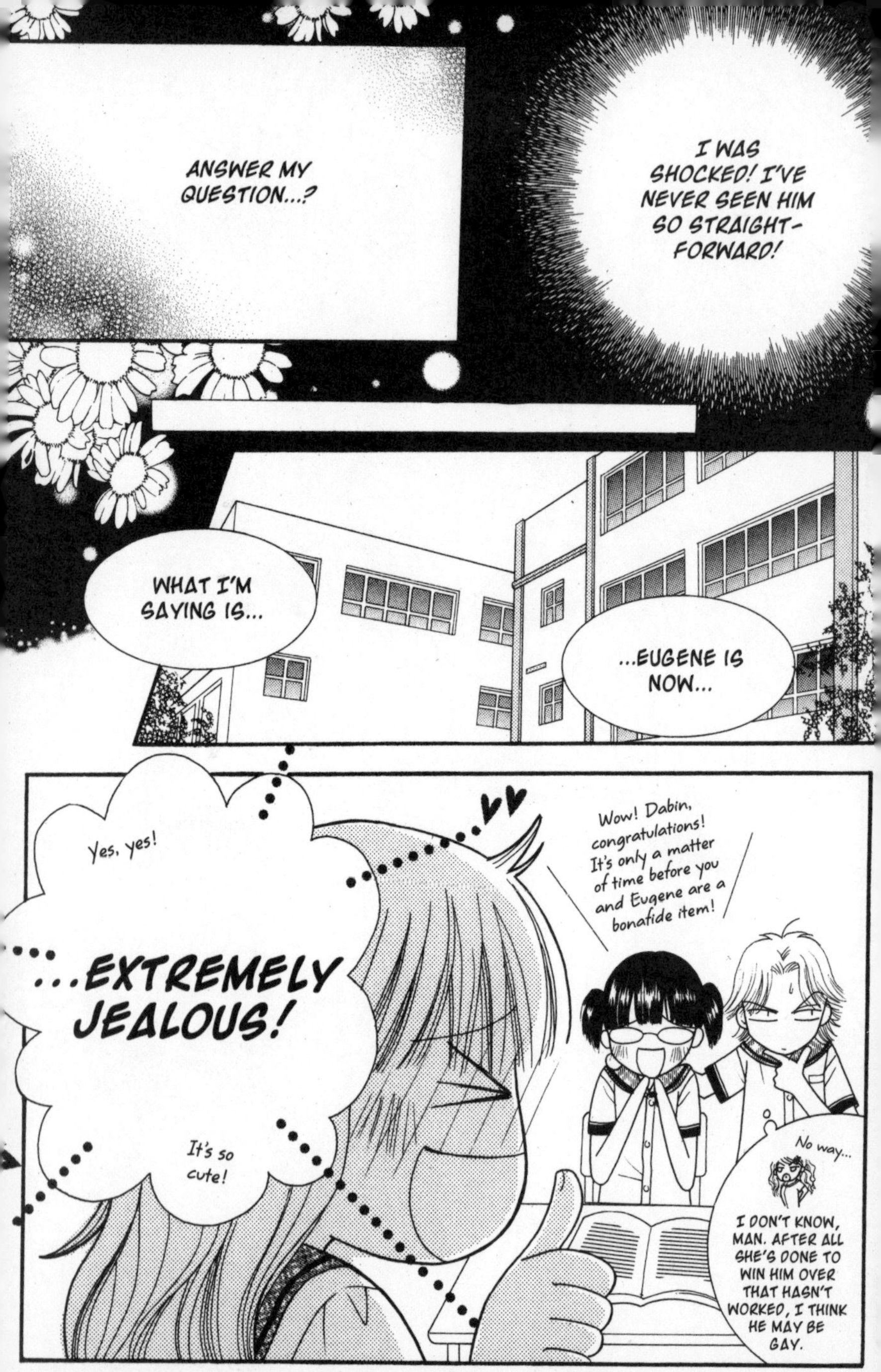
ANSWER MY QUESTION...?
I WAS SHOCKED! I'VE NEVER SEEN HIM SO STRAIGHT-FORWARD!
WHAT I'M SAYING IS...
...EUGENE IS NOW...
Yes, yes!
...EXTREMELY JEALOUS!
It's so cute!
Wow! Dabin, congratulations! It's only a matter of time before you and Eugene are a bonafide item!
No way...
I DON'T KNOW, MAN. AFTER ALL SHE'S DONE TO WIN HIM OVER THAT HASN'T WORKED, I THINK HE MAY BE GAY.

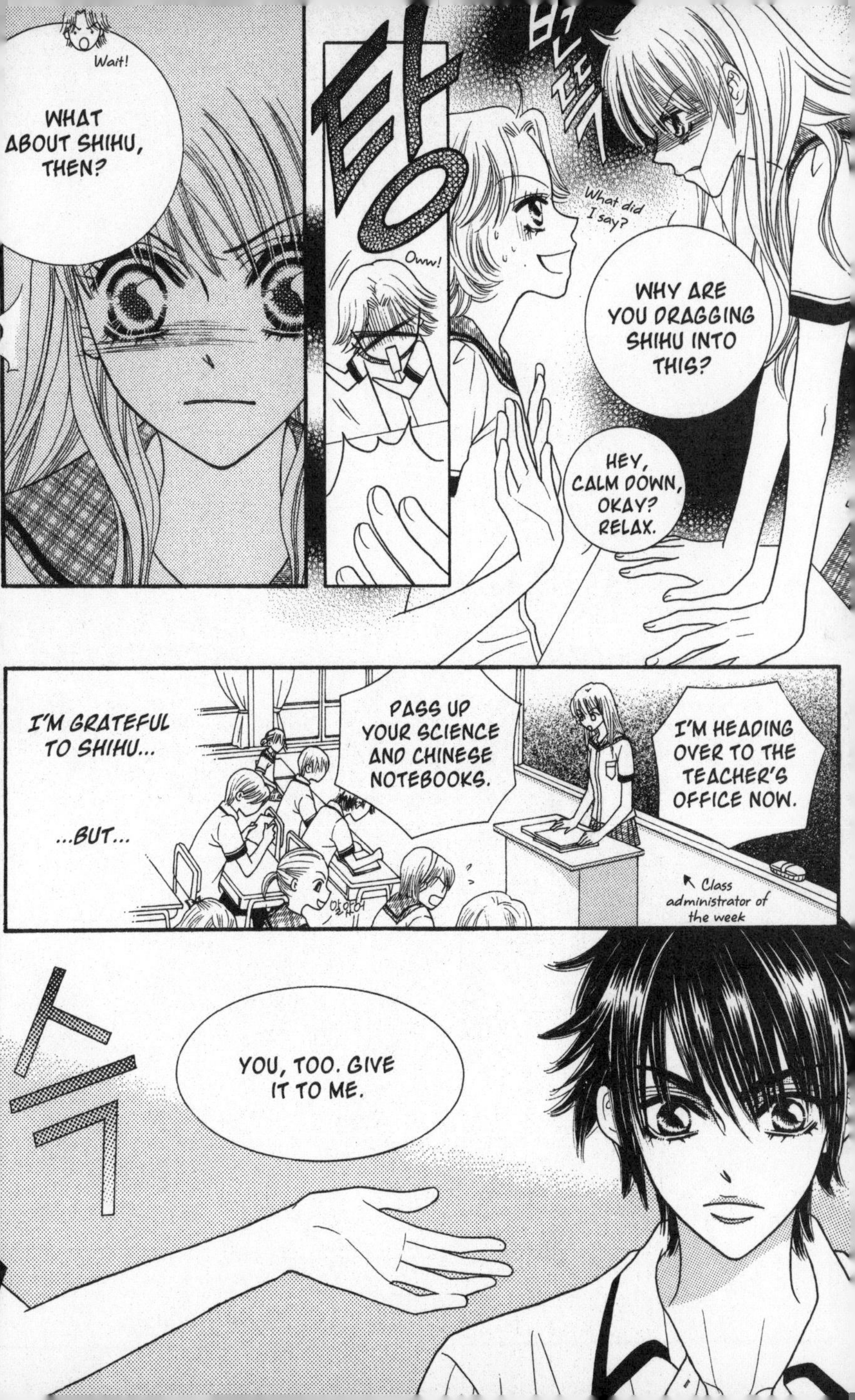

Wait!
WHAT ABOUT SHIHU, THEN?
탕
Oww!
What did I say?
WHY ARE YOU DRAGGING SHIHU INTO THIS?
HEY, CALM DOWN, OKAY? RELAX.
I'M GRATEFUL TO SHIHU...
...BUT...
PASS UP YOUR SCIENCE AND CHINESE NOTEBOOKS.
I'M HEADING OVER TO THE TEACHER'S OFFICE NOW.
↖ Class administrator of the week
YOU, TOO. GIVE IT TO ME.

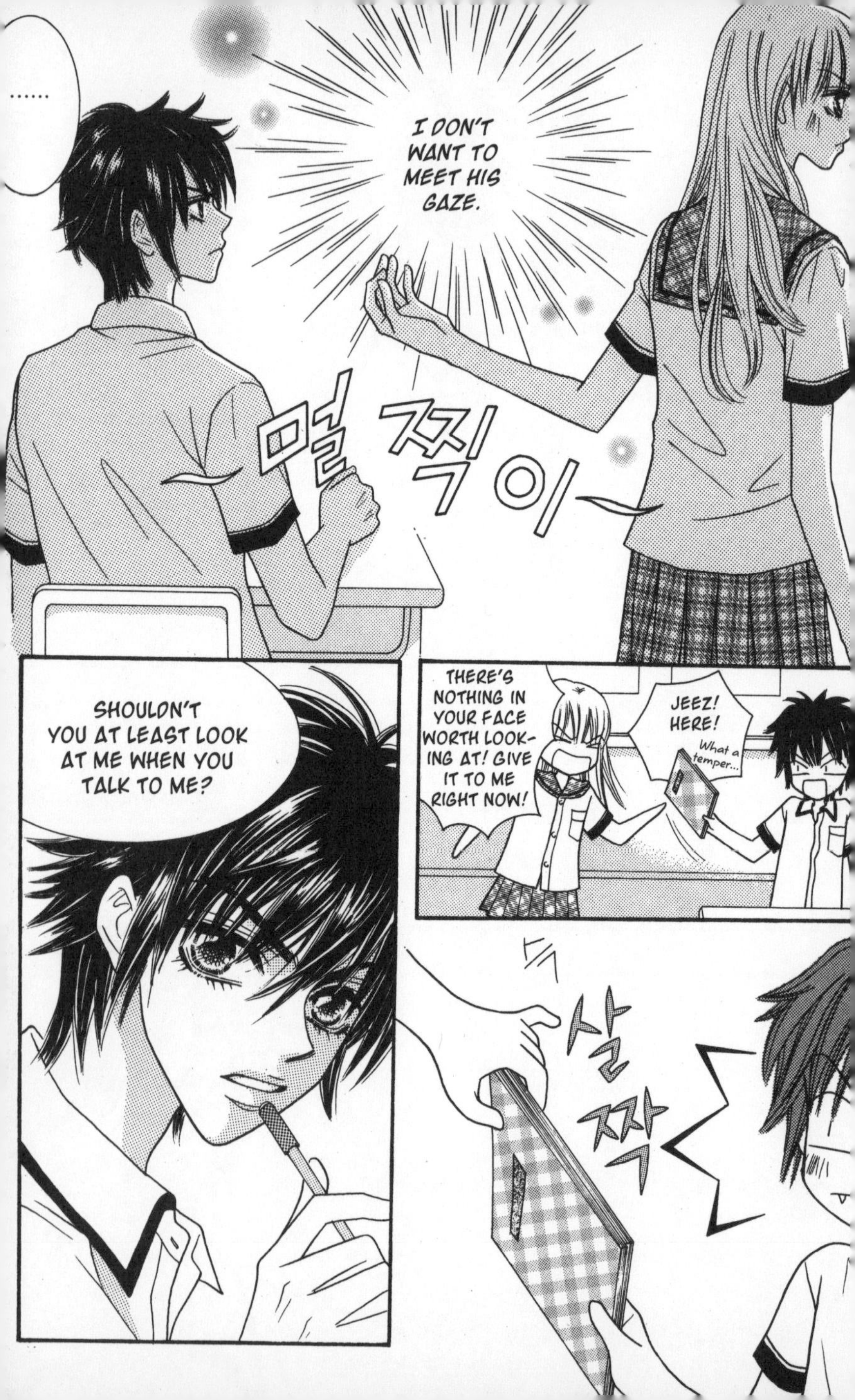
......
I DON'T WANT TO MEET HIS GAZE.
멀찍이~
SHOULDN'T YOU AT LEAST LOOK AT ME WHEN YOU TALK TO ME?
THERE'S NOTHING IN YOUR FACE WORTH LOOKING AT! GIVE IT TO ME RIGHT NOW!
JEEZ! HERE!
What a temper...
살짝

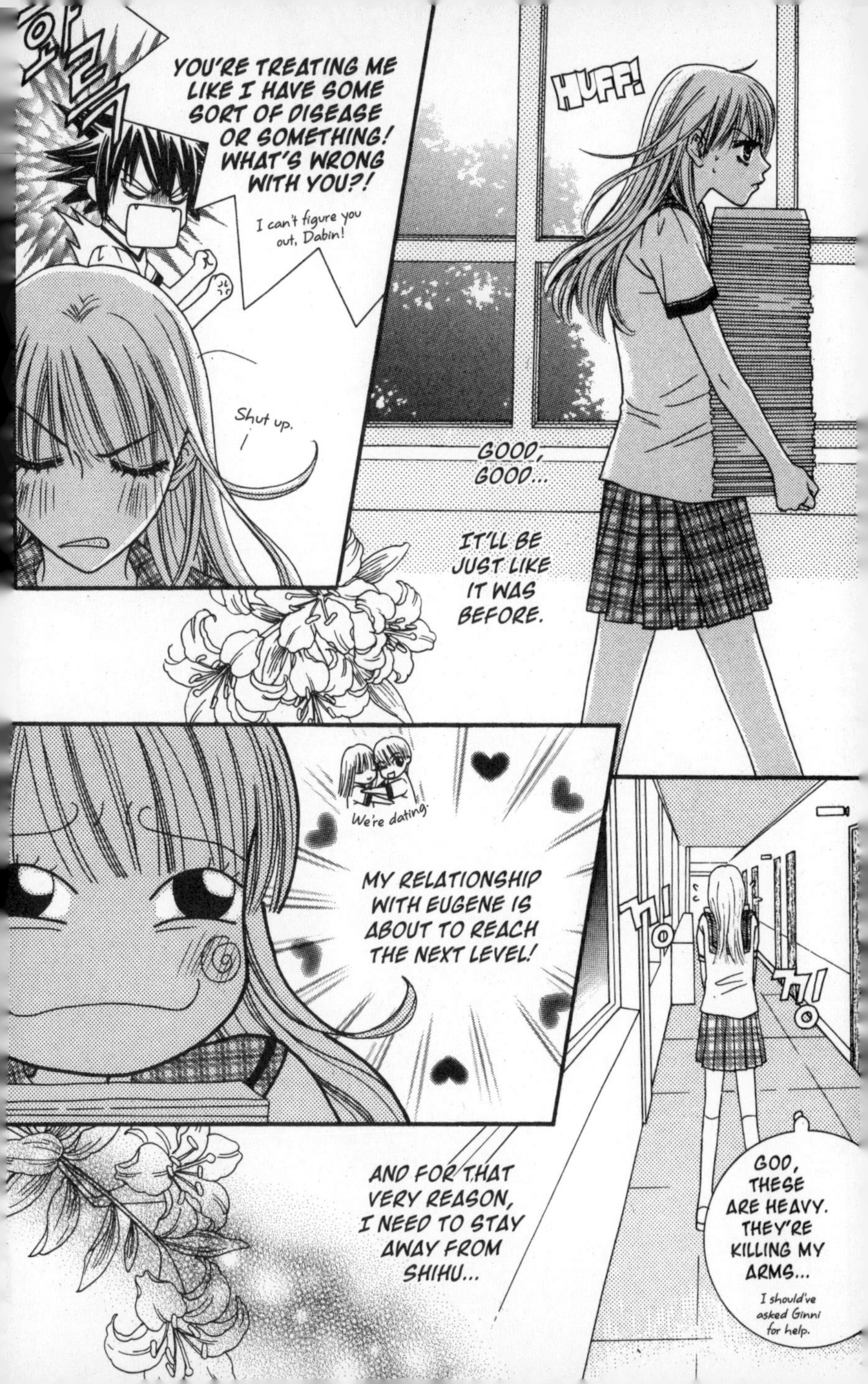
YOU'RE TREATING ME LIKE I HAVE SOME SORT OF DISEASE OR SOMETHING! WHAT'S WRONG WITH YOU?!
I can't figure you out, Dabin!
Shut up.
HUFF!
GOOD, GOOD...
IT'LL BE JUST LIKE IT WAS BEFORE.
We're dating.
MY RELATIONSHIP WITH EUGENE IS ABOUT TO REACH THE NEXT LEVEL!
AND FOR THAT VERY REASON, I NEED TO STAY AWAY FROM SHIHU...
GOD, THESE ARE HEAVY. THEY'RE KILLING MY ARMS...
I should've asked Ginni for help.

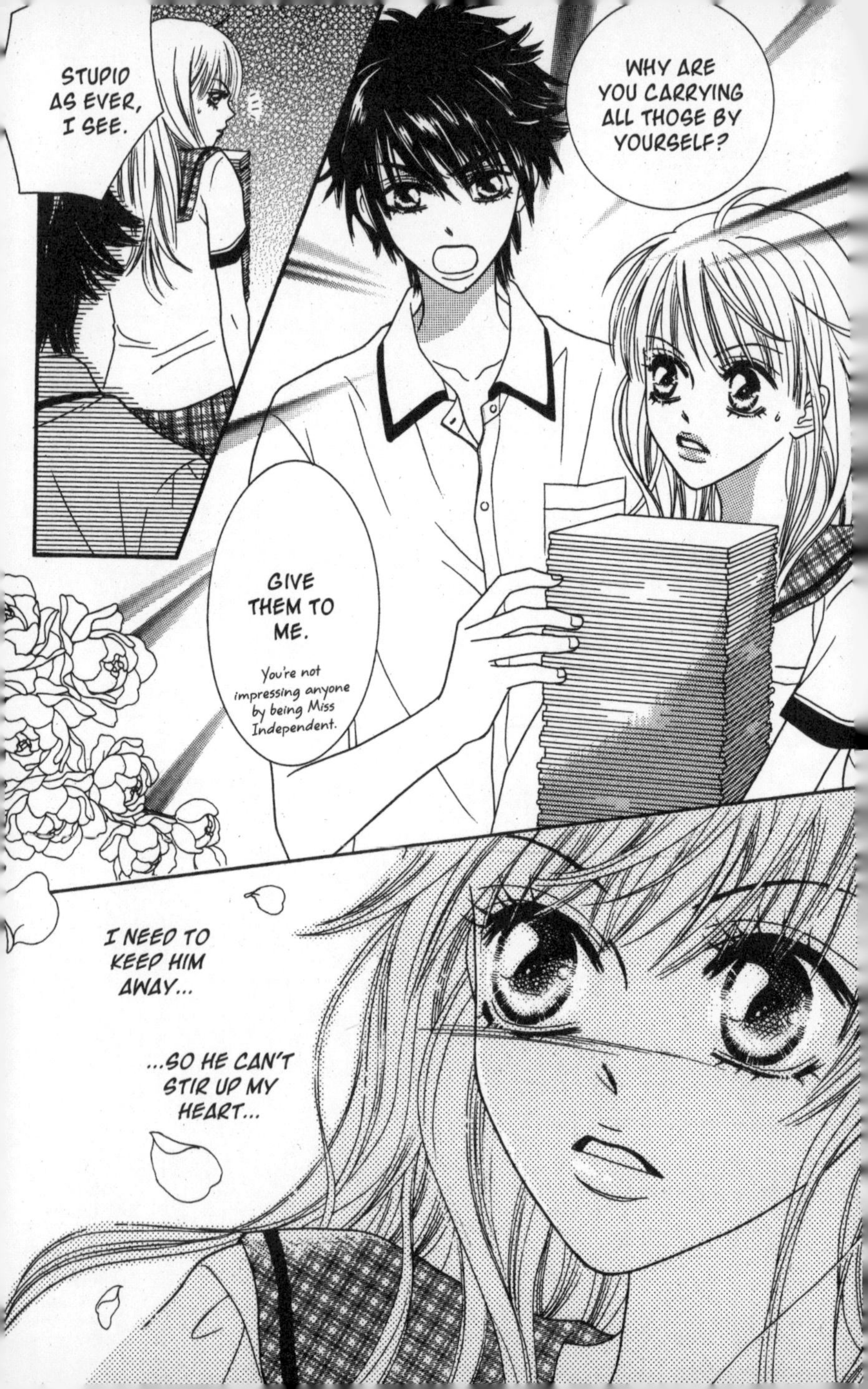
STUPID AS EVER, I SEE.
WHY ARE YOU CARRYING ALL THOSE BY YOURSELF?
GIVE THEM TO ME.
You're not impressing anyone by being Miss Independent.
I NEED TO KEEP HIM AWAY...
...SO HE CAN'T STIR UP MY HEART...

| Cute | Sweet | Bright | Fresh |

| Cute | Sweet | Bright | Fresh |

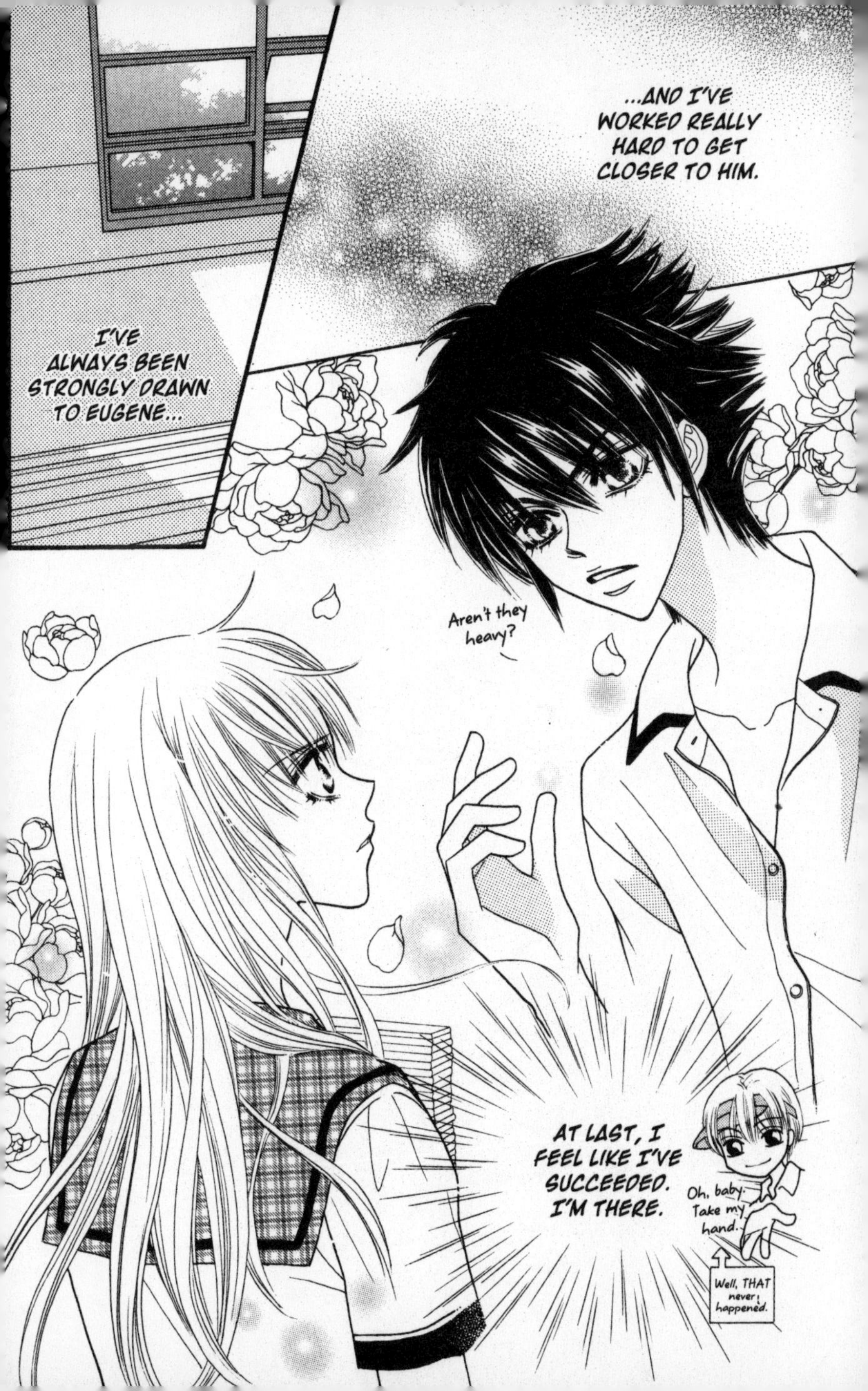
I'VE ALWAYS BEEN STRONGLY DRAWN TO EUGENE...
...AND I'VE WORKED REALLY HARD TO GET CLOSER TO HIM.
Aren't they heavy?
AT LAST, I FEEL LIKE I'VE SUCCEEDED. I'M THERE.
Oh, baby. Take my hand.
Well, THAT never happened.

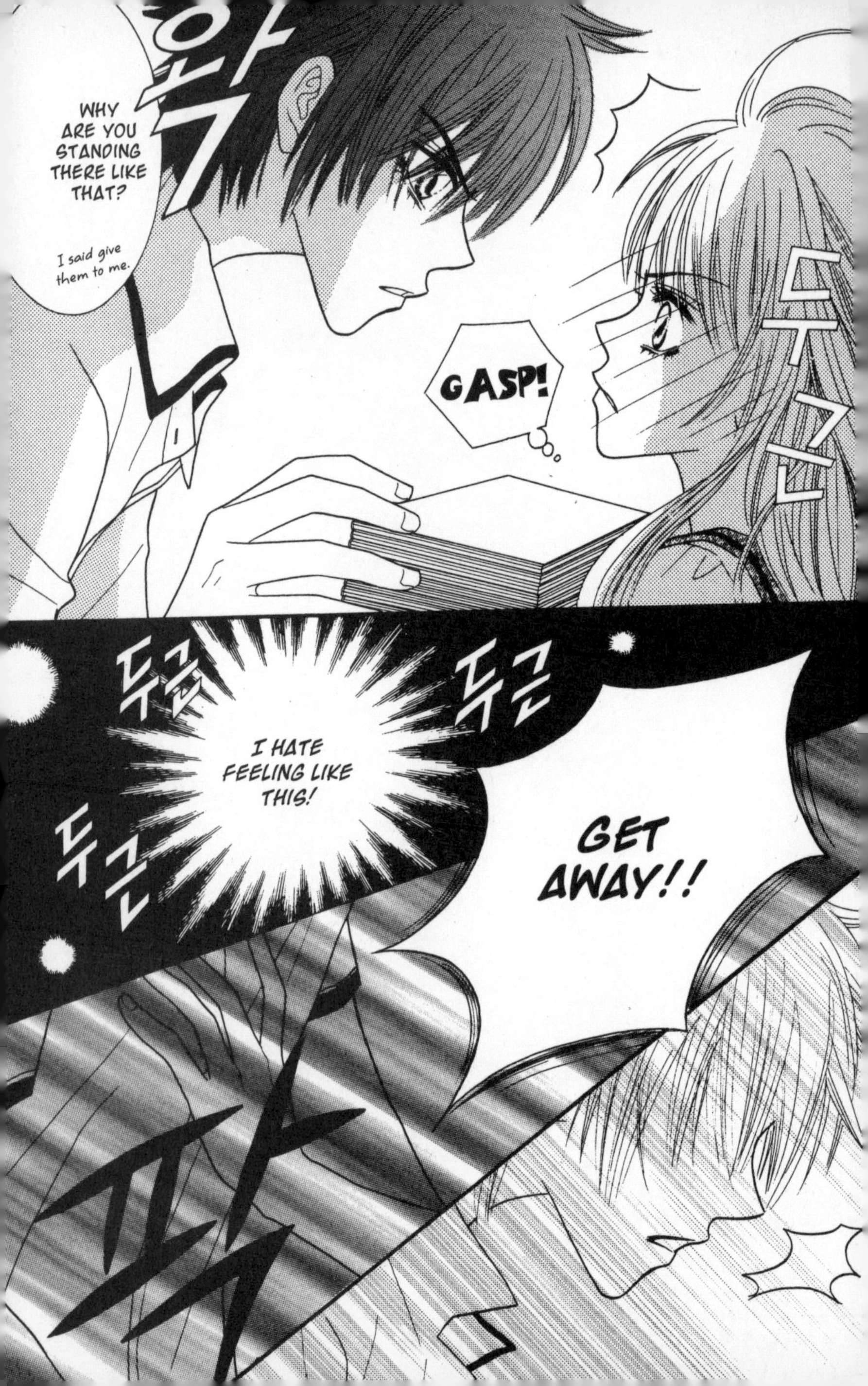
WHY ARE YOU STANDING THERE LIKE THAT?
I said give them to me.
GASP!
I HATE FEELING LIKE THIS!
GET AWAY!!

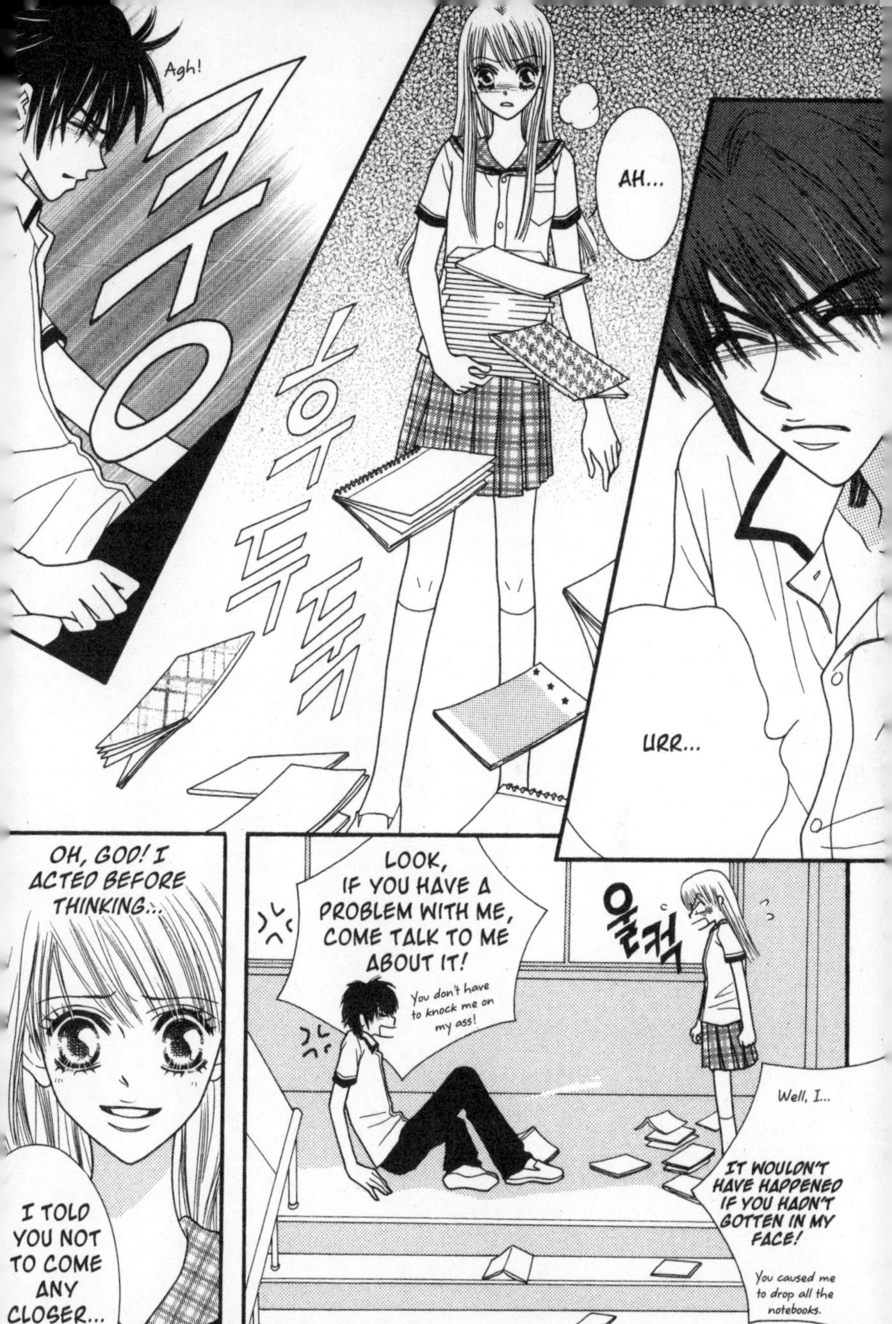
Agh!
AH...
URR...
OH, GOD! I ACTED BEFORE THINKING...
I TOLD YOU NOT TO COME ANY CLOSER...
LOOK, IF YOU HAVE A PROBLEM WITH ME, COME TALK TO ME ABOUT IT!
You don't have to knock me on my ass!
울컥
Well, I...
IT WOULDN'T HAVE HAPPENED IF YOU HADN'T GOTTEN IN MY FACE!
You caused me to drop all the notebooks.

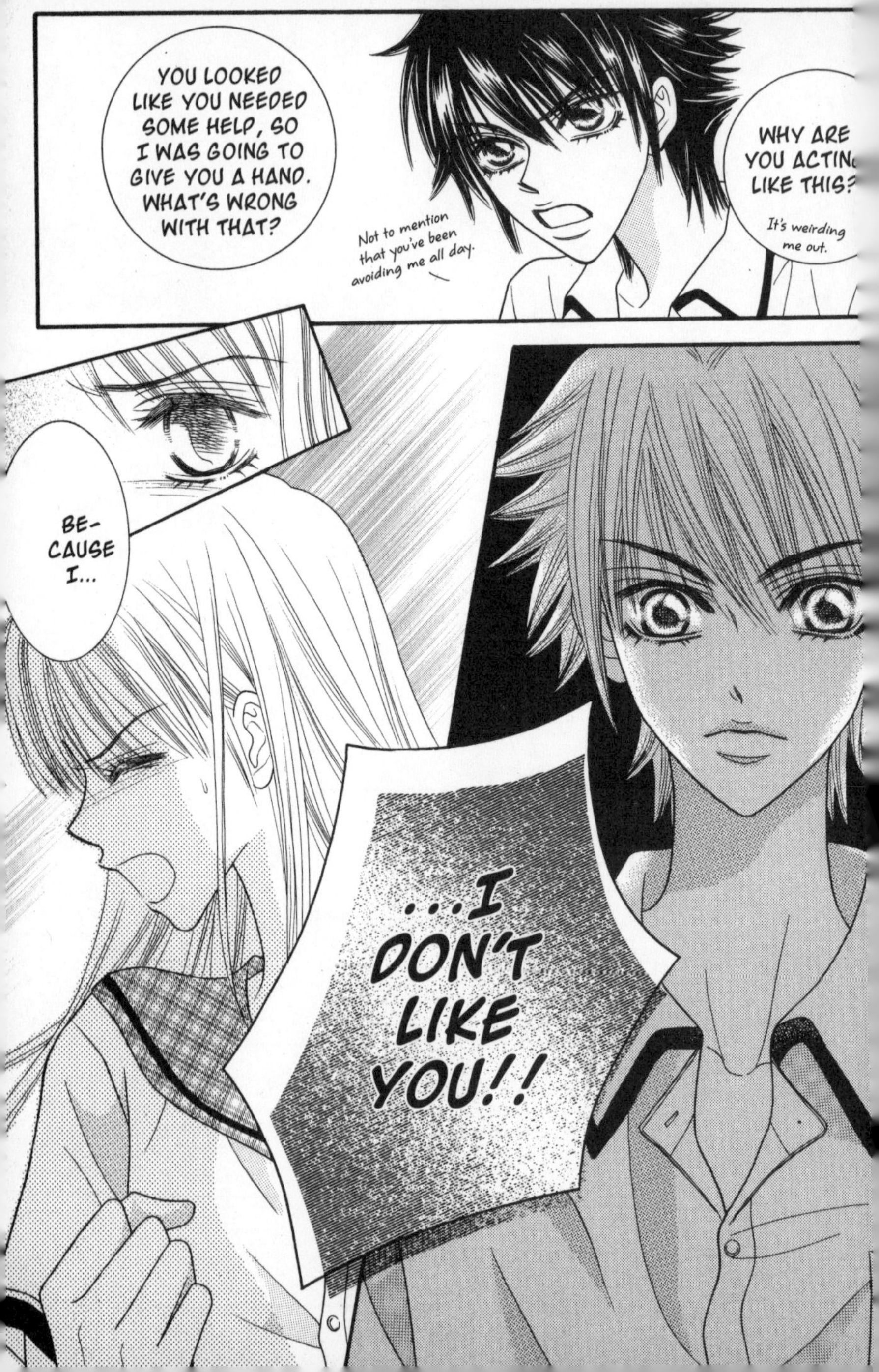
YOU LOOKED LIKE YOU NEEDED SOME HELP, SO I WAS GOING TO GIVE YOU A HAND. WHAT'S WRONG WITH THAT?
Not to mention that you've been avoiding me all day.
WHY ARE YOU ACTING LIKE THIS?
It's weirding me out.
BE-CAUSE I...
...I DON'T LIKE YOU!!

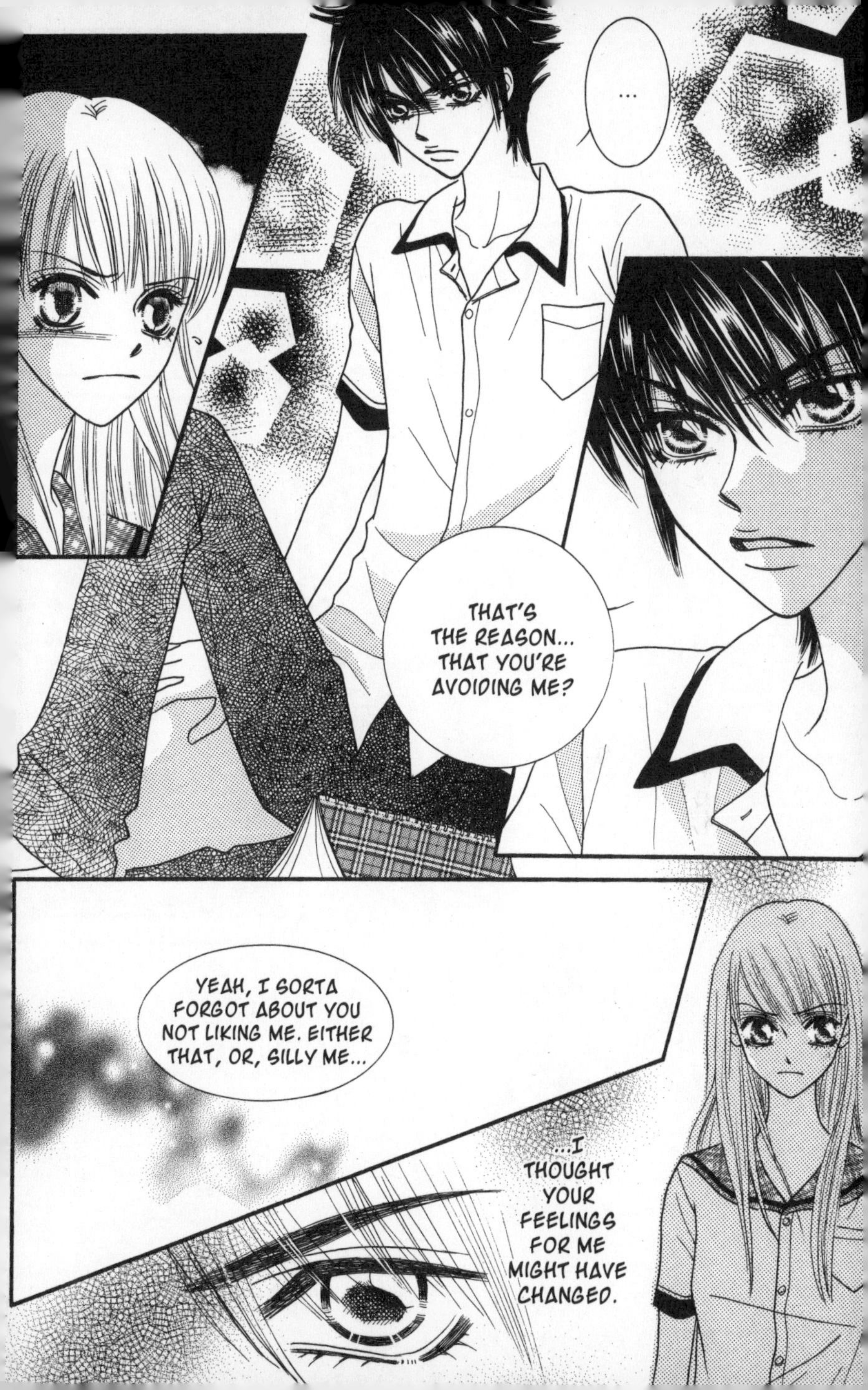
...
THAT'S THE REASON... THAT YOU'RE AVOIDING ME?
YEAH, I SORTA FORGOT ABOUT YOU NOT LIKING ME. EITHER THAT, OR, SILLY ME...
...I THOUGHT YOUR FEELINGS FOR ME MIGHT HAVE CHANGED.

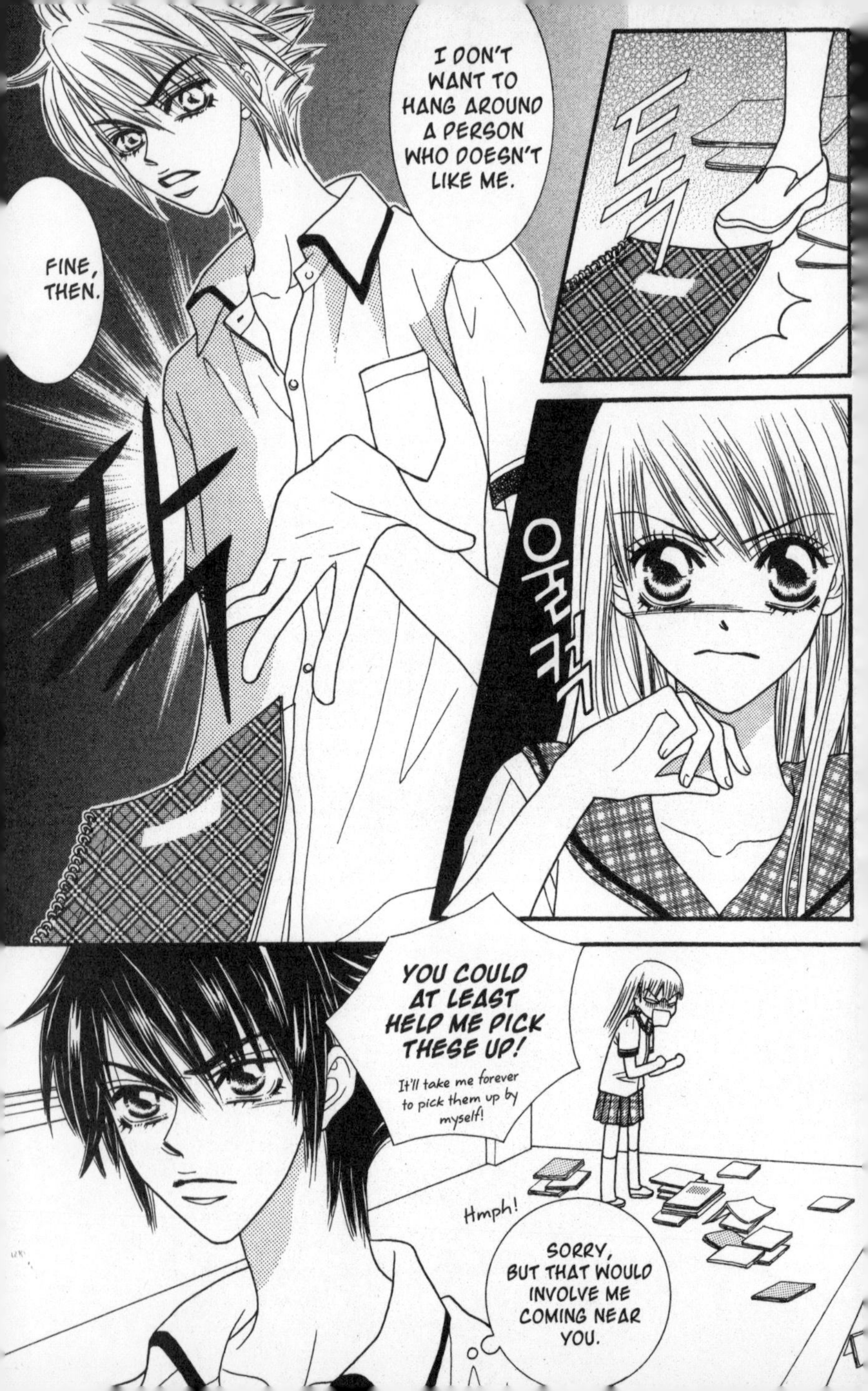
FINE, THEN.
I DON'T WANT TO HANG AROUND A PERSON WHO DOESN'T LIKE ME.
YOU COULD AT LEAST HELP ME PICK THESE UP!
It'll take me forever to pick them up by myself!
Hmph!
SORRY, BUT THAT WOULD INVOLVE ME COMING NEAR YOU.

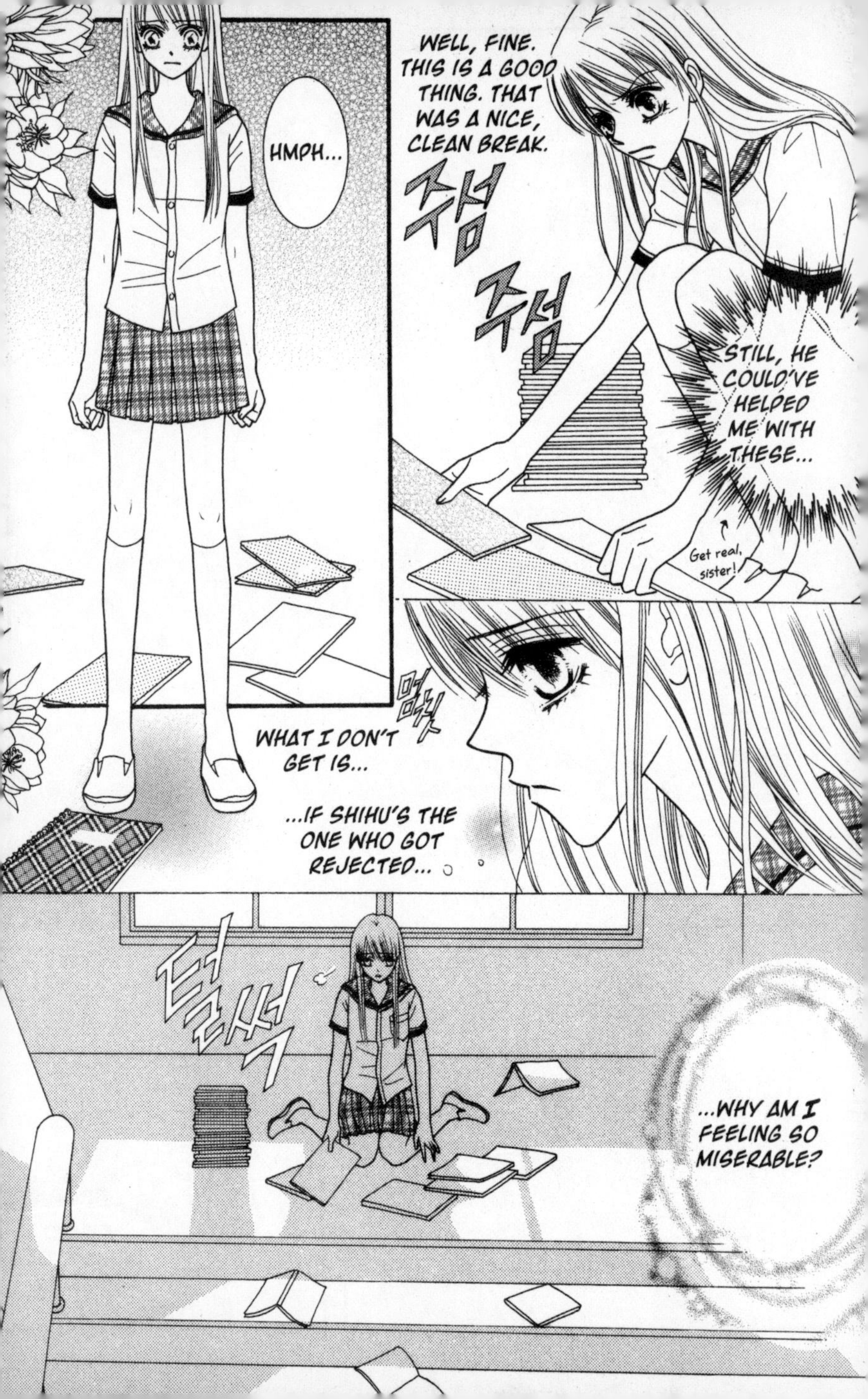
HMPH...
WELL, FINE. THIS IS A GOOD THING. THAT WAS A NICE, CLEAN BREAK.
주섬
주섬
STILL, HE COULD'VE HELPED ME WITH THESE...
Get real, sister!
멈칫
WHAT I DON'T GET IS...
...IF SHIHU'S THE ONE WHO GOT REJECTED...
털썩
...WHY AM I FEELING SO MISERABLE?

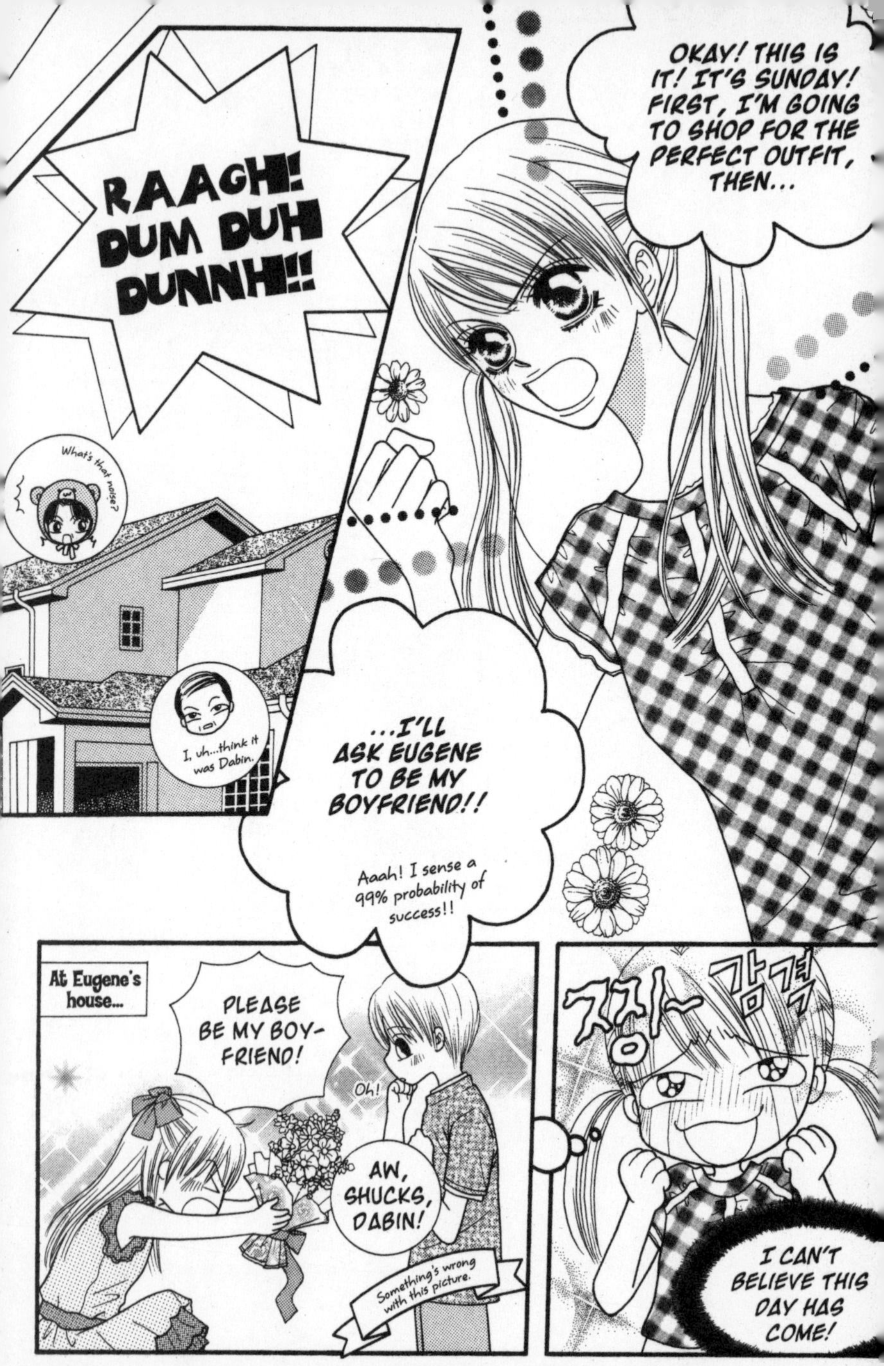
RAAGH! DUM DUH DUNNH!!
What's that noise?
I, uh...think it was Dabin.
OKAY! THIS IS IT! IT'S SUNDAY! FIRST, I'M GOING TO SHOP FOR THE PERFECT OUTFIT, THEN...
...I'LL ASK EUGENE TO BE MY BOYFRIEND!!
Aaah! I sense a 99% probability of success!!
At Eugene's house...
PLEASE BE MY BOY-FRIEND!
Oh!
AW, SHUCKS, DABIN!
Something's wrong with this picture.
감격
I CAN'T BELIEVE THIS DAY HAS COME!

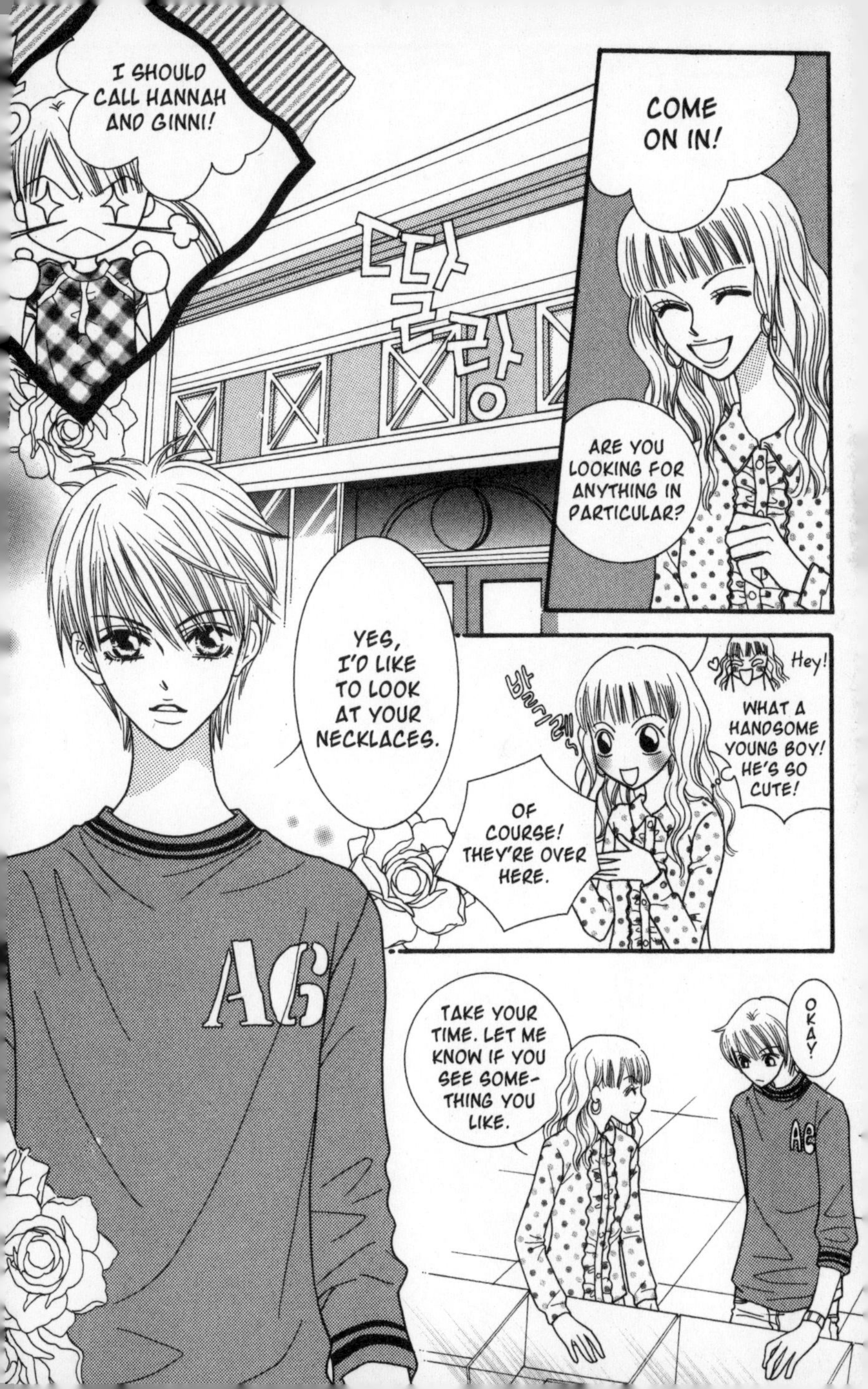

I SHOULD CALL HANNAH AND GINNI!
COME ON IN!
ARE YOU LOOKING FOR ANYTHING IN PARTICULAR?
YES, I'D LIKE TO LOOK AT YOUR NECKLACES.
Hey!
WHAT A HANDSOME YOUNG BOY! HE'S SO CUTE!
OF COURSE! THEY'RE OVER HERE.
TAKE YOUR TIME. LET ME KNOW IF YOU SEE SOME-THING YOU LIKE.
OKAY.

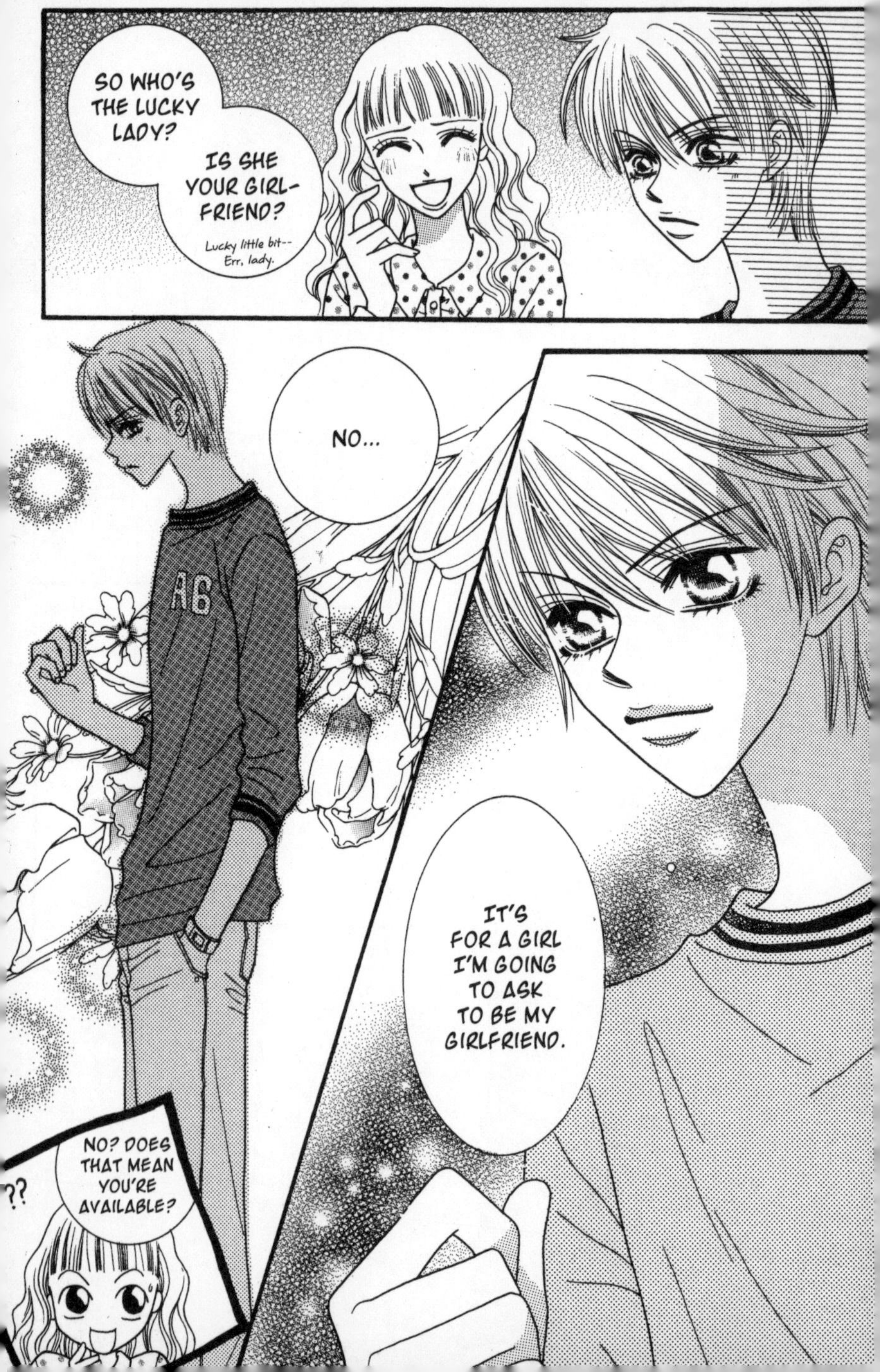
SO WHO'S THE LUCKY LADY?
IS SHE YOUR GIRL-FRIEND?
Lucky little bit-- Err, lady.
NO...
IT'S FOR A GIRL I'M GOING TO ASK TO BE MY GIRLFRIEND.
??
NO? DOES THAT MEAN YOU'RE AVAILABLE?
A6

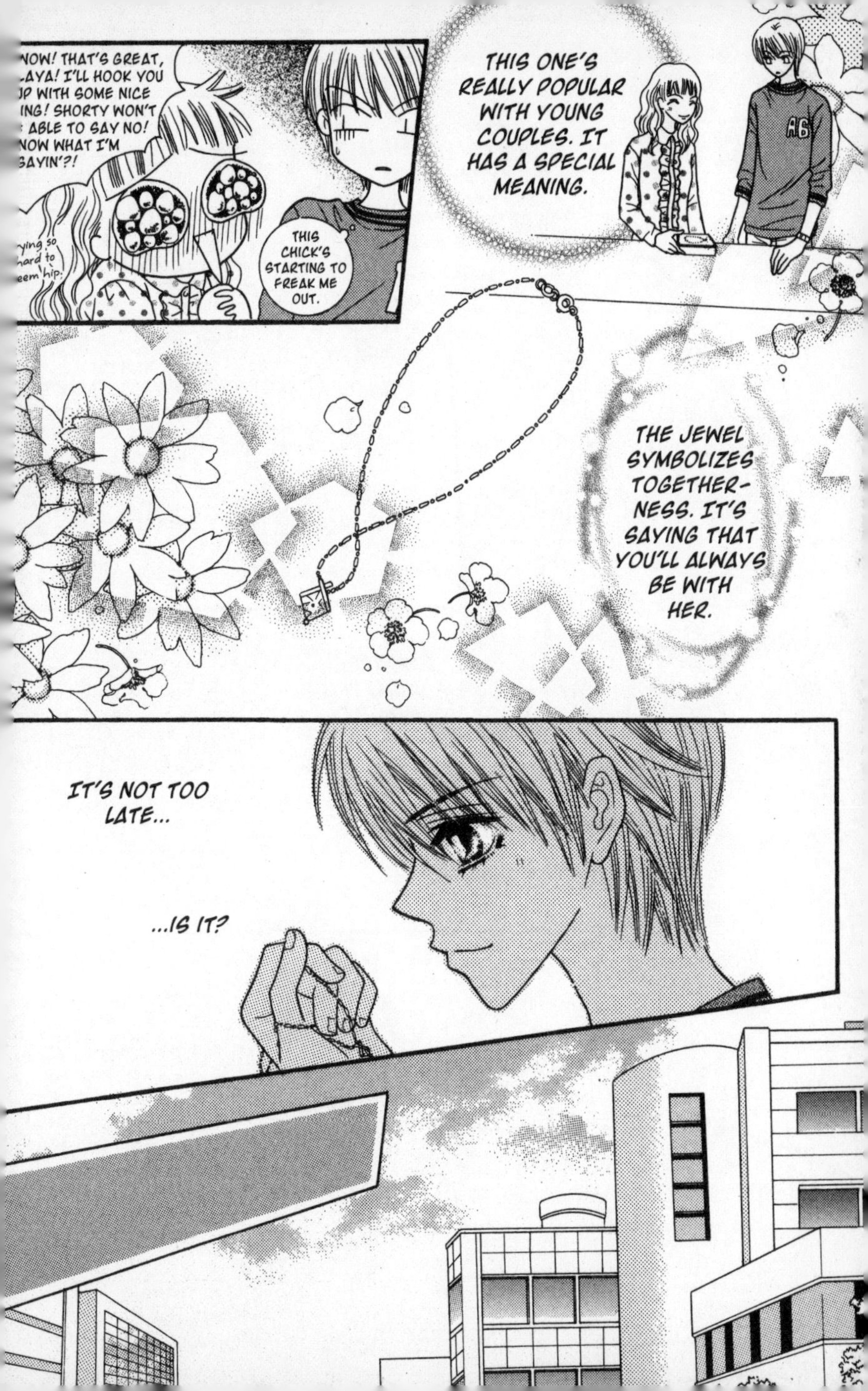
NOW! THAT'S GREAT, LAYA! I'LL HOOK YOU UP WITH SOME NICE ING! SHORTY WON'T ABLE TO SAY NO! NOW WHAT I'M SAYIN'?!
ying so hard to eem hip.
THIS CHICK'S STARTING TO FREAK ME OUT.
THIS ONE'S REALLY POPULAR WITH YOUNG COUPLES. IT HAS A SPECIAL MEANING.
THE JEWEL SYMBOLIZES TOGETHER-NESS. IT'S SAYING THAT YOU'LL ALWAYS BE WITH HER.
IT'S NOT TOO LATE...
...IS IT?

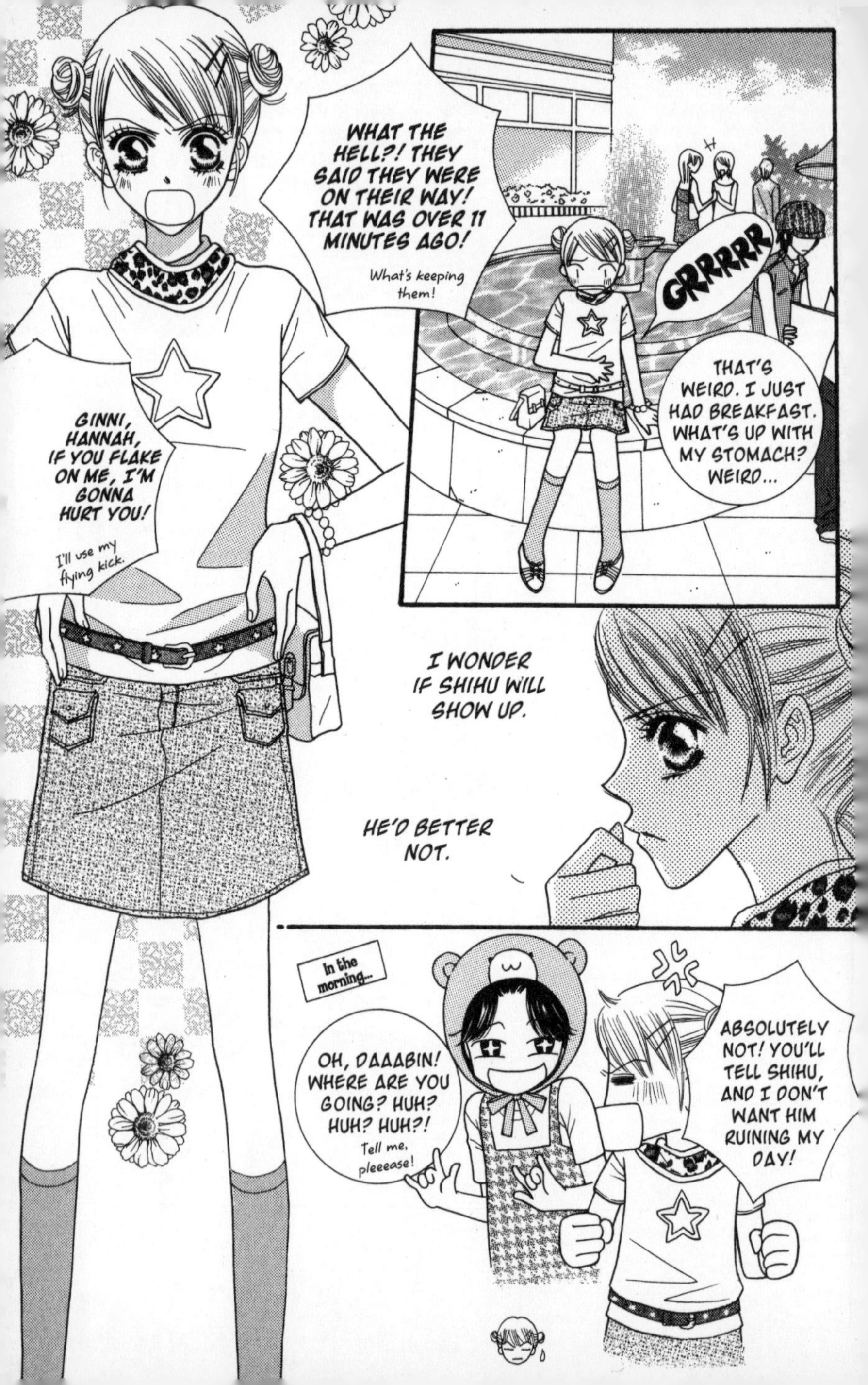
WHAT THE HELL?! THEY SAID THEY WERE ON THEIR WAY! THAT WAS OVER 11 MINUTES AGO!
What's keeping them!
GINNI, HANNAH, IF YOU FLAKE ON ME, I'M GONNA HURT YOU!
I'll use my flying kick.
GRRRRR
THAT'S WEIRD. I JUST HAD BREAKFAST. WHAT'S UP WITH MY STOMACH? WEIRD...
I WONDER IF SHIHU WILL SHOW UP.
HE'D BETTER NOT.
In the morning...
OH, DAAABIN! WHERE ARE YOU GOING? HUH? HUH? HUH?!
Tell me, pleeease!
ABSOLUTELY NOT! YOU'LL TELL SHIHU, AND I DON'T WANT HIM RUINING MY DAY!

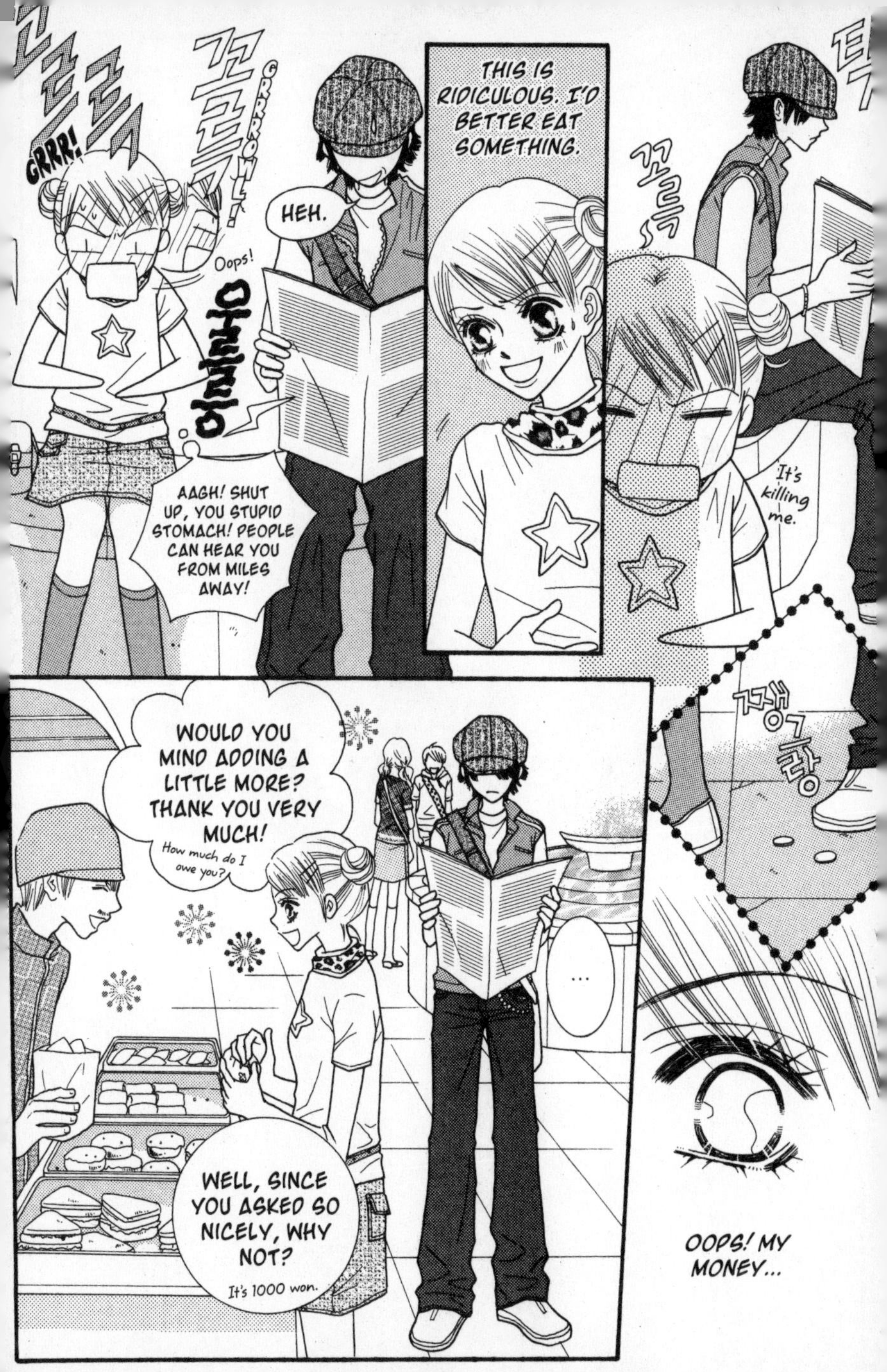
GRRR!
GRRROWL!
Oops!
HEH.
AAGH! SHUT UP, YOU STUPID STOMACH! PEOPLE CAN HEAR YOU FROM MILES AWAY!
THIS IS RIDICULOUS. I'D BETTER EAT SOMETHING.
It's killing me.
WOULD YOU MIND ADDING A LITTLE MORE? THANK YOU VERY MUCH!
How much do I owe you?
WELL, SINCE YOU ASKED SO NICELY, WHY NOT?
It's 1000 won.
...
OOPS! MY MONEY...

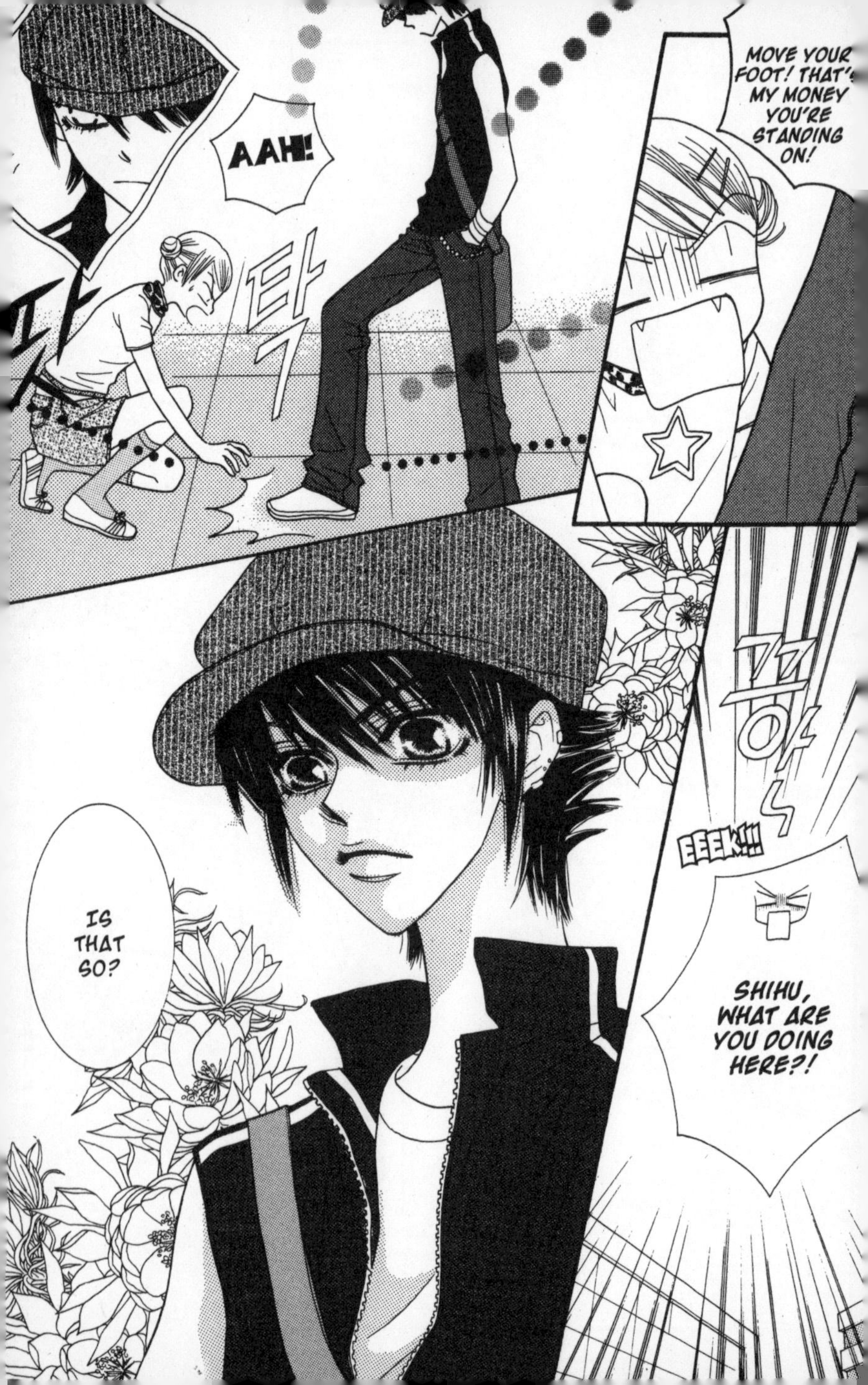
AAH!
탁
MOVE YOUR FOOT! THAT'S MY MONEY YOU'RE STANDING ON!
IS THAT SO?
EEEK!!!
SHIHU, WHAT ARE YOU DOING HERE?!

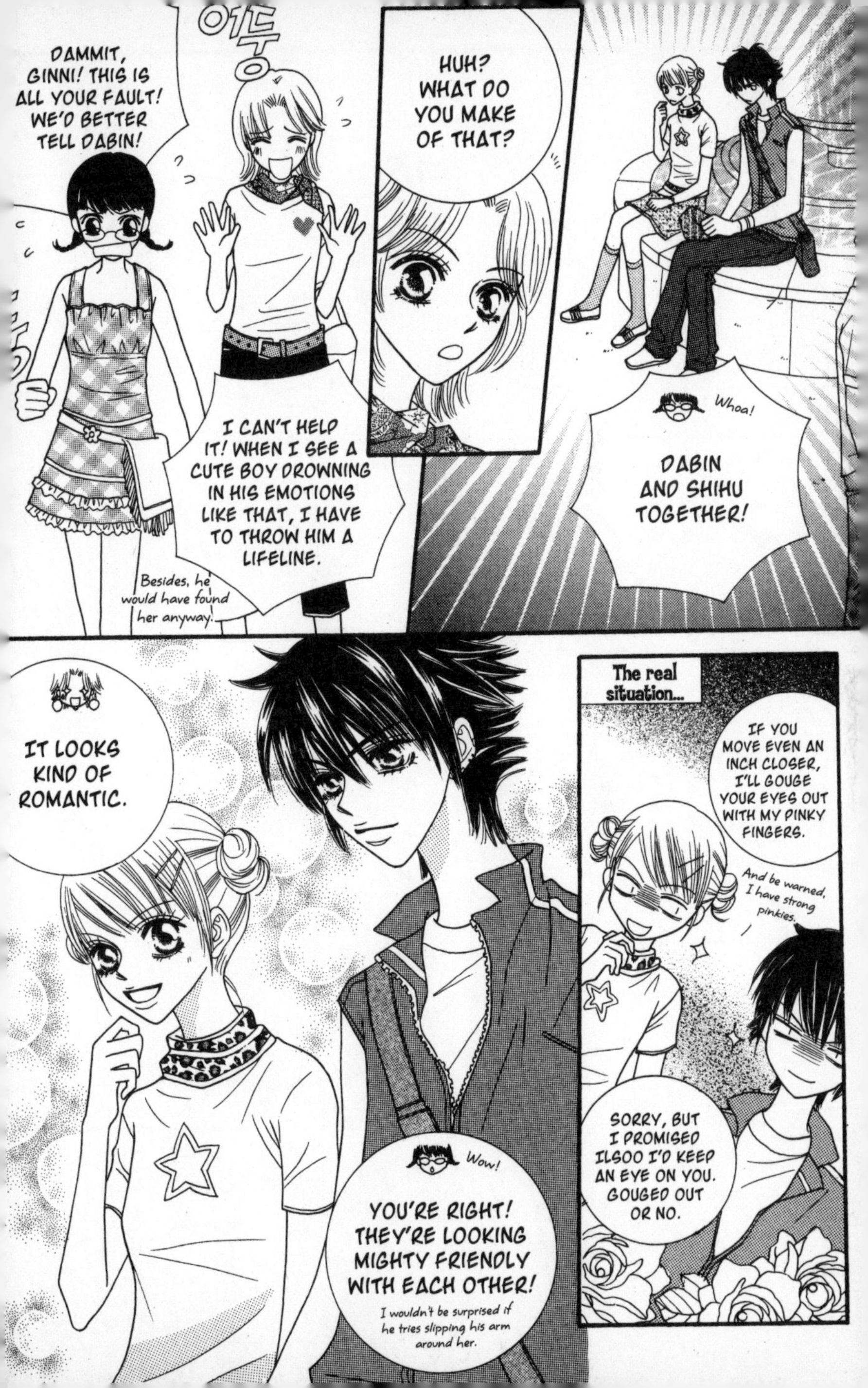
DAMMIT, GINNI! THIS IS ALL YOUR FAULT! WE'D BETTER TELL DABIN!
I CAN'T HELP IT! WHEN I SEE A CUTE BOY DROWNING IN HIS EMOTIONS LIKE THAT, I HAVE TO THROW HIM A LIFELINE.
Besides, he would have found her anyway.
HUH? WHAT DO YOU MAKE OF THAT?
Whoa!
DABIN AND SHIHU TOGETHER!
IT LOOKS KIND OF ROMANTIC.
Wow!
YOU'RE RIGHT! THEY'RE LOOKING MIGHTY FRIENDLY WITH EACH OTHER!
I wouldn't be surprised if he tries slipping his arm around her.
The real situation...
IF YOU MOVE EVEN AN INCH CLOSER, I'LL GOUGE YOUR EYES OUT WITH MY PINKY FINGERS.
And be warned, I have strong pinkies.
SORRY, BUT I PROMISED ILSOO I'D KEEP AN EYE ON YOU. GOUGED OUT OR NO.

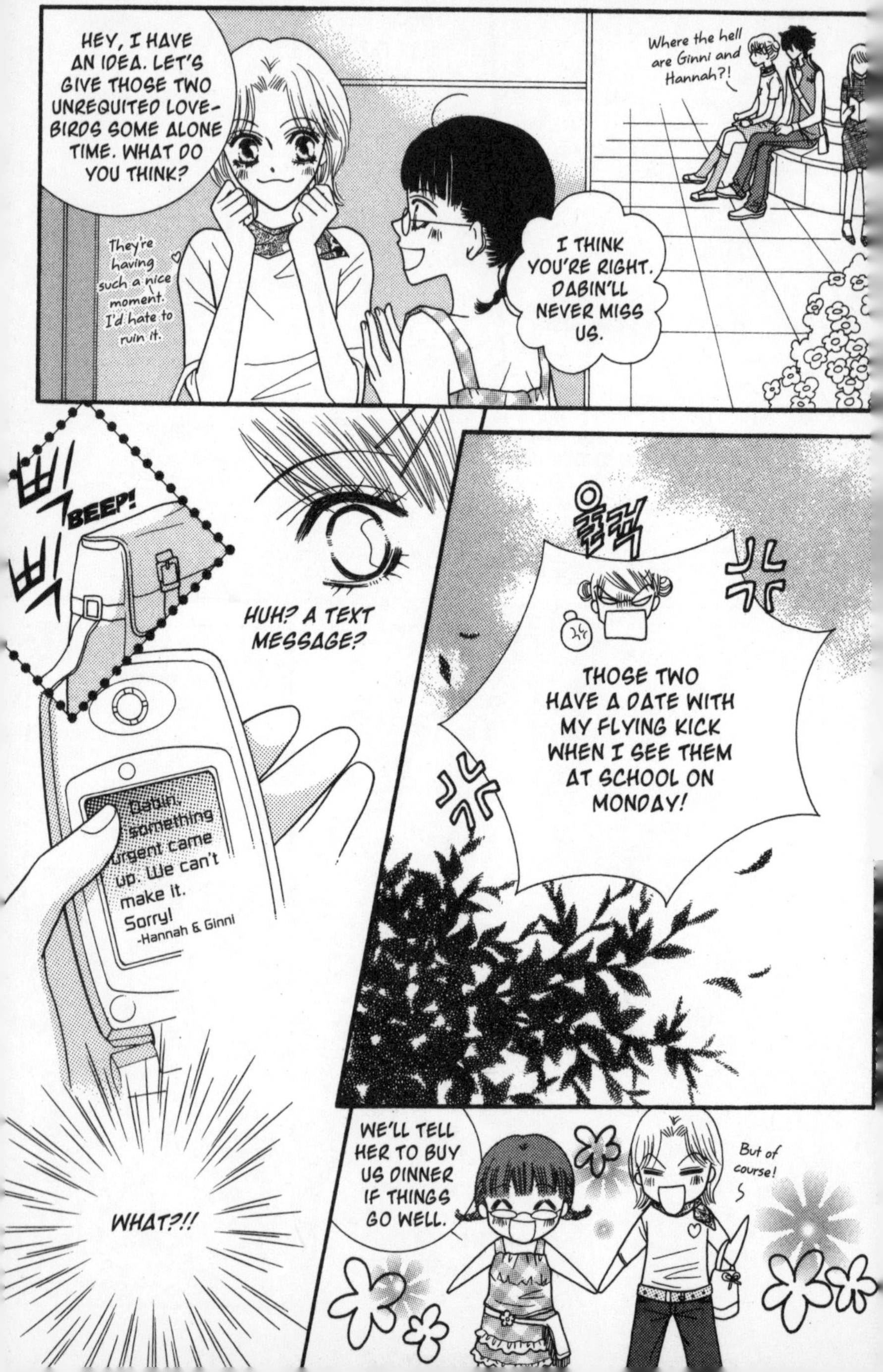
HEY, I HAVE AN IDEA. LET'S GIVE THOSE TWO UNREQUITED LOVE-BIRDS SOME ALONE TIME. WHAT DO YOU THINK?
They're having such a nice moment. I'd hate to ruin it.
I THINK YOU'RE RIGHT. DABIN'LL NEVER MISS US.
Where the hell are Ginni and Hannah?!
BEEP!
HUH? A TEXT MESSAGE?
Dabin, something urgent came up. We can't make it. Sorry! -Hannah & Ginni
WHAT?!!
THOSE TWO HAVE A DATE WITH MY FLYING KICK WHEN I SEE THEM AT SCHOOL ON MONDAY!
WE'LL TELL HER TO BUY US DINNER IF THINGS GO WELL.
But of course!

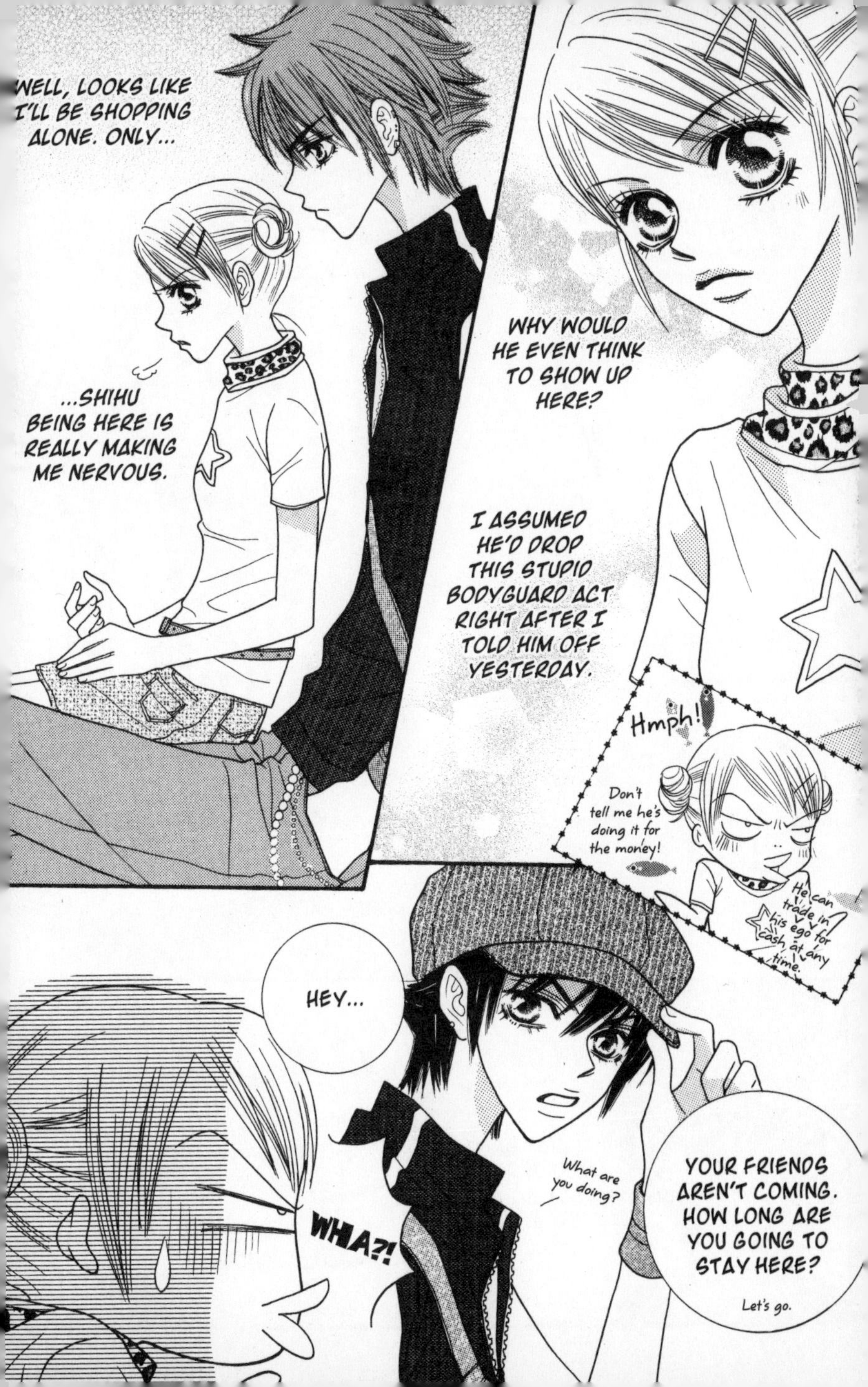
WELL, LOOKS LIKE I'LL BE SHOPPING ALONE. ONLY...
...SHIHU BEING HERE IS REALLY MAKING ME NERVOUS.
WHY WOULD HE EVEN THINK TO SHOW UP HERE?
I ASSUMED HE'D DROP THIS STUPID BODYGUARD ACT RIGHT AFTER I TOLD HIM OFF YESTERDAY.
Hmph!
Don't tell me he's doing it for the money!
He can trade in his ego for cash at any time.
HEY...
What are you doing?
WHA?!
YOUR FRIENDS AREN'T COMING. HOW LONG ARE YOU GOING TO STAY HERE?
Let's go.

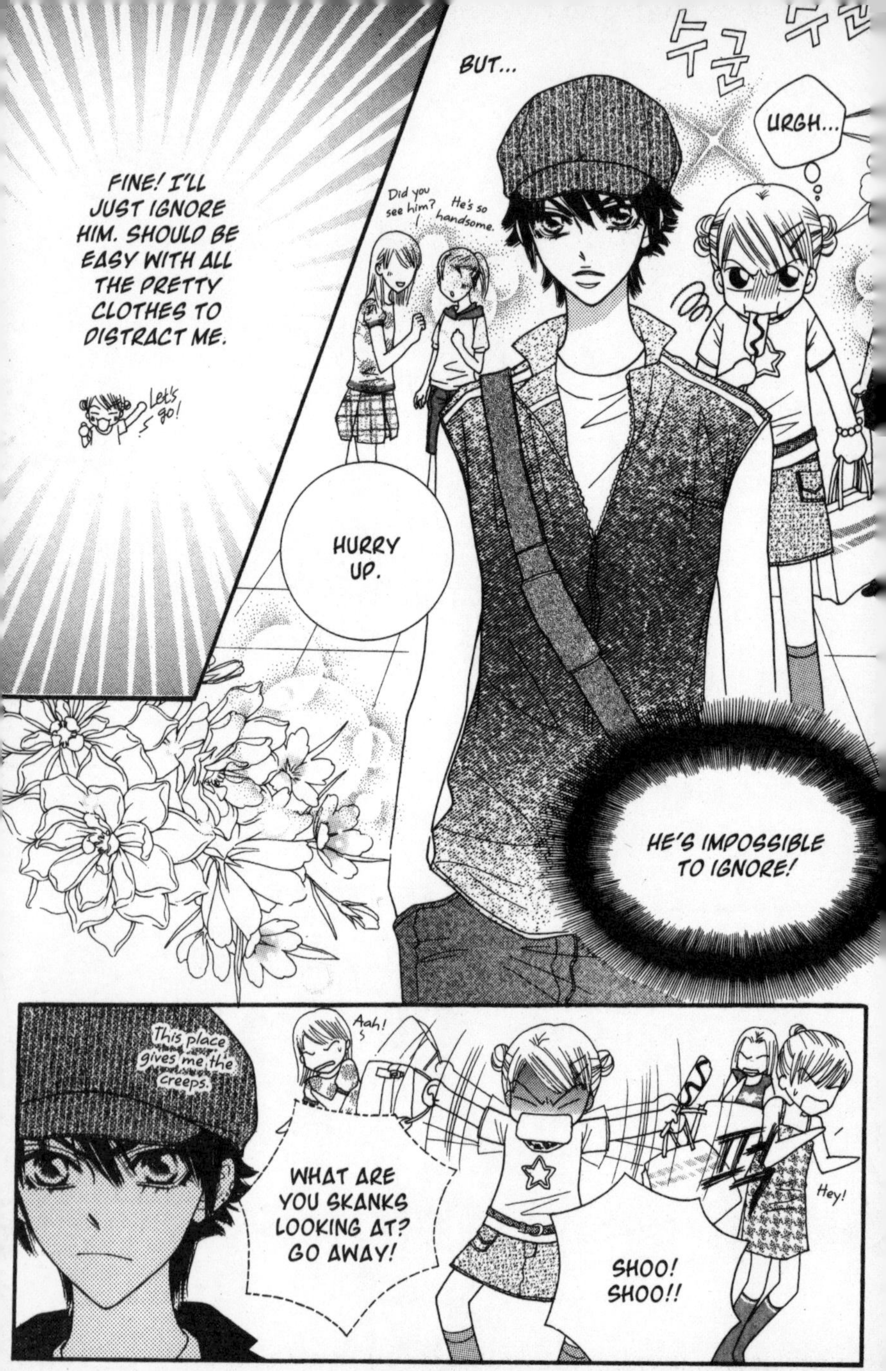
FINE! I'LL JUST IGNORE HIM. SHOULD BE EASY WITH ALL THE PRETTY CLOTHES TO DISTRACT ME.
Let's go!
BUT...
수군 수군
Did you see him?
He's so handsome.
URGH...
HURRY UP.
HE'S IMPOSSIBLE TO IGNORE!
This place gives me the creeps.
Aah!
WHAT ARE YOU SKANKS LOOKING AT? GO AWAY!
SHOO! SHOO!!
Hey!

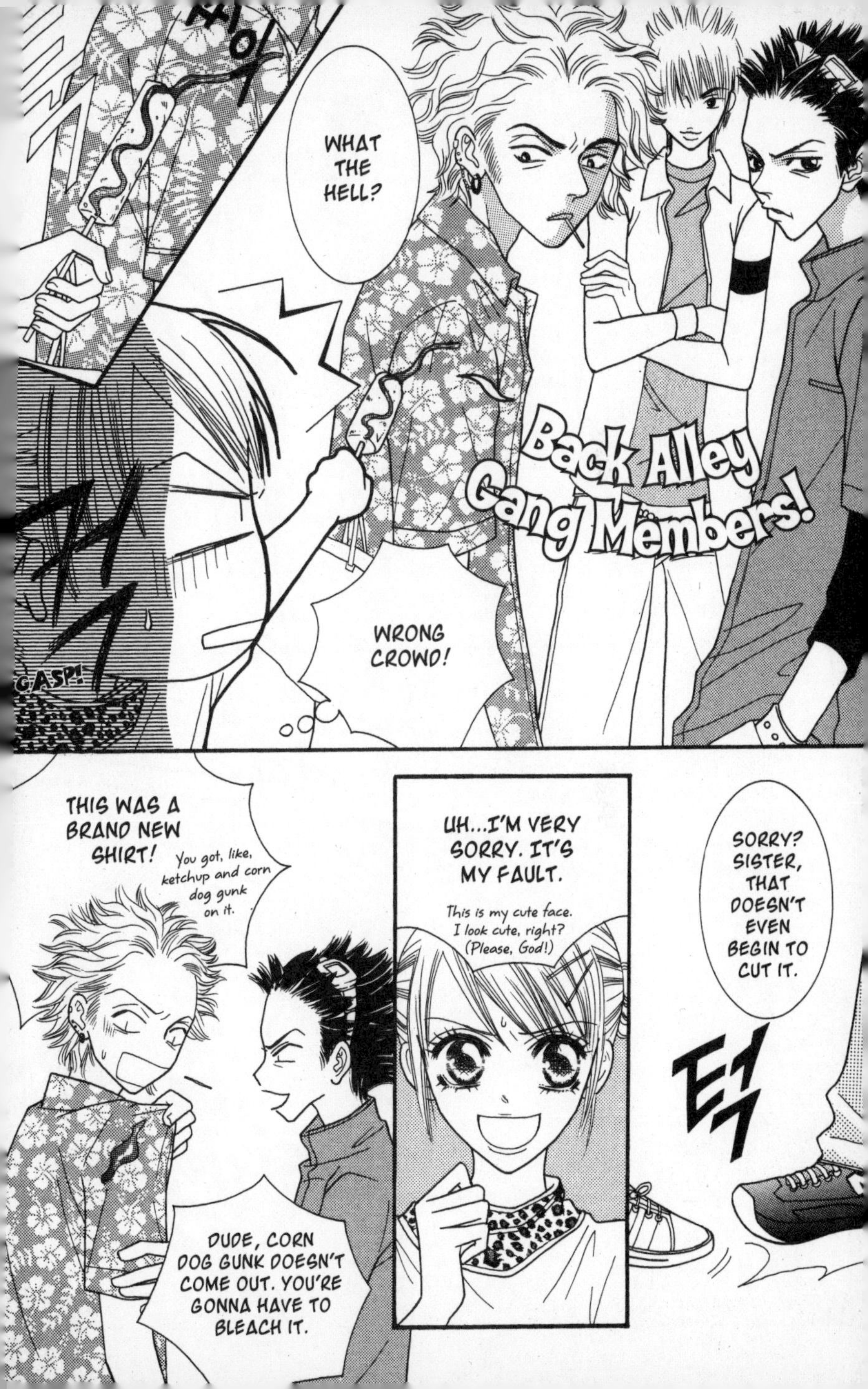
WHAT THE HELL?
Back Alley Gang Members!
WRONG CROWD!
GASP!
THIS WAS A BRAND NEW SHIRT!
You got, like, ketchup and corn dog gunk on it.
DUDE, CORN DOG GUNK DOESN'T COME OUT. YOU'RE GONNA HAVE TO BLEACH IT.
UH...I'M VERY SORRY. IT'S MY FAULT.
This is my cute face. I look cute, right? (Please, God!)
SORRY? SISTER, THAT DOESN'T EVEN BEGIN TO CUT IT.

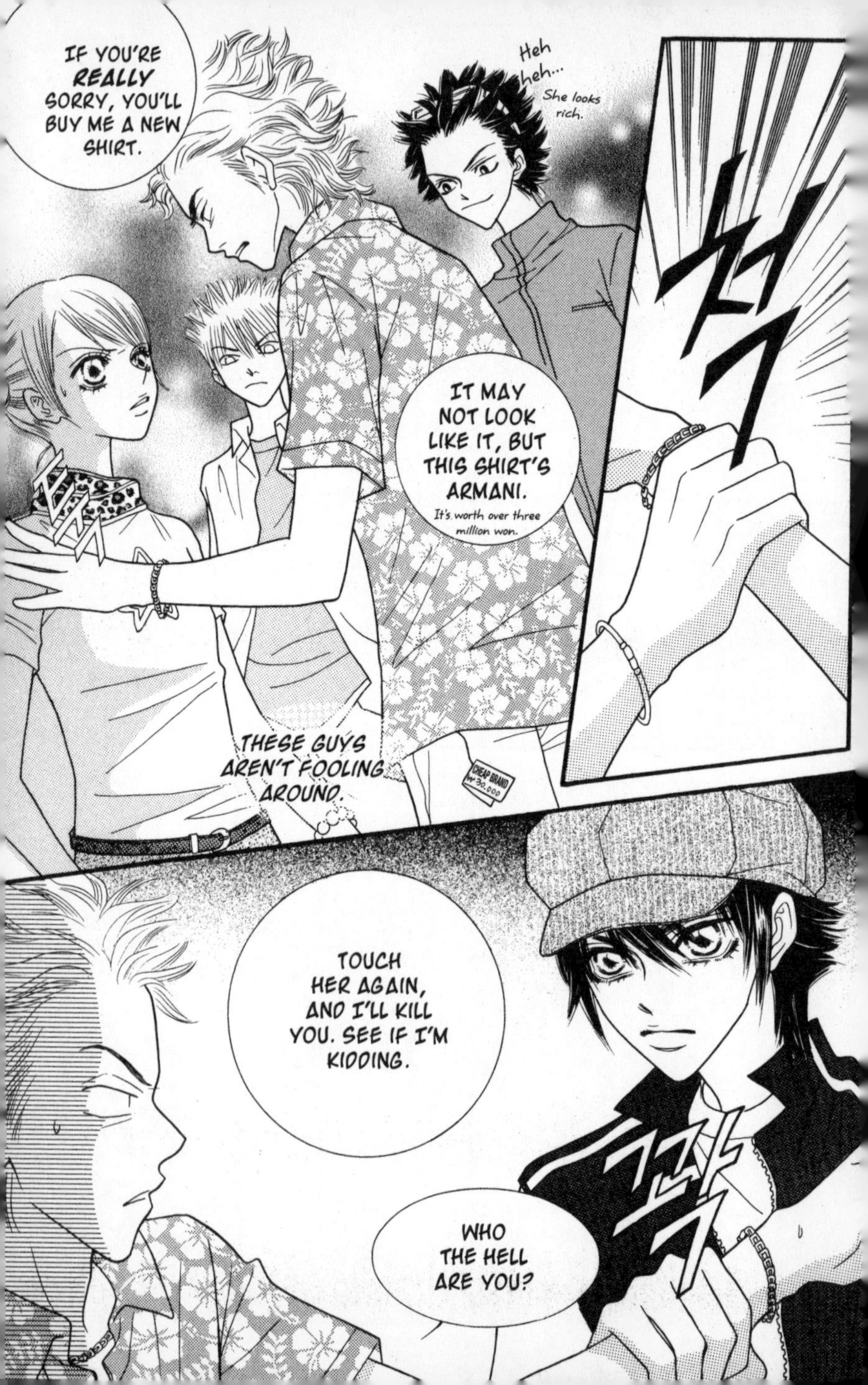
IF YOU'RE REALLY SORRY, YOU'LL BUY ME A NEW SHIRT.
Heh heh...
She looks rich.
IT MAY NOT LOOK LIKE IT, BUT THIS SHIRT'S ARMANI.
It's worth over three million won.
THESE GUYS AREN'T FOOLING AROUND.
CHEAP BRAND ₩30,000
TOUCH HER AGAIN, AND I'LL KILL YOU. SEE IF I'M KIDDING.
WHO THE HELL ARE YOU?

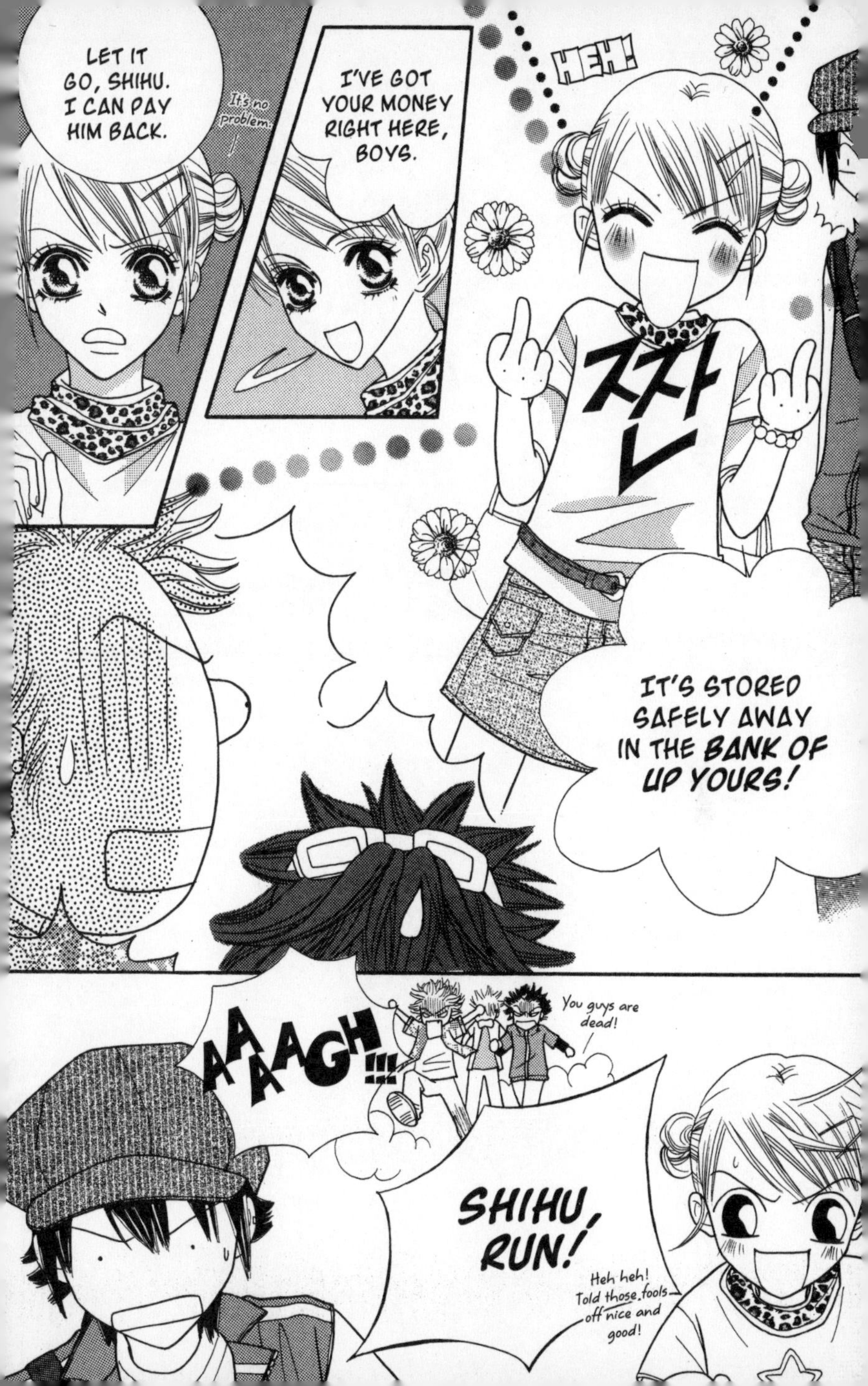
LET IT GO, SHIHU. I CAN PAY HIM BACK.
It's no problem.
I'VE GOT YOUR MONEY RIGHT HERE, BOYS.
HEH!
IT'S STORED SAFELY AWAY IN THE BANK OF UP YOURS!
AAAAGH!!!
You guys are dead!
SHIHU, RUN!
Heh heh! Told those fools off nice and good!

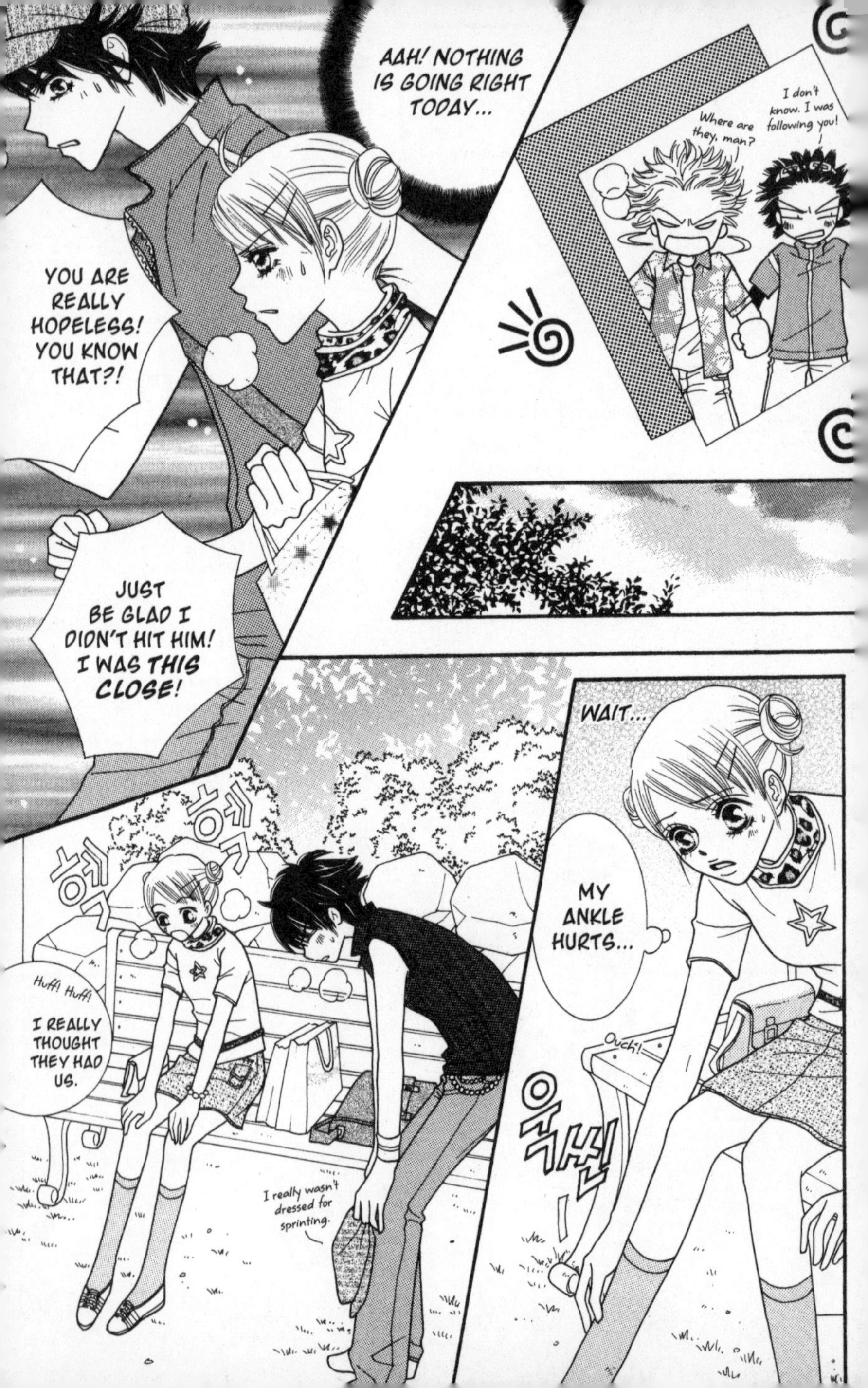
YOU ARE REALLY HOPELESS! YOU KNOW THAT?!
AAH! NOTHING IS GOING RIGHT TODAY...
JUST BE GLAD I DIDN'T HIT HIM! I WAS THIS CLOSE!
Where are they, man?
I don't know. I was following you!
Huff! Huff!
I REALLY THOUGHT THEY HAD US.
I really wasn't dressed for sprinting.
WAIT...
MY ANKLE HURTS...
Ouch!

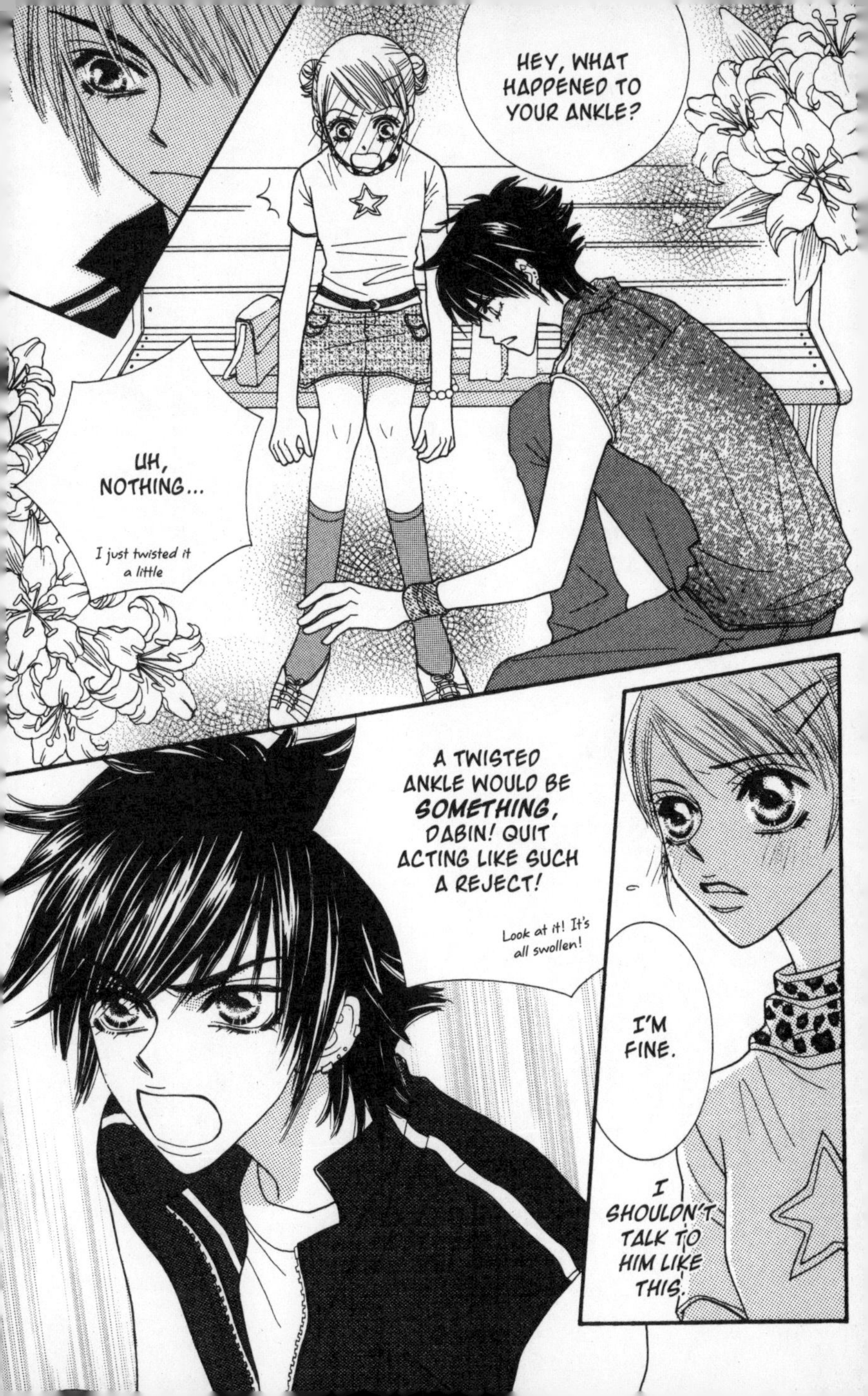
HEY, WHAT HAPPENED TO YOUR ANKLE?
UH, NOTHING...
I just twisted it a little
A TWISTED ANKLE WOULD BE SOMETHING, DABIN! QUIT ACTING LIKE SUCH A REJECT!
Look at it! It's all swollen!
I'M FINE.
I SHOULDN'T TALK TO HIM LIKE THIS.

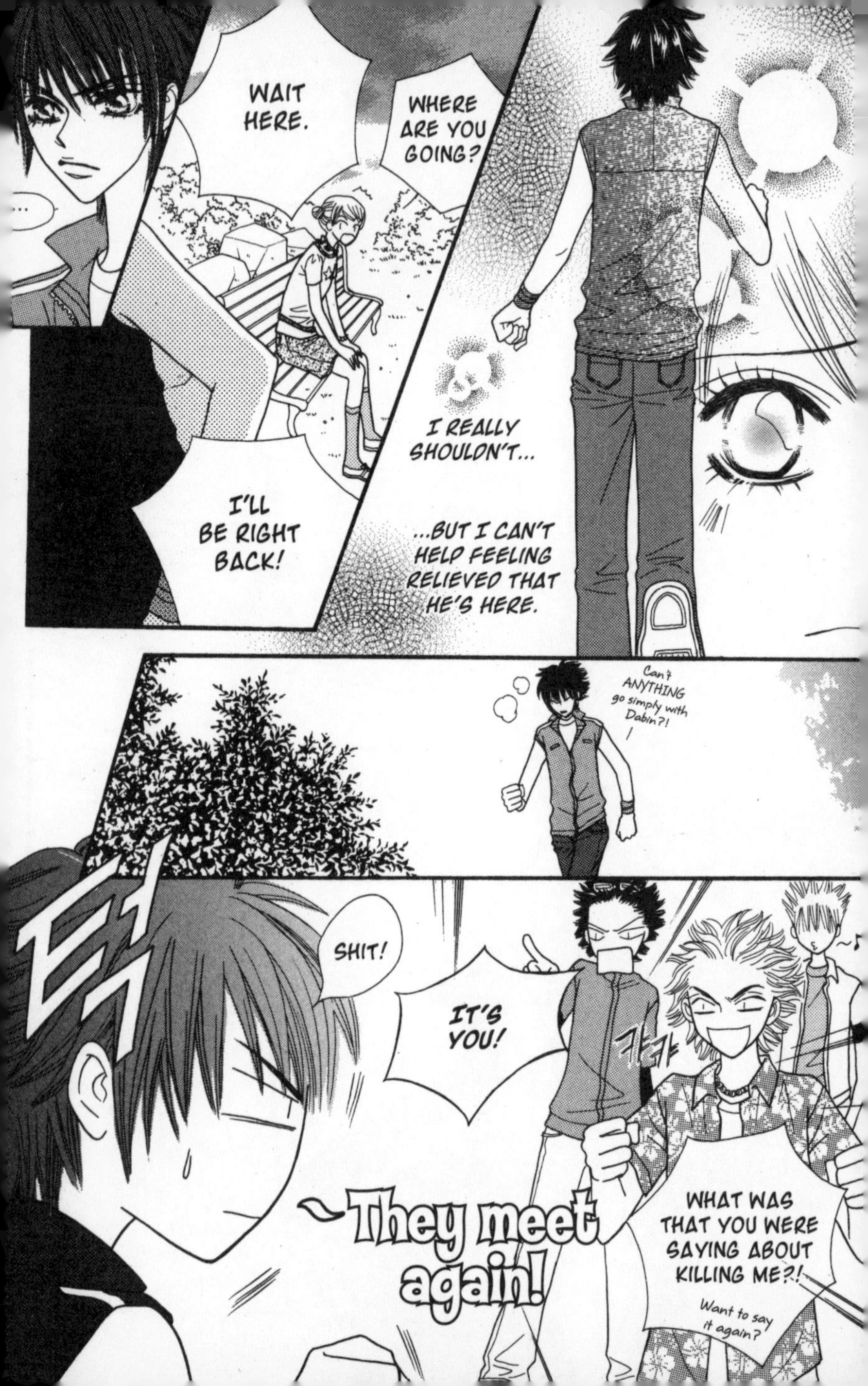
WAIT HERE.
...
WHERE ARE YOU GOING?
I'LL BE RIGHT BACK!
I REALLY SHOULDN'T...
...BUT I CAN'T HELP FEELING RELIEVED THAT HE'S HERE.
Can't ANYTHING go simply with Dabin?!
SHIT!
IT'S YOU!
~They meet again!
WHAT WAS THAT YOU WERE SAYING ABOUT KILLING ME?!
Want to say it again?

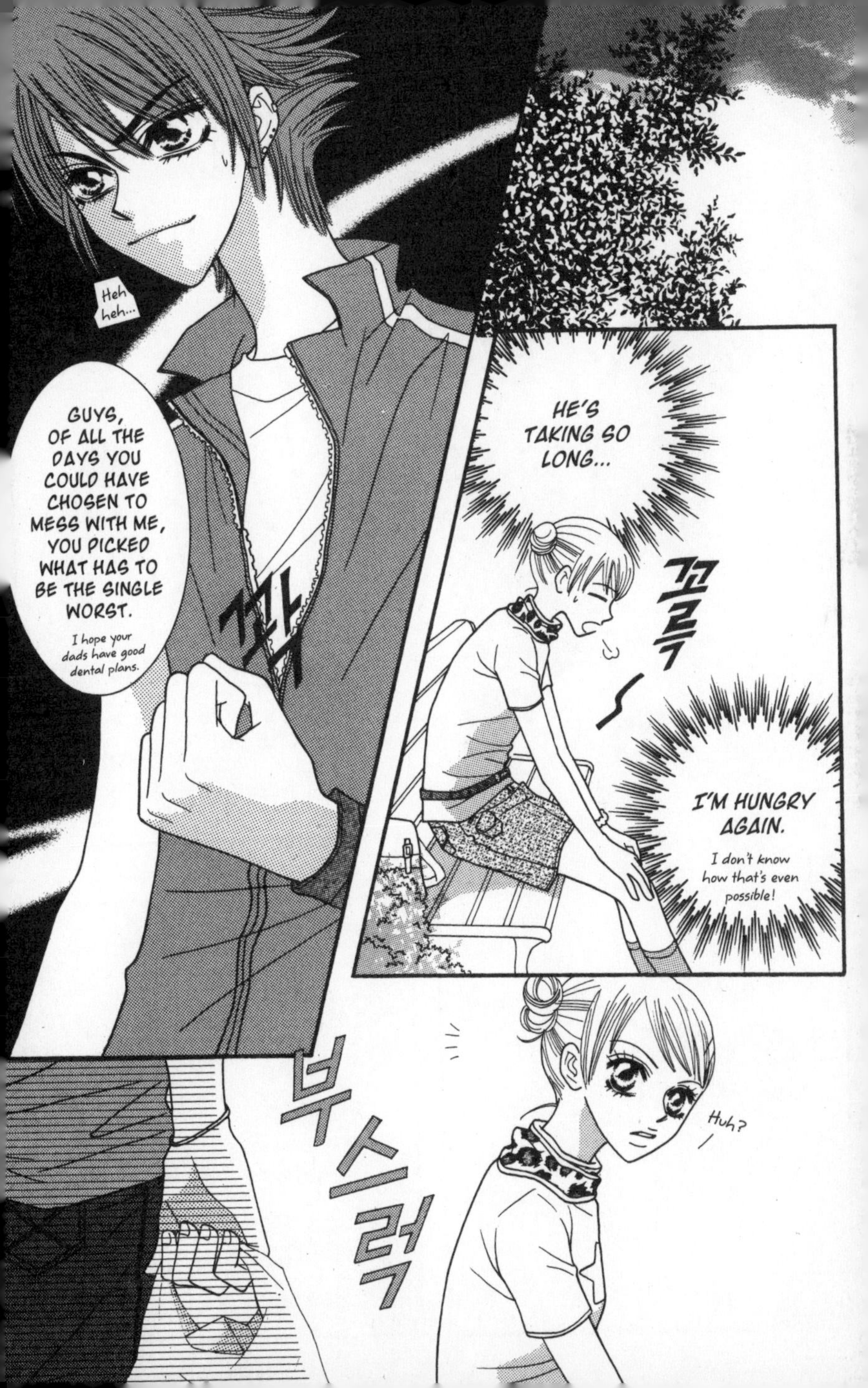
Heh heh...
GUYS, OF ALL THE DAYS YOU COULD HAVE CHOSEN TO MESS WITH ME, YOU PICKED WHAT HAS TO BE THE SINGLE WORST.
I hope your dads have good dental plans.
HE'S TAKING SO LONG...
꼬르륵
I'M HUNGRY AGAIN.
I don't know how that's even possible!
부스럭
Huh?

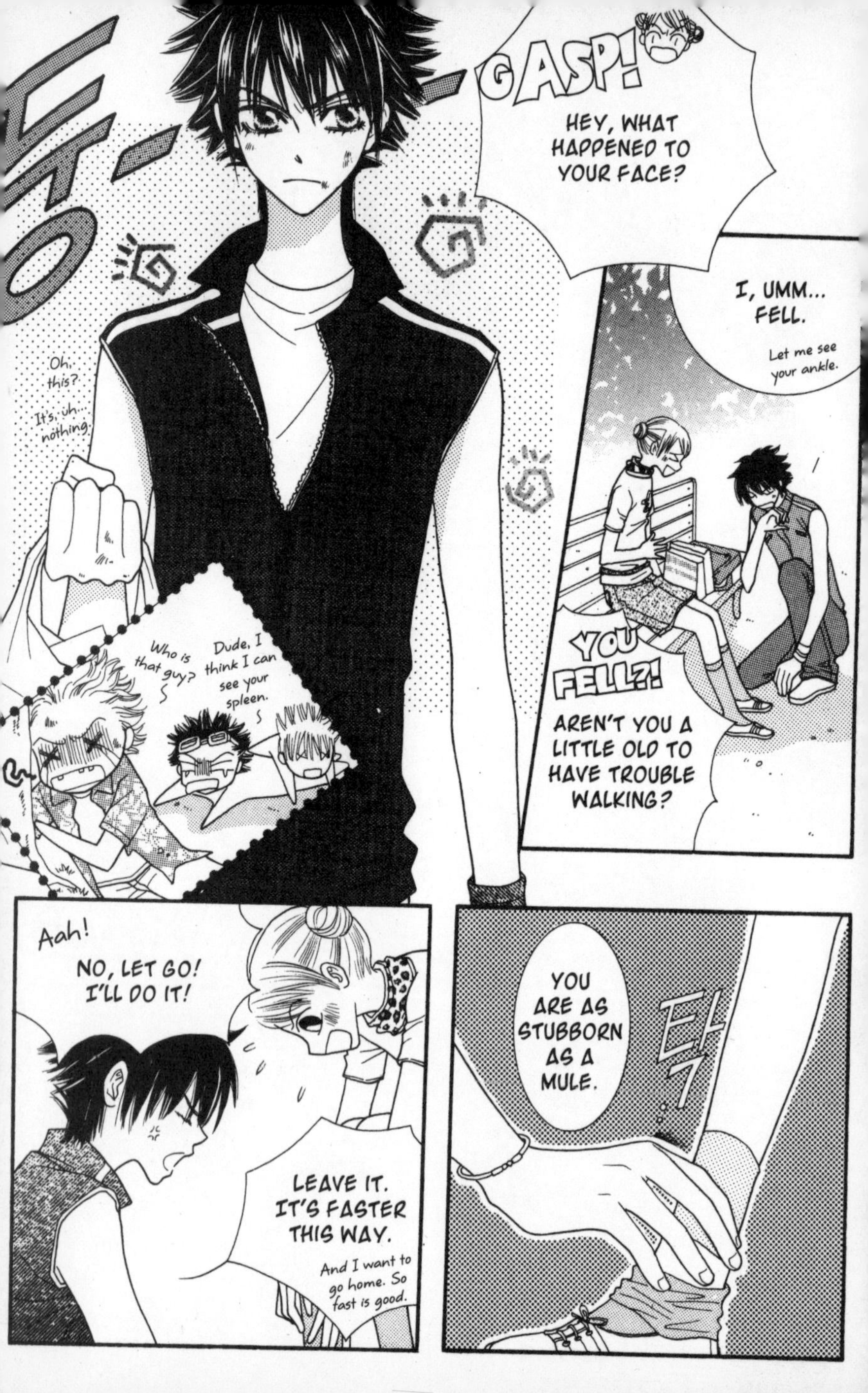
Oh, this?
It's, uh... nothing.
Who is that guy?
Dude, I think I can see your spleen.
GASP!
HEY, WHAT HAPPENED TO YOUR FACE?
I, UMM... FELL.
Let me see your ankle.
YOU FELL?!
AREN'T YOU A LITTLE OLD TO HAVE TROUBLE WALKING?
Aah!
NO, LET GO! I'LL DO IT!
LEAVE IT. IT'S FASTER THIS WAY.
And I want to go home. So fast is good.
YOU ARE AS STUBBORN AS A MULE.

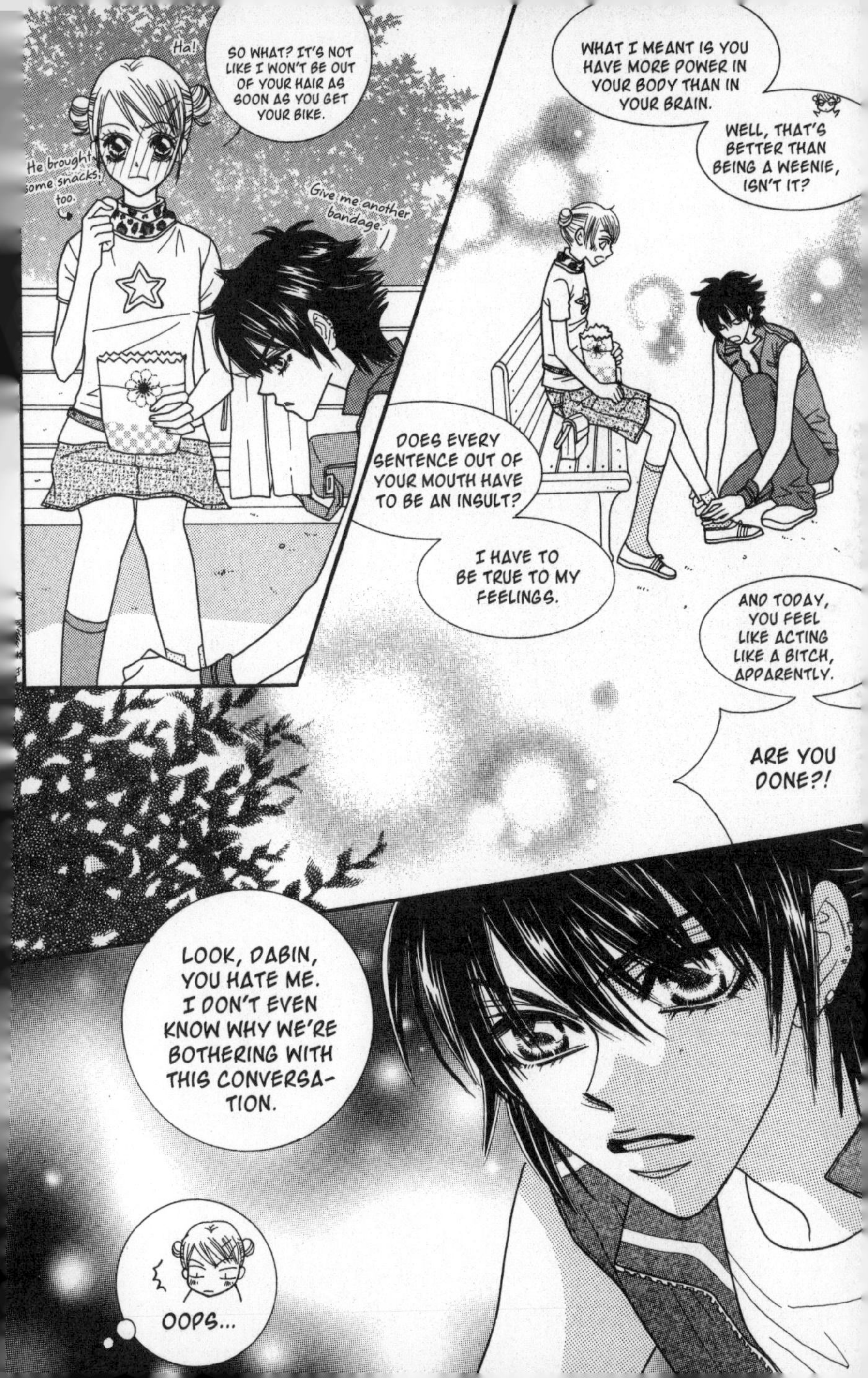
Ha!
SO WHAT? IT'S NOT LIKE I WON'T BE OUT OF YOUR HAIR AS SOON AS YOU GET YOUR BIKE.
He brought some snacks, too.
Give me another bandage.
WHAT I MEANT IS YOU HAVE MORE POWER IN YOUR BODY THAN IN YOUR BRAIN.
WELL, THAT'S BETTER THAN BEING A WEENIE, ISN'T IT?
DOES EVERY SENTENCE OUT OF YOUR MOUTH HAVE TO BE AN INSULT?
I HAVE TO BE TRUE TO MY FEELINGS.
AND TODAY, YOU FEEL LIKE ACTING LIKE A BITCH, APPARENTLY.
ARE YOU DONE?!
LOOK, DABIN, YOU HATE ME. I DON'T EVEN KNOW WHY WE'RE BOTHERING WITH THIS CONVERSA-TION.
OOPS...

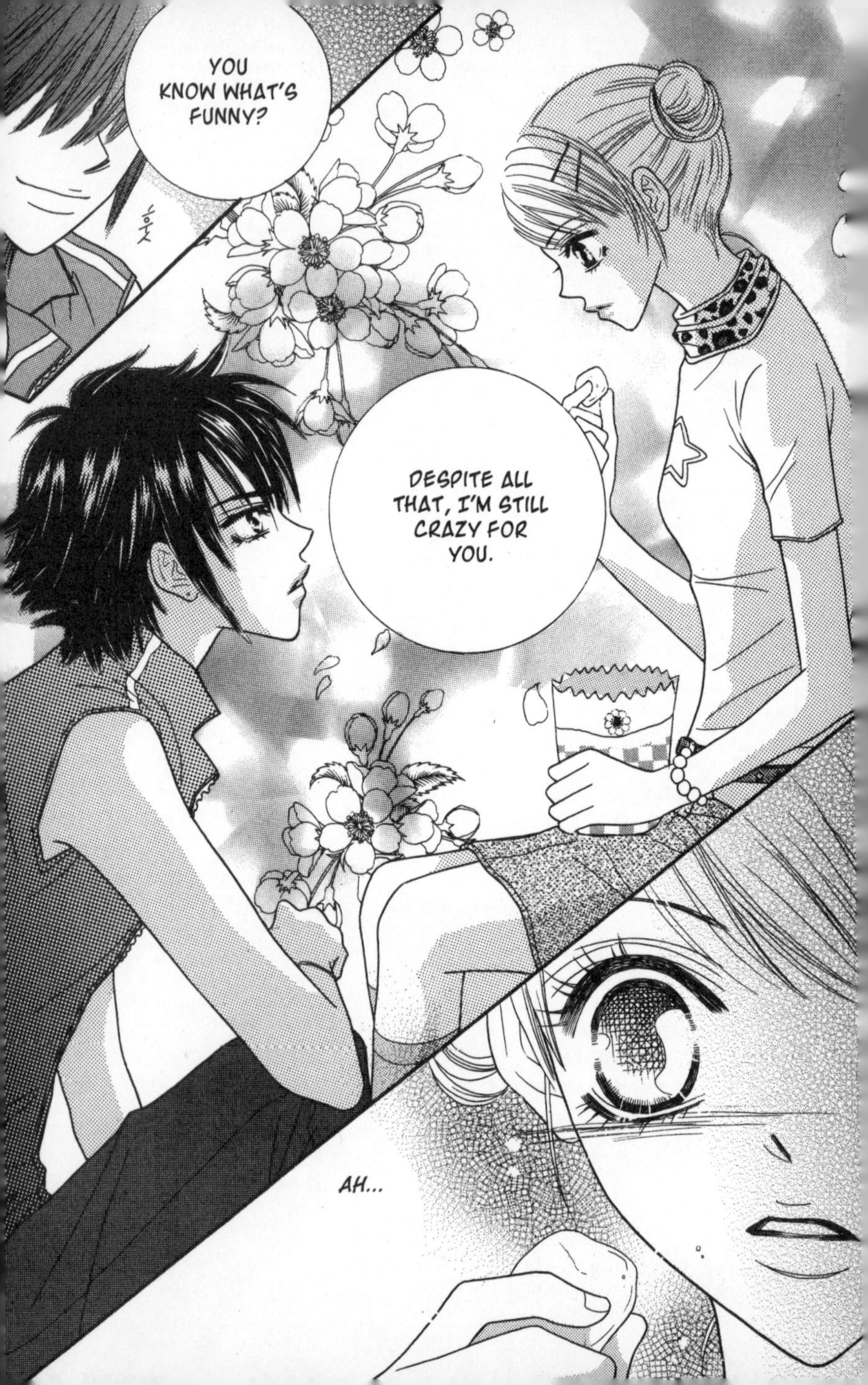
YOU KNOW WHAT'S FUNNY?
DESPITE ALL THAT, I'M STILL CRAZY FOR YOU.
AH...

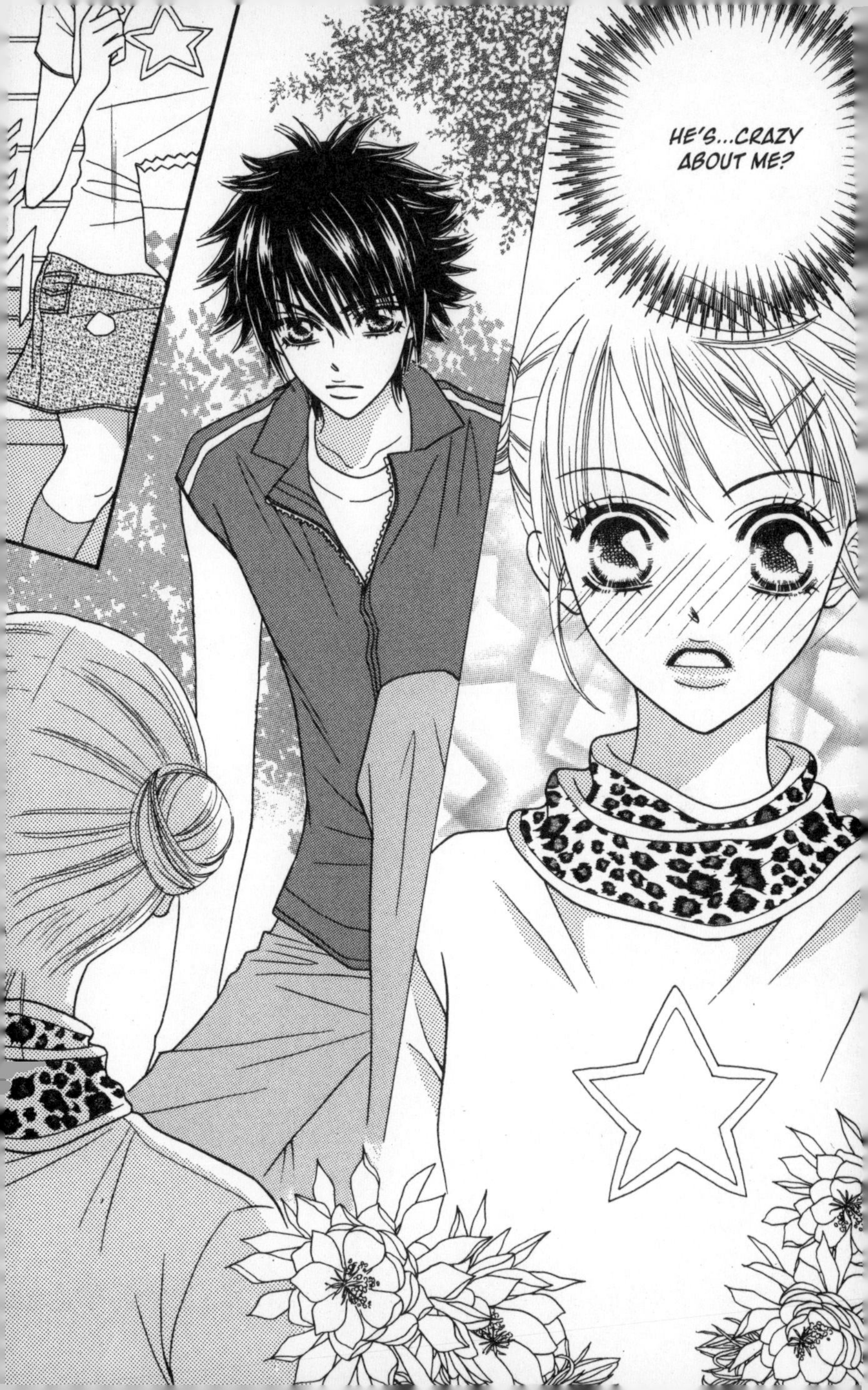
HE'S...CRAZY ABOUT ME?

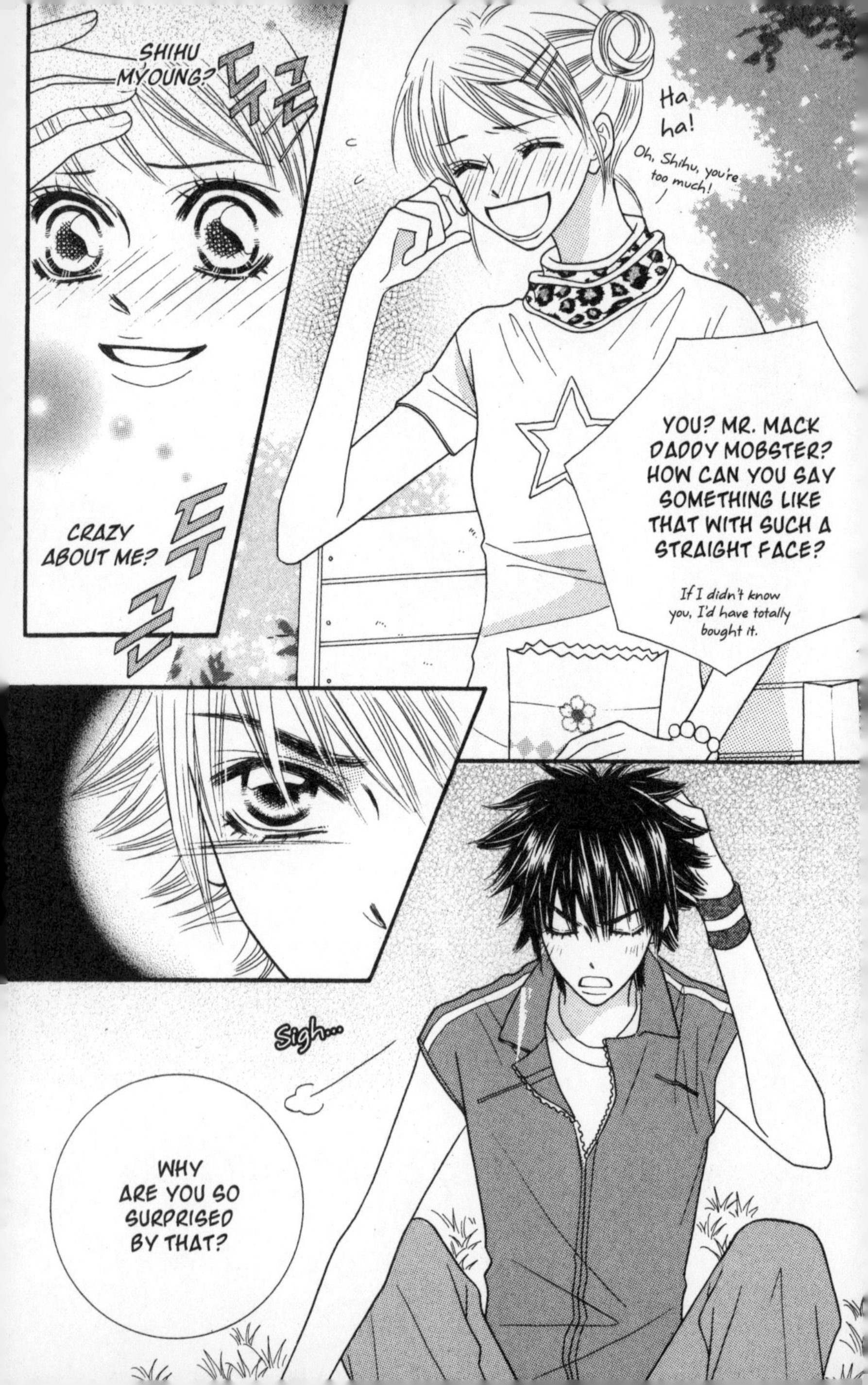
SHIHU MYOUNG?
CRAZY ABOUT ME?
Ha ha!
Oh, Shihu, you're too much!
YOU? MR. MACK DADDY MOBSTER? HOW CAN YOU SAY SOMETHING LIKE THAT WITH SUCH A STRAIGHT FACE?
If I didn't know you, I'd have totally bought it.
Sigh...
WHY ARE YOU SO SURPRISED BY THAT?

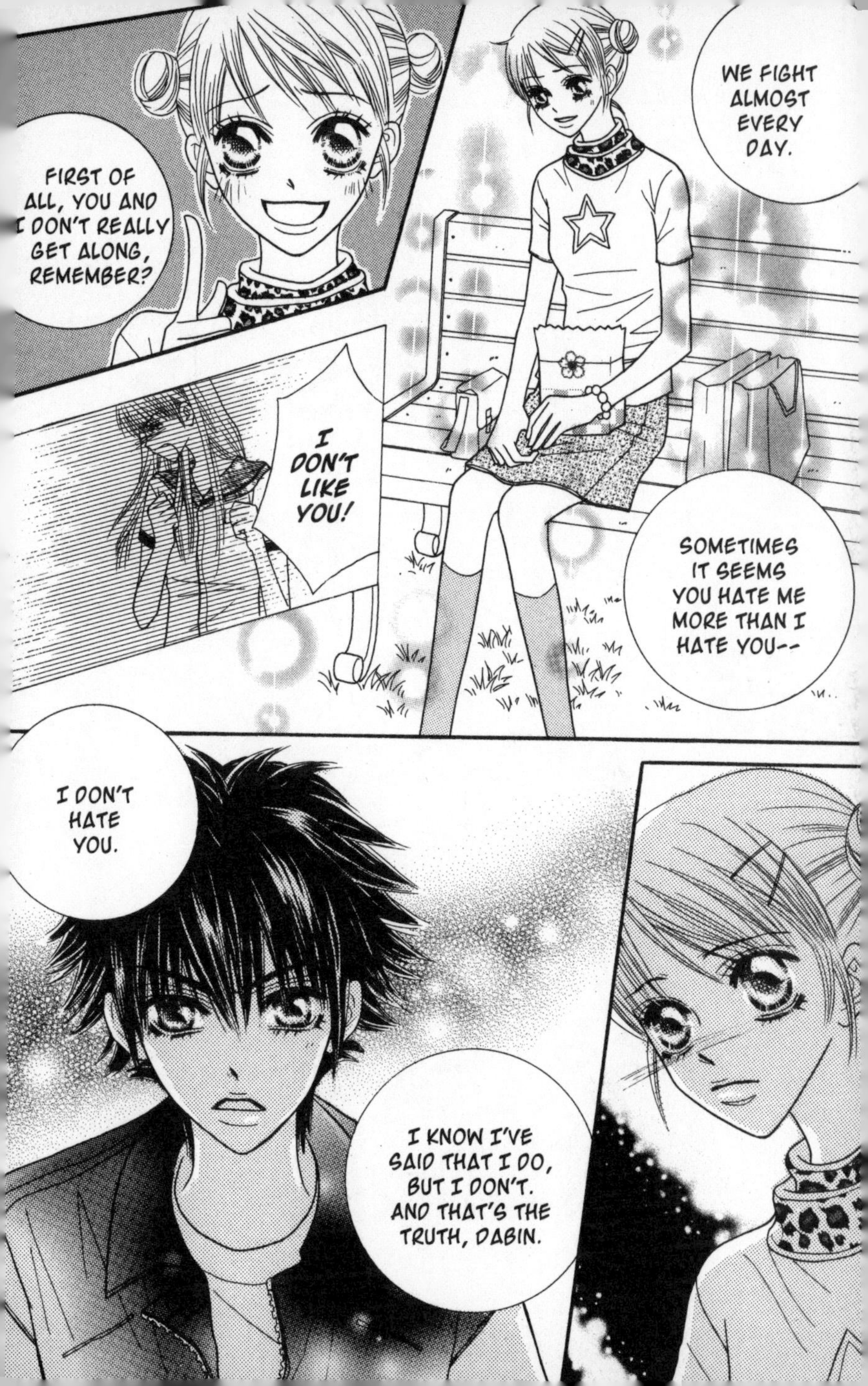
FIRST OF ALL, YOU AND I DON'T REALLY GET ALONG, REMEMBER?
WE FIGHT ALMOST EVERY DAY.
I DON'T LIKE YOU!
SOMETIMES IT SEEMS YOU HATE ME MORE THAN I HATE YOU--
I DON'T HATE YOU.
I KNOW I'VE SAID THAT I DO, BUT I DON'T. AND THAT'S THE TRUTH, DABIN.

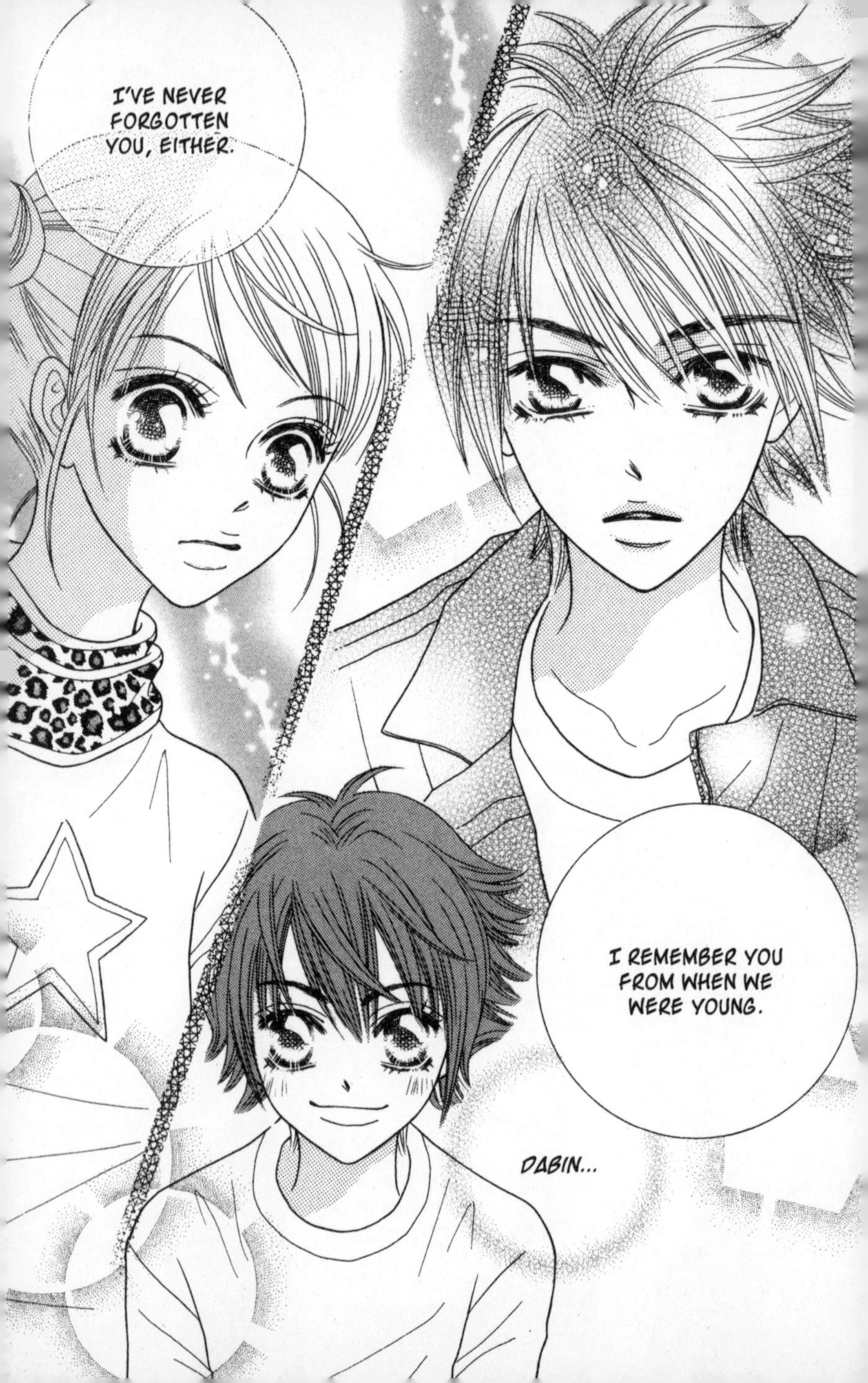
I'VE NEVER FORGOTTEN YOU, EITHER.
I REMEMBER YOU FROM WHEN WE WERE YOUNG.
DABIN...

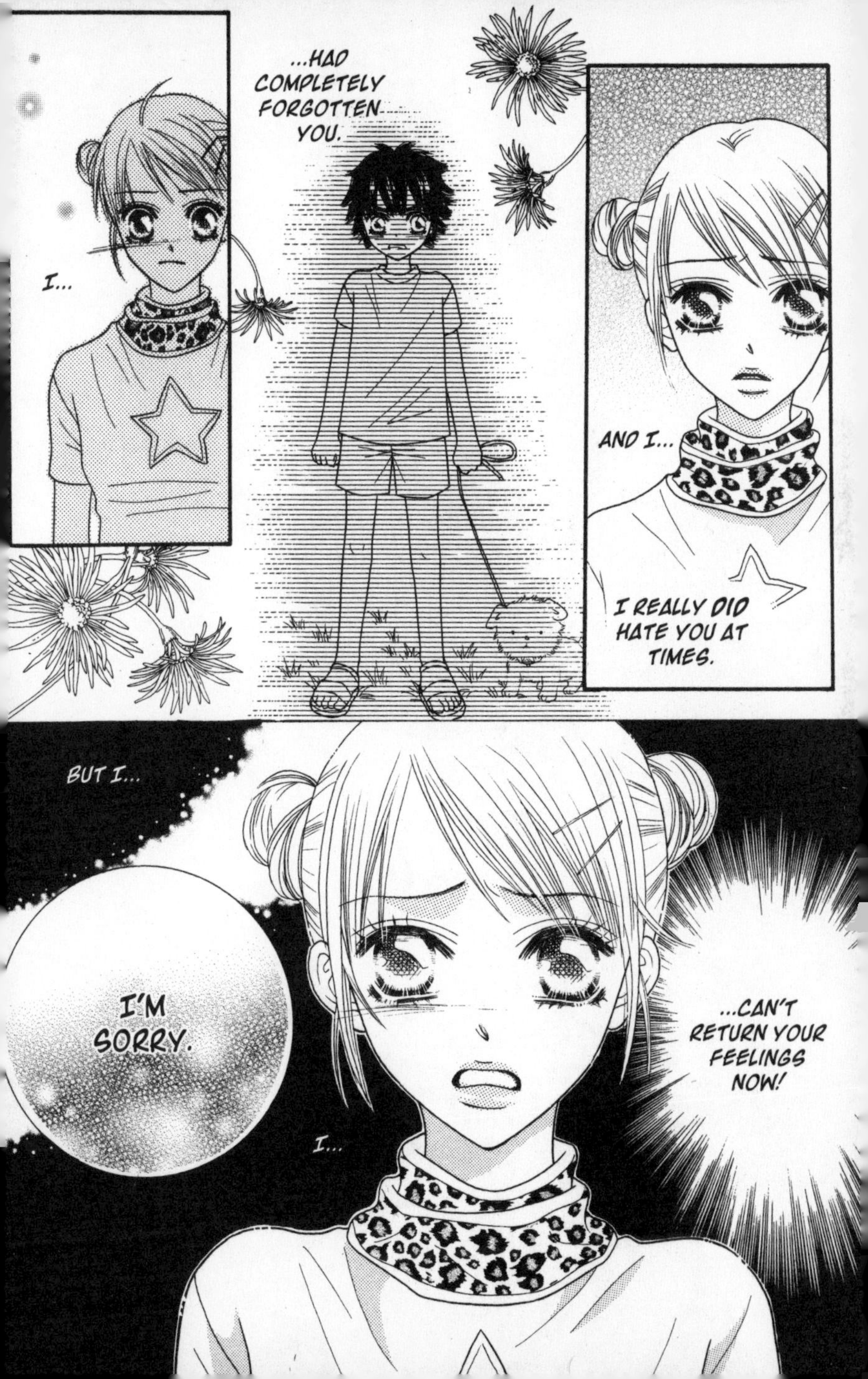
I...
...HAD COMPLETELY FORGOTTEN YOU.
AND I...
I REALLY DID HATE YOU AT TIMES.
BUT I...
I'M SORRY.
I...
...CAN'T RETURN YOUR FEELINGS NOW!

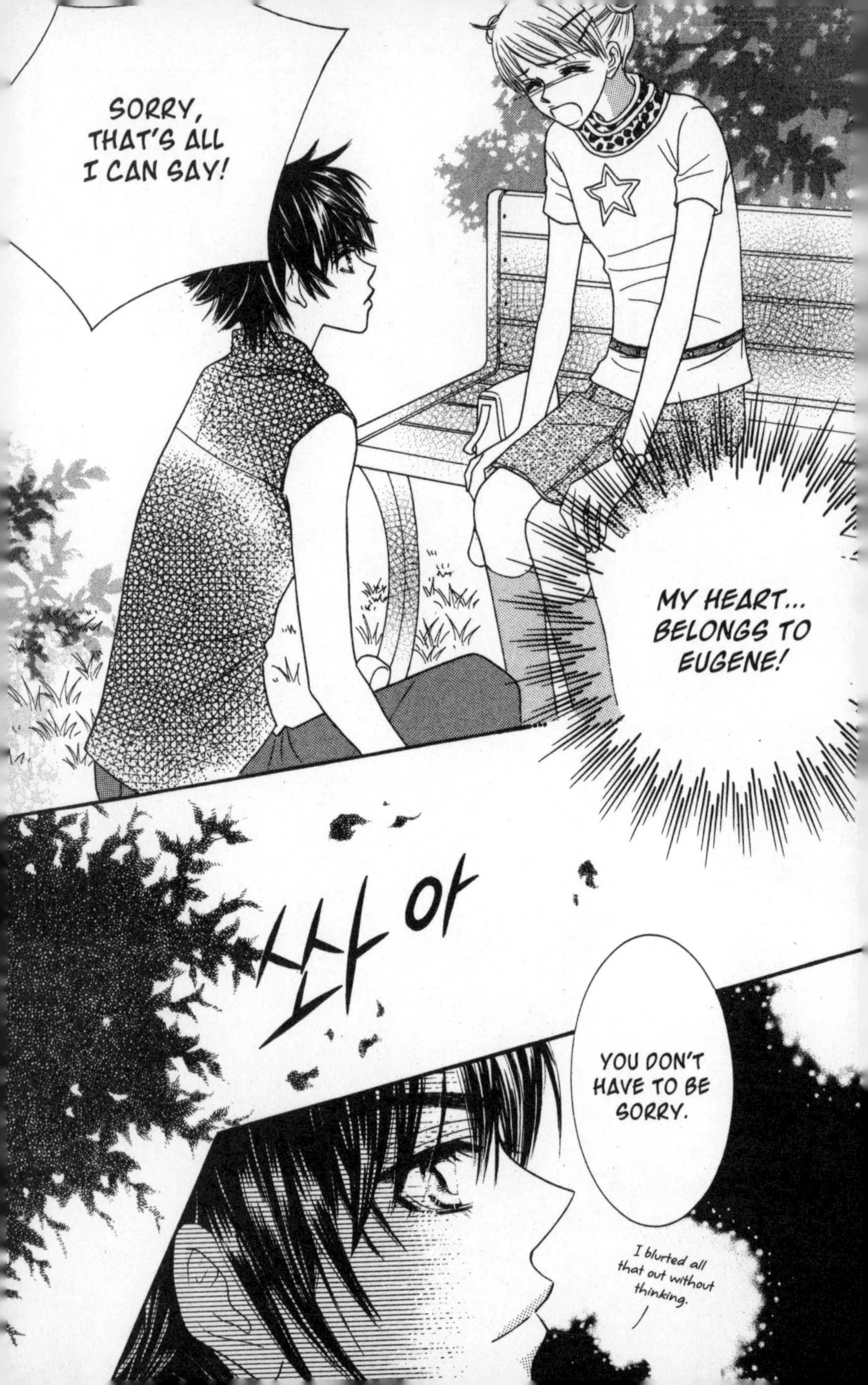
SORRY, THAT'S ALL I CAN SAY!
MY HEART... BELONGS TO EUGENE!
쏴아
YOU DON'T HAVE TO BE SORRY.
I blurted all that out without thinking.

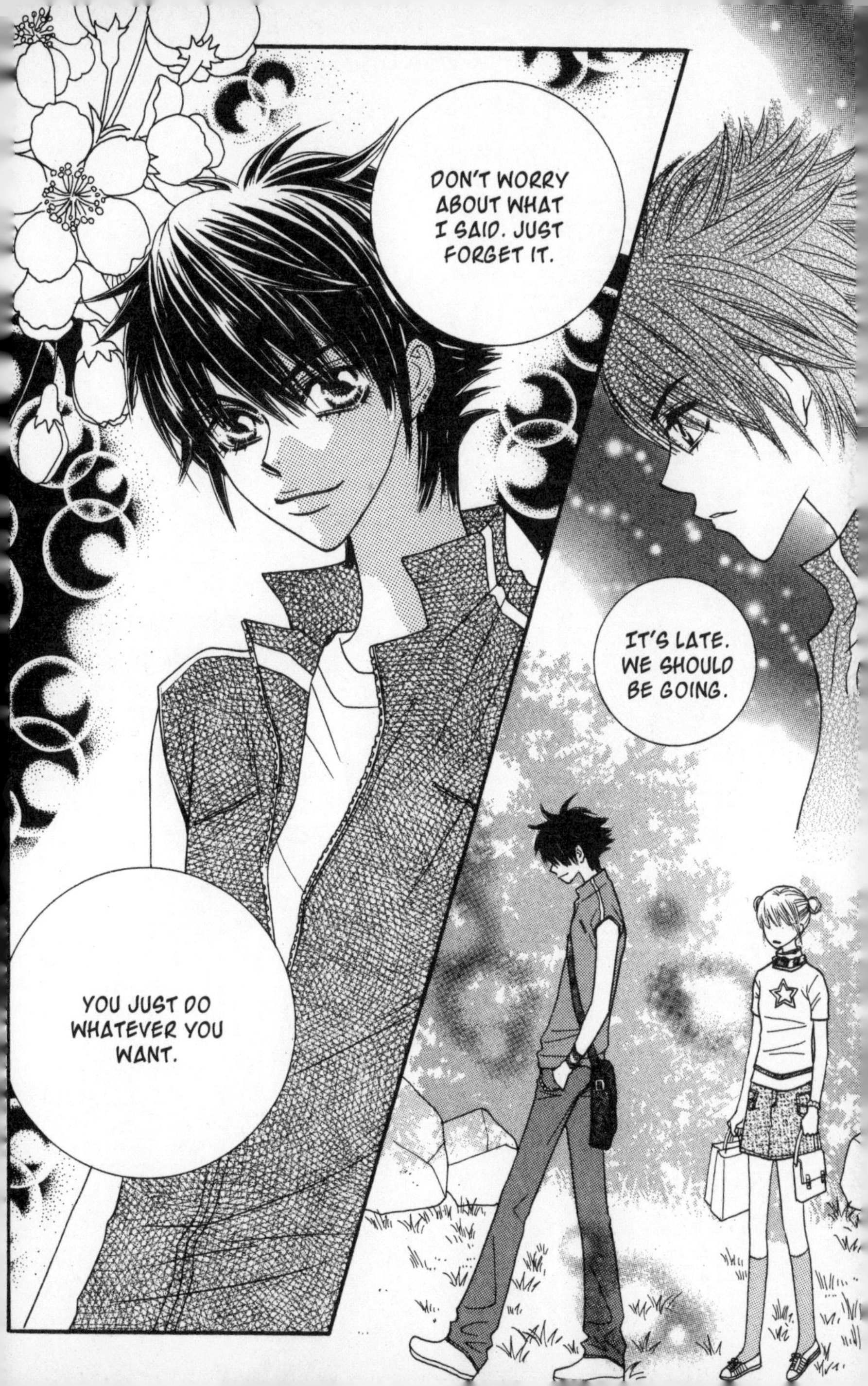
DON'T WORRY ABOUT WHAT I SAID. JUST FORGET IT.
YOU JUST DO WHATEVER YOU WANT.
IT'S LATE. WE SHOULD BE GOING.

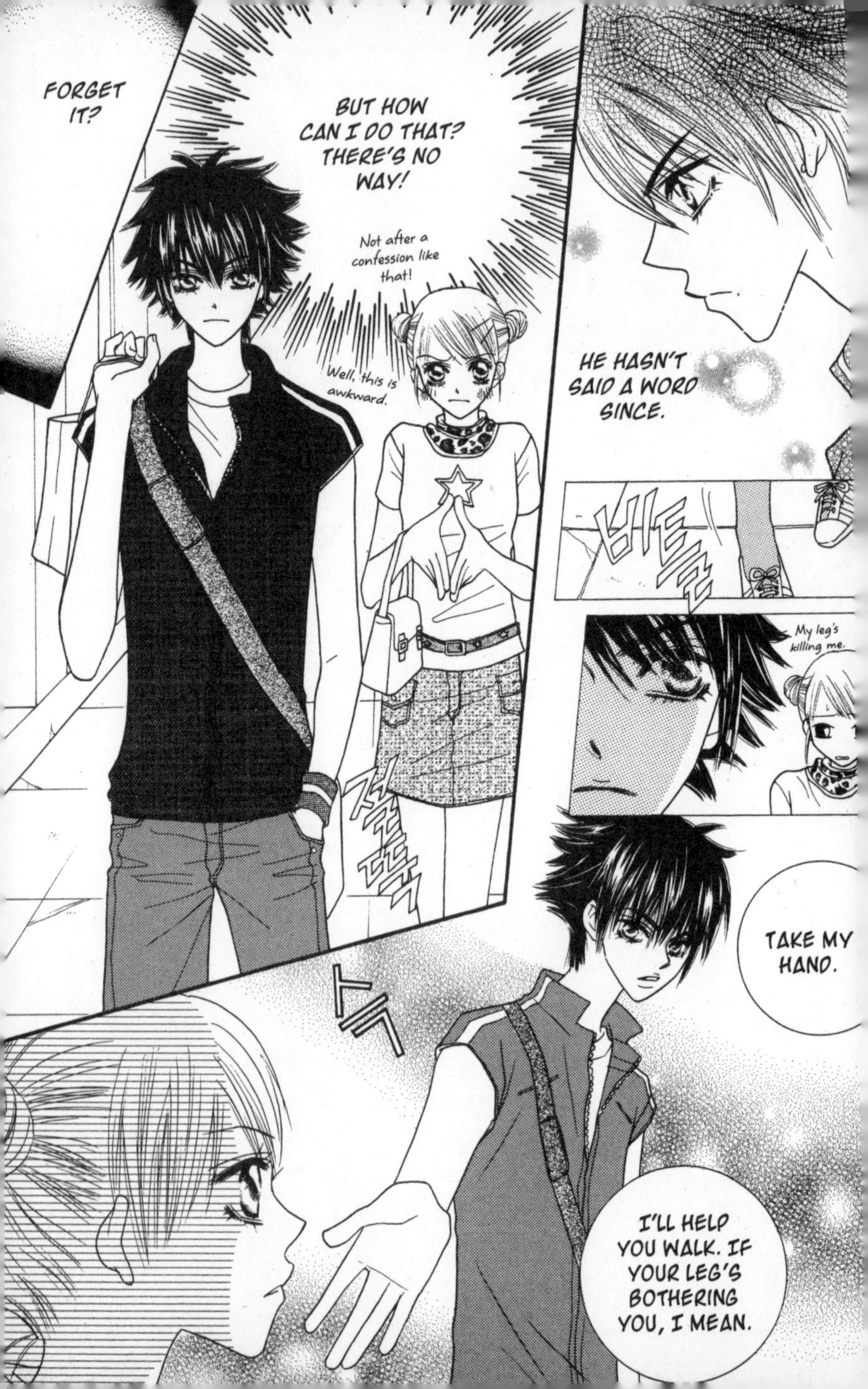
FORGET IT?
BUT HOW CAN I DO THAT? THERE'S NO WAY!
Not after a confession like that!
Well, this is awkward.
HE HASN'T SAID A WORD SINCE.
My leg's killing me.
TAKE MY HAND.
I'LL HELP YOU WALK. IF YOUR LEG'S BOTHERING YOU, I MEAN.

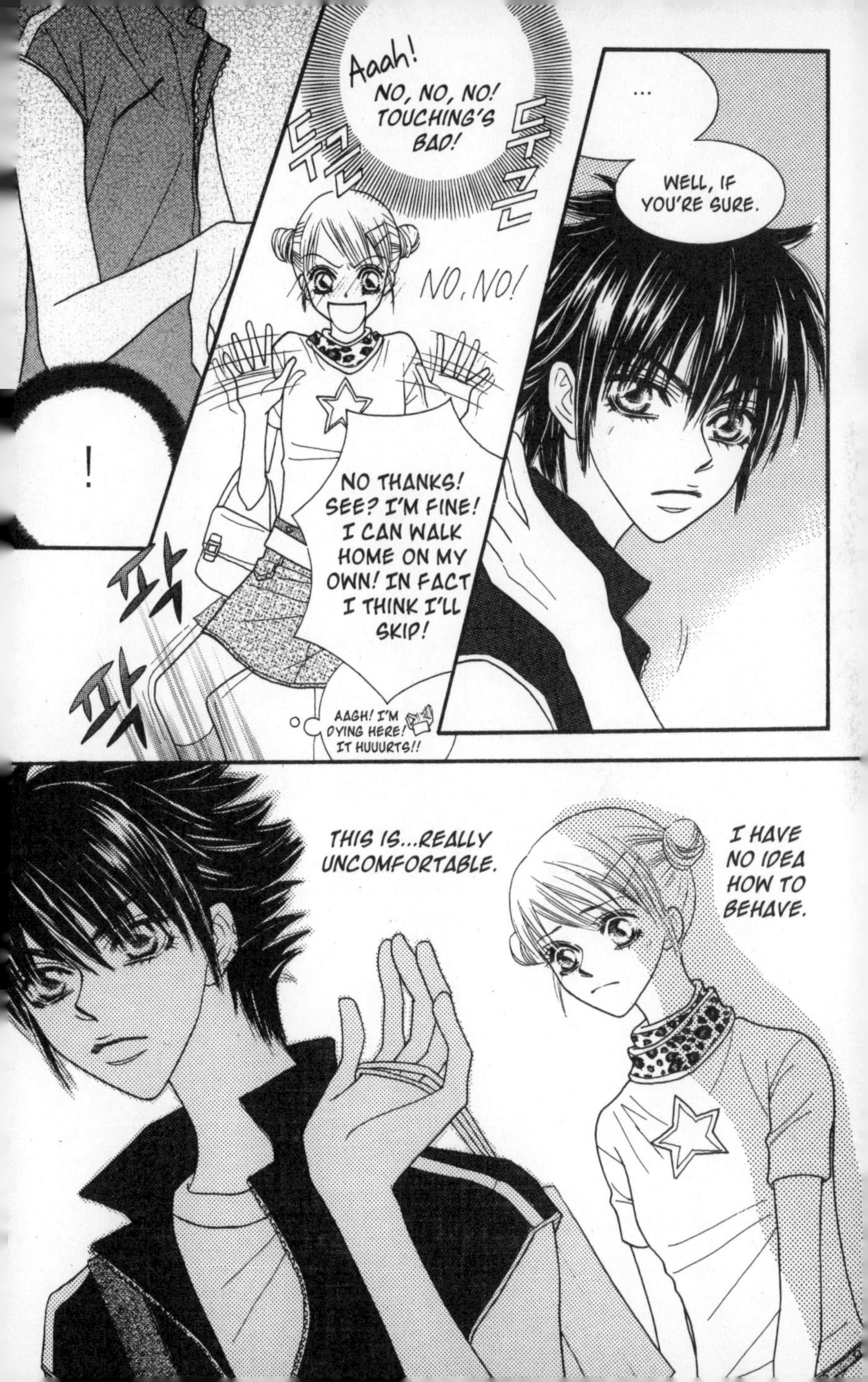
!
Aaah!
NO, NO, NO! TOUCHING'S BAD!
NO, NO!
NO THANKS! SEE? I'M FINE! I CAN WALK HOME ON MY OWN! IN FACT I THINK I'LL SKIP!
AAGH! I'M DYING HERE! IT HUUURTS!!
...
WELL, IF YOU'RE SURE.
THIS IS...REALLY UNCOMFORTABLE.
I HAVE NO IDEA HOW TO BEHAVE.

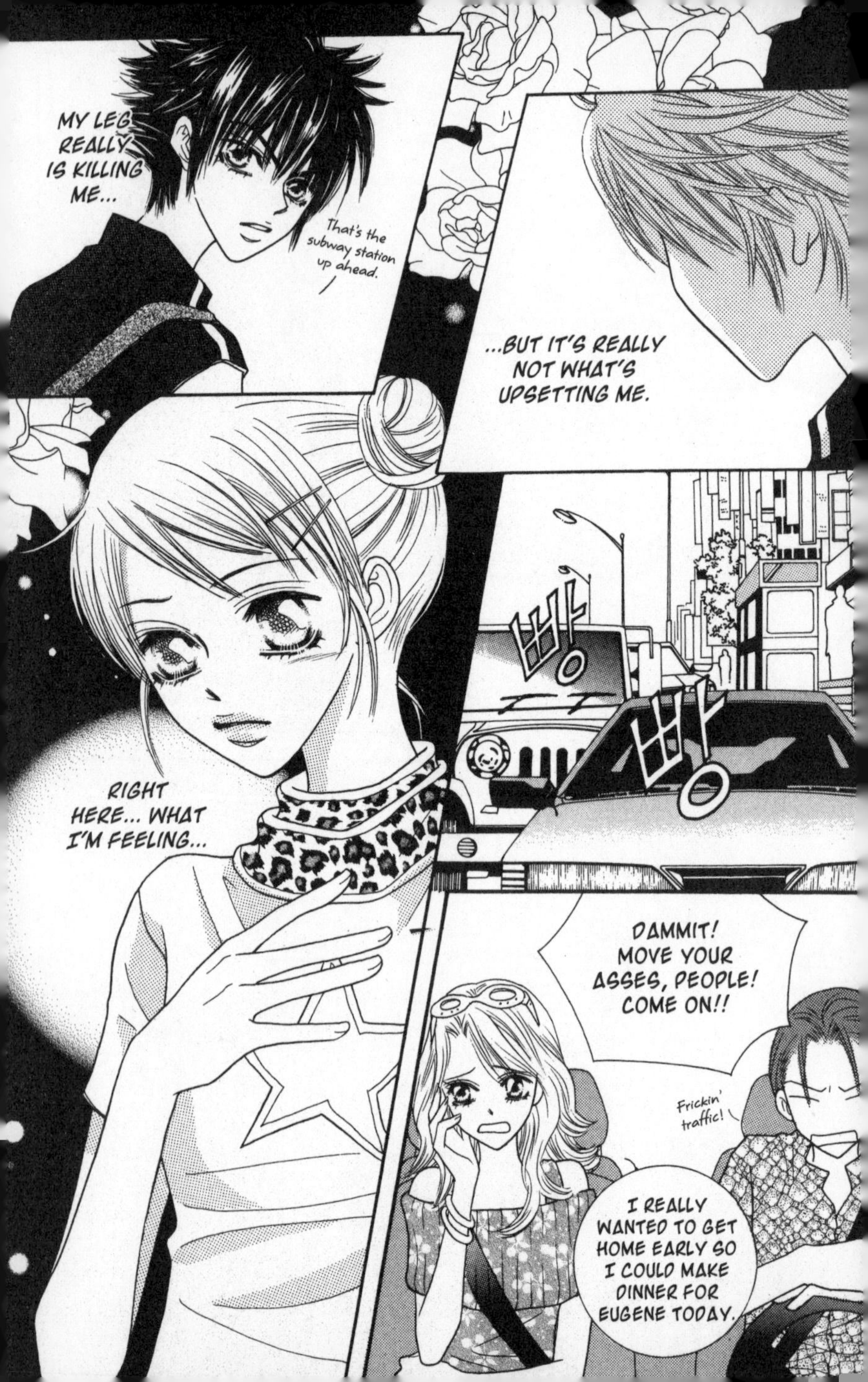
MY LEG REALLY IS KILLING ME...
That's the subway station up ahead.
...BUT IT'S REALLY NOT WHAT'S UPSETTING ME.
RIGHT HERE... WHAT I'M FEELING...
빵
빵
DAMMIT! MOVE YOUR ASSES, PEOPLE! COME ON!!
Frickin' traffic!
I REALLY WANTED TO GET HOME EARLY SO I COULD MAKE DINNER FOR EUGENE TODAY.

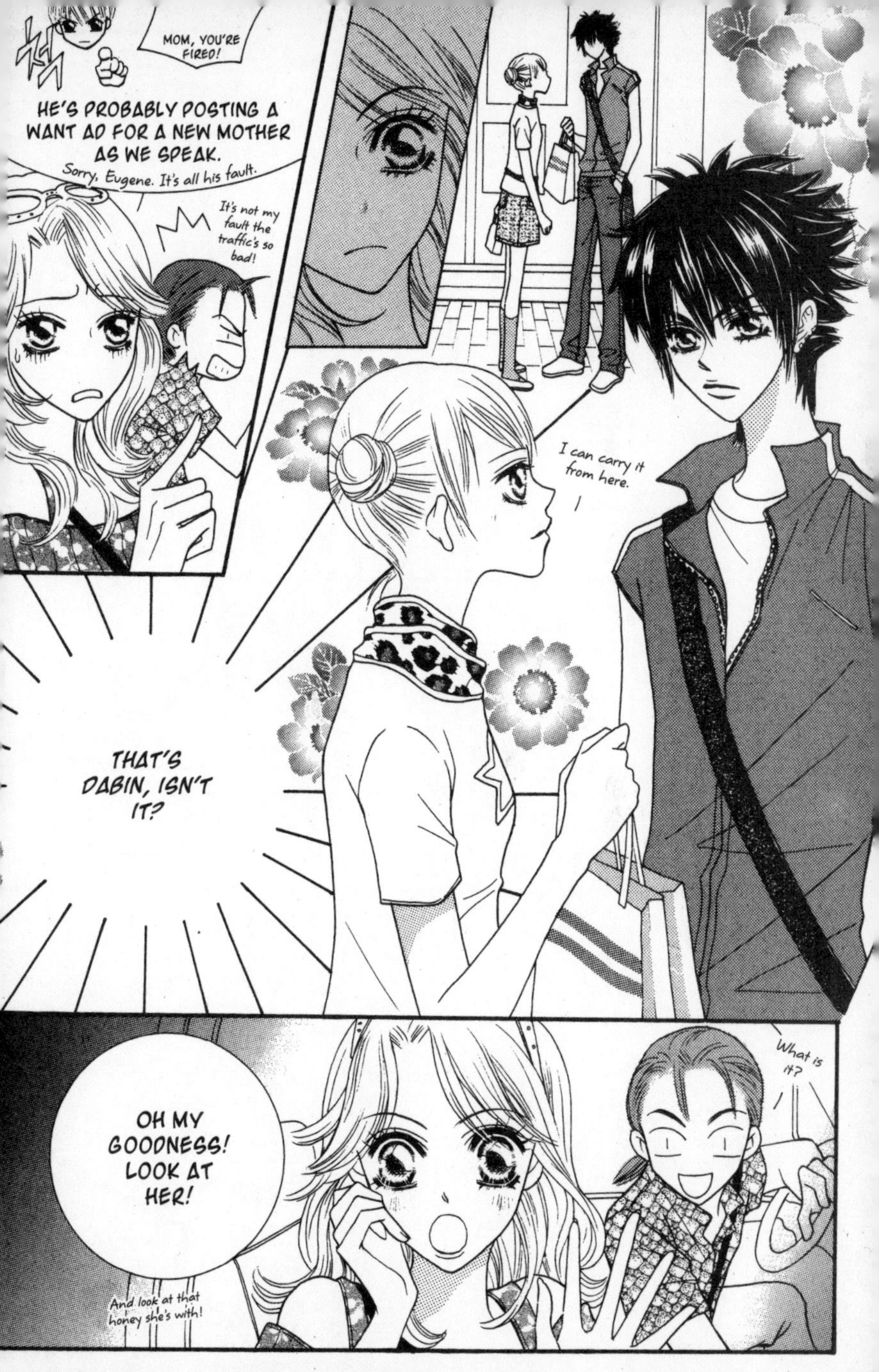

MOM, YOU'RE FIRED!
HE'S PROBABLY POSTING A WANT AD FOR A NEW MOTHER AS WE SPEAK.
Sorry, Eugene. It's all his fault.
It's not my fault the traffic's so bad!
I can carry it from here.
THAT'S DABIN, ISN'T IT?
OH MY GOODNESS! LOOK AT HER!
And look at that honey she's with!
What is it?

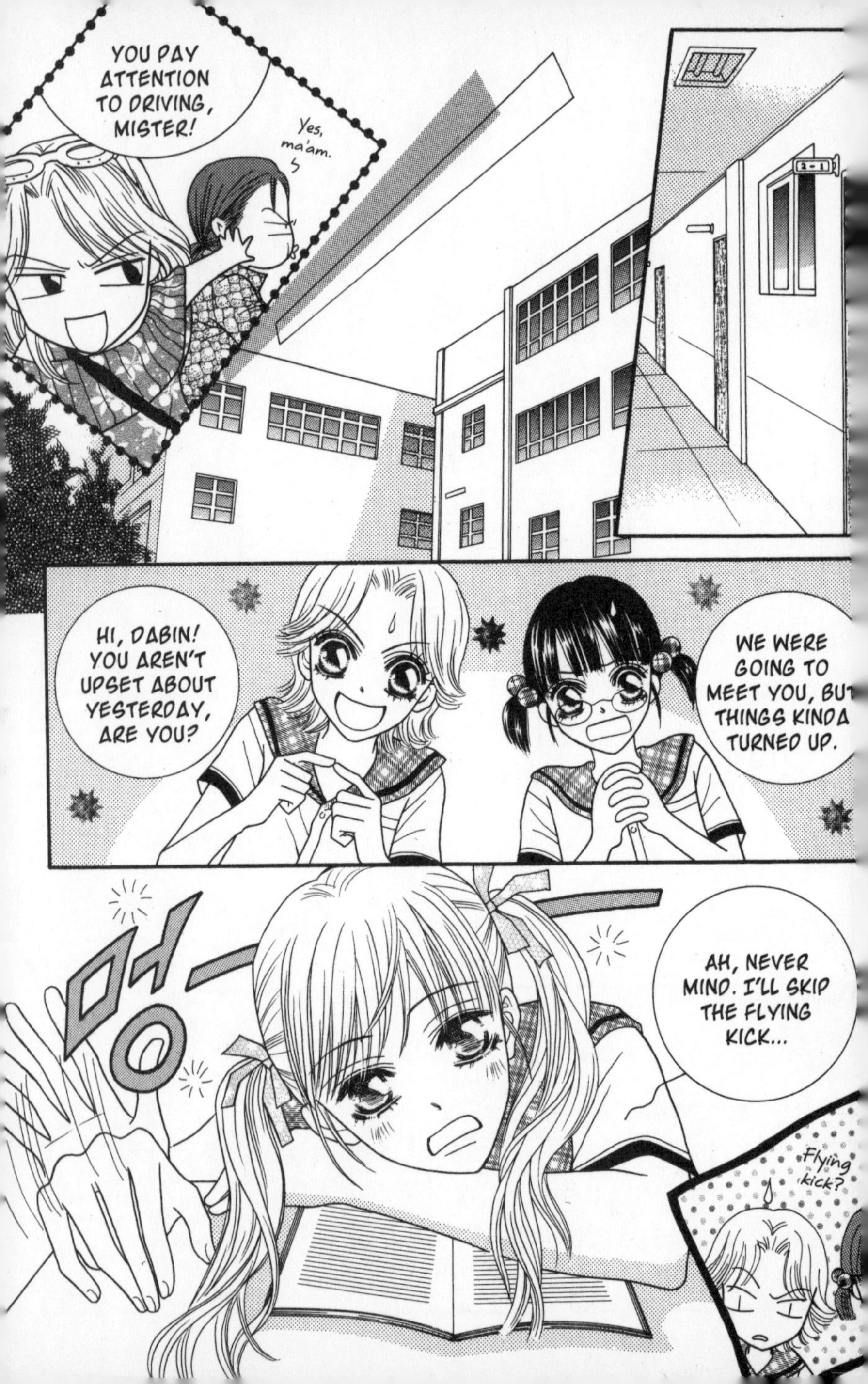
YOU PAY ATTENTION TO DRIVING, MISTER!
Yes, ma'am.
HI, DABIN! YOU AREN'T UPSET ABOUT YESTERDAY, ARE YOU?
WE WERE GOING TO MEET YOU, BUT THINGS KINDA TURNED UP.
AH, NEVER MIND. I'LL SKIP THE FLYING KICK...
Flying kick?

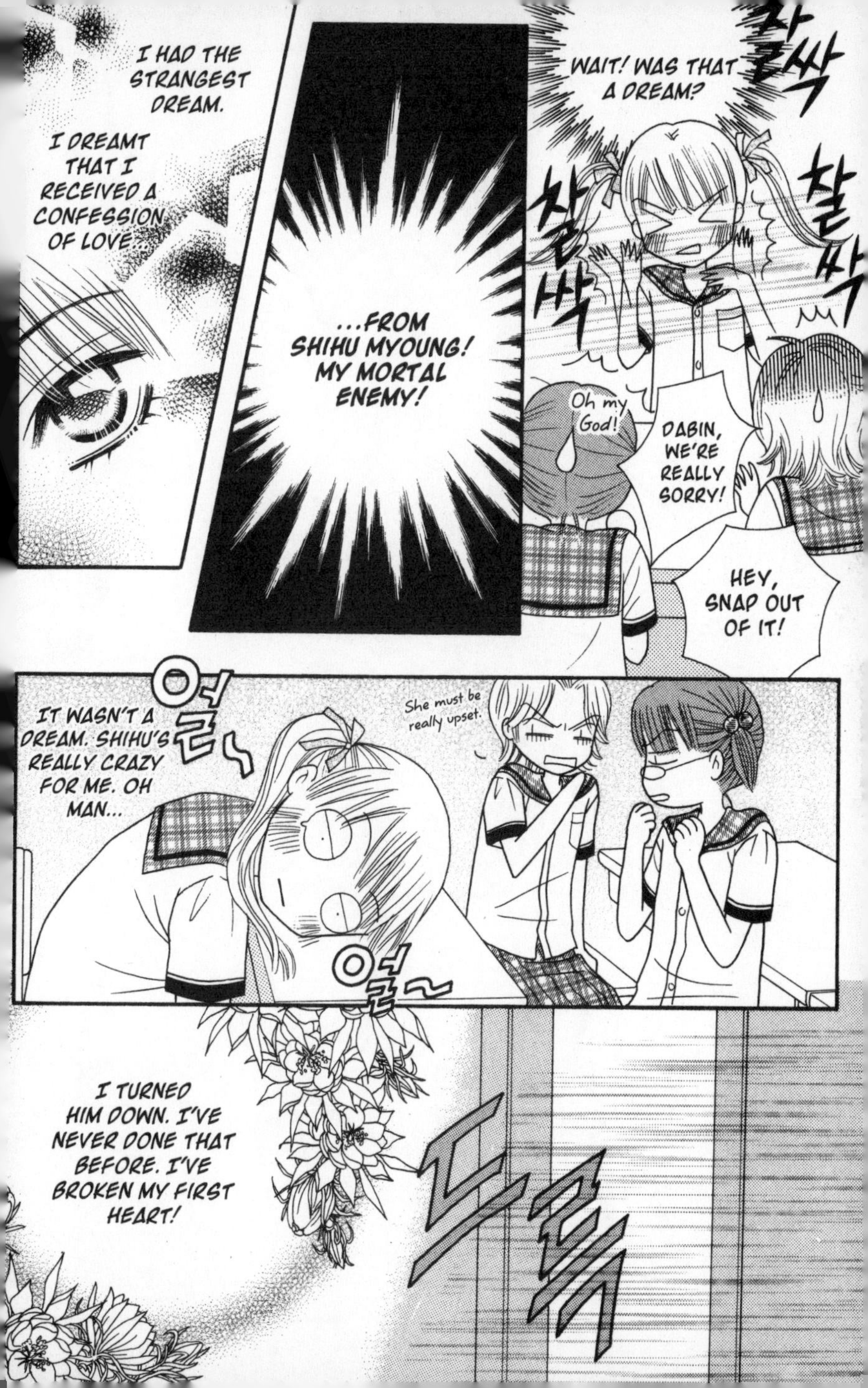
I HAD THE STRANGEST DREAM.
I DREAMT THAT I RECEIVED A CONFESSION OF LOVE...
...FROM SHIHU MYOUNG! MY MORTAL ENEMY!
찰싹
WAIT! WAS THAT A DREAM?
찰싹
찰싹
Oh my God!
DABIN, WE'RE REALLY SORRY!
HEY, SNAP OUT OF IT!
IT WASN'T A DREAM. SHIHU'S REALLY CRAZY FOR ME. OH MAN...
She must be really upset.
I TURNED HIM DOWN. I'VE NEVER DONE THAT BEFORE. I'VE BROKEN MY FIRST HEART!

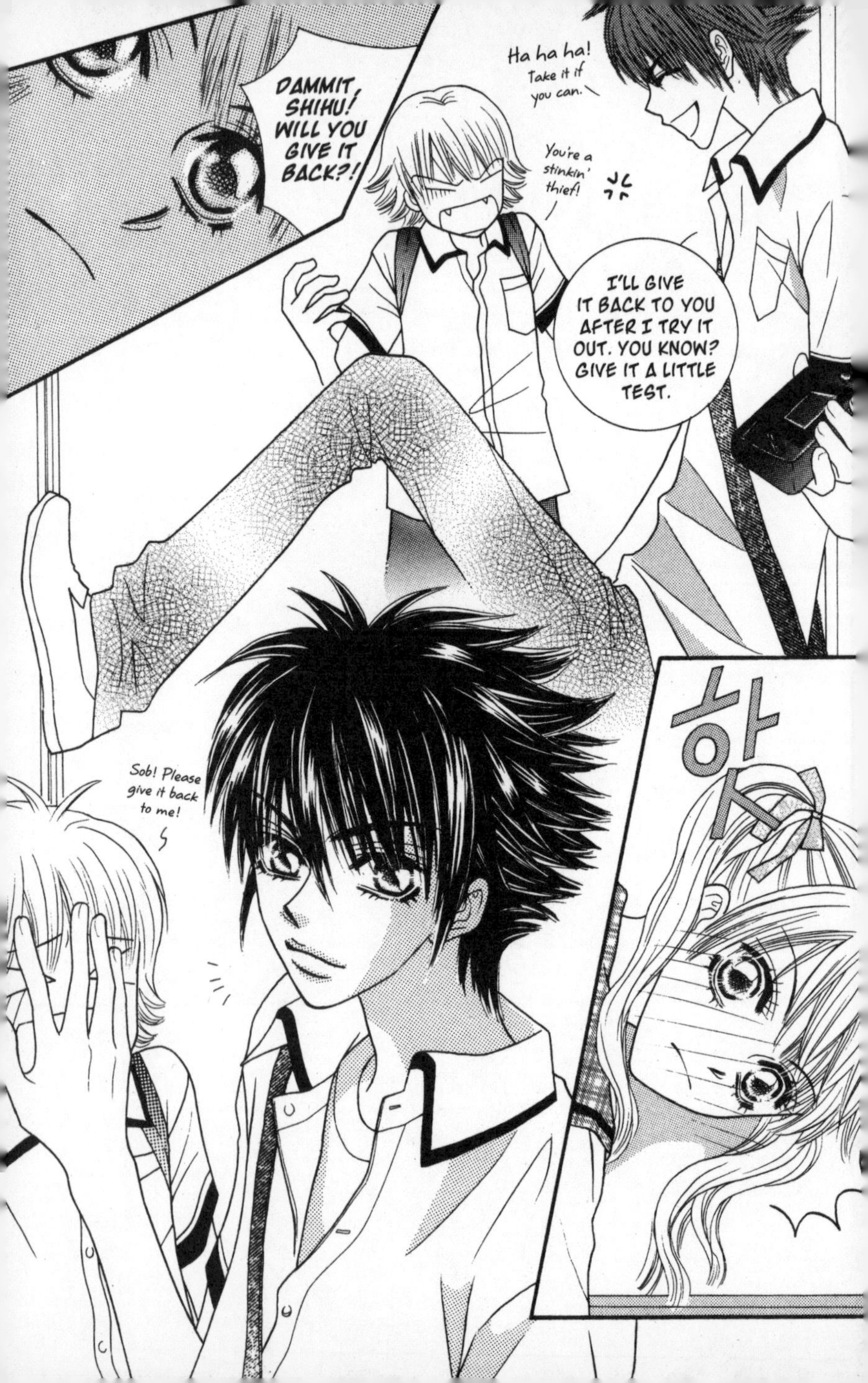
DAMMIT, SHIHU! WILL YOU GIVE IT BACK?!
Ha ha ha! Take it if you can.
You're a stinkin' thief!
I'LL GIVE IT BACK TO YOU AFTER I TRY IT OUT. YOU KNOW? GIVE IT A LITTLE TEST.
Sob! Please give it back to me!
하

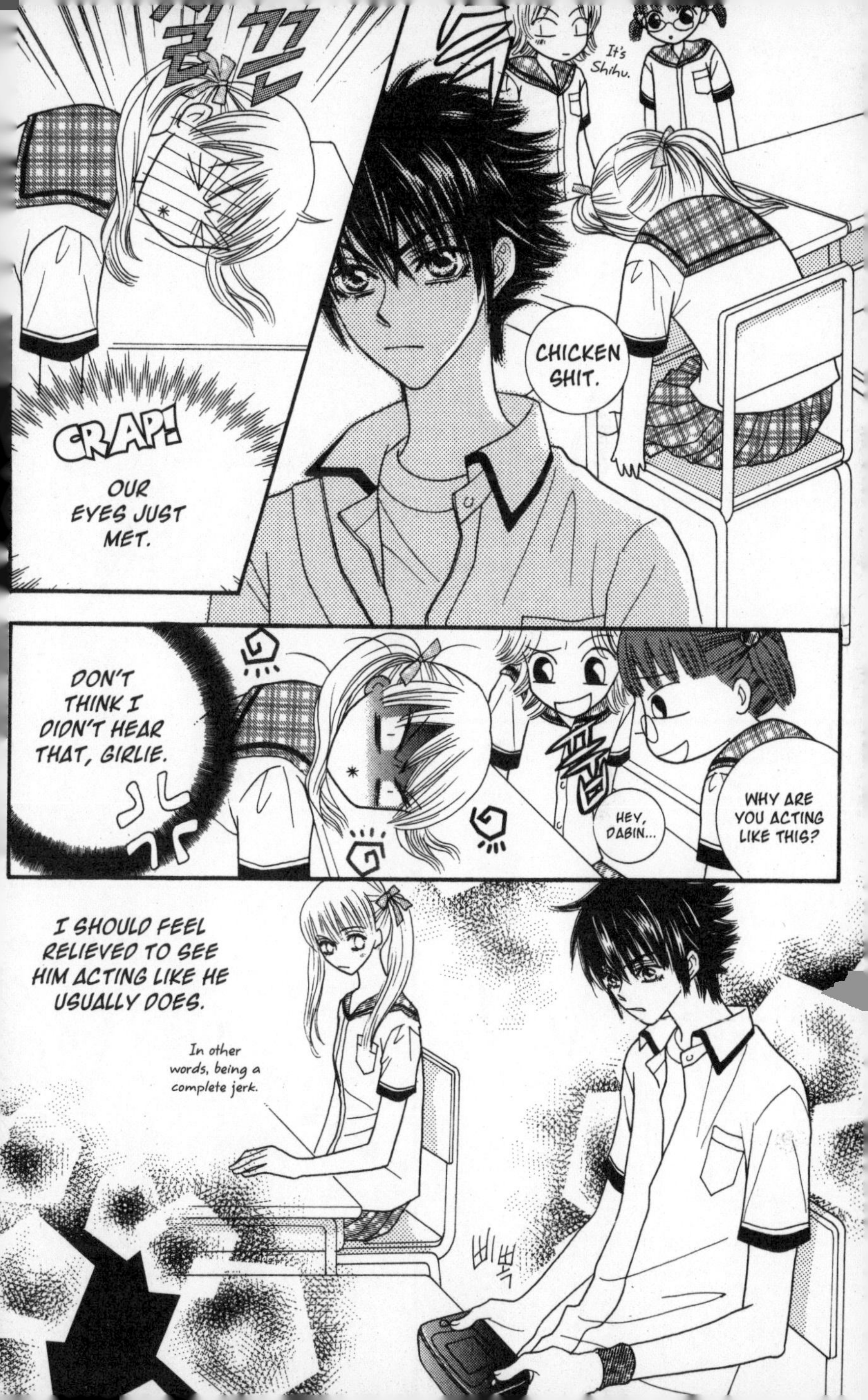
CRAP!
OUR EYES JUST MET.
It's Shihu.
CHICKEN SHIT.
DON'T THINK I DIDN'T HEAR THAT, GIRLIE.
HEY, DABIN...
WHY ARE YOU ACTING LIKE THIS?
I SHOULD FEEL RELIEVED TO SEE HIM ACTING LIKE HE USUALLY DOES.
In other words, being a complete jerk.

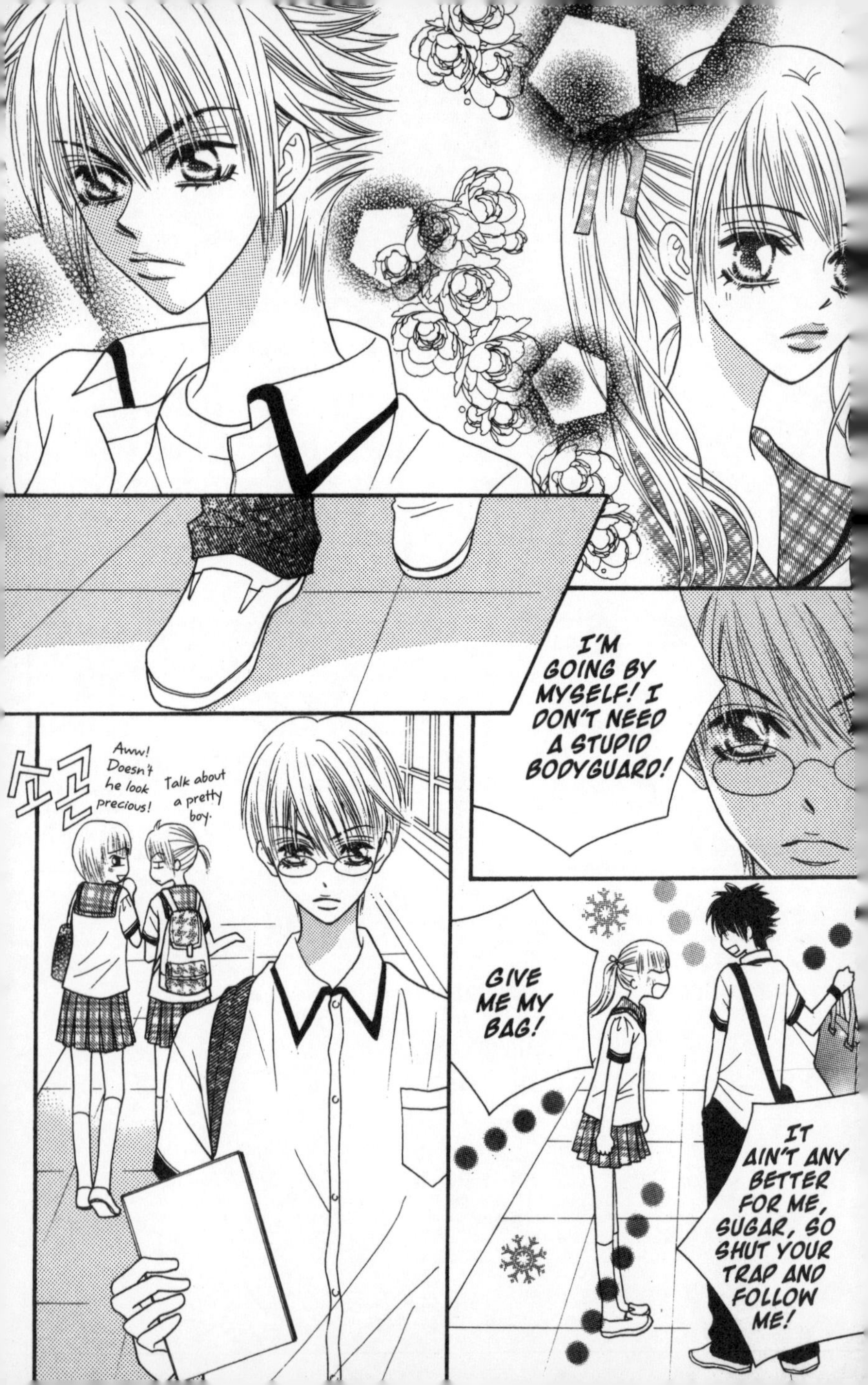
I'M GOING BY MYSELF! I DON'T NEED A STUPID BODYGUARD!
쇼곤
Aww! Doesn't he look precious!
Talk about a pretty boy.
GIVE ME MY BAG!
IT AIN'T ANY BETTER FOR ME, SUGAR, SO SHUT YOUR TRAP AND FOLLOW ME!

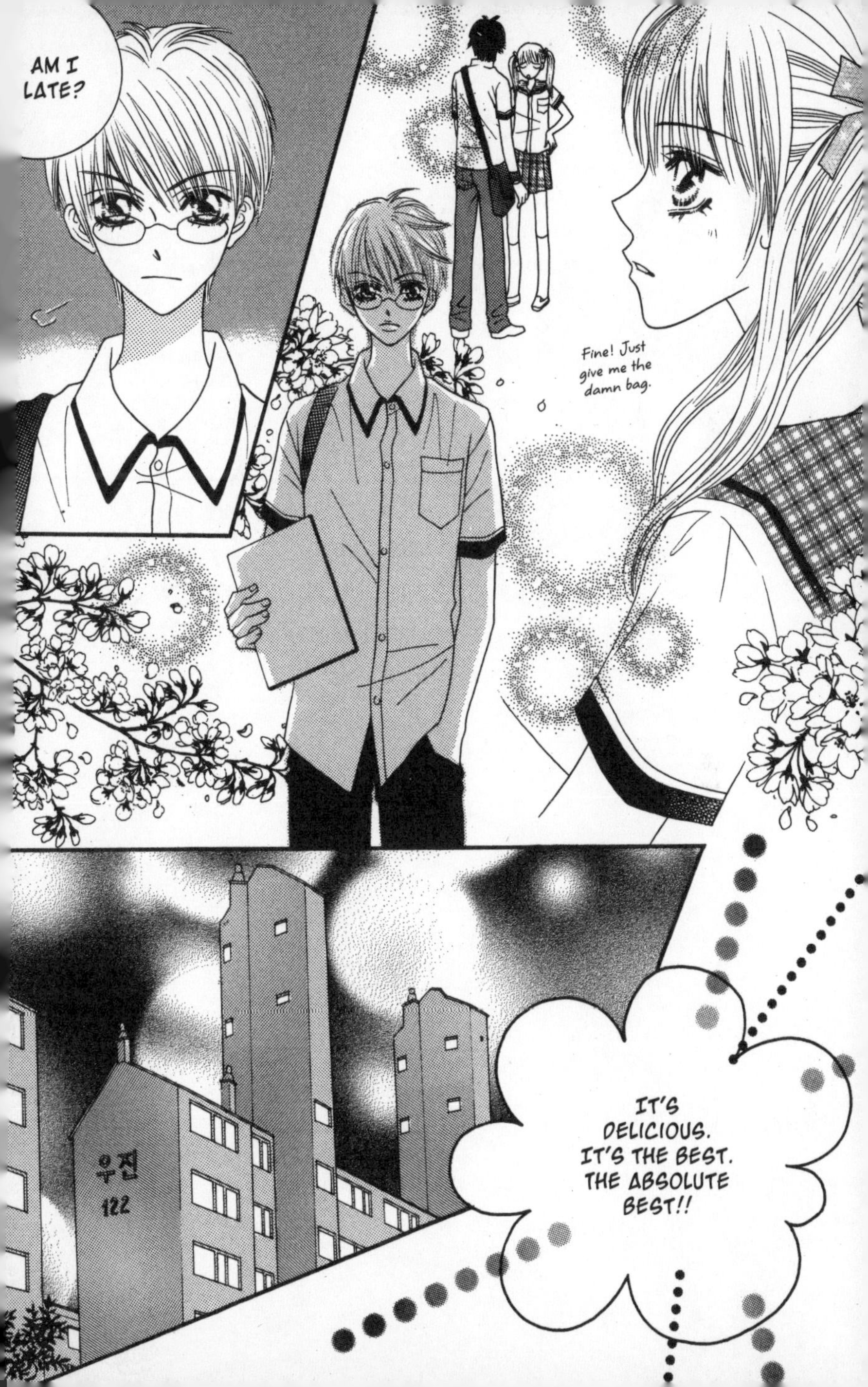
AM I LATE?
Fine! Just give me the damn bag.
우전
122
IT'S DELICIOUS. IT'S THE BEST. THE ABSOLUTE BEST!!

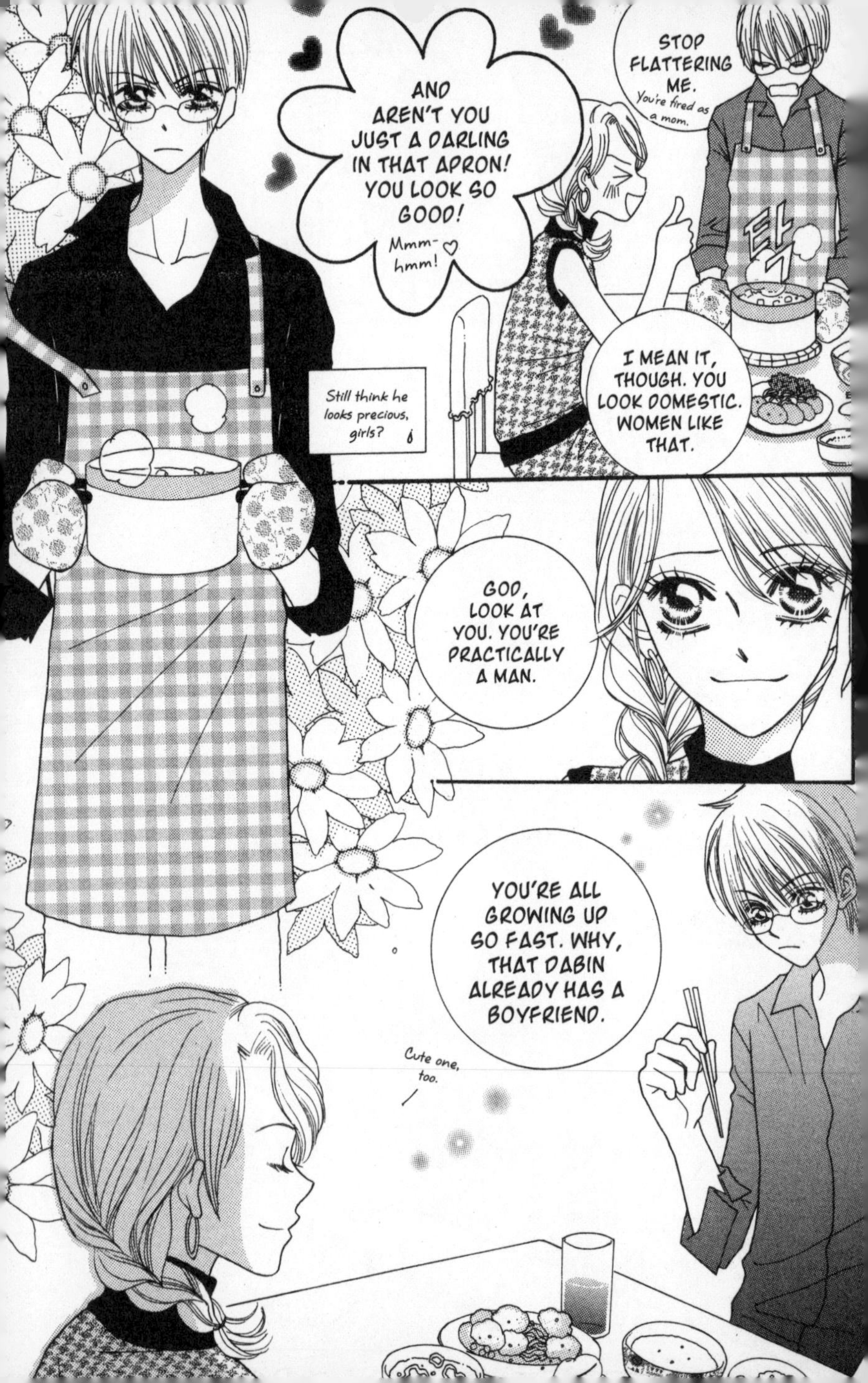
Still think he looks precious, girls?
AND AREN'T YOU JUST A DARLING IN THAT APRON! YOU LOOK SO GOOD!
Mmm-hmm! ♡
STOP FLATTERING ME.
You're fired as a mom.
I MEAN IT, THOUGH. YOU LOOK DOMESTIC. WOMEN LIKE THAT.
GOD, LOOK AT YOU. YOU'RE PRACTICALLY A MAN.
YOU'RE ALL GROWING UP SO FAST. WHY, THAT DABIN ALREADY HAS A BOYFRIEND.
Cute one, too.

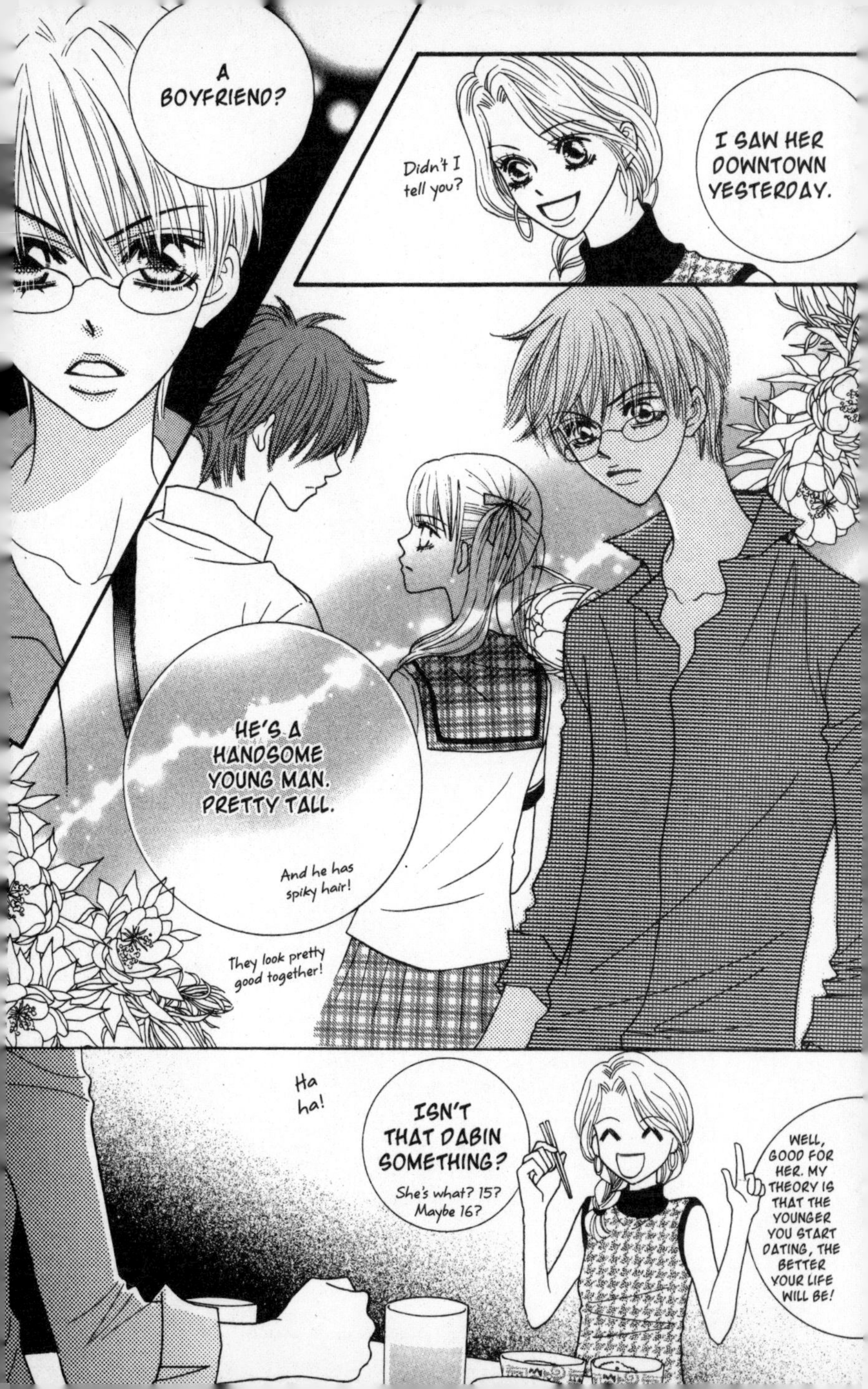
A BOYFRIEND?
Didn't I tell you?
I SAW HER DOWNTOWN YESTERDAY.
HE'S A HANDSOME YOUNG MAN. PRETTY TALL.
And he has spiky hair!
They look pretty good together!
Ha ha!
ISN'T THAT DABIN SOMETHING?
She's what? 15? Maybe 16?
WELL, GOOD FOR HER. MY THEORY IS THAT THE YOUNGER YOU START DATING, THE BETTER YOUR LIFE WILL BE!

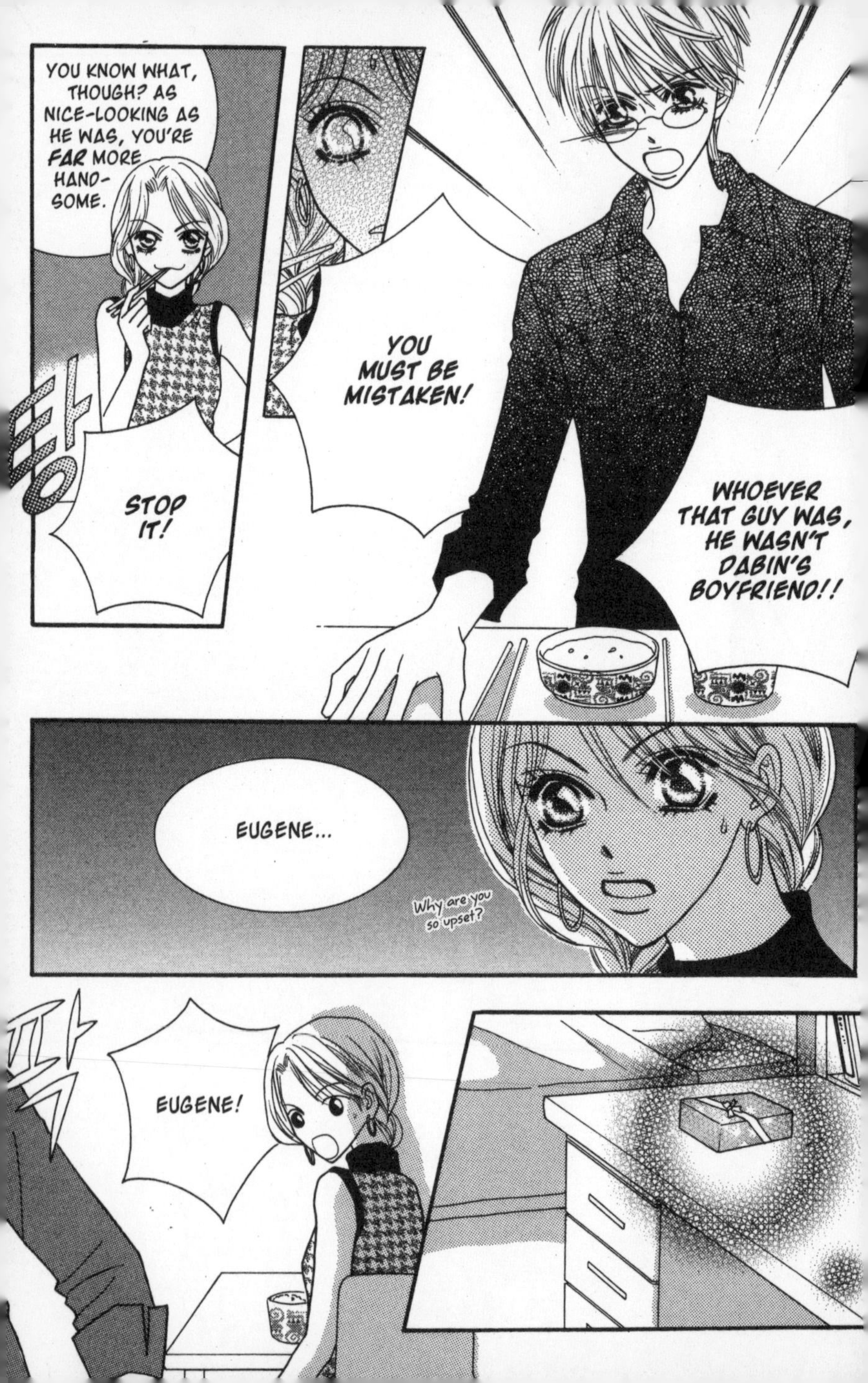

YOU KNOW WHAT, THOUGH? AS NICE-LOOKING AS HE WAS, YOU'RE **FAR** MORE HANDSOME.
STOP IT!
YOU MUST BE MISTAKEN!
WHOEVER THAT GUY WAS, HE WASN'T DABIN'S BOYFRIEND!!
EUGENE...
Why are you so upset?
EUGENE!

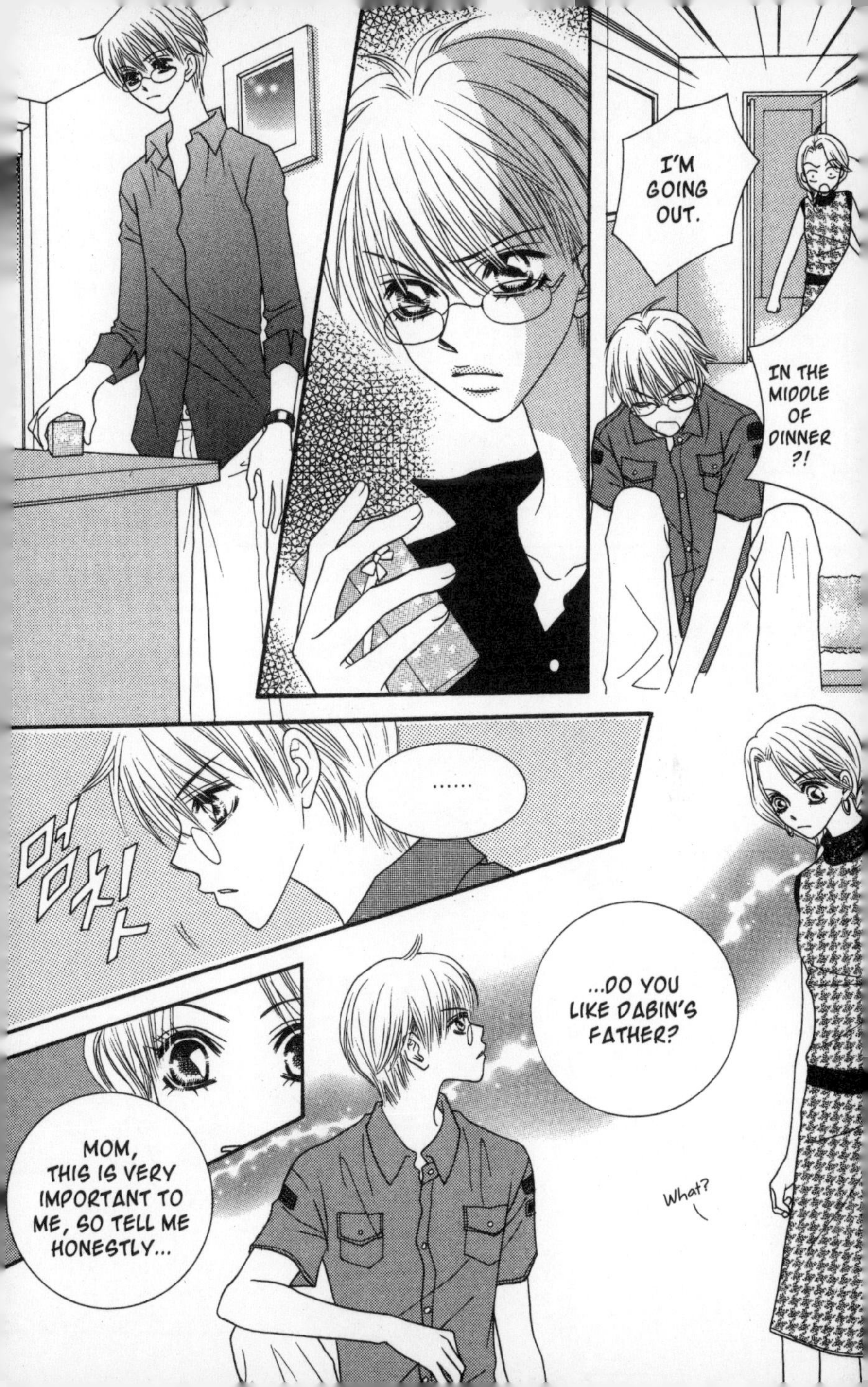
I'M GOING OUT.
IN THE MIDDLE OF DINNER ?!
......
멈칫
MOM, THIS IS VERY IMPORTANT TO ME, SO TELL ME HONESTLY...
...DO YOU LIKE DABIN'S FATHER?
What?

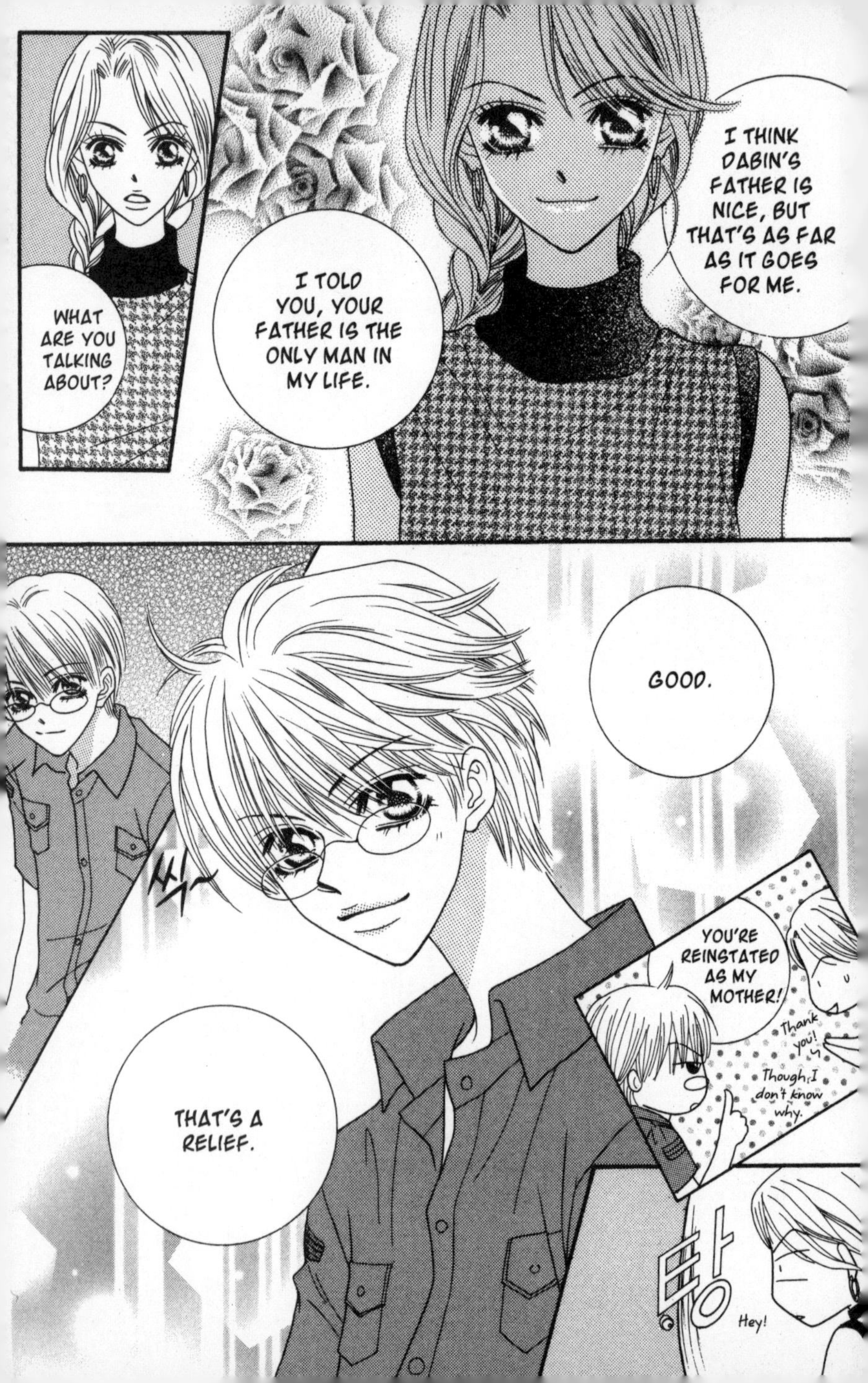

WHAT ARE YOU TALKING ABOUT?
I TOLD YOU, YOUR FATHER IS THE ONLY MAN IN MY LIFE.
I THINK DABIN'S FATHER IS NICE, BUT THAT'S AS FAR AS IT GOES FOR ME.
GOOD.
THAT'S A RELIEF.
YOU'RE REINSTATED AS MY MOTHER!
Thank you!
Though I don't know why.
Hey!

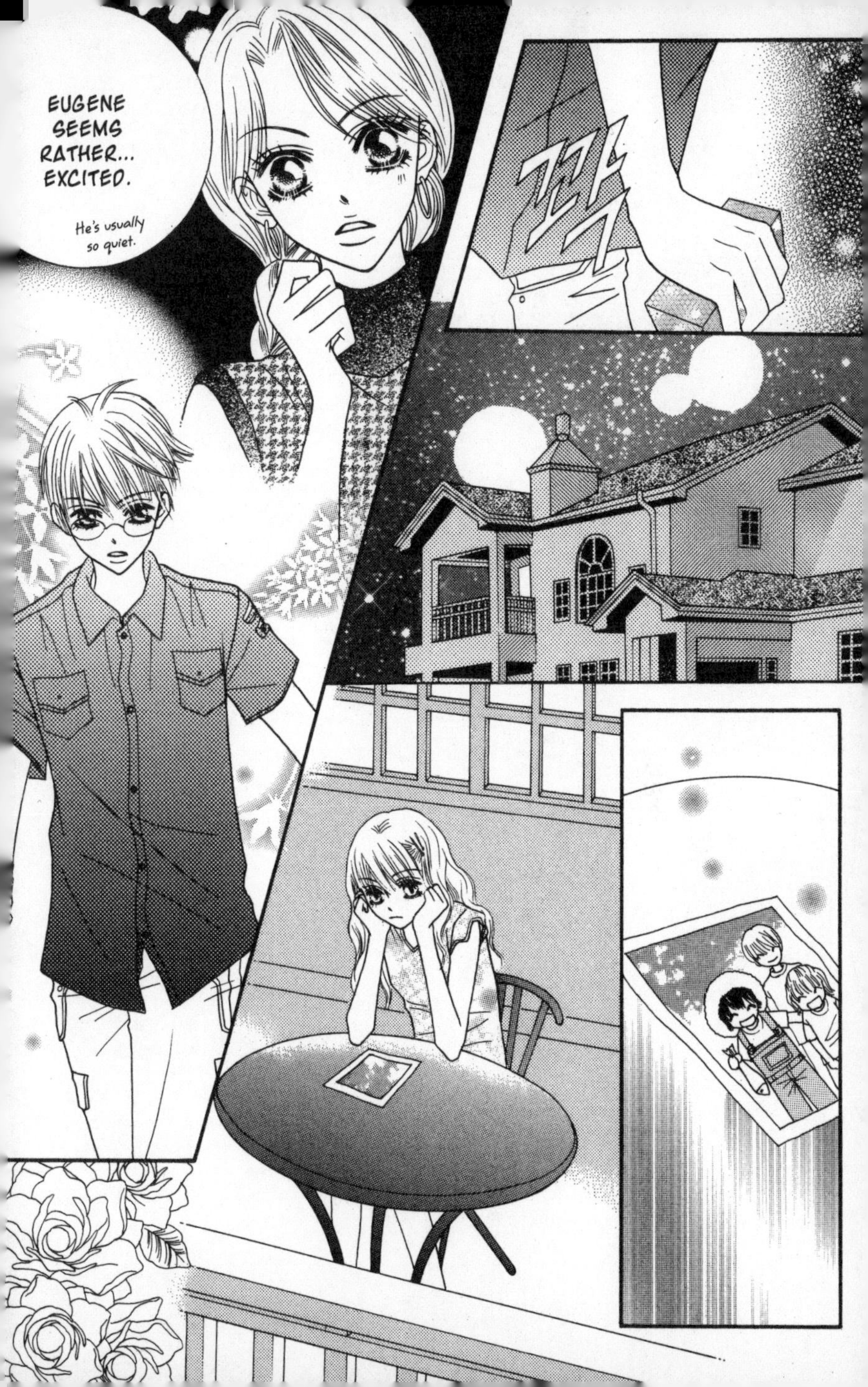
EUGENE SEEMS RATHER... EXCITED.
He's usually so quiet.

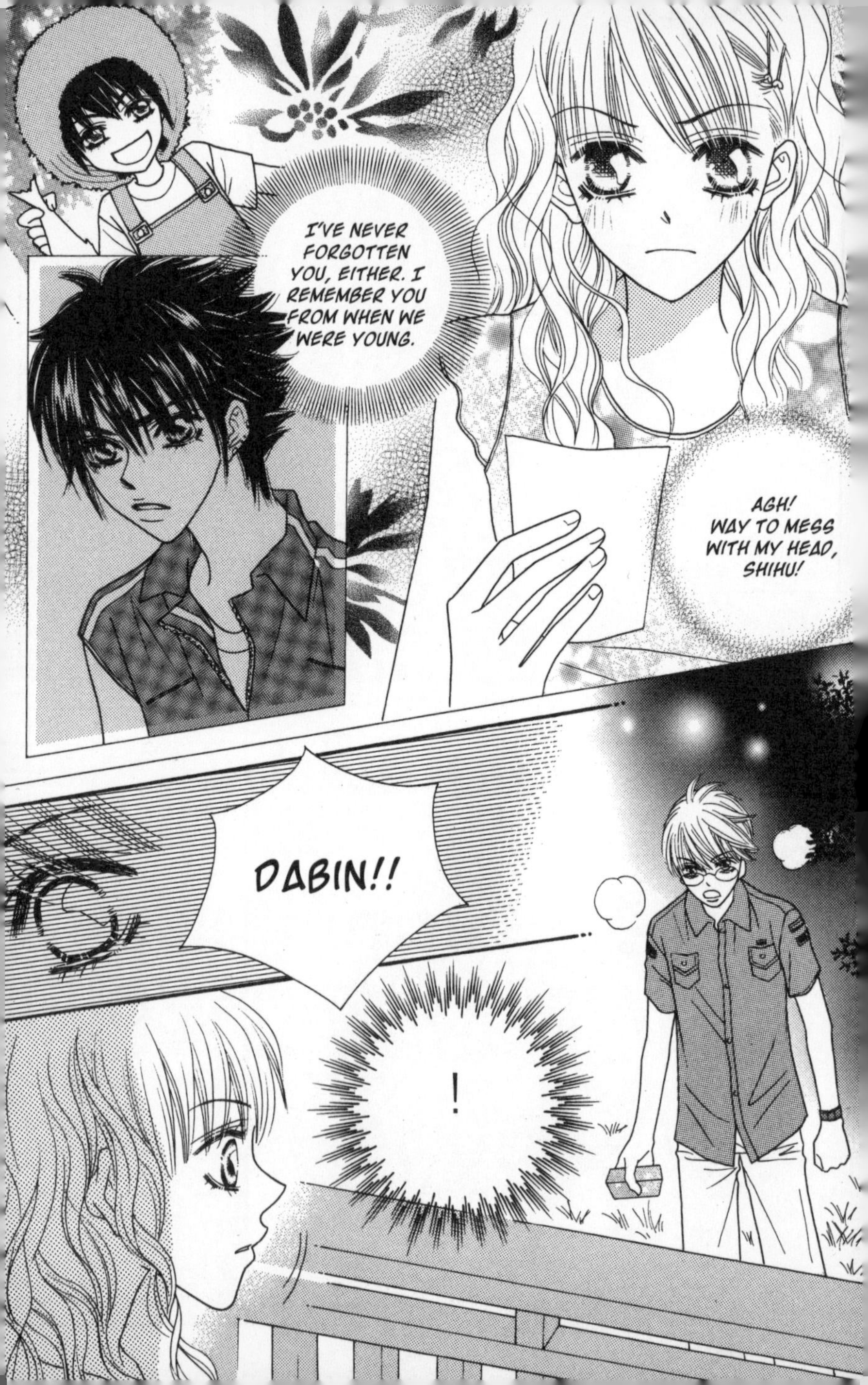
I'VE NEVER FORGOTTEN YOU, EITHER. I REMEMBER YOU FROM WHEN WE WERE YOUNG.
AGH! WAY TO MESS WITH MY HEAD, SHIHU!
DABIN!!
!

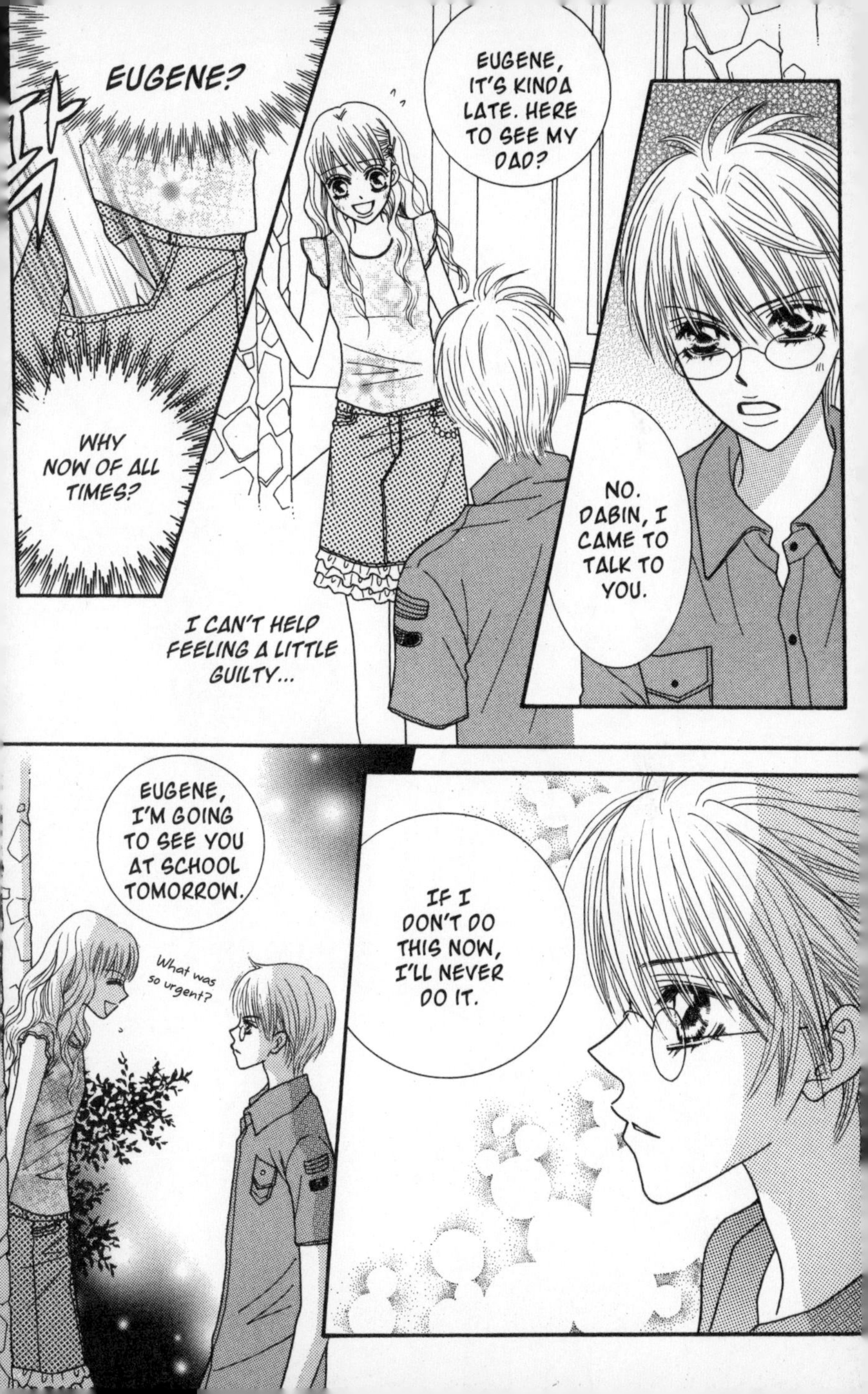
EUGENE?
WHY NOW OF ALL TIMES?
EUGENE, IT'S KINDA LATE. HERE TO SEE MY DAD?
I CAN'T HELP FEELING A LITTLE GUILTY...
NO. DABIN, I CAME TO TALK TO YOU.
EUGENE, I'M GOING TO SEE YOU AT SCHOOL TOMORROW.
What was so urgent?
IF I DON'T DO THIS NOW, I'LL NEVER DO IT.

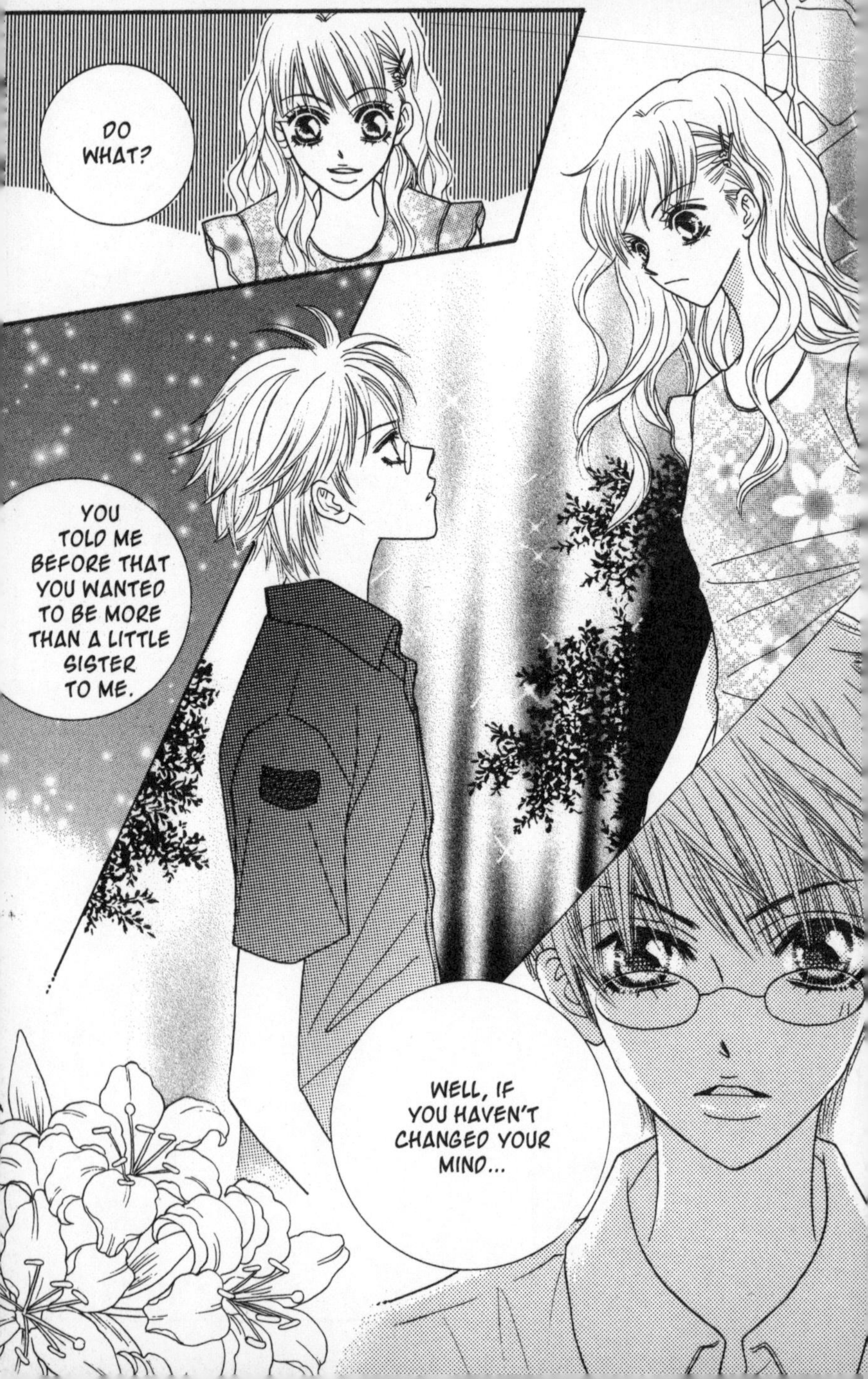
DO WHAT?
YOU TOLD ME BEFORE THAT YOU WANTED TO BE MORE THAN A LITTLE SISTER TO ME.
WELL, IF YOU HAVEN'T CHANGED YOUR MIND...

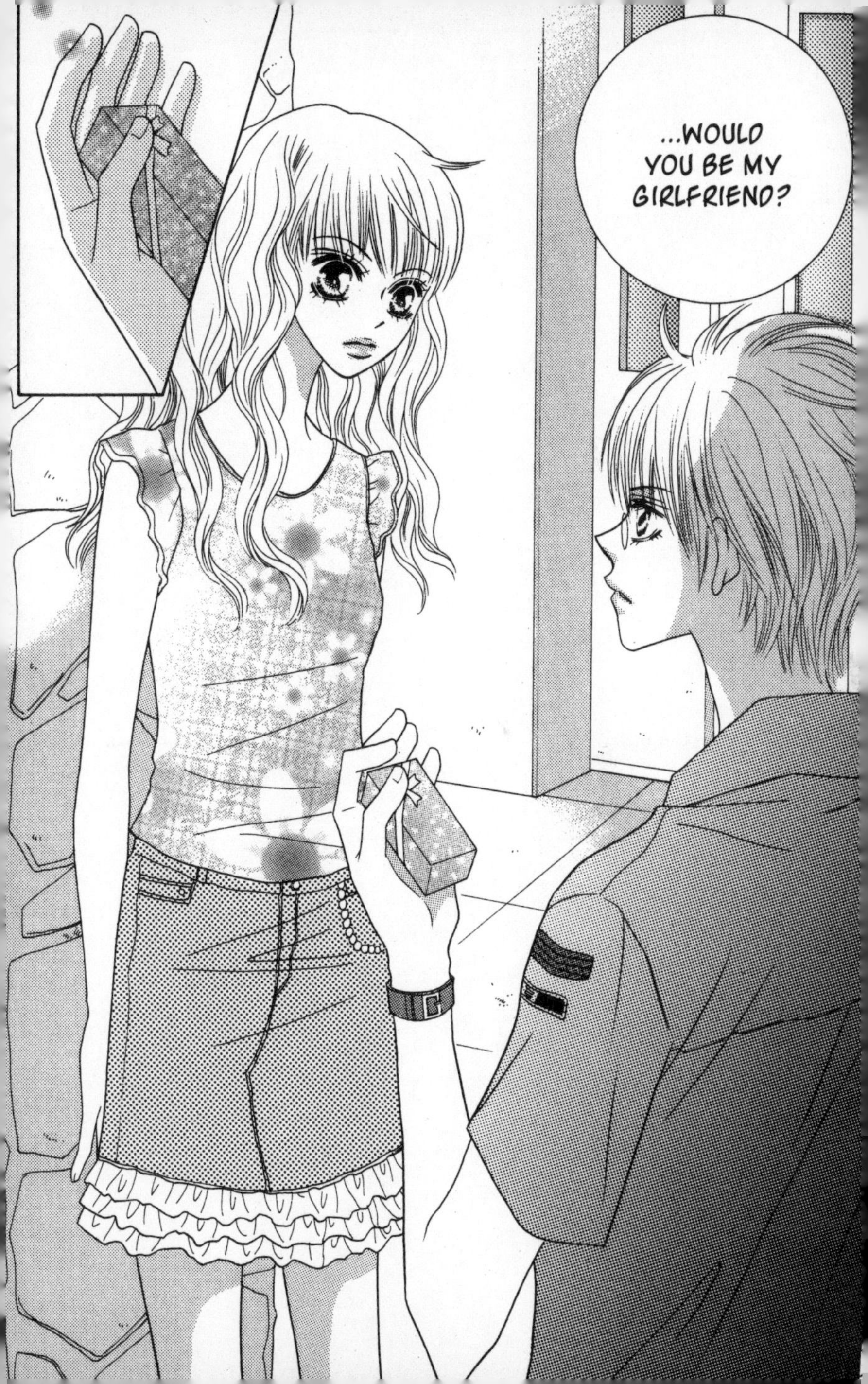
...WOULD YOU BE MY GIRLFRIEND?

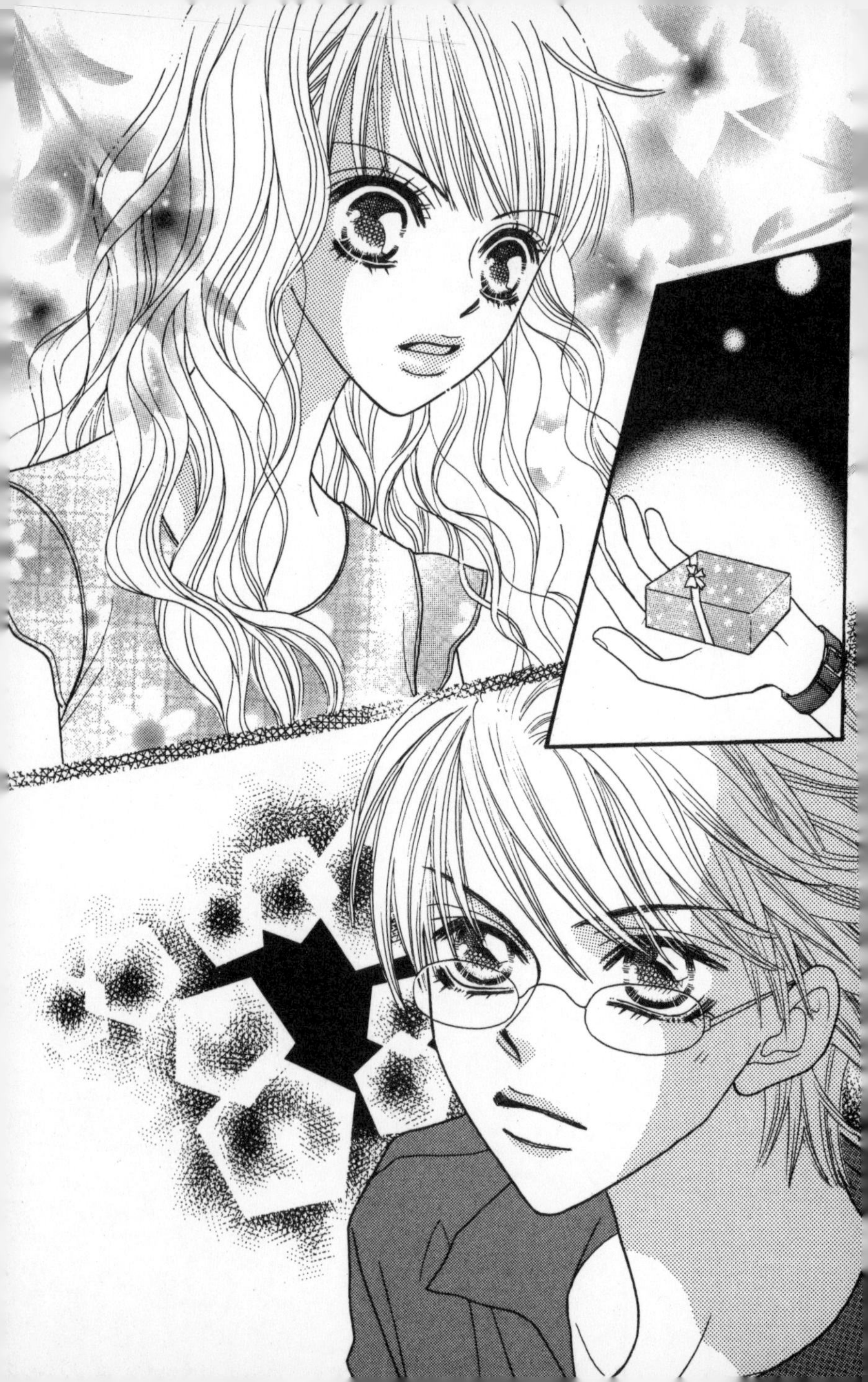

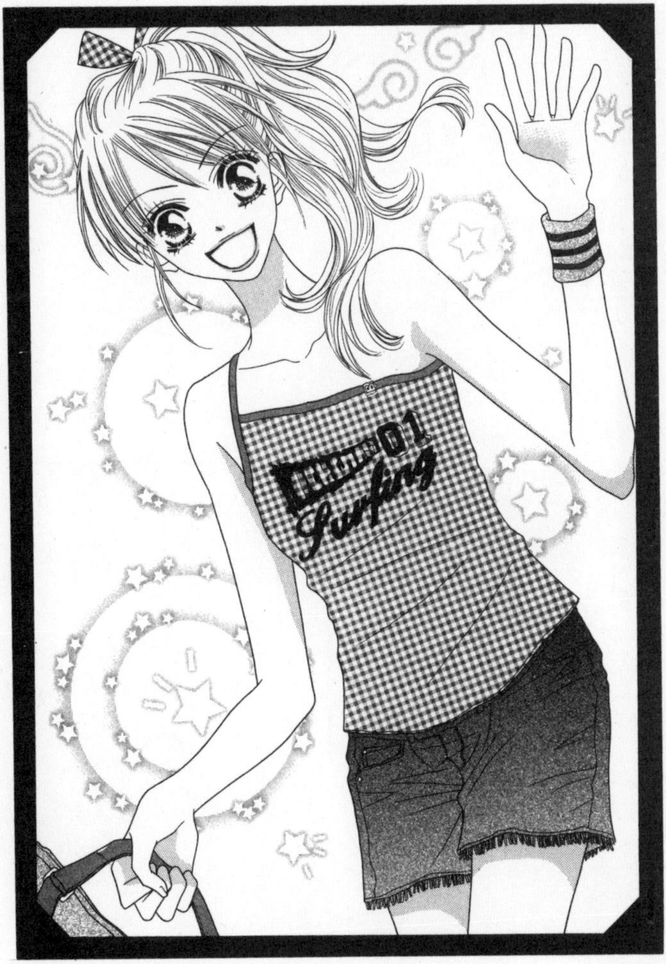
01
Surfing

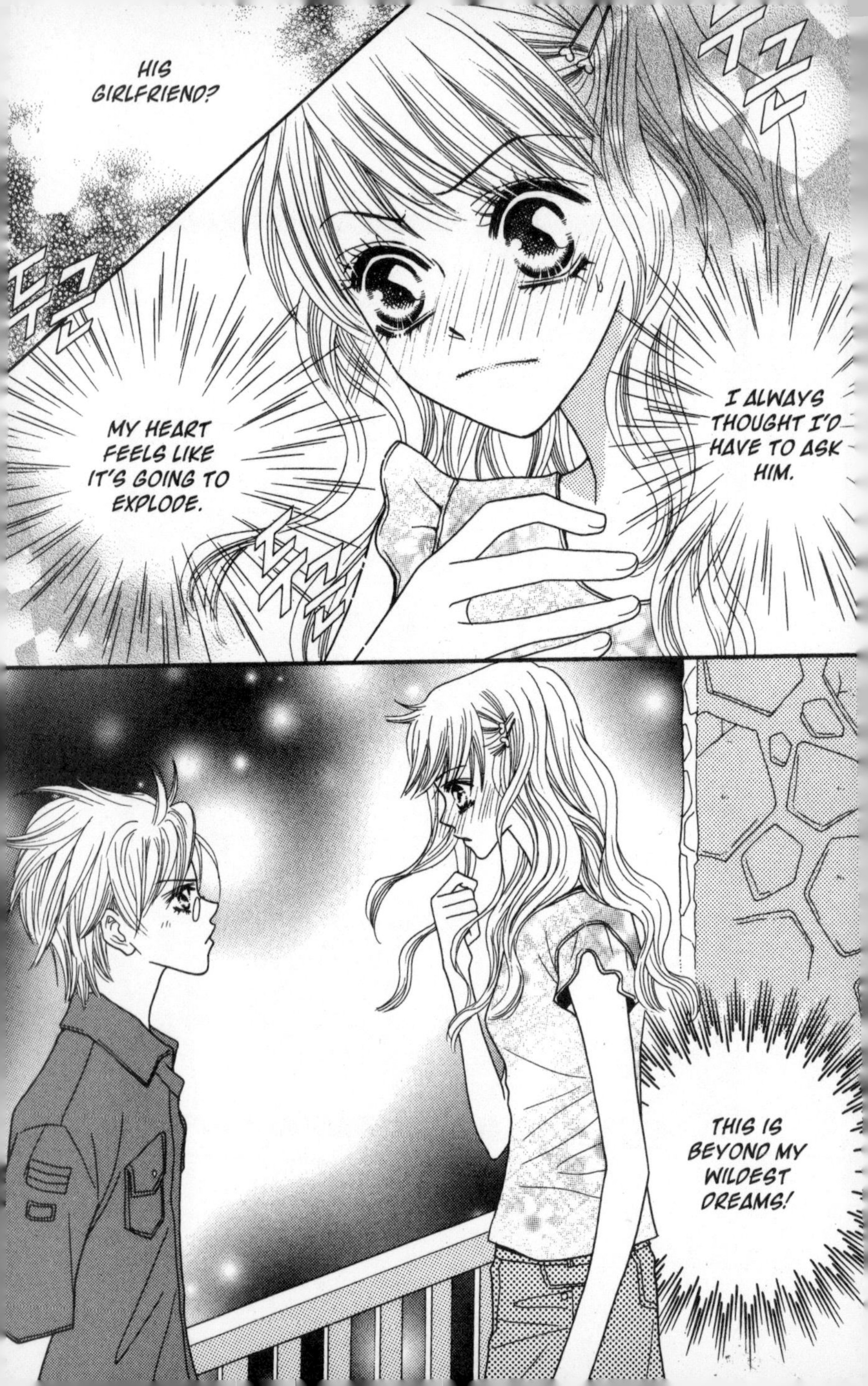
HIS GIRLFRIEND?
I ALWAYS THOUGHT I'D HAVE TO ASK HIM.
MY HEART FEELS LIKE IT'S GOING TO EXPLODE.
THIS IS BEYOND MY WILDEST DREAMS!

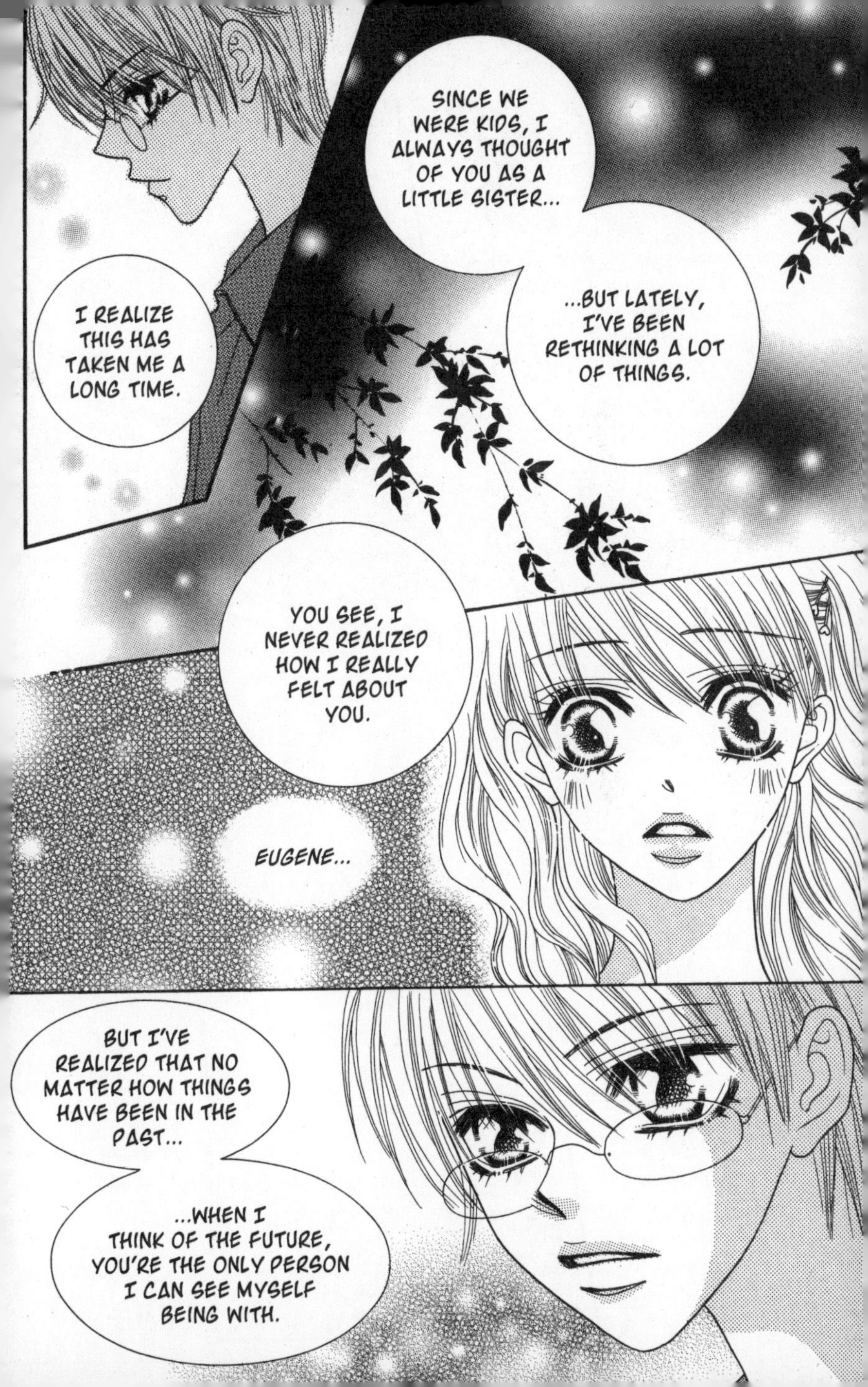
I REALIZE THIS HAS TAKEN ME A LONG TIME.
SINCE WE WERE KIDS, I ALWAYS THOUGHT OF YOU AS A LITTLE SISTER...
...BUT LATELY, I'VE BEEN RETHINKING A LOT OF THINGS.
YOU SEE, I NEVER REALIZED HOW I REALLY FELT ABOUT YOU.
EUGENE...
BUT I'VE REALIZED THAT NO MATTER HOW THINGS HAVE BEEN IN THE PAST...
...WHEN I THINK OF THE FUTURE, YOU'RE THE ONLY PERSON I CAN SEE MYSELF BEING WITH.

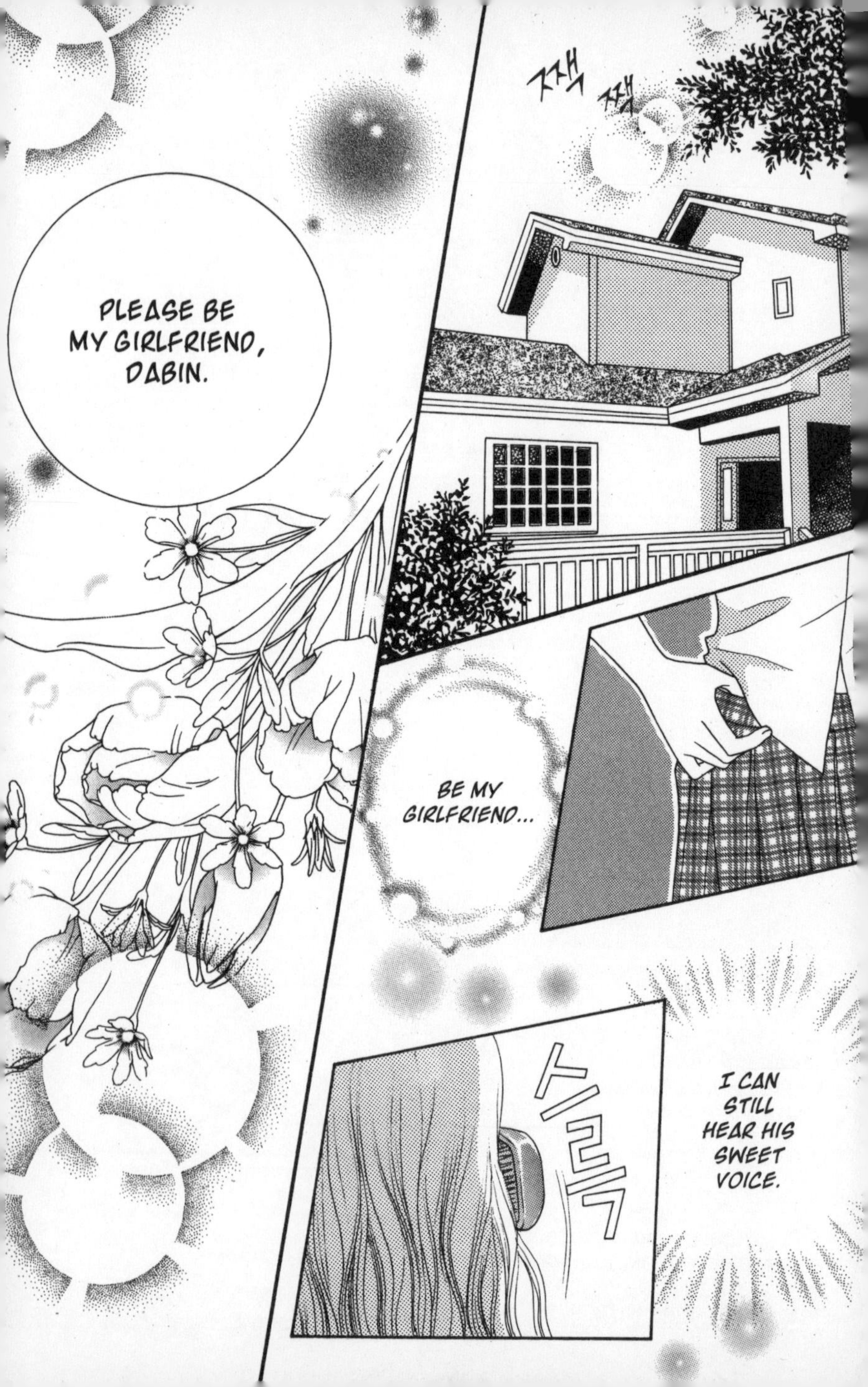
PLEASE BE MY GIRLFRIEND, DABIN.
BE MY GIRLFRIEND...
I CAN STILL HEAR HIS SWEET VOICE.

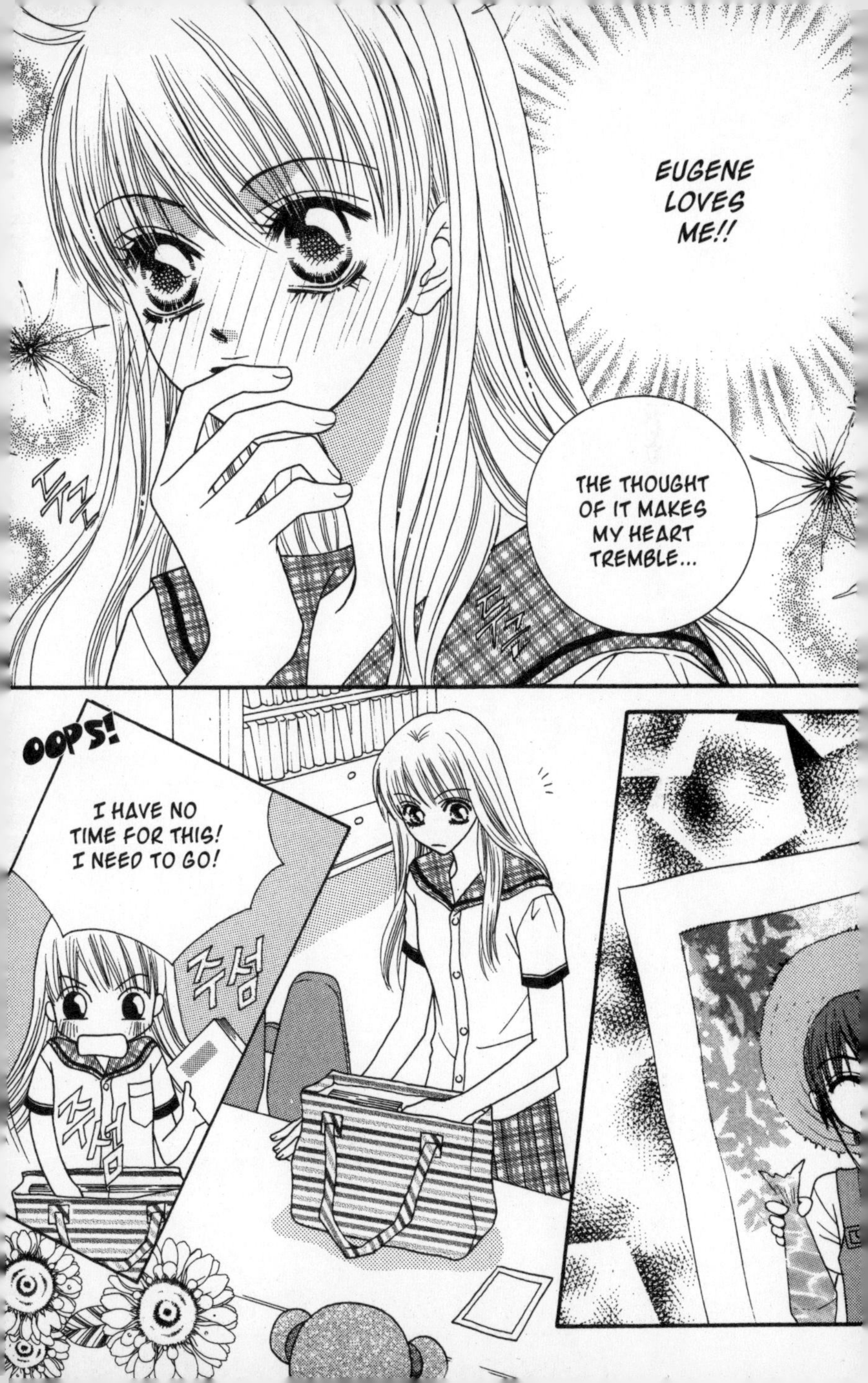
EUGENE LOVES ME!!
THE THOUGHT OF IT MAKES MY HEART TREMBLE...
OOPS!
I HAVE NO TIME FOR THIS! I NEED TO GO!

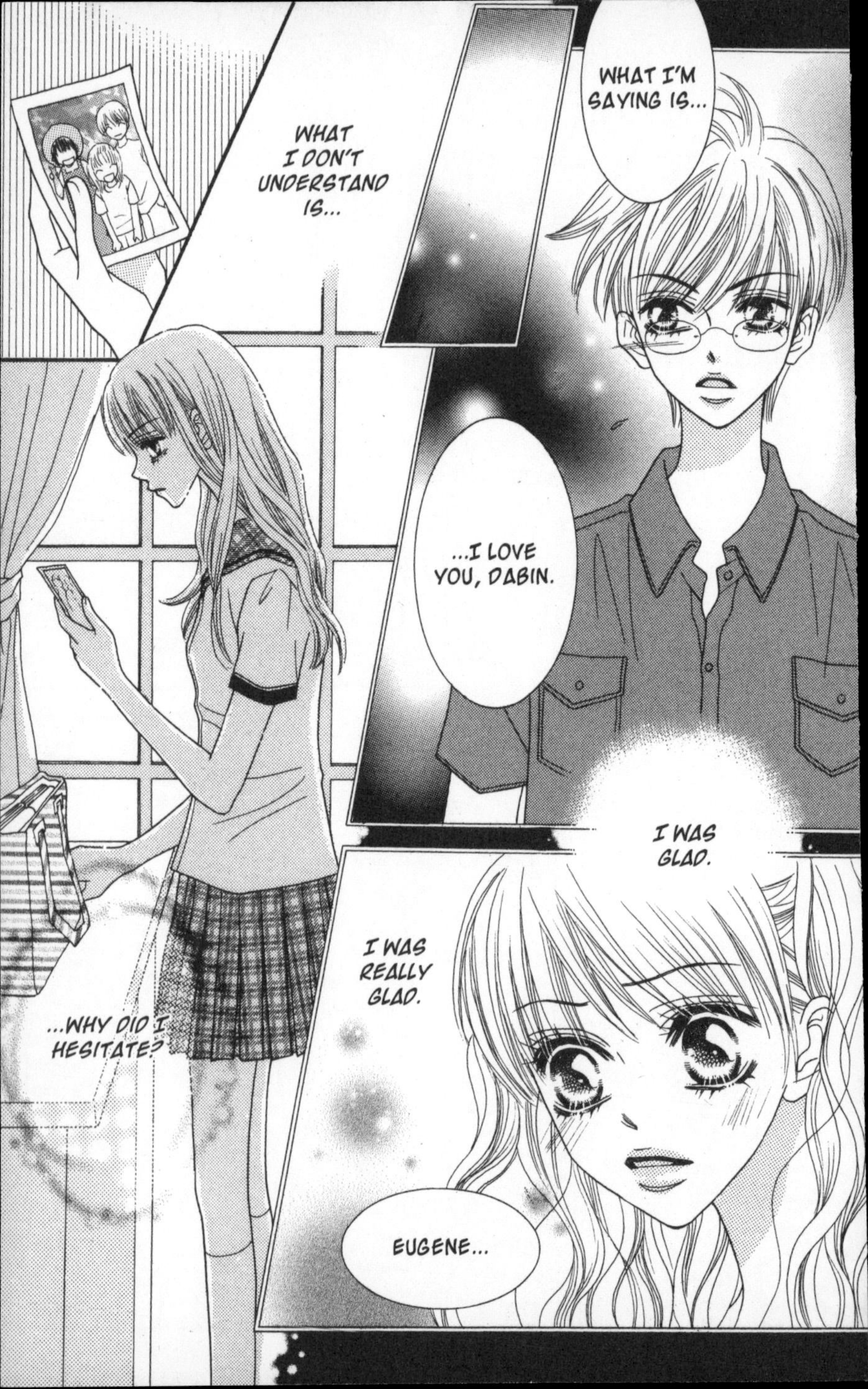
WHAT I DON'T UNDERSTAND IS...
...WHY DID I HESITATE?
WHAT I'M SAYING IS...
...I LOVE YOU, DABIN.
I WAS GLAD.
I WAS REALLY GLAD.
EUGENE...

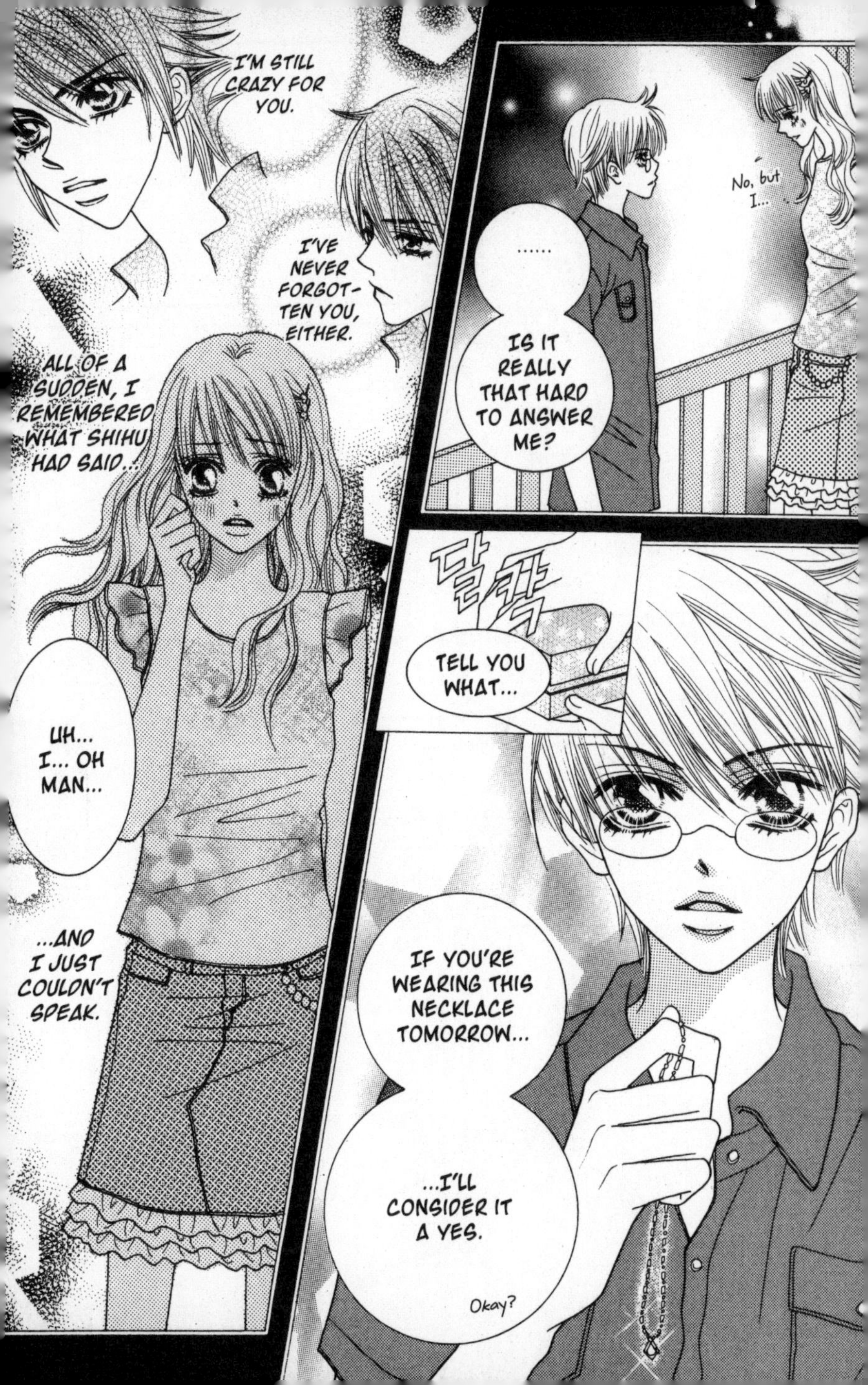
I'M STILL CRAZY FOR YOU.
I'VE NEVER FORGOT-TEN YOU, EITHER.
ALL OF A SUDDEN, I REMEMBERED WHAT SHIHU HAD SAID...
UH... I... OH MAN...
...AND I JUST COULDN'T SPEAK.
......
IS IT REALLY THAT HARD TO ANSWER ME?
No, but I...
달칵
TELL YOU WHAT...
IF YOU'RE WEARING THIS NECKLACE TOMORROW...
...I'LL CONSIDER IT A YES.
Okay?

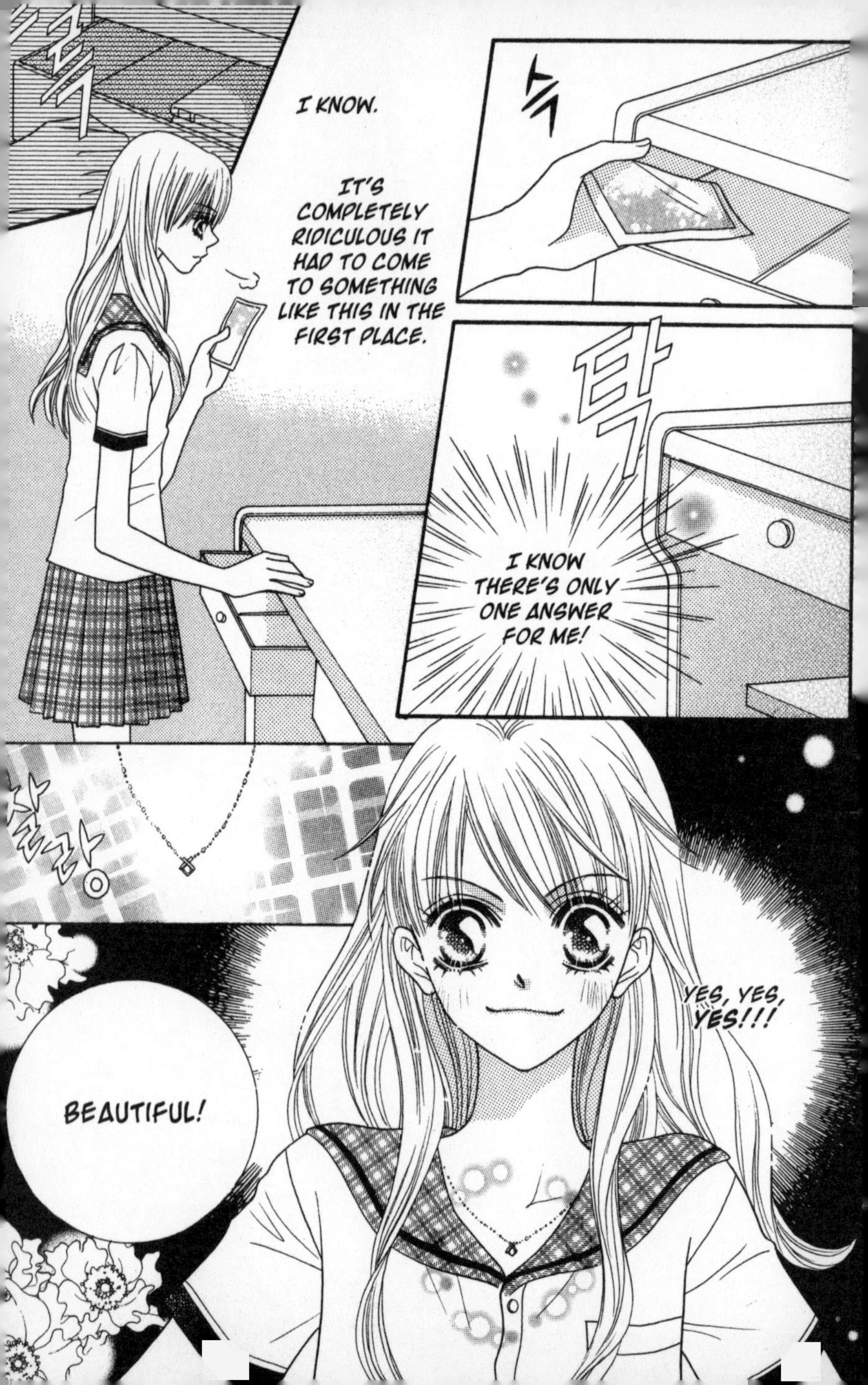
I KNOW.
IT'S COMPLETELY RIDICULOUS IT HAD TO COME TO SOMETHING LIKE THIS IN THE FIRST PLACE.
탁
I KNOW THERE'S ONLY ONE ANSWER FOR ME!
BEAUTIFUL!
YES, YES, YES!!!

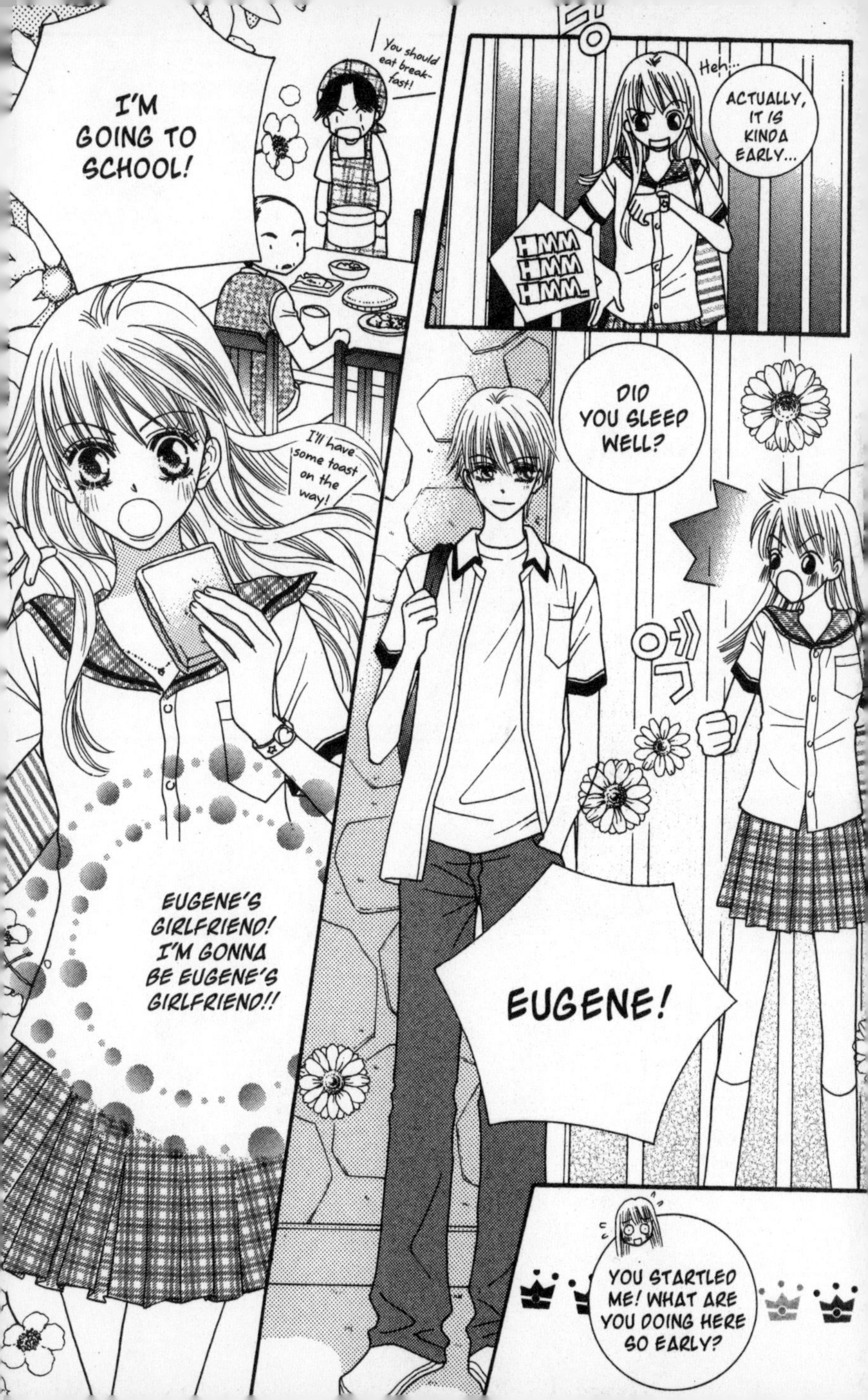

I'M GOING TO SCHOOL!
You should eat breakfast!
I'll have some toast on the way!
EUGENE'S GIRLFRIEND! I'M GONNA BE EUGENE'S GIRLFRIEND!!
Heh...
ACTUALLY, IT IS KINDA EARLY...
HMM HMM HMM...
DID YOU SLEEP WELL?
억
EUGENE!
YOU STARTLED ME! WHAT ARE YOU DOING HERE SO EARLY?

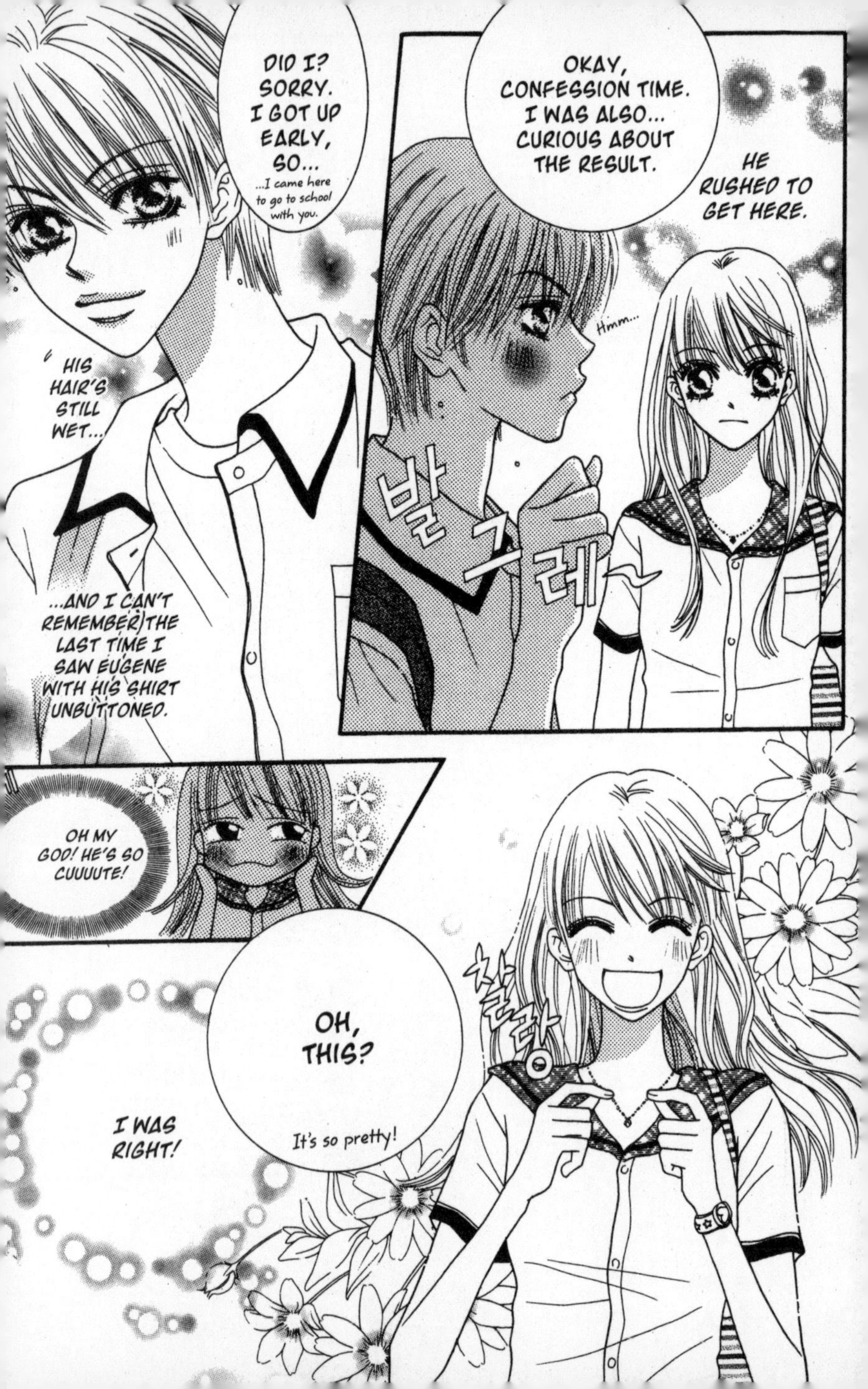
DID I? SORRY. I GOT UP EARLY, SO...
...I came here to go to school with you.
HIS HAIR'S STILL WET...
...AND I CAN'T REMEMBER THE LAST TIME I SAW EUGENE WITH HIS SHIRT UNBUTTONED.
OKAY, CONFESSION TIME. I WAS ALSO... CURIOUS ABOUT THE RESULT.
HE RUSHED TO GET HERE.
Hmm...
발그레~
OH MY GOD! HE'S SO CUUUUTE!
I WAS RIGHT!
OH, THIS?
It's so pretty!
찰랑

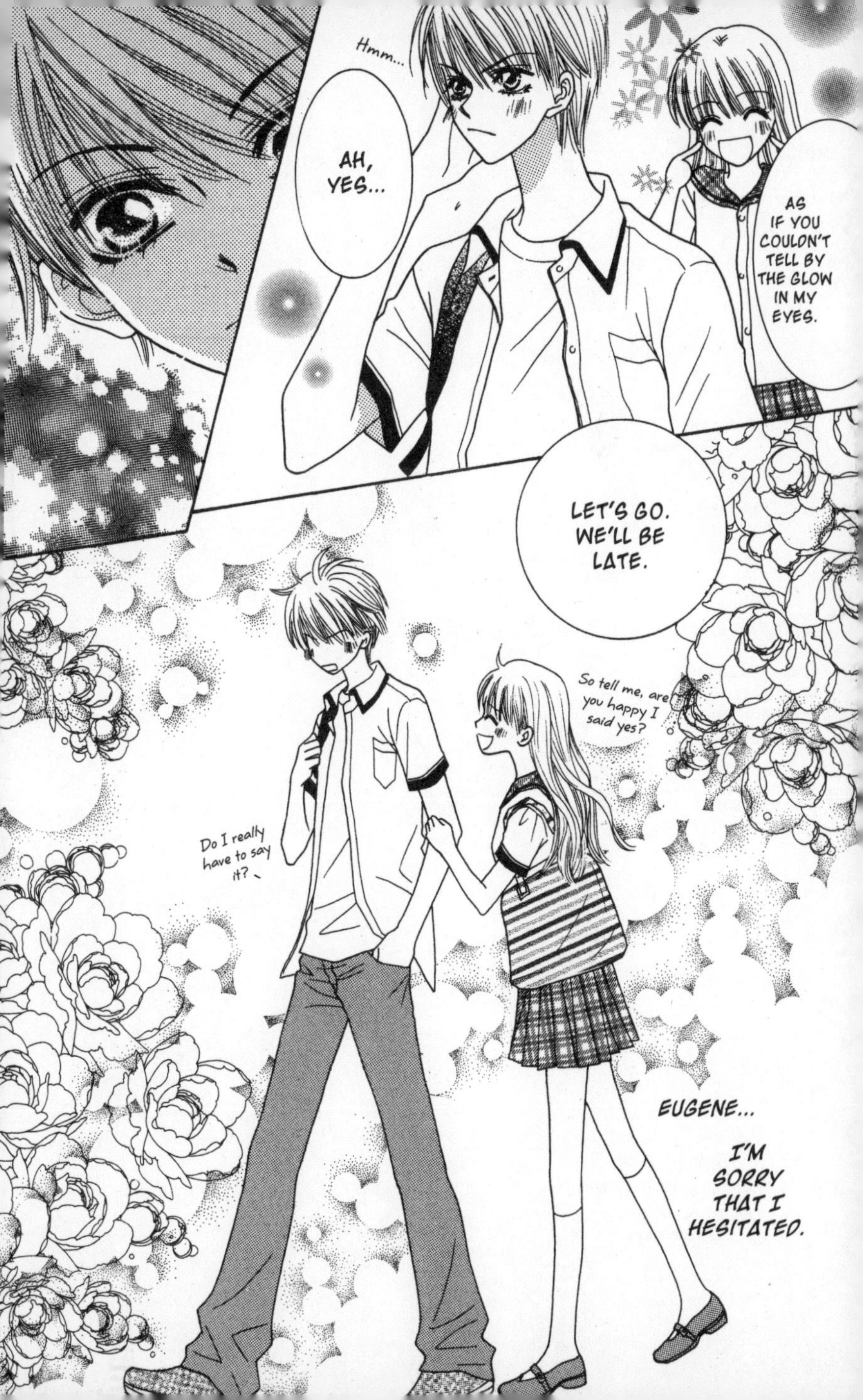
Hmm...
AH, YES...
AS IF YOU COULDN'T TELL BY THE GLOW IN MY EYES.
LET'S GO. WE'LL BE LATE.
So tell me, are you happy I said yes?
Do I really have to say it?
EUGENE...
I'M SORRY THAT I HESITATED.

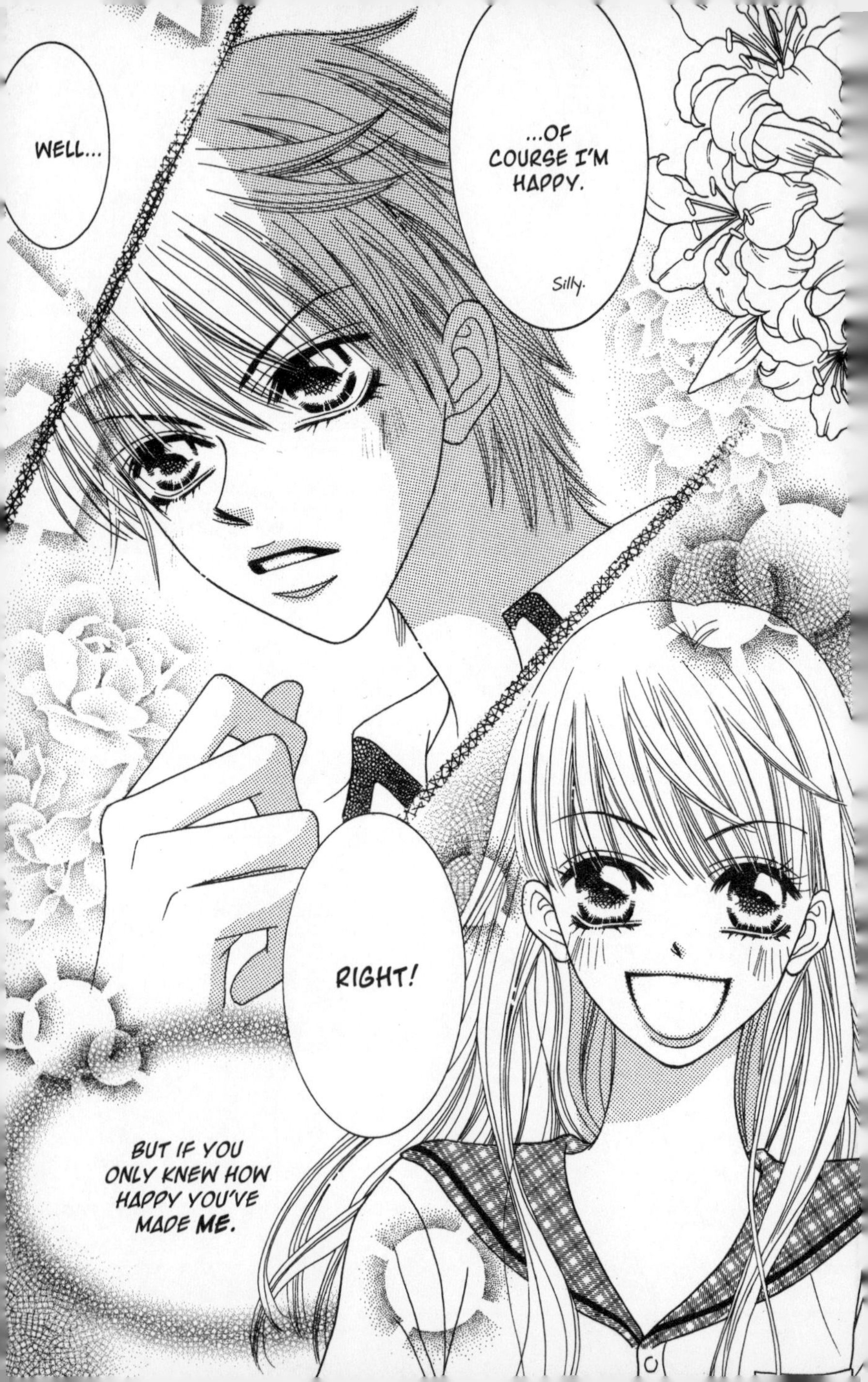
WELL...
...OF COURSE I'M HAPPY.
Silly.
RIGHT!
BUT IF YOU ONLY KNEW HOW HAPPY YOU'VE MADE ME.

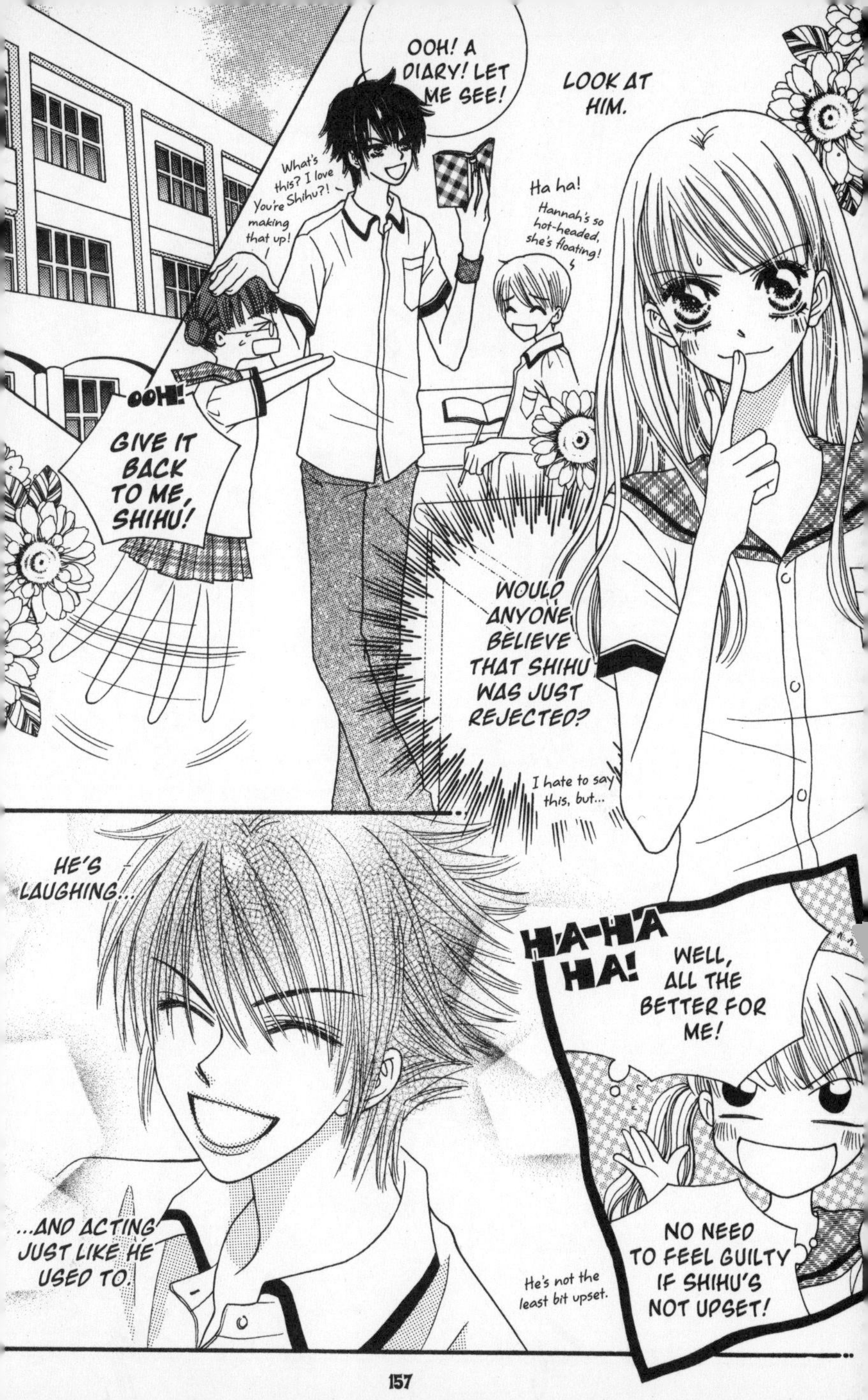

OOH! A DIARY! LET ME SEE!
What's this? I love Shihu?!
You're making that up!
OOH!
GIVE IT BACK TO ME, SHIHU!
Ha ha! Hannah's so hot-headed, she's floating!
LOOK AT HIM.
WOULD ANYONE BELIEVE THAT SHIHU WAS JUST REJECTED?
I hate to say this, but...
HE'S LAUGHING...
...AND ACTING JUST LIKE HE USED TO.
He's not the least bit upset.
HA-HA HA!
WELL, ALL THE BETTER FOR ME!
NO NEED TO FEEL GUILTY IF SHIHU'S NOT UPSET!

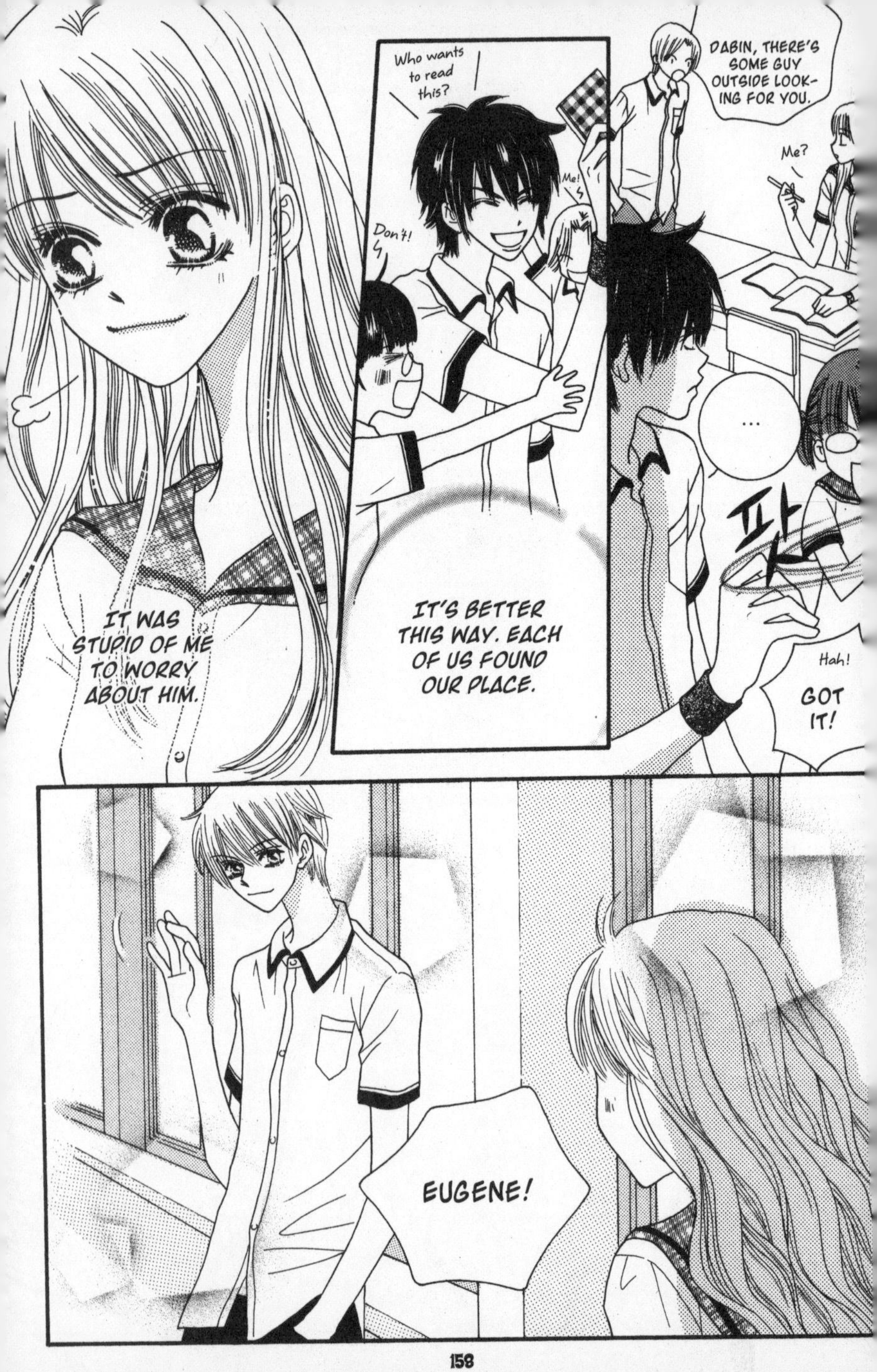
IT WAS STUPID OF ME TO WORRY ABOUT HIM.
Who wants to read this?
Me!
Don't!
IT'S BETTER THIS WAY. EACH OF US FOUND OUR PLACE.
DABIN, THERE'S SOME GUY OUTSIDE LOOKING FOR YOU.
Me?
...
Hah!
GOT IT!
EUGENE!

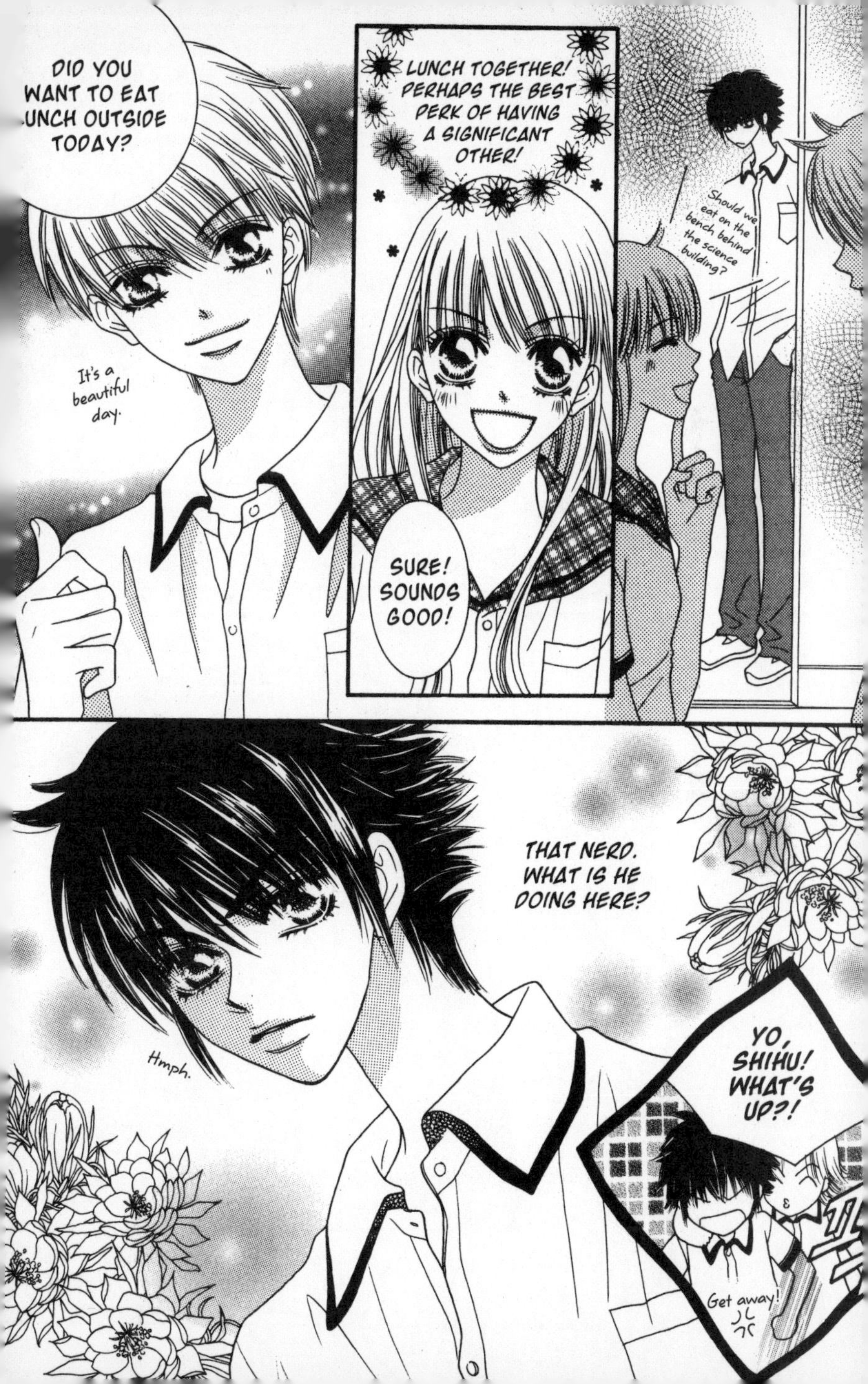
DID YOU WANT TO EAT UNCH OUTSIDE TODAY?
It's a beautiful day.
LUNCH TOGETHER! PERHAPS THE BEST PERK OF HAVING A SIGNIFICANT OTHER!
SURE! SOUNDS GOOD!
Should we eat on the bench behind the science building?
THAT NERD. WHAT IS HE DOING HERE?
Hmph.
YO, SHIHU! WHAT'S UP?!
Get away!

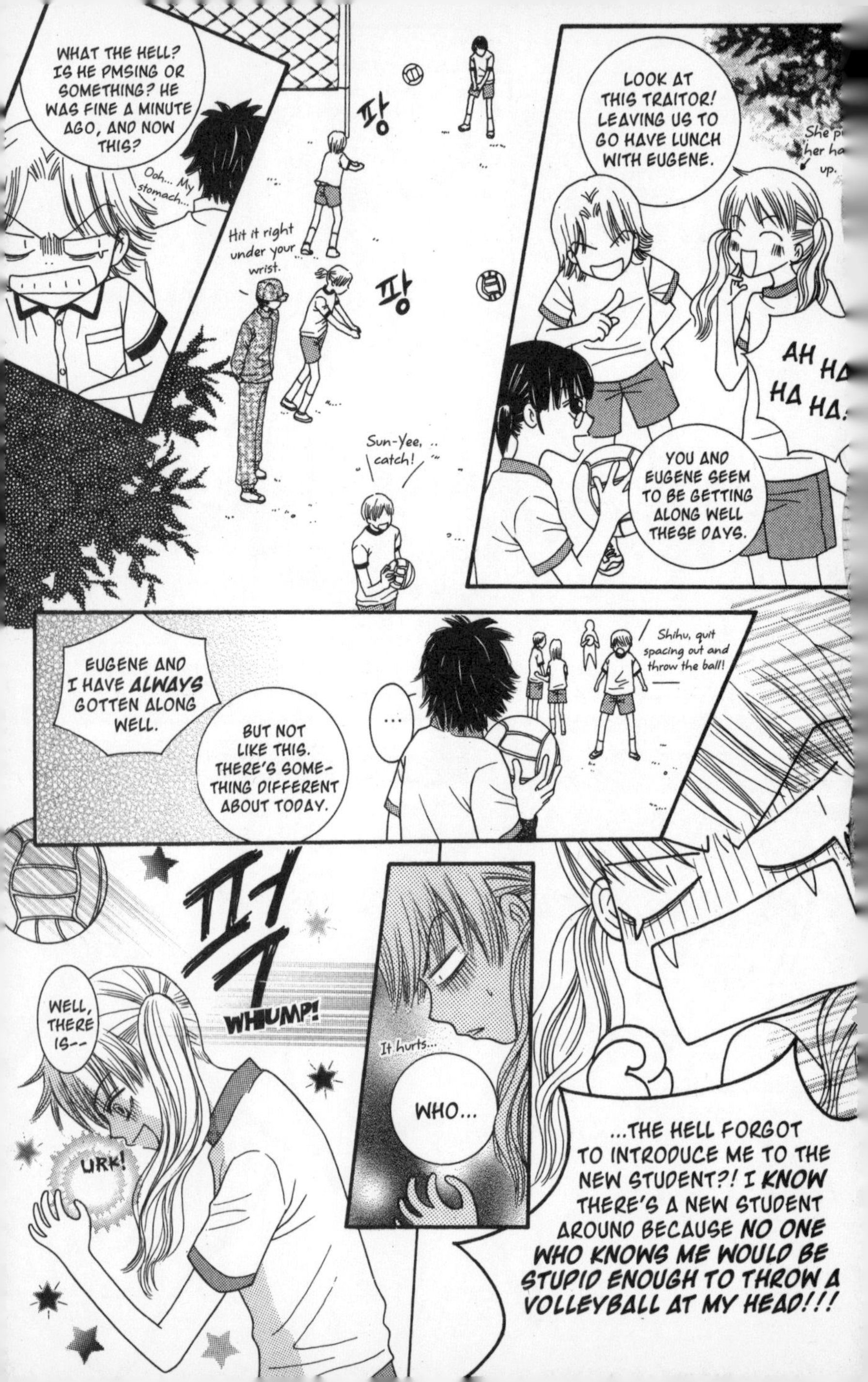
WHAT THE HELL? IS HE PMSING OR SOMETHING? HE WAS FINE A MINUTE AGO, AND NOW THIS?
Ooh... My stomach...
팡
Hit it right under your wrist.
팡
Sun-Yee, catch!
LOOK AT THIS TRAITOR! LEAVING US TO GO HAVE LUNCH WITH EUGENE.
She p her ha up.
AH HA HA HA
YOU AND EUGENE SEEM TO BE GETTING ALONG WELL THESE DAYS.
EUGENE AND I HAVE ALWAYS GOTTEN ALONG WELL.
...
BUT NOT LIKE THIS. THERE'S SOME-THING DIFFERENT ABOUT TODAY.
Shihu, quit spacing out and throw the ball!
퍽
WHUMP!
WELL, THERE IS--
URK!
It hurts...
WHO...
...THE HELL FORGOT TO INTRODUCE ME TO THE NEW STUDENT?! I KNOW THERE'S A NEW STUDENT AROUND BECAUSE NO ONE WHO KNOWS ME WOULD BE STUPID ENOUGH TO THROW A VOLLEYBALL AT MY HEAD!!!

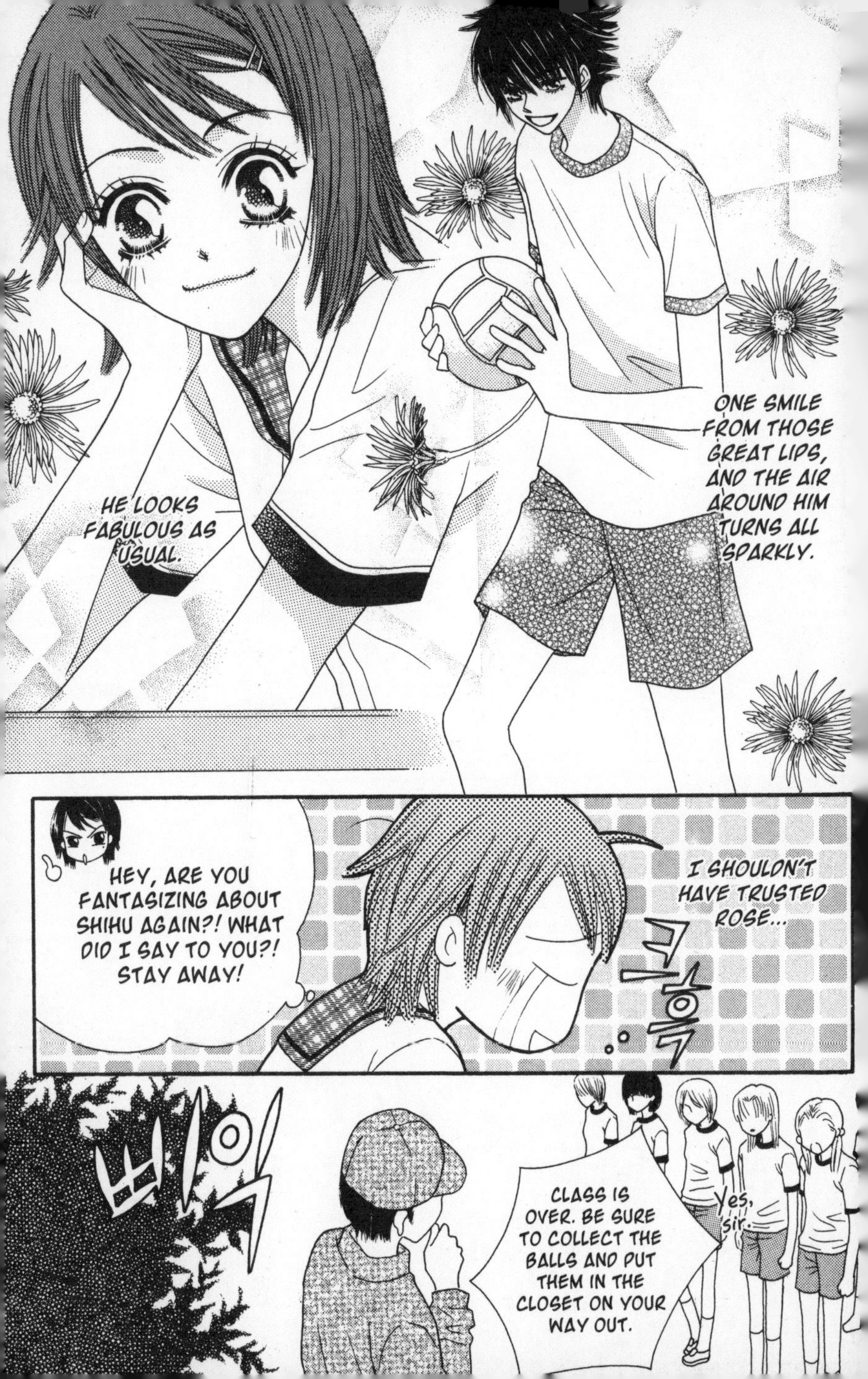

HE LOOKS FABULOUS AS USUAL.
ONE SMILE FROM THOSE GREAT LIPS, AND THE AIR AROUND HIM TURNS ALL SPARKLY.
HEY, ARE YOU FANTASIZING ABOUT SHIHU AGAIN?! WHAT DID I SAY TO YOU?! STAY AWAY!
I SHOULDN'T HAVE TRUSTED ROSE...
CLASS IS OVER. BE SURE TO COLLECT THE BALLS AND PUT THEM IN THE CLOSET ON YOUR WAY OUT.
Yes, sir.

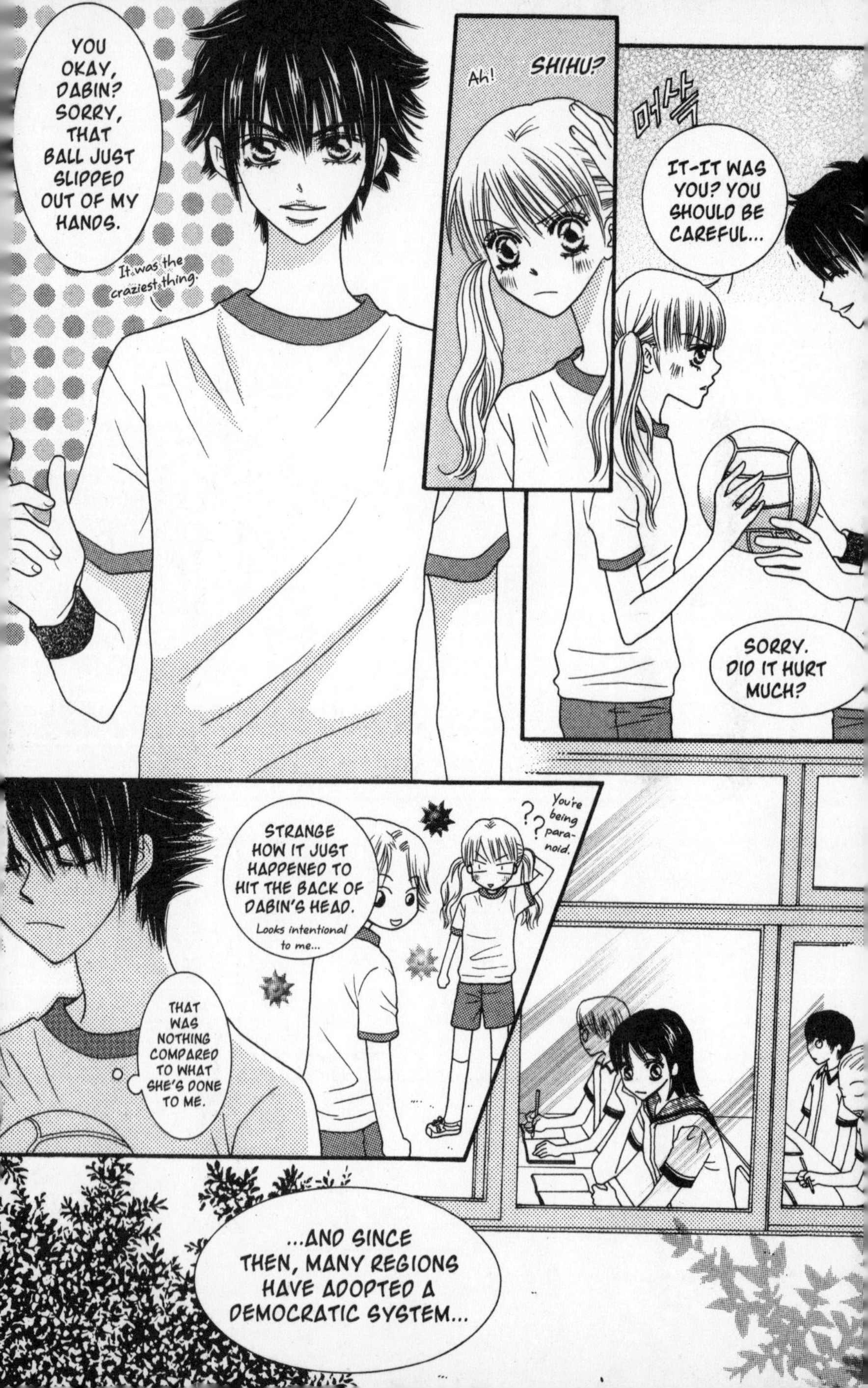
YOU OKAY, DABIN? SORRY, THAT BALL JUST SLIPPED OUT OF MY HANDS.
It was the craziest thing.
Ah!
SHIHU?
머쓱
IT-IT WAS YOU? YOU SHOULD BE CAREFUL...
SORRY. DID IT HURT MUCH?
STRANGE HOW IT JUST HAPPENED TO HIT THE BACK OF DABIN'S HEAD.
Looks intentional to me...
You're being paranoid.
THAT WAS NOTHING COMPARED TO WHAT SHE'S DONE TO ME.
...AND SINCE THEN, MANY REGIONS HAVE ADOPTED A DEMOCRATIC SYSTEM...

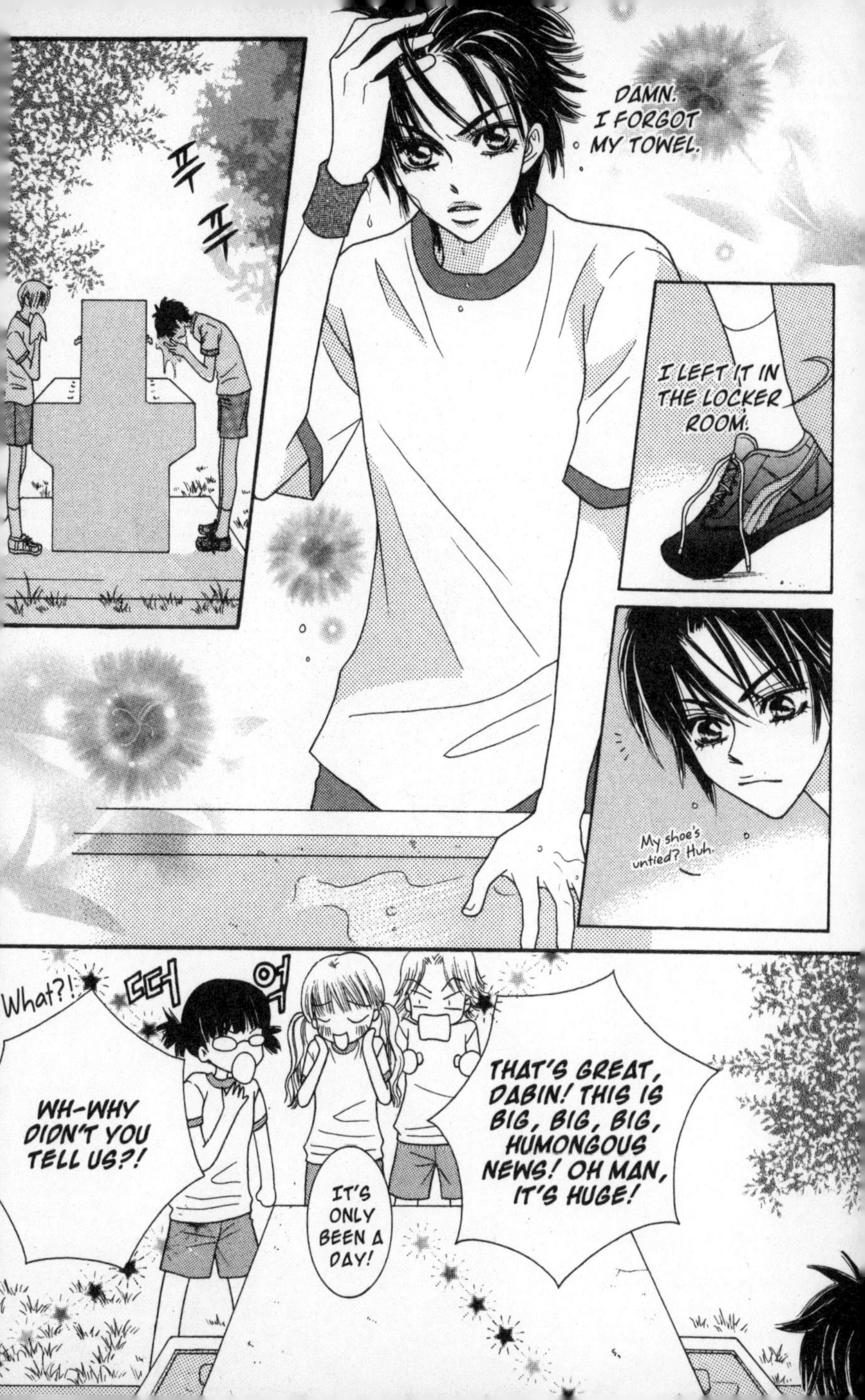
푸 푸
DAMN. I FORGOT MY TOWEL.
I LEFT IT IN THE LOCKER ROOM.
My shoe's untied? Huh.
What?!
떠억
WH-WHY DIDN'T YOU TELL US?!
IT'S ONLY BEEN A DAY!
THAT'S GREAT, DABIN! THIS IS BIG, BIG, BIG, HUMONGOUS NEWS! OH MAN, IT'S HUGE!

SO TELL US HOW IT HAPPENED? HOW DID THE NEW GIRL SNAG THE MOST ELIGIBLE BACHELOR IN SCHOOL?
찰박
C'MON, DABIN, SPILL IT!
HA HA!
Shit.
IS THAT DABIN?
I CAN'T GET UP NOW.
I MEAN, FOR THE LIFE OF ME, I NEVER THOUGHT YOU'D PULL IT OFF. I NEVER FOR ONE MOMENT THOUGHT YOU'D GET EUGENE TO BE YOUR BOYFRIEND.

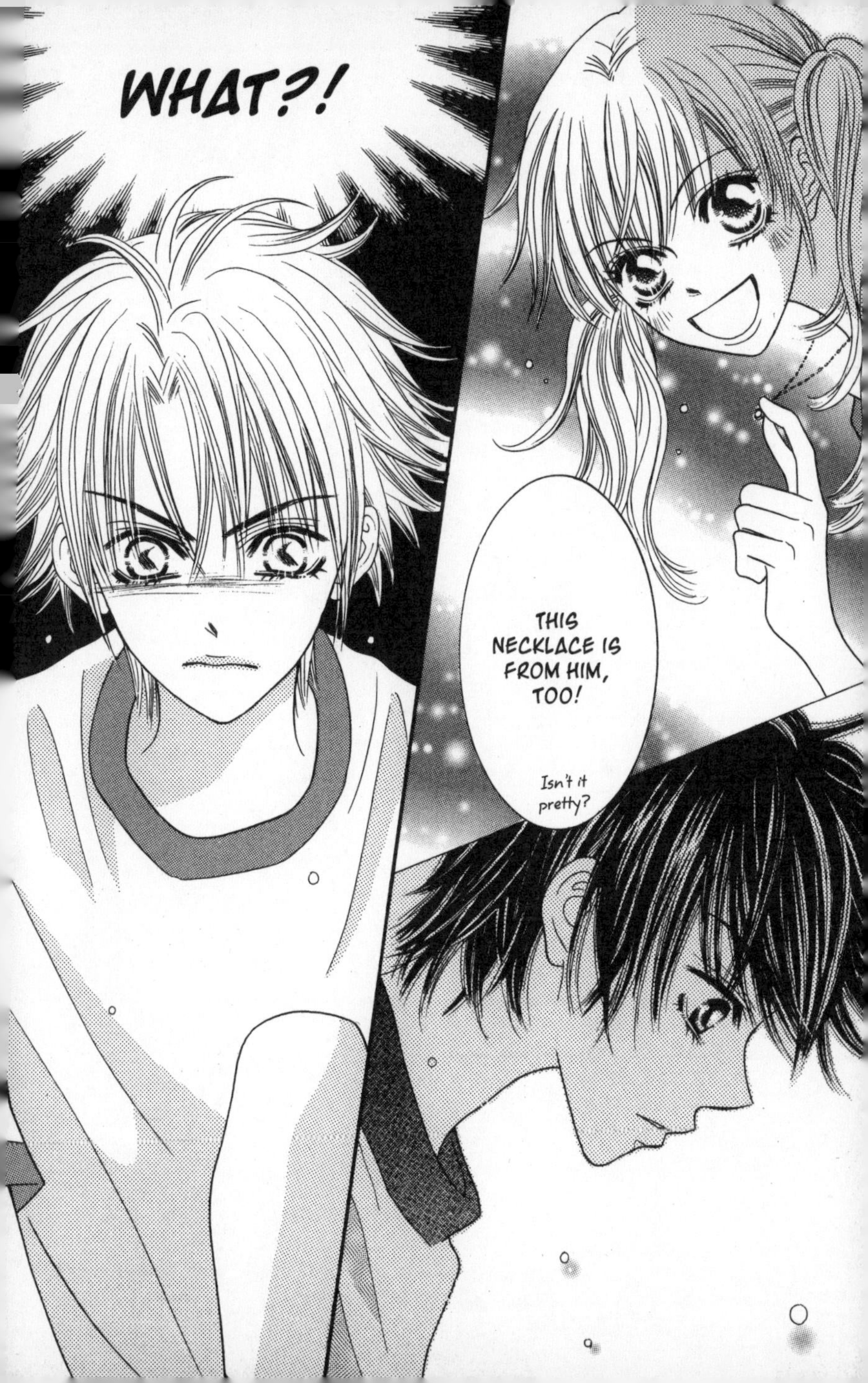
WHAT?!
THIS NECKLACE IS FROM HIM, TOO!
Isn't it pretty?

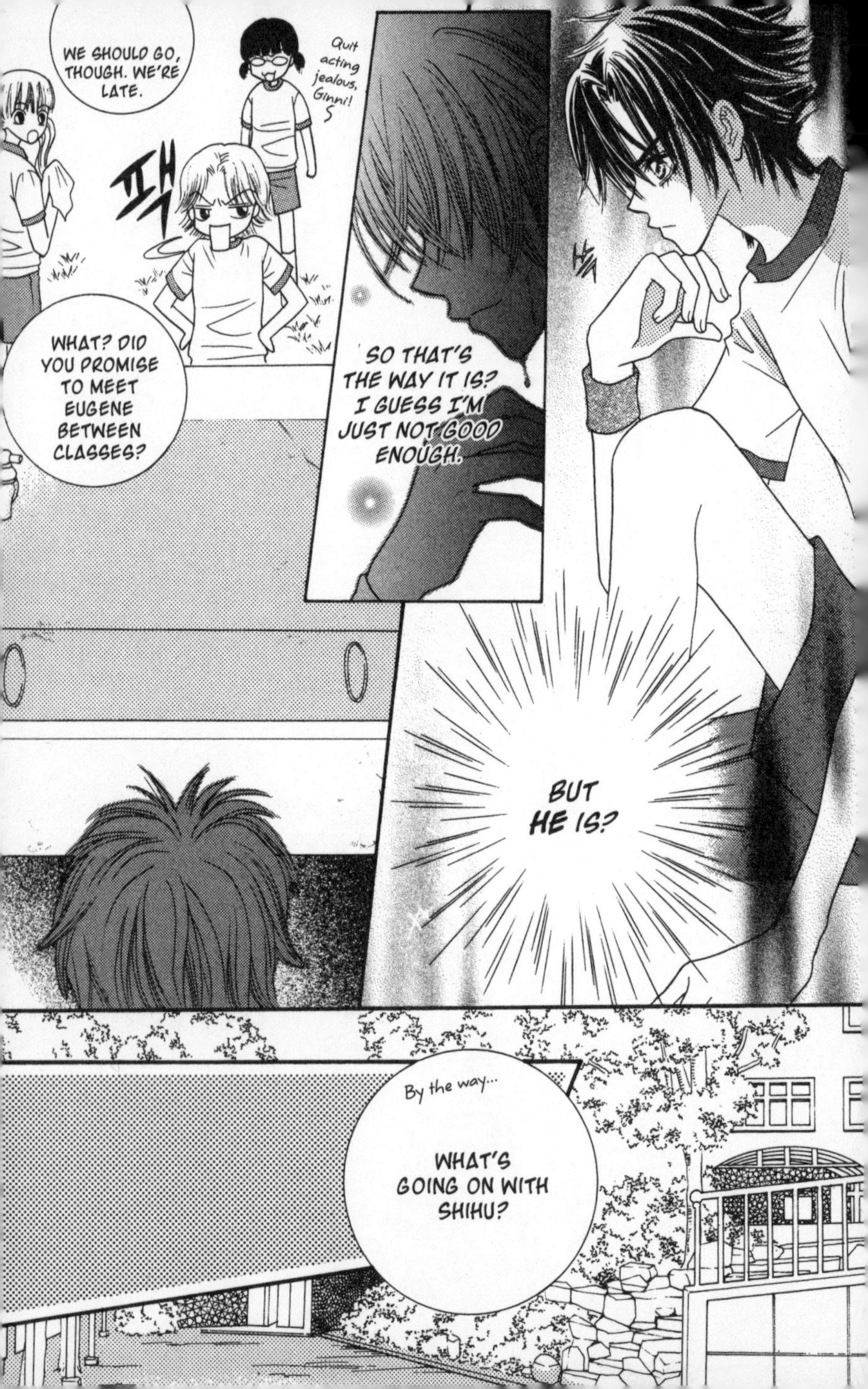
WE SHOULD GO, THOUGH. WE'RE LATE.
Quit acting jealous, Ginni!
WHAT? DID YOU PROMISE TO MEET EUGENE BETWEEN CLASSES?
SO THAT'S THE WAY IT IS? I GUESS I'M JUST NOT GOOD ENOUGH.
BUT HE IS?
By the way...
WHAT'S GOING ON WITH SHIHU?

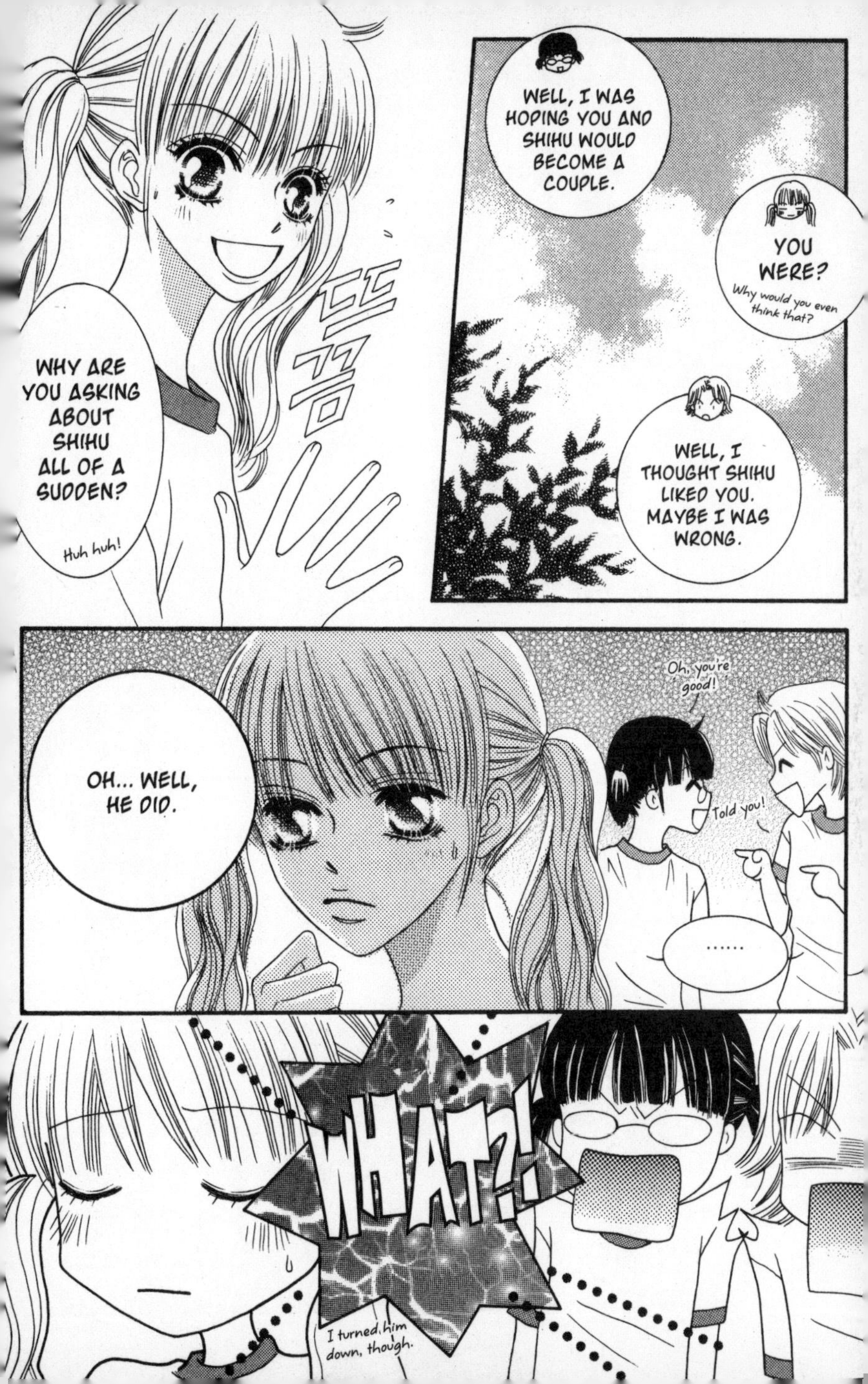
WHY ARE YOU ASKING ABOUT SHIHU ALL OF A SUDDEN?
Huh huh!
뜨끔
WELL, I WAS HOPING YOU AND SHIHU WOULD BECOME A COUPLE.
YOU WERE?
Why would you even think that?
WELL, I THOUGHT SHIHU LIKED YOU. MAYBE I WAS WRONG.
OH... WELL, HE DID.
Oh, you're good!
Told you!
......
WHAT?!
I turned him down, though.

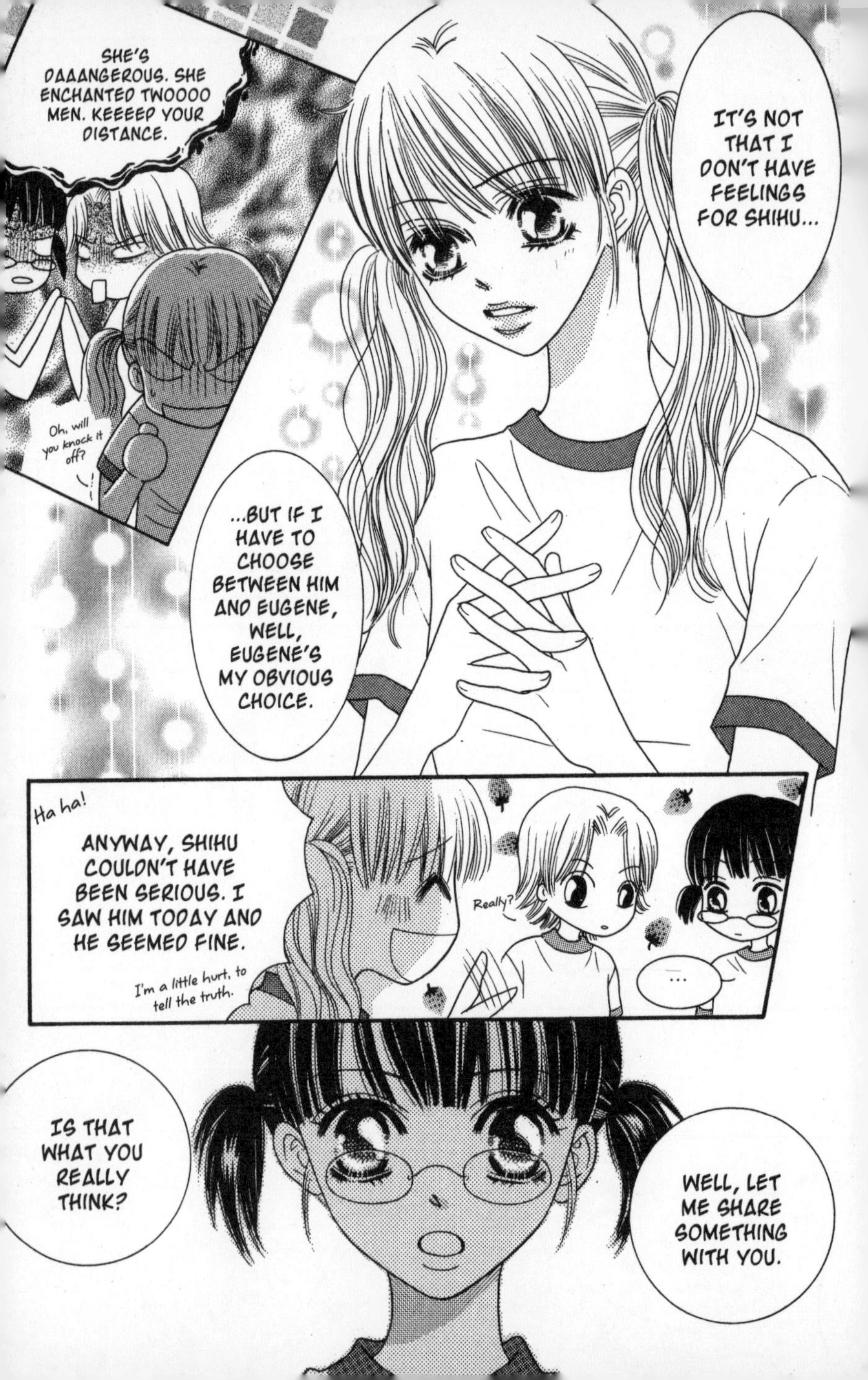

SHE'S DAAANGEROUS. SHE ENCHANTED TWOOOO MEN. KEEEEP YOUR DISTANCE.
Oh, will you knock it off?
IT'S NOT THAT I DON'T HAVE FEELINGS FOR SHIHU...
...BUT IF I HAVE TO CHOOSE BETWEEN HIM AND EUGENE, WELL, EUGENE'S MY OBVIOUS CHOICE.
Ha ha!
ANYWAY, SHIHU COULDN'T HAVE BEEN SERIOUS. I SAW HIM TODAY AND HE SEEMED FINE.
I'm a little hurt, to tell the truth.
Really?
...
IS THAT WHAT YOU REALLY THINK?
WELL, LET ME SHARE SOMETHING WITH YOU.

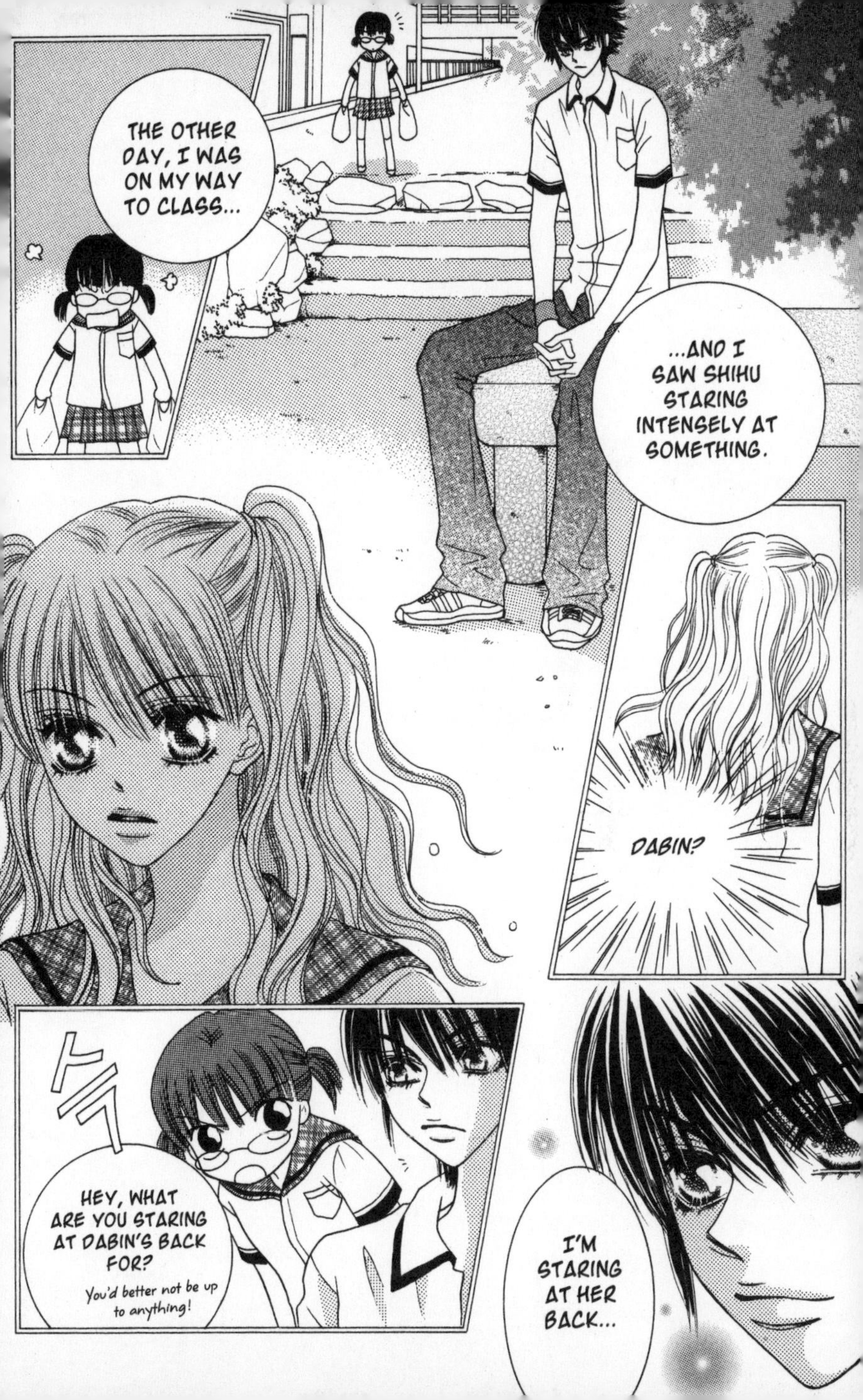
THE OTHER DAY, I WAS ON MY WAY TO CLASS...
...AND I SAW SHIHU STARING INTENSELY AT SOMETHING.
DABIN?
HEY, WHAT ARE YOU STARING AT DABIN'S BACK FOR?
You'd better not be up to anything!
I'M STARING AT HER BACK...

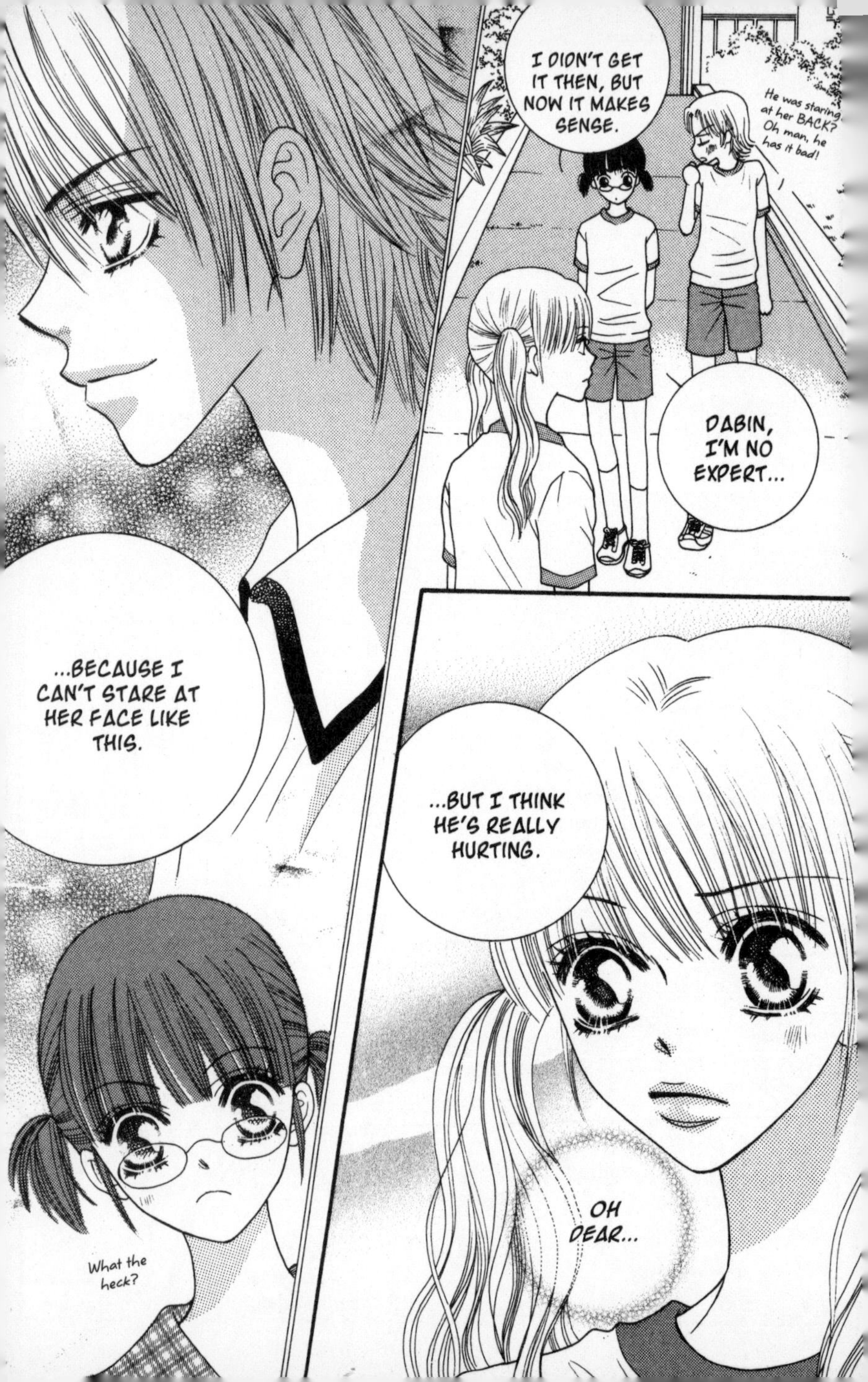
...BECAUSE I CAN'T STARE AT HER FACE LIKE THIS.
What the heck?
I DIDN'T GET IT THEN, BUT NOW IT MAKES SENSE.
He was staring at her BACK? Oh man, he has it bad!
DABIN, I'M NO EXPERT...
...BUT I THINK HE'S REALLY HURTING.
OH DEAR...

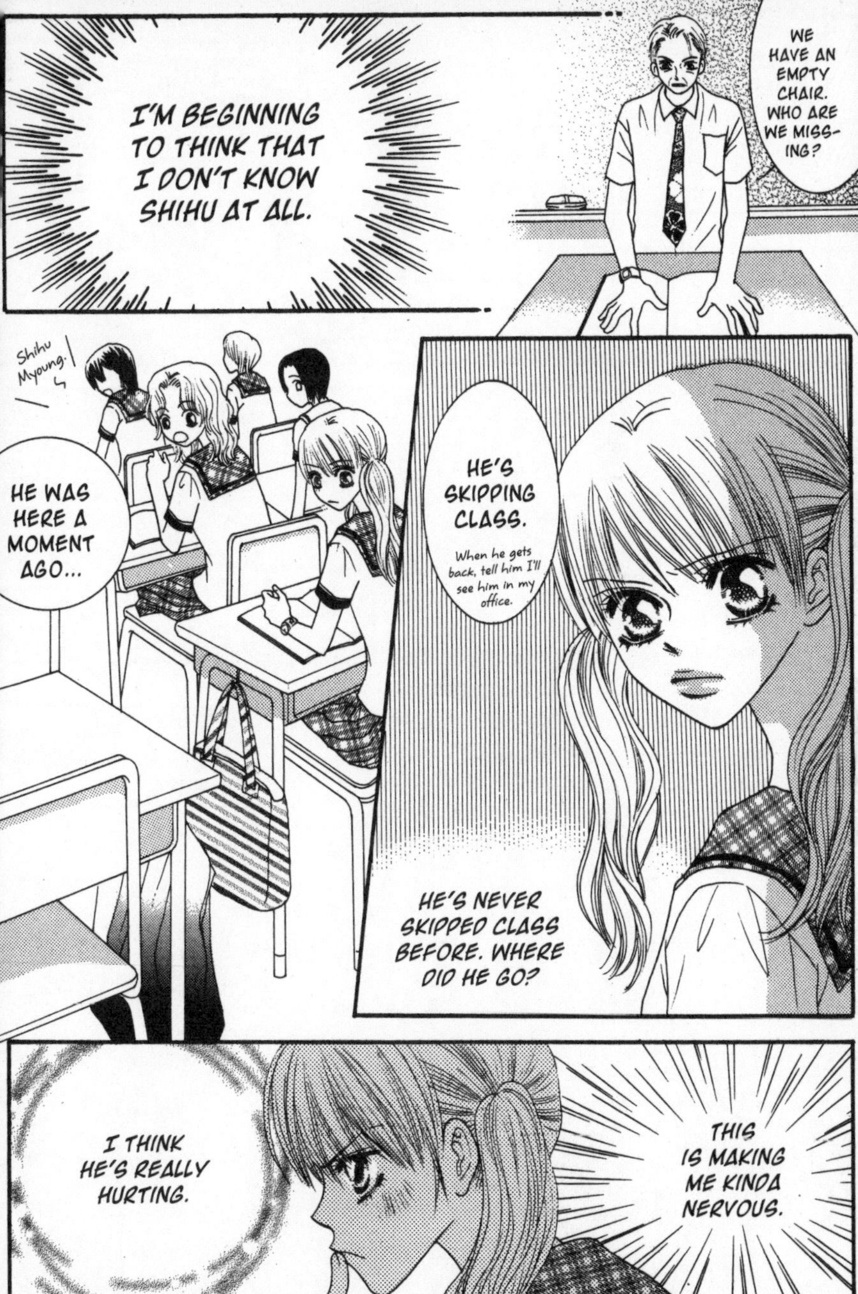
I'M BEGINNING TO THINK THAT I DON'T KNOW SHIHU AT ALL.
WE HAVE AN EMPTY CHAIR. WHO ARE WE MISSING?
Shihu Myoung.
HE WAS HERE A MOMENT AGO...
HE'S SKIPPING CLASS.
When he gets back, tell him I'll see him in my office.
HE'S NEVER SKIPPED CLASS BEFORE. WHERE DID HE GO?
I THINK HE'S REALLY HURTING.
THIS IS MAKING ME KINDA NERVOUS.

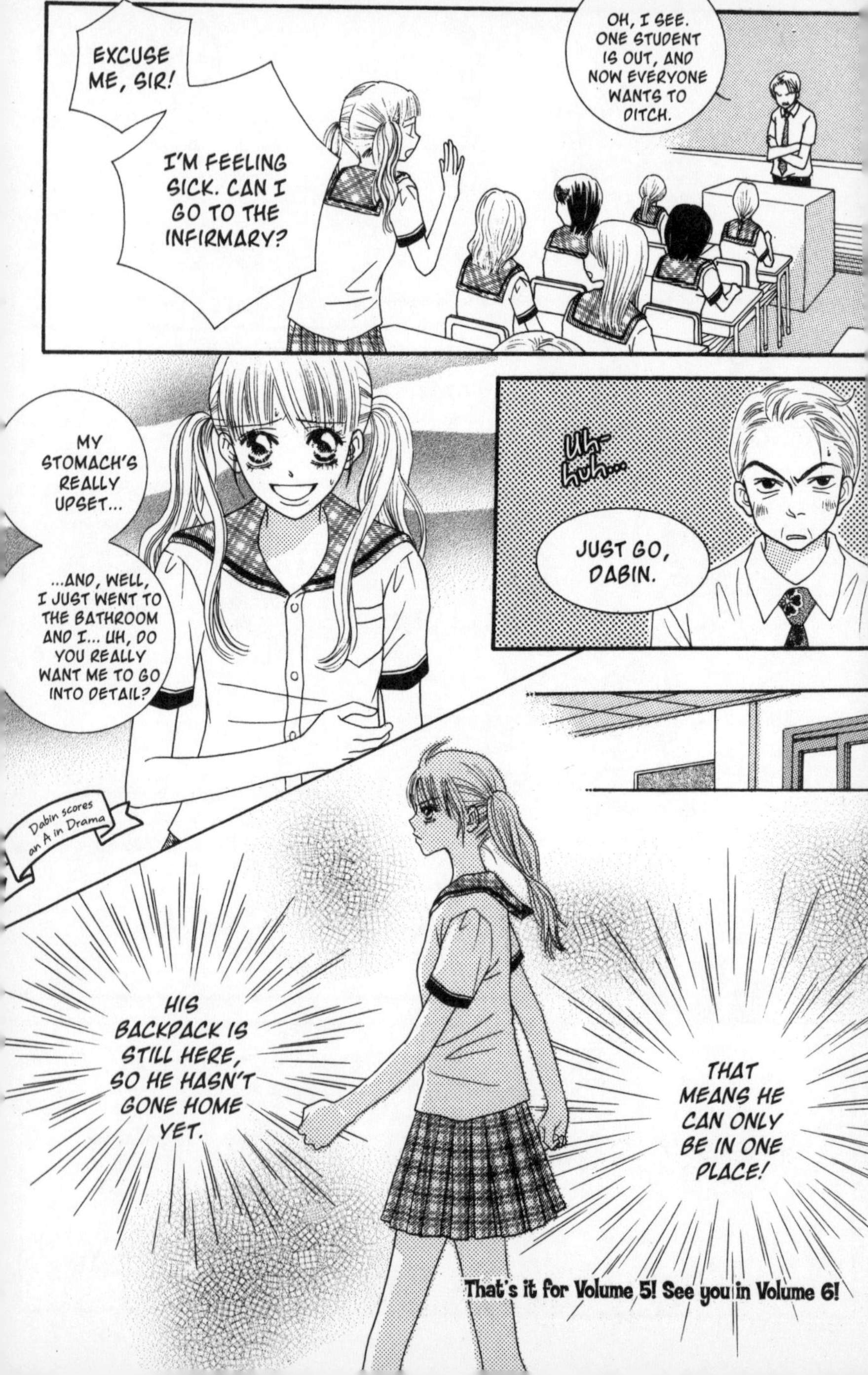
EXCUSE ME, SIR!
I'M FEELING SICK. CAN I GO TO THE INFIRMARY?
OH, I SEE. ONE STUDENT IS OUT, AND NOW EVERYONE WANTS TO DITCH.
MY STOMACH'S REALLY UPSET...
...AND, WELL, I JUST WENT TO THE BATHROOM AND I... UH, DO YOU REALLY WANT ME TO GO INTO DETAIL?
Dabin scores an A in Drama
Uh-huh...
JUST GO, DABIN.
HIS BACKPACK IS STILL HERE, SO HE HASN'T GONE HOME YET.
THAT MEANS HE CAN ONLY BE IN ONE PLACE!
That's it for Volume 5! See you in Volume 6!

Well, that's not ENTIRELY it. Turn the page for a special bonus!

Yeah, turn the page!

| Cute | Sweet | Bright | Fresh |

| Cute | Sweet | Bright | Fresh |

Rose's Story A Tale of Revenge

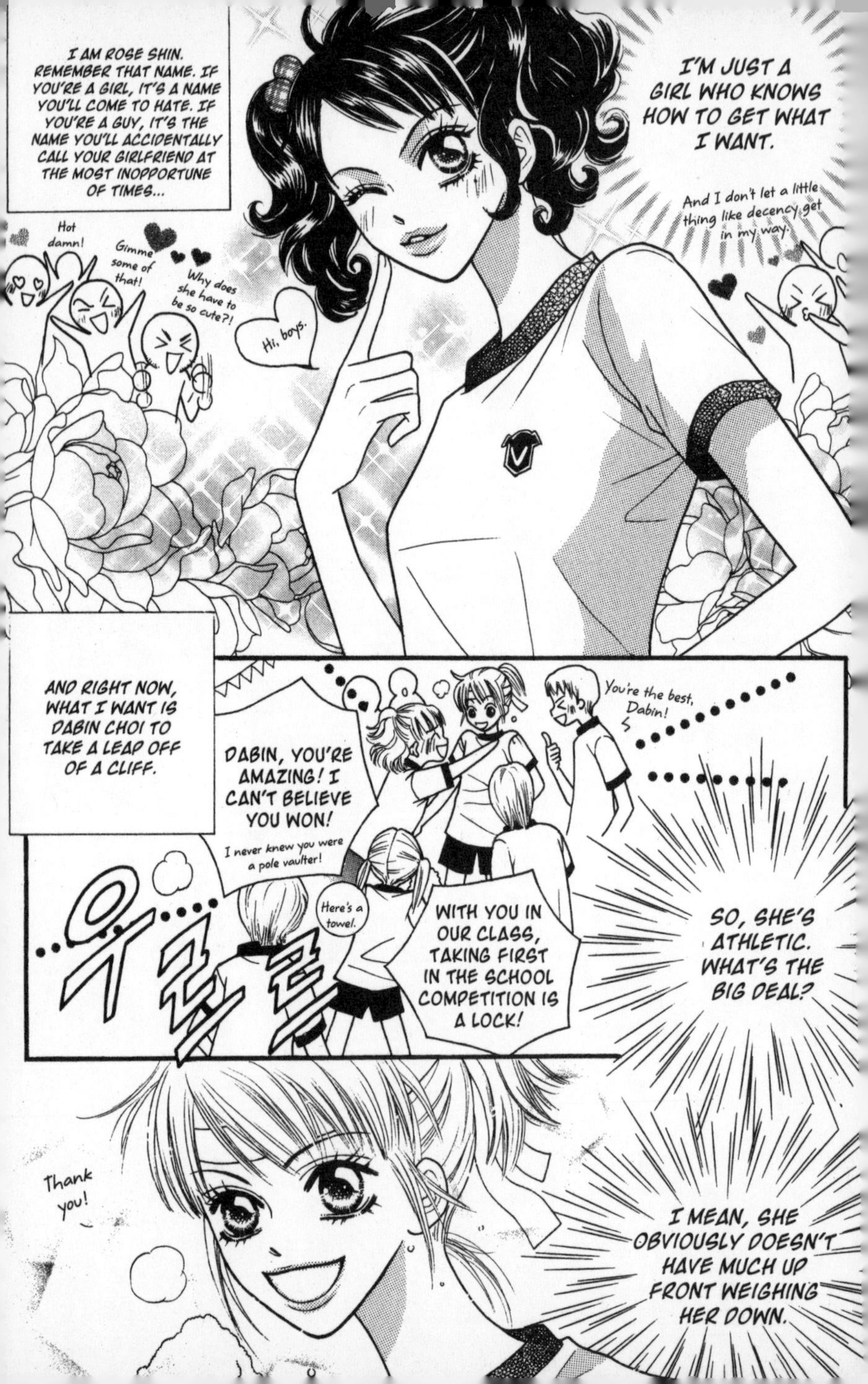

I AM ROSE SHIN. REMEMBER THAT NAME. IF YOU'RE A GIRL, IT'S A NAME YOU'LL COME TO HATE. IF YOU'RE A GUY, IT'S THE NAME YOU'LL ACCIDENTALLY CALL YOUR GIRLFRIEND AT THE MOST INOPPORTUNE OF TIMES...
Hot damn!
Gimme some of that!
Why does she have to be so cute?!
Hi, boys.
I'M JUST A GIRL WHO KNOWS HOW TO GET WHAT I WANT.
And I don't let a little thing like decency get in my way.
AND RIGHT NOW, WHAT I WANT IS DABIN CHOI TO TAKE A LEAP OFF OF A CLIFF.
DABIN, YOU'RE AMAZING! I CAN'T BELIEVE YOU WON!
I never knew you were a pole vaulter!
You're the best, Dabin!
Here's a towel.
WITH YOU IN OUR CLASS, TAKING FIRST IN THE SCHOOL COMPETITION IS A LOCK!
SO, SHE'S ATHLETIC. WHAT'S THE BIG DEAL?
Thank you!
I MEAN, SHE OBVIOUSLY DOESN'T HAVE MUCH UP FRONT WEIGHING HER DOWN.

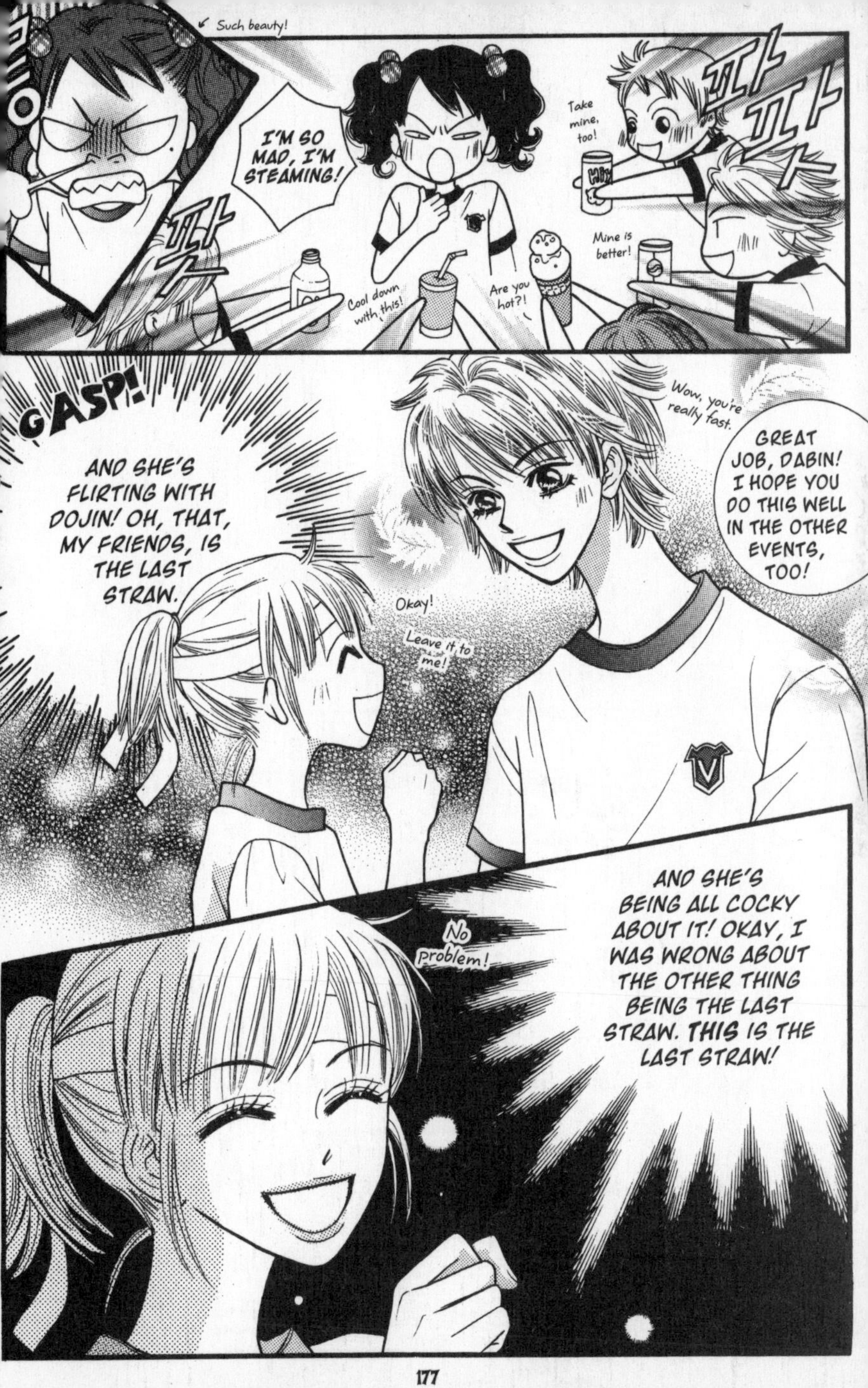
Such beauty!
I'M SO MAD, I'M STEAMING!
Take mine, too!
Cool down with this!
Are you hot?!
Mine is better!
GASP!
AND SHE'S FLIRTING WITH DOJIN! OH, THAT, MY FRIENDS, IS THE LAST STRAW.
Wow, you're really fast.
GREAT JOB, DABIN! I HOPE YOU DO THIS WELL IN THE OTHER EVENTS, TOO!
Okay!
Leave it to me!
No problem!
AND SHE'S BEING ALL COCKY ABOUT IT! OKAY, I WAS WRONG ABOUT THE OTHER THING BEING THE LAST STRAW. THIS IS THE LAST STRAW!

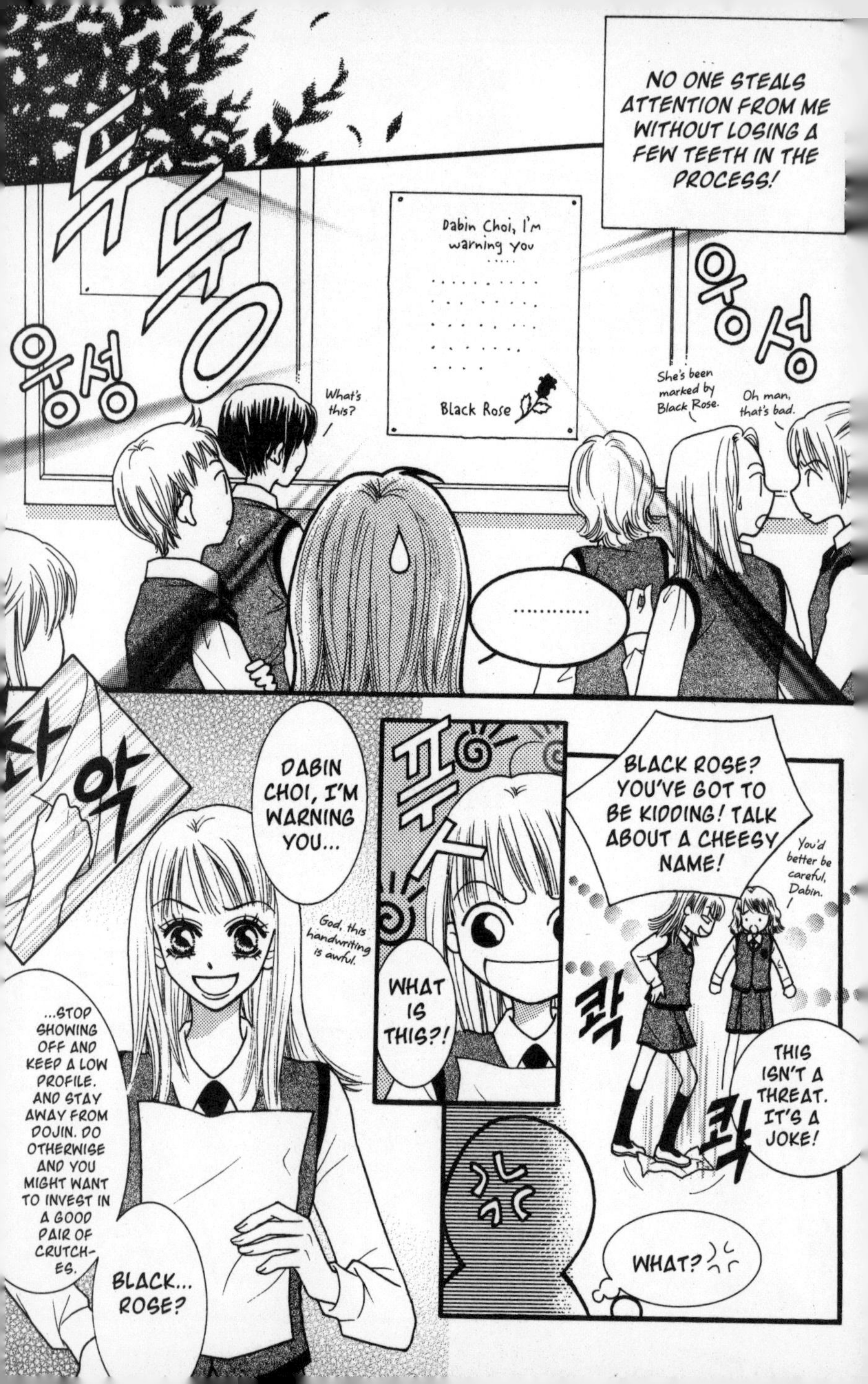

웅성
Dabin Choi, I'm warning you
Black Rose
What's this?
NO ONE STEALS ATTENTION FROM ME WITHOUT LOSING A FEW TEETH IN THE PROCESS!
웅성
She's been marked by Black Rose.
Oh man, that's bad.
....
DABIN CHOI, I'M WARNING YOU...
God, this handwriting is awful.
...STOP SHOWING OFF AND KEEP A LOW PROFILE. AND STAY AWAY FROM DOJIN. DO OTHERWISE AND YOU MIGHT WANT TO INVEST IN A GOOD PAIR OF CRUTCH-ES.
BLACK... ROSE?
WHAT IS THIS?!
BLACK ROSE? YOU'VE GOT TO BE KIDDING! TALK ABOUT A CHEESY NAME!
You'd better be careful, Dabin.
콱
콱
THIS ISN'T A THREAT. IT'S A JOKE!
WHAT?

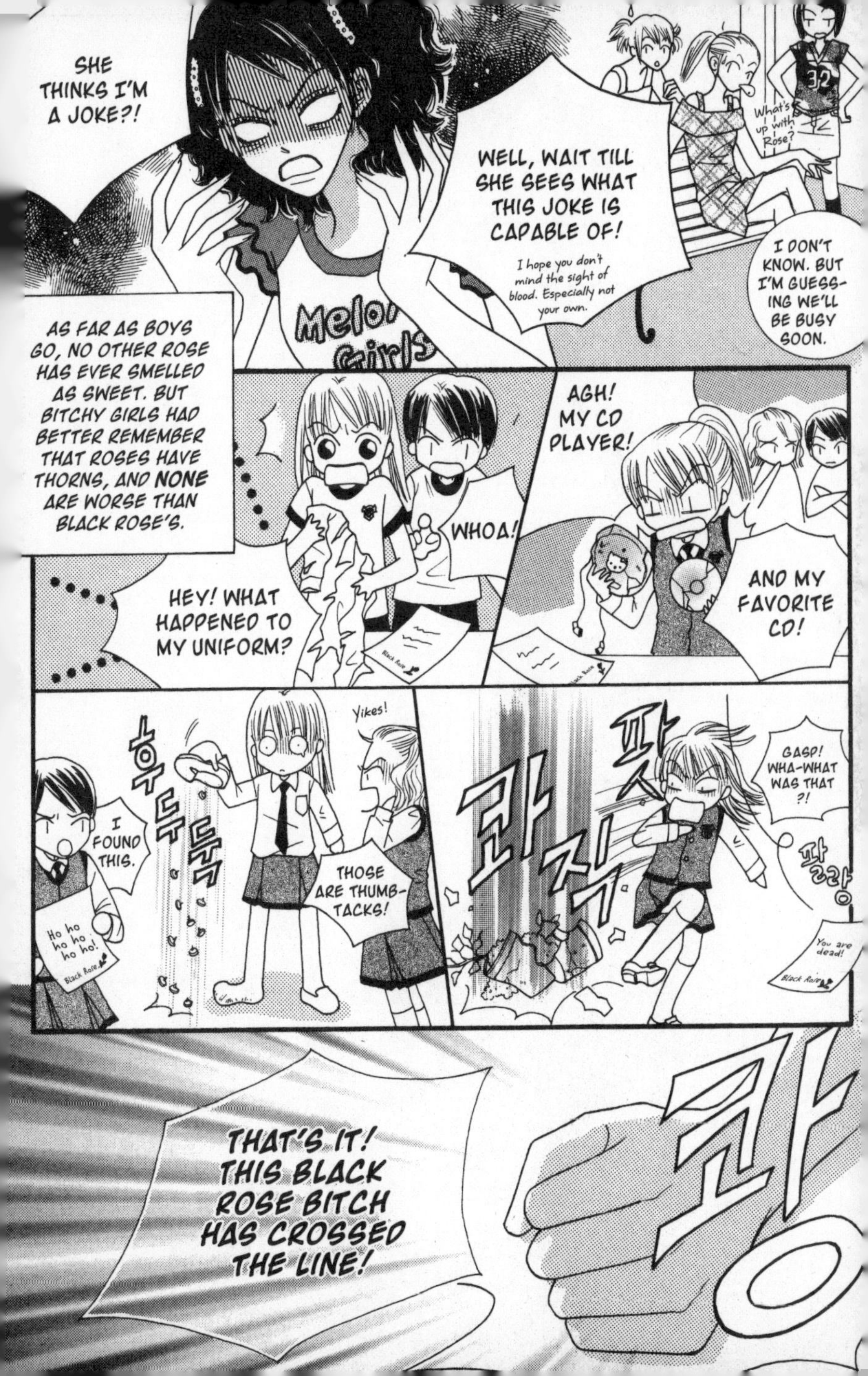
SHE THINKS I'M A JOKE?!
WELL, WAIT TILL SHE SEES WHAT THIS JOKE IS CAPABLE OF!
I hope you don't mind the sight of blood. Especially not your own.
What's up with Rose?
I DON'T KNOW. BUT I'M GUESSING WE'LL BE BUSY SOON.
AS FAR AS BOYS GO, NO OTHER ROSE HAS EVER SMELLED AS SWEET. BUT BITCHY GIRLS HAD BETTER REMEMBER THAT ROSES HAVE THORNS, AND NONE ARE WORSE THAN BLACK ROSE'S.
WHOA!
HEY! WHAT HAPPENED TO MY UNIFORM?
Black Rose
AGH! MY CD PLAYER!
AND MY FAVORITE CD!
Black Rose
I FOUND THIS.
Ho ho ho ho ho!
Black Rose
후두둑
Yikes!
THOSE ARE THUMBTACKS!
GASP! WHA-WHAT WAS THAT?!
You are dead!
Black Rose
THAT'S IT! THIS BLACK ROSE BITCH HAS CROSSED THE LINE!

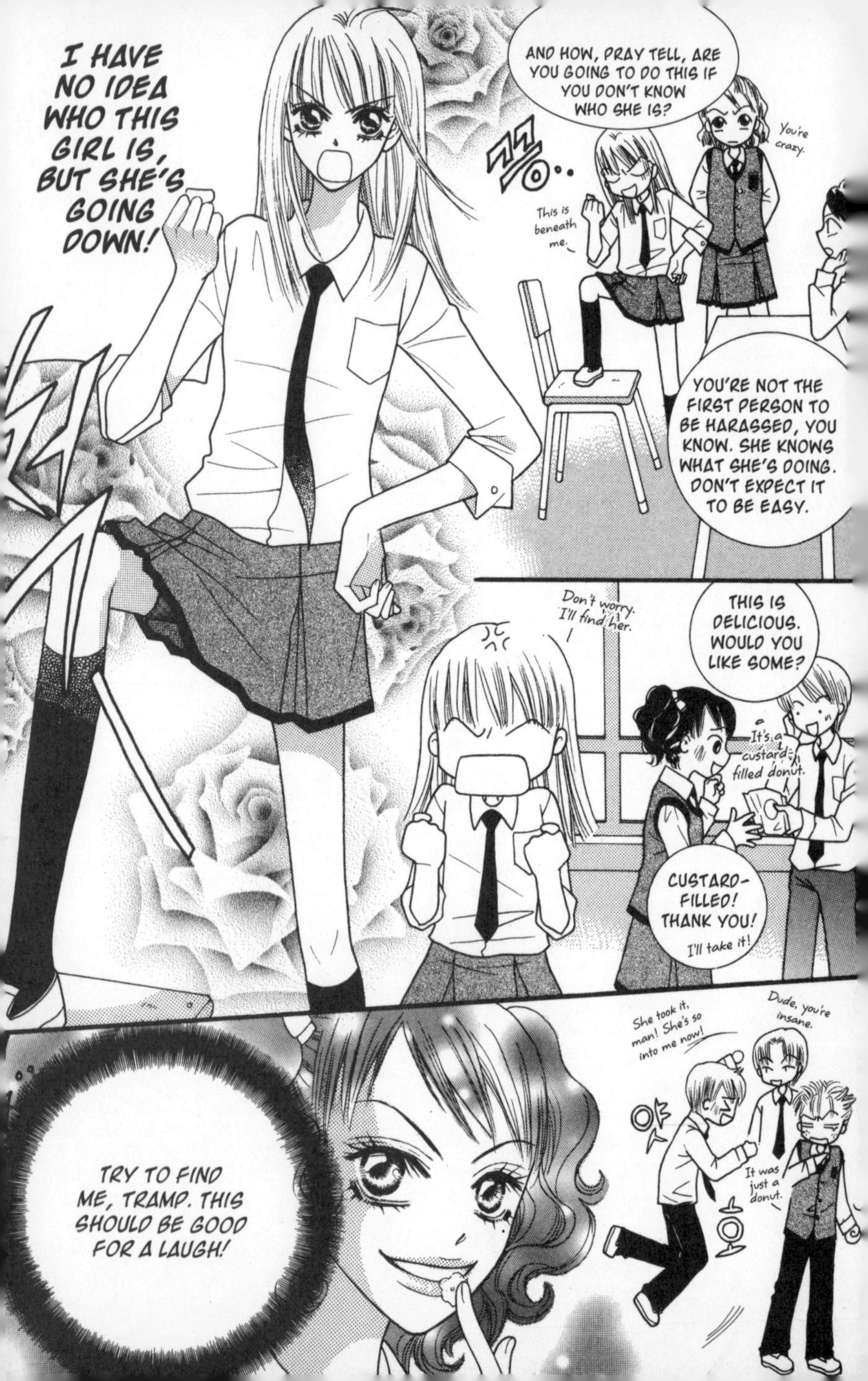
I HAVE NO IDEA WHO THIS GIRL IS, BUT SHE'S GOING DOWN!
AND HOW, PRAY TELL, ARE YOU GOING TO DO THIS IF YOU DON'T KNOW WHO SHE IS?
You're crazy.
This is beneath me.
YOU'RE NOT THE FIRST PERSON TO BE HARASSED, YOU KNOW. SHE KNOWS WHAT SHE'S DOING. DON'T EXPECT IT TO BE EASY.
Don't worry. I'll find her.
THIS IS DELICIOUS. WOULD YOU LIKE SOME?
It's a custard-filled donut.
CUSTARD-FILLED! THANK YOU!
I'll take it!
TRY TO FIND ME, TRAMP. THIS SHOULD BE GOOD FOR A LAUGH!
She took it, man! She's so into me now!
Dude, you're insane.
It was just a donut.

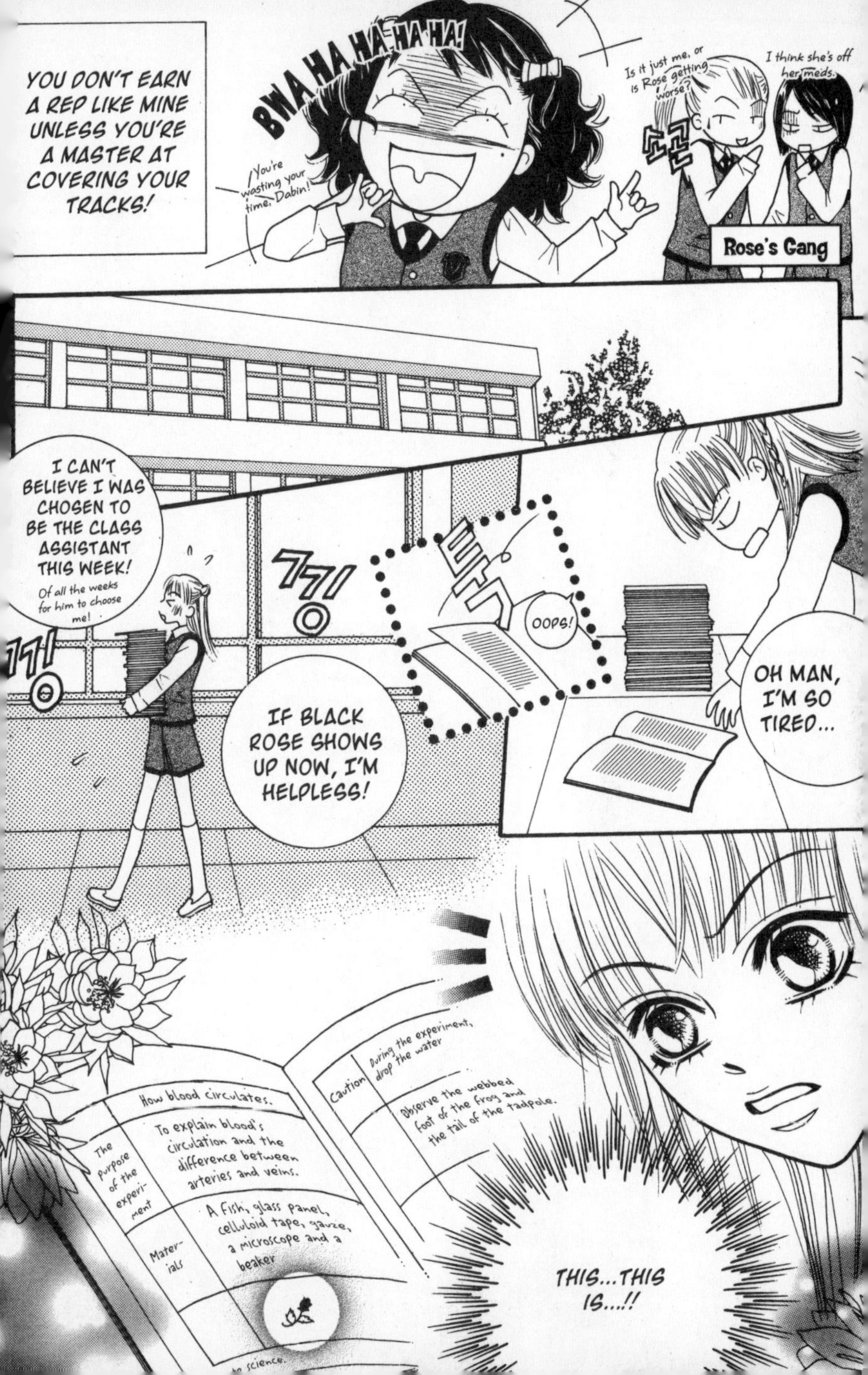
YOU DON'T EARN A REP LIKE MINE UNLESS YOU'RE A MASTER AT COVERING YOUR TRACKS!
BWA HA HA HA HA!
You're wasting your time, Dabin!
Is it just me, or is Rose getting worse?
I think she's off her meds.
Rose's Gang
I CAN'T BELIEVE I WAS CHOSEN TO BE THE CLASS ASSISTANT THIS WEEK!
Of all the weeks for him to choose me!
IF BLACK ROSE SHOWS UP NOW, I'M HELPLESS!
OOPS!
OH MAN, I'M SO TIRED...
How blood circulates.
The purpose of the experiment
To explain blood's circulation and the difference between arteries and veins.
Mater-ials
A fish, glass panel, celluloid tape, gauze, a microscope and a beaker
Caution
During the experiment, drop the water
Observe the webbed foot of the frog and the tail of the tadpole.
THIS...THIS IS...!!

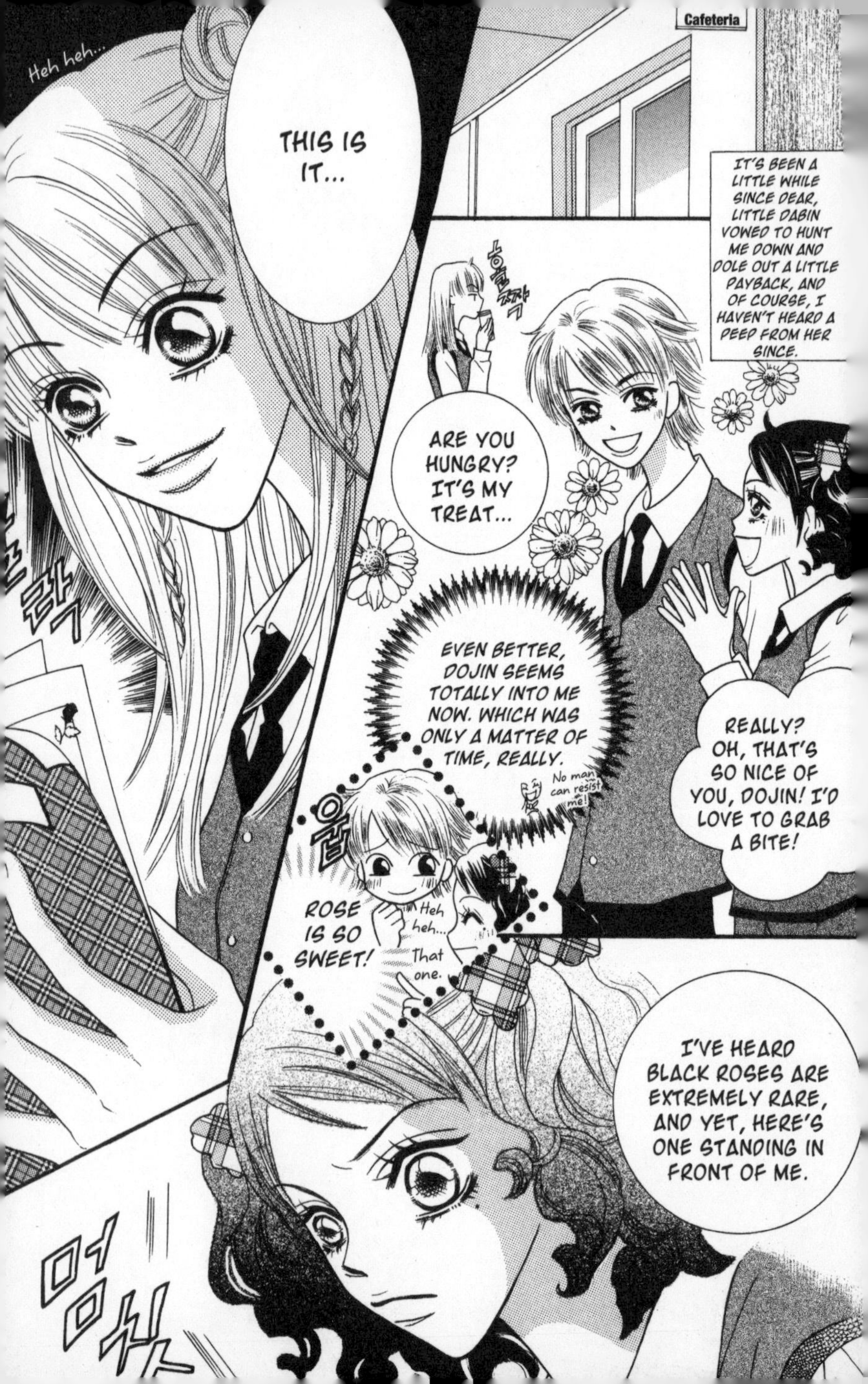
Heh heh...
THIS IS IT...
Cafeteria
IT'S BEEN A LITTLE WHILE SINCE DEAR, LITTLE DABIN VOWED TO HUNT ME DOWN AND DOLE OUT A LITTLE PAYBACK, AND OF COURSE, I HAVEN'T HEARD A PEEP FROM HER SINCE.
ARE YOU HUNGRY? IT'S MY TREAT...
EVEN BETTER, DOJIN SEEMS TOTALLY INTO ME NOW. WHICH WAS ONLY A MATTER OF TIME, REALLY.
No man can resist me!
REALLY? OH, THAT'S SO NICE OF YOU, DOJIN! I'D LOVE TO GRAB A BITE!
ROSE IS SO SWEET!
Heh heh...
That one.
I'VE HEARD BLACK ROSES ARE EXTREMELY RARE, AND YET, HERE'S ONE STANDING IN FRONT OF ME.

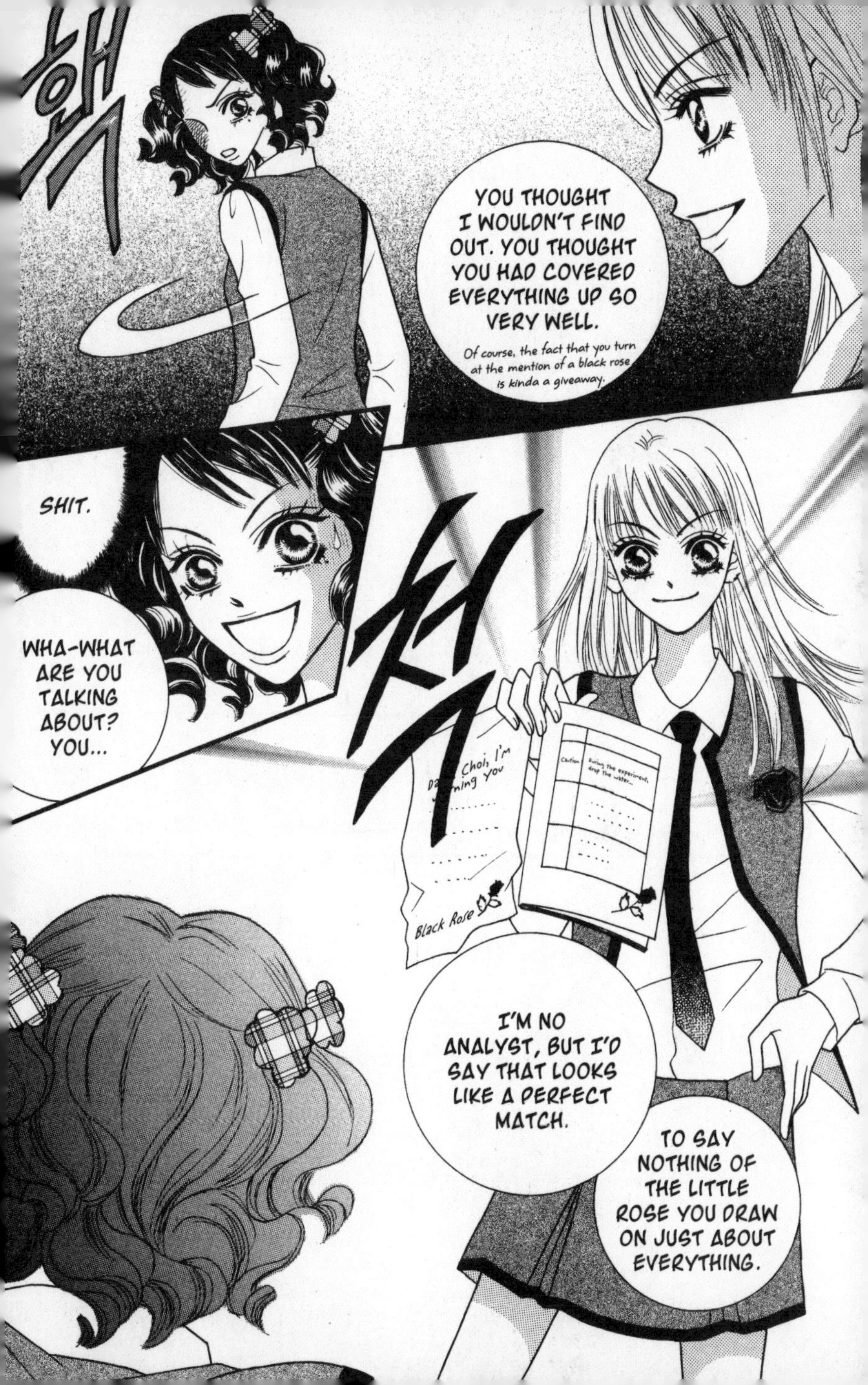

홱
YOU THOUGHT I WOULDN'T FIND OUT. YOU THOUGHT YOU HAD COVERED EVERYTHING UP SO VERY WELL.
Of course, the fact that you turn at the mention of a black rose is kinda a giveaway.
SHIT.
WHA-WHAT ARE YOU TALKING ABOUT? YOU...
Caution
During the experiment, drop the water...
Black Rose
I'M NO ANALYST, BUT I'D SAY THAT LOOKS LIKE A PERFECT MATCH.
TO SAY NOTHING OF THE LITTLE ROSE YOU DRAW ON JUST ABOUT EVERYTHING.

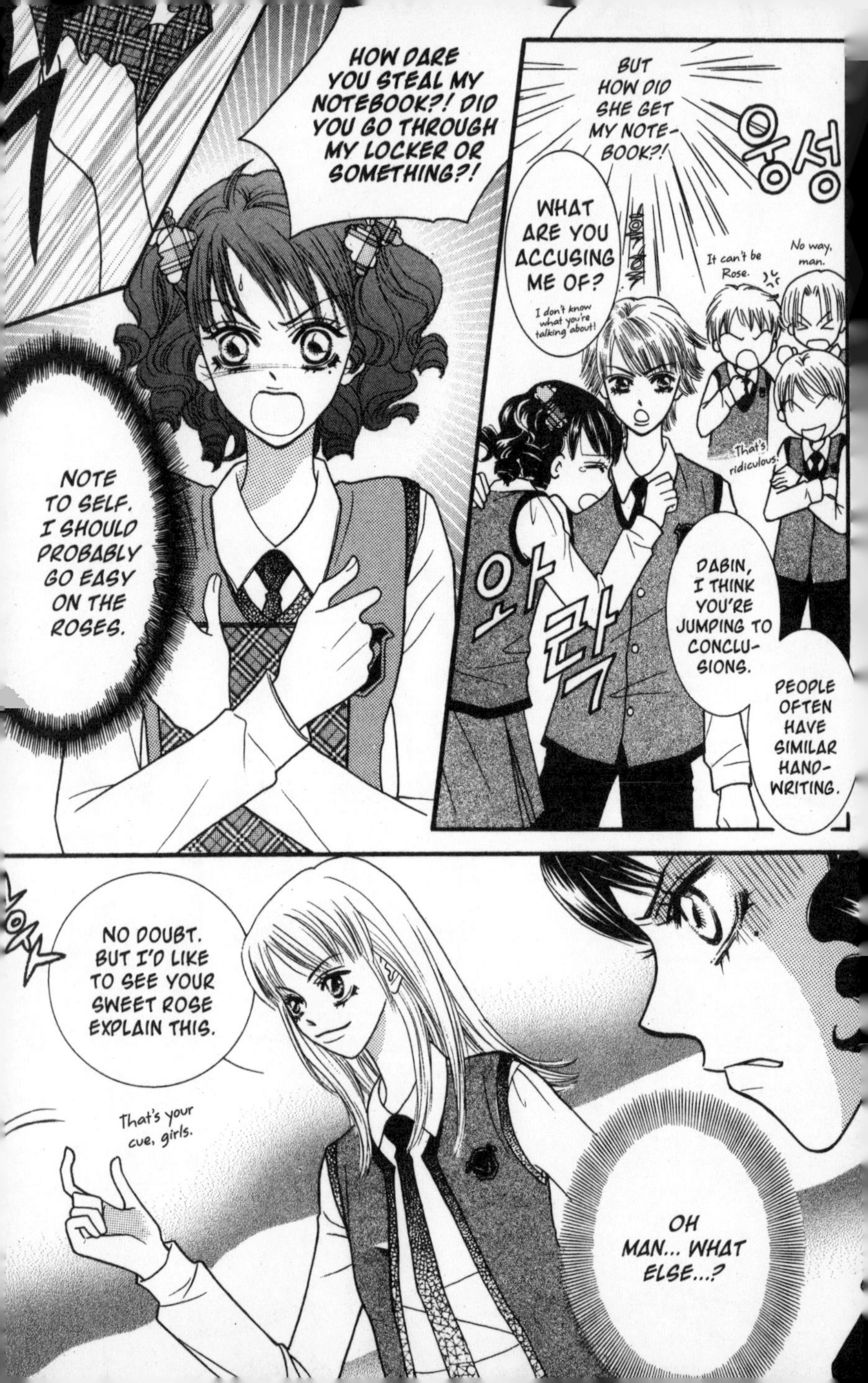
HOW DARE YOU STEAL MY NOTEBOOK?! DID YOU GO THROUGH MY LOCKER OR SOMETHING?!
NOTE TO SELF. I SHOULD PROBABLY GO EASY ON THE ROSES.
BUT HOW DID SHE GET MY NOTE-BOOK?!
WHAT ARE YOU ACCUSING ME OF?
I don't know what you're talking about!
It can't be Rose.
No way, man.
That's ridiculous!
와락
DABIN, I THINK YOU'RE JUMPING TO CONCLU-SIONS.
PEOPLE OFTEN HAVE SIMILAR HAND-WRITING.
NO DOUBT. BUT I'D LIKE TO SEE YOUR SWEET ROSE EXPLAIN THIS.
That's your cue, girls.
OH MAN... WHAT ELSE...?

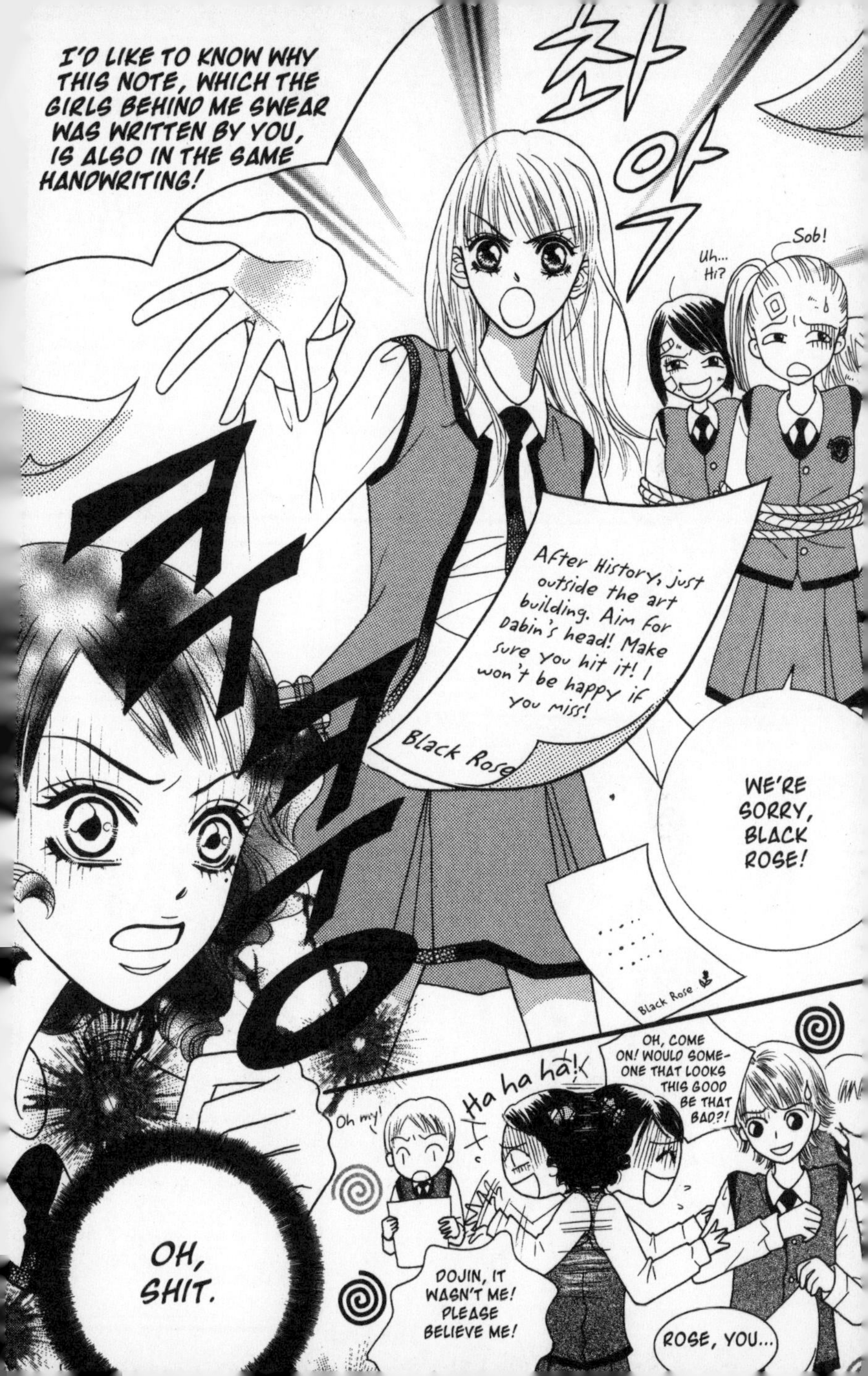
I'D LIKE TO KNOW WHY THIS NOTE, WHICH THE GIRLS BEHIND ME SWEAR WAS WRITTEN BY YOU, IS ALSO IN THE SAME HANDWRITING!
Uh... Hi?
Sob!
After History, just outside the art building. Aim for Dabin's head! Make sure you hit it! I won't be happy if you miss!
Black Rose
WE'RE SORRY, BLACK ROSE!
Black Rose
OH, SHIT.
Oh my!
Ha ha ha!
OH, COME ON! WOULD SOME-ONE THAT LOOKS THIS GOOD BE THAT BAD?!
DOJIN, IT WASN'T ME! PLEASE BELIEVE ME!
ROSE, YOU...

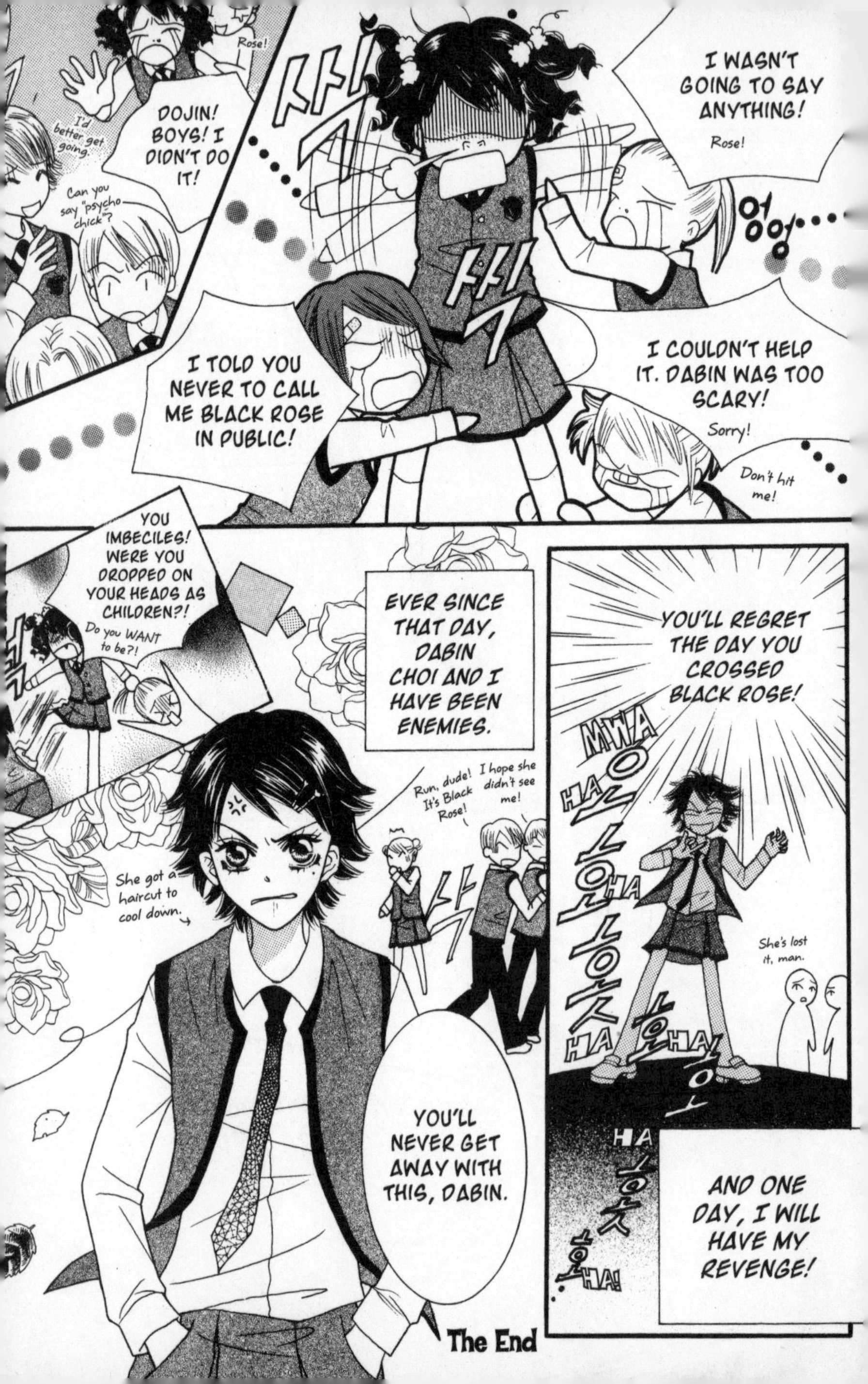
Rose!
DOJIN! BOYS! I DIDN'T DO IT!
I'd better get going.
Can you say "psycho chick"?
I WASN'T GOING TO SAY ANYTHING!
Rose!
I TOLD YOU NEVER TO CALL ME BLACK ROSE IN PUBLIC!
I COULDN'T HELP IT. DABIN WAS TOO SCARY!
Sorry!
Don't hit me!
YOU IMBECILES! WERE YOU DROPPED ON YOUR HEADS AS CHILDREN?!
Do you WANT to be?!
EVER SINCE THAT DAY, DABIN CHOI AND I HAVE BEEN ENEMIES.
She got a haircut to cool down.
Run, dude! It's Black Rose!
I hope she didn't see me!
YOU'LL NEVER GET AWAY WITH THIS, DABIN.
YOU'LL REGRET THE DAY YOU CROSSED BLACK ROSE!
MWA HA HA HA HA HA HA!
She's lost it, man.
AND ONE DAY, I WILL HAVE MY REVENGE!
The End

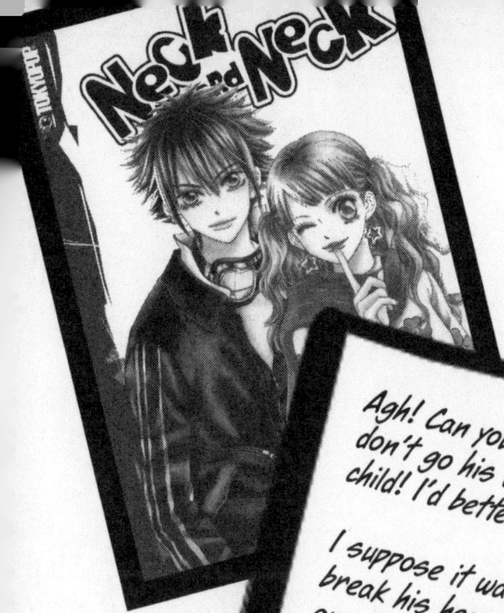
Neck and Neck
TOKYOPOP

Neck and Neck Volume 6 Coming in November 2006

Agh! Can you believe this?! Typical Shihu! Things don't go his way so he runs away and acts like a child! I'd better not get in trouble for this!

I suppose it was kinda naive to think that I could break his heart like I did and not have to deal with any sort of repercussions. I can't help it, though. I'm new to all this relationship stuff. And how was I supposed to know he felt that way?! He sure has a lousy way of showing it!

Are all relationships this complicated? I should be really happy. I'm finally, FINALLY Eugene's girlfriend! But there's just something in the back of my head that won't allow me to let things go with Shihu. There's no reason for me to be getting involved like this, but I can't help it.

I'd imagine things are going to be getting a lot more complicated for me in the future. I'm sure Eugene isn't going to be happy when he finds out that I left class to look for Shihu. Especially since it's only our first day as a couple. Still, I'll figure out some way to handle it. I always do. After all, if our relationship's going to last, it's going to have to withstand a few bumps.

Speaking of bumps, I'll be giving Shihu a few of them on the head when I find him! These childish games of his have GOT to stop!

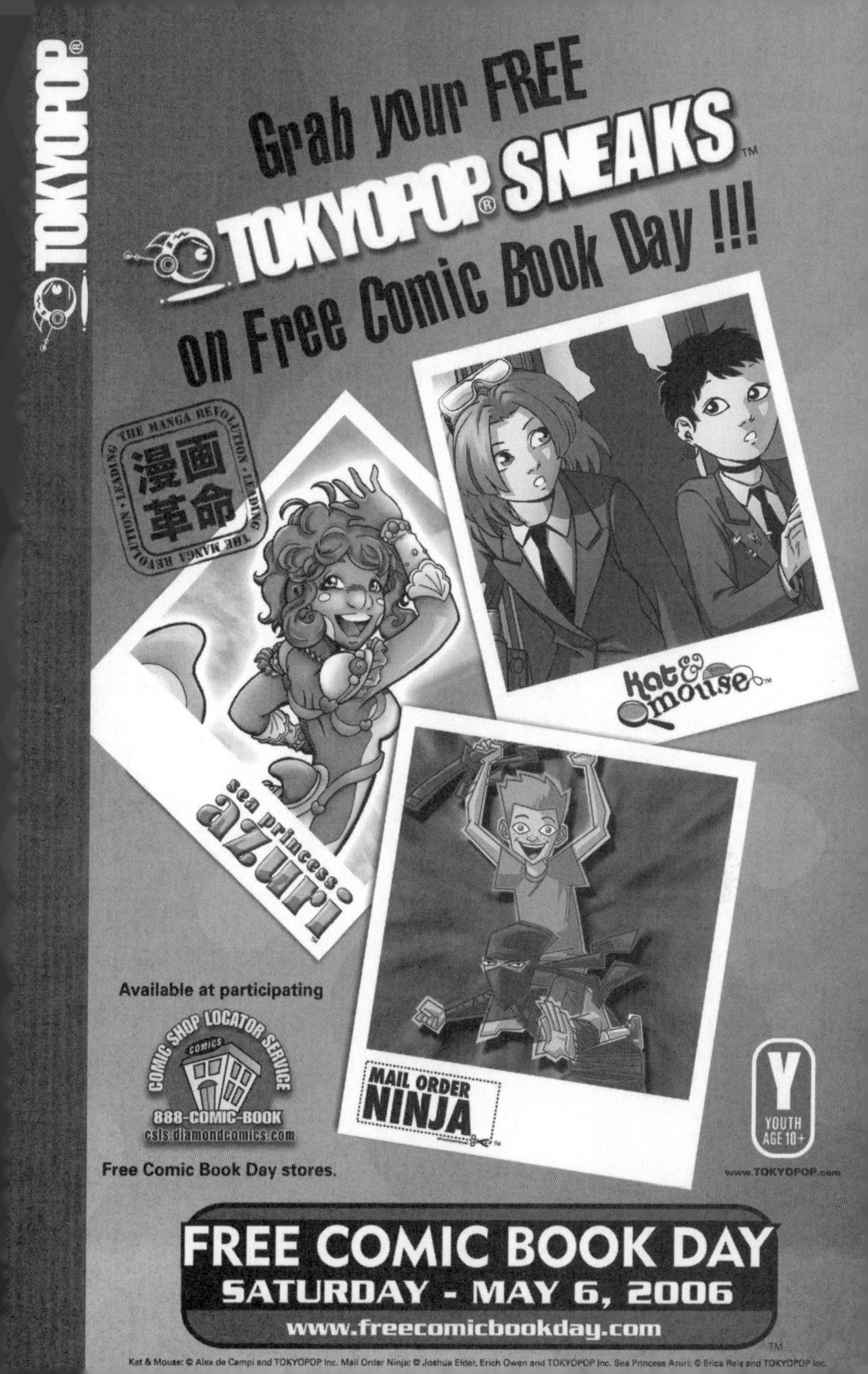
TOKYOPOP
Grab your FREE
TOKYOPOP SNEAKS
on Free Comic Book Day !!!
THE MANGA REVOLUTION · LEADING
漫画革命
Kat & mouse
sea princess azuri
MAIL ORDER NINJA
Available at participating
COMIC SHOP LOCATOR SERVICE
COMICS
888-COMIC-BOOK
csls.diamondcomics.com
Free Comic Book Day stores.
Y
YOUTH
AGE 10+
www.TOKYOPOP.com
FREE COMIC BOOK DAY
SATURDAY - MAY 6, 2006
www.freecomicbookday.com
Kat & Mouse: © Alex de Campi and TOKYOPOP Inc. Mail Order Ninja: © Joshua Elder, Erich Owen and TOKYOPOP Inc. Sea Princess Azuri: © Erica Reis and TOKYOPOP Inc.

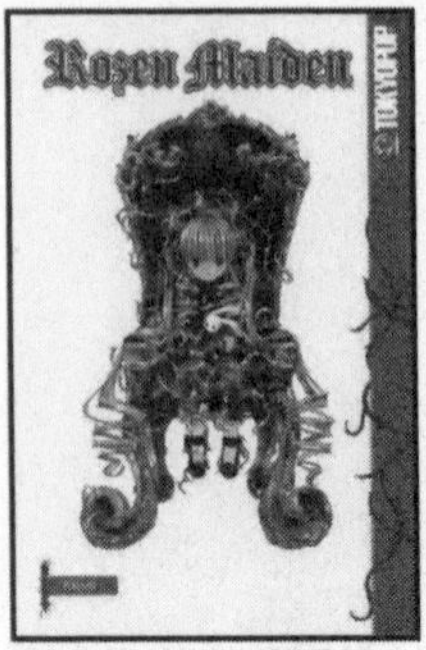
Rozen Maiden
TOKYOPOP
© PEACH-PIT, GENTOSHA COMICS INC.

ROZEN MAIDEN

BY PEACH-PIT

Welcome to the world of *Rozen Maiden* where a boy must enter an all-new reality to protect and serve a living doll!

FANTASY | T TEEN AGE 13+

From the creators of *DearS*!

BOYS OF SUMMER

BY CHUCK AUSTEN AND HIROKI OTSUKA

Just because you strike out on your first attempt at scoring with a girl doesn't mean you won't end up hitting a home run!

COMEDY | OT OLDER TEEN AGE 16+

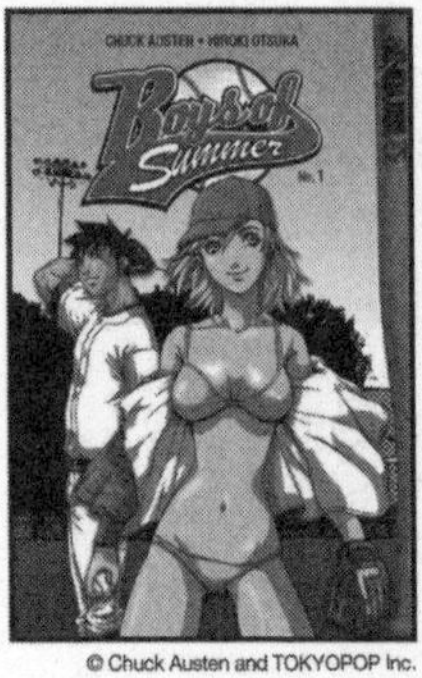
CHUCK AUSTEN + HIROKI OTSUKA
Boys of Summer
No. 1
© Chuck Austen and TOKYOPOP Inc.

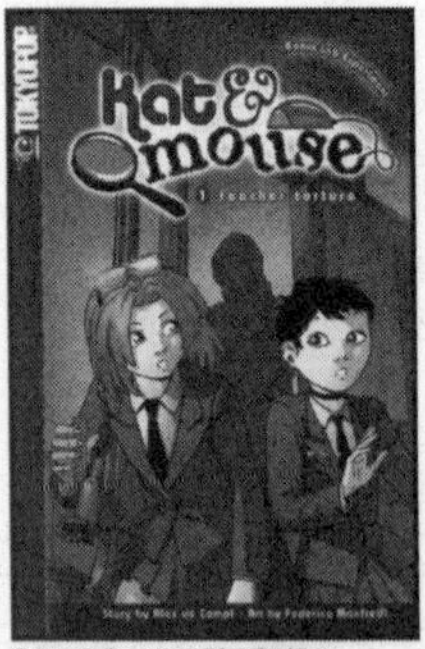
TOKYOPOP
Kat & mouse
1 teacher torture
© Alex de Campi and TOKYOPOP Inc.

KAT & MOUSE

BY ALEX DE CAMPI AND FEDERICA MANFREDI

When science whiz Kat teams up with computer nerd Mouse, bullies and blackmailers don't stand a chance!

MYSTERY | A ALL AGES

SHOWCASE

TOKYOPOP MANGA SUPPLEMENT

SHRINE OF THE MORNING MIST

BY HIROKI UGAWA

When the spirit world suddenly shifts out of balance, it's up to sisters Kurako, Yuzu and Tama to save us—but first they must get through their family drama.

FANTASY

T
TEEN AGE 13+

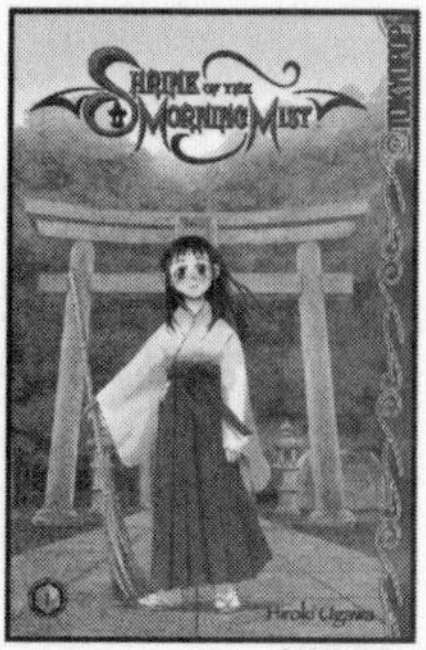

SHRINE OF THE MORNING MIST
TOKYOPOP
Hiroki Ugawa

CONFIDENTIAL CONFESSIONS -DEAI-

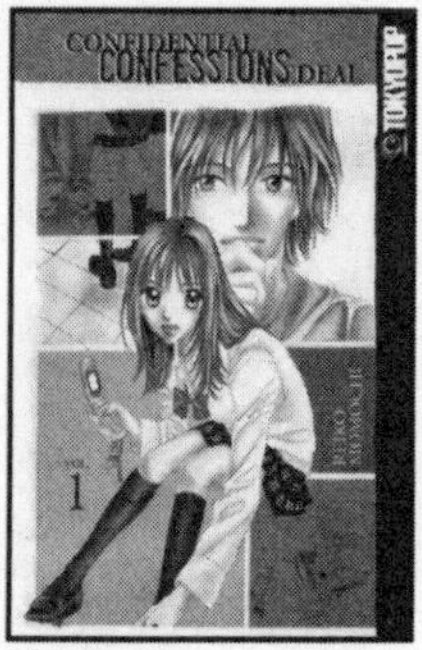

CONFIDENTIAL CONFESSIONS DEAI
TOKYOPOP
1

BY REIKO MOMOCHI

In this unflinching portrayal of teens in crisis, silence isn't always golden...

DRAMA

OT
OLDER TEEN AGE 16+

DEATH JAM

BY JEON SANG YOUNG

Muchaca Smooth is an assassin with just one shot to make it big!

ACTION

OT
OLDER TEEN AGE 16+

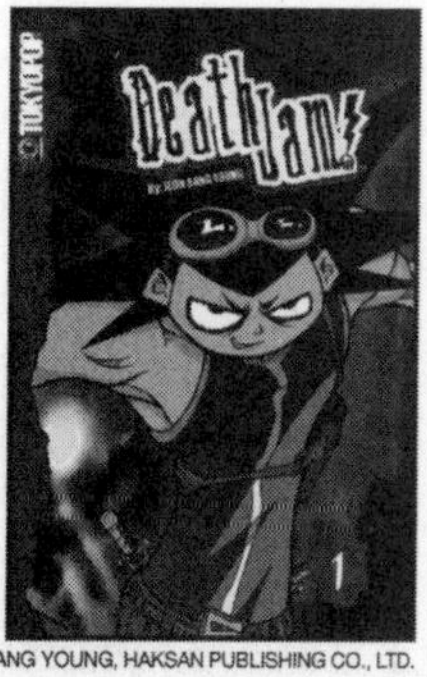

TOKYOPOP
Death Jam!
1

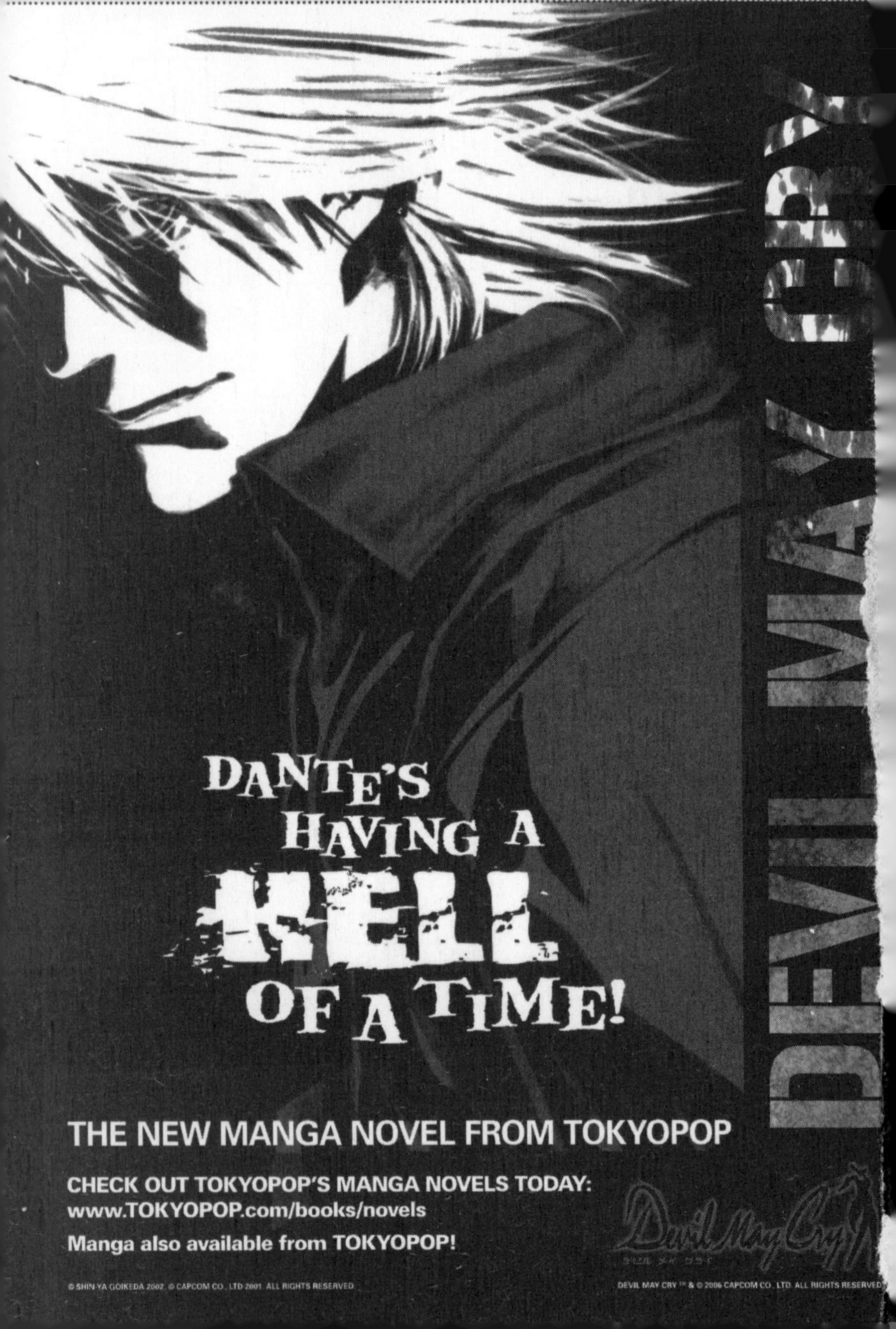
DEVIL MAY CRY
DANTE'S HAVING A HELL OF A TIME!
THE NEW MANGA NOVEL FROM TOKYOPOP
CHECK OUT TOKYOPOP'S MANGA NOVELS TODAY:
www.TOKYOPOP.com/books/novels
Manga also available from TOKYOPOP!
Devil May Cry
© SHIN-YA GOIKEDA 2002. © CAPCOM CO., LTD 2001. ALL RIGHTS RESERVED.
DEVIL MAY CRY ™ & © 2006 CAPCOM CO., LTD. ALL RIGHTS RESERVED.